"Entertaining and instructive . . . especially for its high Washington gossip quotient—and Conant tells it well. . . . A part of Dahl's life that is not generally known."

—Jonathan Yardley, *The Washington Post Book World*

"What more could one wish from a book? Here is a discussion of propaganda and covert actions . . . salacious gossip about the upper circles of Washington's political and media community. A writing style that has one racing from page to page, eager to soak in more details. I thump my desk with glee over Jennet Conant's *The Irregulars*."

—Joseph C. Goulden, *The Washington Times*

"Jennet Conant . . . has found a wonderfully intriguing story to build her new book around—that of one ally actively spying on the citizens of another while a guest in their country, and one that includes a roster of names readers know from activities other than spying."

—Joanne Collings, *Chicago Sun-Times*

"A lively new history. . . . If the British spies in Washington—who included dashing authors Ian Fleming and [Roald] Dahl—did not quite drag America into World War II . . . they effectively wooed and spied upon the press and political establishment."

—Evan Thomas, *Newsweek*

"[B]efore he became a successful writer, Roald Dahl had a very different reputation—as the sexiest British spy in America. A ribald portrait of Dahl's second world war years as an undercover agent attached to the British embassy in Washington. . . . Drawing on a previously unpublished trove of Dahl letters and other documents, Jennet Conant . . . has written what may prove the most comprehensive account of Dahl's raucous wartime exploits as a charming RAF attaché."

—Tony Allen-Mills, *The Sunday Times* (London)

"Conant's prose reads more like a novel than a history book. Well researched and chockfull of intricate history . . . a fresh, engrossing read full of amusing anecdotes."

—Jessica Harrison, *Deseret Morning News* (Salt Lake City)

"Conant . . . has a gift for writing large stories based on the activities of seemingly minor figures. . . . Explores the never-ending battle between isolationism and globalism in a way that makes her story surprisingly relevant to contemporary readers. . . . *The Irregulars* makes a persuasive argument that Stephenson acolyte Dahl and other figures with a literary bent (including Fleming and Noël Coward) were critical to the effort to end U.S. isolationism. . . . In addition to her colorful evocation of a complex city in a singularly tense time, Conant conjures a glamorous, fashionable world in which fidelity took a backseat to power."

—Carlo Wolff, *The Christian Science Monitor*

"Editor's choice"

—*The New York Times Book Review*

"[A] wonderfully rendered history of British spy jinks in Washington, D.C. . . . [A] merry tale of money, powers, and politics. . . . [A] thoroughly enjoyable book."

—David Walton, *St. Petersburg Times*

"Intriguing. . . . Conant's account is calm and superbly informed."

—Robert Winder, *The New York Sun*

"Editor's choice."

—*The Vancouver Sun*

"A book as entertaining for its inside Washington gossip and scandal as it is for its clarifying picture of how espionage was conducted in America during the war. . . . An engaging tale."

—*America in WWII* magazine

"Conant . . . knows a good story when she finds one and she's found one here."

—Scott Eyman, *Palm Beach Post*

"What could be more intriguing than the young writer Roald Dahl—destined to create such classics as *Charlie and the Chocolate Factory*—assigned by His Majesty's Government to Washington, D.C., as a diplomat in the spring of 1942, charged with a secret mission?"

—*Publishers Weekly* (starred review)

"In her enjoyable popular history, Conant keeps the narrative moving at a brisk pace, including adequate doses of serious information and juicy gossip. . . . She ably captures the complexity and paradox of the era as she depicts the spies' active professional and social lives. . . . Entertaining social history that also reveals a little-known aspect of an important literary figure's life."

—*Kirkus Reviews*

"A fascinating glimpse of the intrigue and spying inside the British-American alliance in wartime Washington."

—Ben Bradlee

"Jennet Conant's new book is pure pleasure. Immensely intelligent and entertaining, with a narrative so strongly fashioned it reads, and compels, like the best fiction. All the complexities of friends spying on friends, yet as good a weekend companion as you'll find this year."

—Alan Furst, author of *The Spies of Warsaw*

"With grace and insight and an unerring eye for the telling human detail, Jennet Conant has given us an entertaining and enlightening account of a long-forgotten but essential chapter of the Second World War: the British espionage operations based in Washington during those epic days. By recovering Roald Dahl, the man at the center of seemingly everything, and placing him and his shadowy work in historical context, Conant has shed fresh light on the complexities and contradictions of the 'special relationship' between Roosevelt and Churchill and their nations. This is a terrific tale—and it's all true, proving anew that history trumps even the most vivid fiction."

—Jon Meacham, author of *American Gospel: God, the Founding Fathers, and the Making of a Nation* and *Franklin and Winston: An Intimate Portrait of an Epic Friendship*

ALSO BY JENNET CONANT

109 East Palace:
Robert Oppenheimer and the Secret City of Los Alamos

Tuxedo Park:
A Wall Street Tycoon and the Secret Palace of Science
That Changed the Course of World War II

THE
IRREGULARS

Roald Dahl and the British Spy Ring in Wartime Washington

Jennet Conant

SIMON & SCHUSTER PAPERBACKS
New York   London   Toronto   Sydney

SIMON & SCHUSTER PAPERBACKS
1230 Avenue of the Americas
New York, NY 10020

First Simon & Schuster trade paperback edition September 2009

SIMON & SCHUSTER PAPERBACKS and colophon are registered trademarks
of Simon & Schuster, Inc.

For information about special discounts for bulk purchases,
please contact Simon & Schuster Special Sales at 1-866-506-1949
or business@simonandschuster.com.

The Simon & Schuster Speakers Bureau can bring authors
to your live event. For more information or to book an event
contact the Simon & Schuster Speakers Bureau at
1-866-248-3049 or visit our website at www.simonspeakers.com.

Designed by Dana Sloan

Manufactured in the United States of America

10 9 8 7 6 5 4

The Library of Congress has cataloged the hardcover edition as follows:
Conant, Jennet.
  The irregulars : Roald Dahl and the British spy ring in wartime
Washington / Jennet Conant.
     p.   cm.
Includes index.
  1. Dahl, Roald—Career in espionage. 2. Great Britain. British
Security Coordination. 3. World War, 1939–1945—Secret service—Great
Britain. 4. World War, 1939–1945—Secret service—United States.
5. World War, 1939–1945—Propaganda. 6. Propaganda, British—
United States. I. Title.
D810.S8D234 2008
940.54'86410973—dc22   2008012483

ISBN 978-0-7432-9458-4
ISBN 978-0-7432-9459-1 (pbk)
ISBN 978-1-4165-8032-4 (ebook)

"No, it's not quite so bad as that. It's the unofficial force—
the Baker Street irregulars. . . .

"They can go everywhere, see everything, overhear every one."

—ARTHUR CONAN DOYLE,
The Sign of the Four

"Say from whence you owe this strange intelligence. . . ."

—*Macbeth* I, iii

CONTENTS

CONTENTS

PREFACE

Though fraud in other activities be detestable, in the
management of war it is laudable and glorious, and he
who overcomes an enemy by fraud is as much to be
praised as he who does so by force.

— MACHIAVELLI,
Discourses, Book III, Chapter XL

THIS BOOK IS AN attempt to reconstruct, as accurately as possible,
the infamous exploits of a group of spies who served with the
secret intelligence organization known as British Security Coordination (BSC), which set up shop in America during World War II and
remains one of the most controversial, and probably one of the most
successful, covert action campaigns in the annals of espionage. The
relentless duplicity of the BSC agents is not without precedent—ruses
de guerre have been part of a long tradition in warfare that dates as far
back as the Trojan horse, if not earlier—but until Winston Churchill
dispatched William Stephenson, aka Intrepid, to America as part of his
plan to prod the country into action, no one had ever dared to mount

such a large shadow force to wage war by means of sabotage, propaganda, and political subversion. As director of the BSC, Stephenson, according to the organization's official history, was empowered to "do all that was not being done and could not be done by overt means" to assure aid for Britain and counter the enemy's plans in the Western Hemisphere.

By the spring of 1942, when Roald Dahl, a dashing young RAF pilot, arrived in Washington as an assistant air attaché at the British Embassy, the BSC's vast network of spies was already in place and had established a remarkably effective propaganda machine that rallied American public opinion behind active support of England. Dahl would soon be caught up in the complex web of intrigue masterminded by Stephenson, the legendary Canadian spymaster, who outmaneuvered the FBI and State Department and managed to create an elaborate clandestine organization whose purpose was to weaken the isolationist forces in America and influence U.S. policy in favor of Britain.

Tall, handsome, and intelligent, Dahl had all the makings of an ideal operative. A courageous officer wounded in battle, smashing looking in his dress uniform, he was everything England could have asked for as a romantic representative of that imperiled island. He was also arrogant, idiosyncratic, and incorrigible, and probably the last person anyone would have considered reliable enough to be trusted with anything secret. Above all, however, Dahl was a survivor. When he got into trouble, he was shrewd enough to make himself useful to British intelligence, providing them with gossipy items that proved he had a nose for scandal and the writer's ear for damning detail. Already attached to the British Air Mission in Washington, he came equipped with the perfect cover story, and his easy wit and conspicuous charm guaranteed him entrée to the drawing rooms—and bedrooms—of the rich and powerful.

Dahl quickly infiltrated the upper reaches of Washington society and government, ingratiating himself with influential wartime leaders from Henry Wallace to Henry Morgenthau, captivating the heiress Evalyn Walsh McLean, and seducing the glamorous congresswoman Clare Boothe Luce. Encouraged by his superiors to cultivate friendships with important American publishers, Dahl became so close to the Texas newspaper tycoon Charles Marsh that he was virtually adopted into the family. As a result of his burgeoning fame as a writer, he was recommended to the First Lady, Eleanor Roosevelt, and before long was a regular guest at the White House, as well as at the presidential retreat, Hyde Park. All the while he was rubbing shoulders with the American elite, Dahl was reporting to his contacts at the BSC on everything he heard and saw.

Dahl and colorful coconspirators—including Noël Coward, Ian Fleming, David Ogilvy, and Ivar Bryce—were all rank amateurs, recruited for their clever minds and connections rather than any real experience in the trade of spying. These "Baker Street Irregulars," as they were dubbed in honor of the mischievous street urchins who aided the famous literary sleuth Sherlock Holmes, were Churchill's underground army in America, an "invisible fortress" that would help forestall the enemy and help England secure victory. They planted propaganda in American newspapers, radio stations, and wire services; co-opted leading columnists from Drew Pearson to Walter Lippmann and Walter Winchell; harassed prominent isolationists and anti–New Dealers; exposed Nazi sympathizers and fifth columnists; and plotted against corporations that were working against British interests.

While it may not have been the most honorable way to fight a war, Churchill was convinced he had no alternative—his country's very existence was at stake. By the winter of 1940, England faced an entrenched enemy and stood on the brink of collapse. The Nazis were sweeping across Europe and preparing to invade. Britain's only hope of survival hinged on America's assistance, and Churchill—with the tacit permission of President Roosevelt, who was privately in favor of intervention despite the overwhelming public opposition—instructed the BSC to do everything possible "to drag" their reluctant ally into the war against Germany.

The BSC succeeded not only in mystifying and misdirecting its political enemies but also in manipulating the policies of its greatest wartime ally in favor of England, changing the course of the United States forever. By pushing Roosevelt to create a transatlantic intelligence alliance in the form of the OSS, to be headed by London's "man in Washington" William "Wild Bill" Donovan, Stephenson effectively made the U.S. intelligence service the willing handmaiden of the British. Not surprisingly, this episode of history, which lay the foundation for the CIA, comes in many versions, with Stephenson and the BSC cast either as heroes or as villains depending on the author's ties to either the American or British intelligence establishments and the degree of moral discomfort with their devious activities and methods. Because of the outrageous lengths to which Stephenson and his dirty tricks squad resorted in their efforts to confound and defeat the Nazis—an end that, no matter how noble, did not necessarily justify the means—the BSC became an embarrassment to both America and England, charged with having a sinister influence on foreign affairs and immeasurably complicating relations between the two countries in the years to come.

There is no end to the mysteries, rumors, and hostile criticism that still enshroud the BSC's covert operation in America. To some extent, the problem is endemic to the intelligence services, where the successors always feel the need to rewrite the history of their predecessors and regard everyone who came before with suspicion, so that no one's reputation is safe. But it is especially acute in the case of the BSC, which was conceived of as a black, or unofficial, operation, precisely so that if any of Stephenson's boys were caught, they could be disowned by everyone. At every step along the way, they took meticulous care to cover their tracks, both to keep the enemy from picking up their scent and to prevent outraged American officials in the FBI and State Department from giving the show away. For practical purposes, it meant they left virtually no paper trail in this country. What few documents may exist in the classified archives of MI6 in London, the British have declined to release.

Complicating matters, Stephenson began securing his legacy well before the fighting was over, and he commissioned a number of reports, written by his own handpicked officers—including Dahl—so as to guarantee that his accomplishments would not be lost to time or jealous peers. Compiled into a 536-page book entitled *British Security Coordination: The Secret History of British Intelligence in the Americas, 1940–1945*, it lays bare both the audacity and achievements of the BSC spy network and the shocking willingness of the American press to peddle foreign propaganda aimed at leading the country into war. While parts of this top-secret "official history" were leaked over the years, and quoted and misquoted in countless books and articles, it was not made public until 1998, when it was copyrighted and published in Britain by St. Ermin's Press. How the classified document was obtained—was it a photocopy of Sir William's personal edition, as rumored, or one of the few remaining original volumes?—and whether it is in fact in its complete and unexpurgated form, has yet to be determined. The book comes with a disclaimer: "This publication has not been officially endorsed by Her Majesty's Government."

During the more than fifty years this secret history was suppressed, it became a tantalizing subject of speculation, what the former CIA officer and intelligence historian Thomas F. Troy described as a kind of "forbidden fruit." In its absence, far more thrilling and sensational narratives thrived. Stephenson went on to achieve outsize postwar celebrity—in not one but three tell-all books, a documentary, and a television movie—forever fixing the myth of the "superspy" in the popular imagination and kicking off a furious debate over his more dramatic claims and the true extent of his role as Churchill's personal representative in America. While serious historians do not question his remarkable contribution early in the war, at a time when many Americans believed the Nazi conquest of Britain was inevitable, those who have sought to discredit his legendary heroics have accused him of taking credit for others' work and attacked him as a self-promoting fraud. Unfortunately, after the publication of the first book, *The Quiet Canadian,* in 1962, which was written by H. Montgomery Hyde, a member of his BSC staff, Stephenson suffered a series of strokes, yet he continued to grant interviews to reporters and authors. His exaggerated claims in the 1976 best seller *A Man Called Intrepid* further undermined his credibility. Over the years, dozens of books on American and British intelligence activities in World War II have reexamined this fraught period, each of them marshaling documents, parsing quotes, and debunking previous accounts in order to argue their own conclusions. One of the most thorough and well reasoned of these is Troy's *Wild Bill and Intrepid,* which attempts to address the questions and inconsistencies that have "ignited controversies."

I⸀T is extremely difficult to write about any secret operation, let alone one that is still partly obscured in the murky netherworld of espionage. I have endeavored to pull the curtain back on one small part of this shadowy episode in order to tell the story of young Dahl's incredible experience as one of Stephenson's "agents of influence" in America. My task was greatly facilitated by the discovery of a large cache of wartime letters between Dahl and Charles Marsh, who became one of the BSC's valuable sources in the press, as well as a horde of carefully preserved minutes, memos, notes, files, and assorted correspondence with third parties. I also benefited from the surprising number of firsthand accounts of these events I was able to unearth, including diaries, private reminiscences, and numerous memoirs, in addition to published and unpublished interviews with many of the principal participants before they died. While these direct sources have the advantage of being uncensored, they are also unchecked and unsubstantiated. As a result, I had to sift through a wealth of material, some of it conflicting; and in the end some gaps were unavoidable and, as indicated in footnotes, a number of discrepancies could not be satisfactorily explained. In order to tell a compelling story, and not interrupt the narrative with too many caveats, I have also used my own judgment about the veracity of some of the events that follow and apologize in advance if it turns out I, too, have amplified any myths in the process.

To that end, it should be noted that spies are notoriously unreliable narrators. It would be unfair, perhaps, to suggest that they are all natural-born liars, but surely they are more facile than most. The BSC agents emerged from the war practiced in the arts of deception, obfuscation, and seduction—skills that no doubt contributed to their great success in civilian life. They all played the game so long and so well that it could not have been easy to stop. Fabricating can be habit-forming; surely it is no accident that three of them—Dahl, Fleming, and Ogilvy—would all make their fortunes as fabulists of sorts. It would therefore be naïve to assume that the principal participants in this story were ever entirely honest and forthright, even in their most intimate correspondence and conversations. Interviews given years after the fact are problematic in their own way, given the tendency of wartime figures to forget embarrassing details and embellish their records. While they did what they had to in their country's hour of need, after years of peacetime reflection they might have become understandably reticent about discussing the more unsavory aspects of their undercover assignments. They were also bound, even decades later, by the Official Secrets Act, so that even the most scrupulous among them might have felt it necessary to omit details. As Louis Franck, the wealthy Belgian banker who became head of the BSC's Special Operations Section, often reminded his men, "Truth is far too precious a commodity to be used lightly."

1

THE USUAL DRILL

"Don't you think that you or some other regular officer
should be doing this job?"
"We've all got our hands full," the Captain said.

—ROALD DAHL, *Going Solo*

I T WAS AN unseasonably warm spring evening in 1942, and between
the cherry blossoms and soldiers in uniform, brightly lit shopwin-
dows and partly darkened government buildings, wartime Washington
was a strange sight. Four months had passed since the Japanese attack
on Pearl Harbor. The grim task of mobilization had clearly begun, and
the streets were riddled with Quonset huts and hastily constructed
plywood office complexes. But these were the only outward signs of
conflict. In the eyes of a newly arrived Englishman, life in the capital
appeared almost normal. Back in London, there was not a light to be
seen in the bomb-shattered streets, where blackout shades were kept
drawn against the nightly air attacks, and people fumbled home from
work in the permanent gloom. The Battle of Britain, Germany's first air
assault on England, intended to pummel them into submission prior to

invasion, had been won the previous fall, but only just, and the city had paid a hell of a price. Here in America, among all the cheery reminders of the uninterrupted Easter holiday, it was hard to tell that there was a war on and that there were far-flung battlegrounds—desert, jungle, and ocean—where England had been fighting for her life the past two and a half years.

Flight Lieutenant Roald Dahl had decidedly mixed feelings about his new posting in the United States. He had turned twenty-five that September and was thoroughly disgusted with himself for being invalided out of the war so soon. His sense of failure was only intensified by the thought of the friends in his old squadron who were still in the thick of it. He knew that at one level he should be grateful. The life expectancy of an RAF pilot was not long, and he was lucky to be alive. On the other hand, the idea that he might have to sit out the rest of the war as a spectator, one of the "whiskey warriors" in Washington, was too awful to contemplate. Everyone knew the diplomatic service was just one of the more respectable ways of dodging the draft. It was "a rotten job," and he wanted no part of it, but then he was in no position to argue.

Dahl had been working for the Shell Oil Company in East Africa when England declared war on Germany in September 1939, and like most men of his age, he had been in a hurry to enlist. Two months after the fighting started, he quit his job and drove six hundred miles across jungle roads from Dar es Salaam to Nairobi to report to the small headquarters the Royal Air Force maintained in Kenya. After taking one look at him, the medical officer advised that at six feet six inches, Dahl was not exactly "the ideal height" for a fighter pilot. It was not hard to see what they were getting at: in order to fit his attenuated frame into the tiny cockpit of a military airplane, he was forced to curl up almost into a fetal position, with his knees tucked tightly under his chin. When he climbed into the open cockpit of a Tiger Moth for the first time and took his seat on the regulation parachute pack, his entire head stuck out above the windshield like some kind of cartoon character. But he was not easily deterred. The war had just begun, pilots were in demand, and in the end the RAF was not too fussy to take him.

Dahl spent the next two months at the RAF's run-down, little initial training school learning to fly over the dusty plains of Kenya. He discovered that flying the aerobatic Tiger Moths was easier than it looked, and he quickly learned to coax the small, single-engine biplanes into vertical spins, flips, and graceful loop-the-loops at a touch of the rudder bar, all of which, he wrote home, "was marvelous fun." Once he had mastered the basics, he was sent on to Iraq, to a large, desolate RAF outpost in Habbaniya, about one hundred miles south of Baghdad, where it was so fiendishly hot that the pilots could practice flying only from dawn to ten A.M. He spent another six months there learning how to handle Hawker Harts, military aircraft with machine guns in their wings, and practiced shooting down Germans by firing at canvas targets towed behind another airplane.

With barely a year's worth of formal training, Dahl was made a pilot officer and judged ready to join a squadron and face the enemy. He was sent to Libya to fight the Italians, who were attempting to seize control of the Mediterranean and were amassing their forces prior to advancing into Egypt. He made his way to Abu Sueir, a large RAF airfield on the Suez Canal, where he was given a Gladiator, an antiquated single-seat biplane that he had absolutely no idea how to operate, and told to fly it across the Nile delta to a forward base in the Western Desert, stopping twice to refuel along the way and receive directions to his new squadron's whereabouts. Needless to say, he never made it. Lost and low on fuel, he made what the RAF squadron report termed "an unsuccessful forced landing" and crashed headlong into the desert floor at seventy-five miles on hour. Despite the impact, he remained conscious long enough to free himself from his seat straps and parachute harness and drag himself from the fuselage before the gas tanks exploded. His overalls caught fire, but he somehow managed to smother the flames by rolling in the sand and suffered only minor burns. Luckily for him, he was picked up not long afterward by a British patrol that spotted the wreck and, when darkness fell, sneaked into enemy territory to check for survivors. All in all, it was a very close call.

Dahl was sent to a naval hospital in Alexandria, where he spent six months recovering from a severe concussion sustained when his face smashed into the aircraft's reflector sight. His skull was fractured, and the swelling from the massive contusion rendered him blind for weeks, and he suffered splitting headaches for months after that. His nose, which had been reduced to a bloody stump, was rebuilt by a famous Harley Street plastic surgeon who was out there doing his part for the war, and according to an informal poll of the nurses, Dahl's profile looked slightly better than before. The most lasting damage was done to his spine, which had been violently crunched in the collision and would never be entirely free of pain.

The entire time he was laid up in the hospital, Dahl could not wait to go back. It was not just the excitement he missed, though he had come to love flying. He had not been able to escape the feeling that he had failed everyone—failed himself—by ditching his plane on his very first trip to the front lines, and he was determined to redeem himself. The doctors had told him that in time his vision would clear, and the headaches would lessen, but the waiting was agony. Dahl was so worried about not being cleared for combat duty again that when informed that he was scheduled to return home on the next convoy, he refused to go. "Who wants to be invalided home anyway," he wrote his mother. "When I go I want to go normally."

It was a sign of just how badly the war was going that in April 1941, despite the injury to his head, he was cleared for operational flying. He was told to rejoin 80 Squadron, which was now in Greece. While convalescing in Alexandria, Dahl had kept up with the news and was aware that things were not going at all well for the token British expeditionary force that had been sent to Greece to repel the invading Italians. By the time the British decided to recall their army, the Italians had brought in German reinforcements, and as they rolled across the Greek frontier, the British found themselves outnumbered and outmaneuvered. Unless they could extricate their 53,000 troops in a hurry, it promised to be a bitter defeat, another Dunkirk in the making. Dahl realized that the two paltry RAF squadrons assigned to provide air cover for the retreat, of which 80 Squadron was one, were no match for the enemy and were being used as cannon fodder in an utterly hopeless and ill-conceived campaign. But he had his orders. There was nothing to do but get on with it.

Once again Dahl took off from Abu Sueir in an unfamiliar plane, a Mark I Hurricane, a powerful fighter with a big Rolls-Royce Merlin engine and eight Browning machine guns. This time, however, he managed to find his way north across the sea and landed safely on Elevsis, near Athens, less than five hours later. Almost immediately upon landing, his worst fears were confirmed when he learned that England was attempting to defend the whole of Greece with a total of eighteen Hurricanes, against a huge German air invasion force of well over one thousand Messerschmitt 109s and 110s, Ju 88s, and Stuka dive-bombers. Any dreams of glory Dahl had entertained while lying in his hospital bed vanished at the prospect of such daunting odds.

When he arrived on Elevsis, Dahl had never been in a dogfight, never shot down a kraut, never seen a friend die. By April 24, after almost two weeks of intensive flying, engaging the enemy as many as three or four times a day, and culminating in a prolonged siege known as the Battle of Athens, he had seen more air-to-air combat than he cared to remember, racked up his share of kills and many times more unconfirmeds, and watched as the better part of his squadron was wiped out. In the end, they were down to a handful of bullet-ridden planes and battle-shocked pilots and were forced to hide from the swarms of German patrols in a grove of olive trees at Argos. After German planes strafed their camp and destroyed their fuel and ammunition stores, the most senior pilots took off for Crete in the five serviceable Hurricanes, while the remaining survivors of 80 Squadron were flown out of the country. By April 30 the Germans expelled the British from Greece and by May had won Crete. The retreating British divisions crawled slowly toward Athens and suffered extremely heavy losses before they were finally evacuated by the navy. Roughly 13,000 men were killed, wounded, or taken prisoner. It was a debacle from start to finish.

The 80 Squadron was re-formed and sent on to Haifa, on the coast of Palestine, where they engaged the Germans again in the Syrian campaign. They had a full-time job trying to protect the British destroyers stationed in the harbor, which were also under attack from Vichy French forces. Dropping a brief line to his mother, Dahl bragged that he had managed to bag five enemy planes and probably many more on the ground. He participated in another three weeks of fierce fighting, during which the Vichy French succeeded in shooting down four out of nine pilots in his squadron, before his headaches returned with a vengeance. The blinding pain tended to hit when he was in the middle of a dogfight, just as he was diving or doing a steep turn, and on more than one occasion brought on a blackout that caused him to lose consciousness for several seconds. The squadron doctor ascribed the episodes to gravitational pressure and the toll it was taking on his old head injury. Dahl had become a danger not only to himself, but to his airplane, which the RAF regarded as valuable property. He had flown his last sortie. He was declared unfit to fly and at the end of June shipped home as a noncombatant.

Dahl had been on leave, convalescing at his mother's small cottage in the rural village of Grendon Underwood, in Buckinghamshire, and pondering his future in some dreary ministry office in London, when he was summoned to the London office of Harold Balfour, the undersecretary of state for air, and informed that he was being sent to the United States as part of a diplomatic delegation. Dahl was stunned. He had known his present state of limbo could not continue indefinitely, that eventually he would have to find something to do, but he was back in the bosom of his family, and that had seemed like enough after what he had been through. He had been away from England for almost three years, first for the Shell Oil Company and then for the RAF, and it had been an emotional homecoming. He was one of seven children, including two from a previous marriage, and his mother's only son, and he had been raised in a household of women, fussed over and adored his entire life, and his safe return had been cause for great relief.

While his mother was a singularly stoic Norwegian, he knew his extended absence had been difficult for her. She had seen too many of those she held most dear snatched away unexpectedly not to find good-byes, even temporary ones, painful. Sofie Magdalene Hesselberg was twenty-six when she married Roald's father, Harald Dahl, and left Norway to go live with him in the small fishing village of Cardiff, in the south of Wales, where he owned a prosperous shipping supply firm. She became a mother to her husband's young son and daughter by his first wife, who had died in childbirth, and in quick succession bore him another four children, two girls, a boy (Roald), and another daughter. Then, when Roald was three, tragedy struck. In the space of only a few weeks, his mother lost the eldest of her three girls, seven-year-old Astri, who died of appendicitis, followed by the death of her fifty-seven-year-old husband, whose heartbreak had been compounded by pneumonia. A woman of rare courage and resolve, she never gave way to despair, even though she had been left alone with five children to care for and was expecting another baby in a few months' time. She also never wavered in her determination to see her children properly educated. It had been her late husband's deepest conviction that the English preparatory schools had no equal in the world, and he had left her sufficiently well off to see his wishes carried out. According to the hard British tradition, Dahl was sent away to school in England at the age of nine, first to St. Peter's, and then to Repton, which ranked a notch or two below Eton in social standing but nevertheless had a solid reputation.

It had been expected that he would go on to university, to Oxford or Cambridge, but he had set his heart on adventure abroad. Mother and son were very close—she had moved the whole family from Wales to England to be nearer his school—and when he broke the news that he had signed a contract with the Shell Oil Company for a three-year tour in Africa, she had been careful not to betray any hint of emotion. He was more boy than man when he left, and he had been bursting with excitement and too full of thoughts of "palm-trees and coconuts and coral reefs" to feel any guilt as he waved a last farewell to his mother and sisters at the London docks. He had not known then that the war would intervene and that the three years would seem much, much longer—more like a lifetime.

Dahl was not a demonstrative man, but after barely getting out of Egypt in one piece, he had been desperate to be reunited with his family. The harrowing journey home on the bomb-threatened troopship, which was chased by German submarines in the Atlantic, and by Focke-Wulf aircraft on the last leg of the voyage from Lagos to Liverpool, only heightened his sense of urgency. He had not had an easy time of it. After working so hard to overcome his injuries and return to his squadron, it had been a bitter pill to be grounded after barely a month. On top of his disappointment at being discharged was the disconcerting knowledge that the complications from his concussion were not completely behind him and would most likely bar him from any other frontline service in the war. It was hard to believe that his days of fighting Germans had come to such a quick end, harder still to take leave of his gallant comrades, who would continue with the squadron without him. When he said good-bye to his closest friend, David Coke, the Earl of Leicester's youngest son, who had been kind enough to show a green recruit the ropes, it was impossible not to wonder if they would ever see each other again.*

To keep his mother from worrying, Dahl had sent her a brief cable from Egypt telling her he was coming home, adding with false bravado that he was "very fit" and the Syrian campaign had been "fun." He still had not received any word from her when his ship sailed from Freetown for Liverpool, but mail service to Haifa was hardly reliable, and he had had no news from England for some time. As a consequence, he had a bad scare when he arrived at Liverpool and attempted to phone his mother's house in Kent, only to be told by the operator that the number was disconnected months ago. The operator had said, "She'll probably have been bombed out like all the rest of them," and speculated that she had moved elsewhere. An awful lot hung on that "probably." The confusion caused by the blitz, where family members were killed or injured in blasts, buried in rubble, or lost as they scrambled from one temporary shelter to another, made for a nightmarish twenty-four hours until he finally succeeded in tracking them down. It turned out that his mother and two of his sisters had been hiding in the cellar when their house was hit and had promptly packed the dogs and what was left of their belongings into the car and driven around the countryside until they had found a suitable cottage in Grendon Underwood. When the bus ferrying him to the tiny village finally pulled to a halt, Dahl spotted a familiar figure standing patiently by the road and, as he

---

*David Coke was decorated for bravery, and as Dahl later wrote in *Going Solo*, "tragically but almost inevitably, he would be shot down and killed."

later wrote, "flew down the steps of the bus straight into the arms of the waiting mother."

He had been home only a few short months when he learned that the undersecretary for air planned to send him away again. Dahl had met Harold Balfour quite by chance that fall, when a colleague had invited him to dine at Pratt's, one of the better-known men's clubs in London. During the course of the evening, Dahl had done his best to impress the senior official with his battle stories and his skill at bridge. Balfour must have taken it upon himself to arrange a cushy assignment for the disabled flier, because the next day he summoned Dahl to his office and informed him that he would be joining the British Embassy in Washington D.C. as an assistant air attaché. When he heard the news, Dahl protested, "Oh no, sir, please, sir—anything but that, sir!" Balfour would not be moved: "He said it was an order, and the job was jolly important."

On March 24, 1942, the Foreign Office issued Dahl a visa and diplomatic identification card and handed him his travel orders. Three days later, per his instructions, he took a train to Glasgow, where he boarded a Polish ship bound for Canada. During the uneventful two-week crossing, he contemplated his new government appointment with a heavy heart. He passed the time trading war stories with a fellow passenger, a RAF pilot by the name of Douglas Bisgood who was, worse luck, being sent to an officer training camp on the east coast of Canada. After being told he could no longer fly combat missions, Dahl had declined the RAF's offer to become an instructor and spend the rest of the war training new pilots. If the RAF training camps in Nairobi and Iraq were any indication, he would have been stuck in some abominable hellhole with nothing more than a strip of hangars and Nissan huts to remind him of civilization. Despite his reservations about his upcoming desk duty, he did not envy Bisgood one bit.

By the time Dahl made his way to Washington and assumed his duties at the British Embassy in late April, he found the capital already in the full bloom of spring and exuding an almost devil-may-care optimism. The restaurants, stores, and theaters were flourishing, and the streets were crowded with happy throngs enjoying all the comforts and amenities of modern urban life. Everyone in America looked prosperous, well dressed, and almost indecently healthy. The bullish mood in Washington, so different from downtrodden London, seemed to stem from the American certainty that they would win the day. There was historical precedent for such confidence—the United States had never lost a war. Thanks to the strength of their armed forces, industry, and abundant resources, the Americans were convinced that victory was a question not of "if" but of "how long." A war was raging, but most people he met seemed chiefly concerned with gas rationing, the availability of summer suits, and the rumored shortage of cigarettes.

Everywhere he went, people wanted to talk to him about Winston Churchill, whose Christmas visit, just weeks after Pearl Harbor, had aroused great interest. It had been the prime minister's first meeting with President Roosevelt since their dramatic rendezvous at sea in August 1941, when Churchill had hoped to come away with a declaration of war and instead had to settle for the disappointing eight-point joint declaration of peace aims known as the Atlantic Charter. Since then the Japanese attack had destroyed much of the U.S. Navy and demonstrated that even the wide Pacific could not keep the enemy from America's shores. The Japanese had dealt England a terrible blow as well: on December 10 they had sunk two of Britain's largest warships, the *Prince of Wales* and *Repulse*. Almost immediately after declaring war on the Japanese, Churchill had crossed the Atlantic to show his solidarity with Roosevelt and the United States. But he had also come, pink-faced and bow-tied, full of fighting spirit and rolling cadences, to marshal the country's immense strength on behalf of the Allied coalition in what was now a global war.

Churchill's yuletide call on the White House had been a well-publicized goodwill tour with a deadly serious purpose—to convince Roosevelt it was time for the machinery of combined action to slip into high gear. Military secrecy, of course, dictated that the details of their conversations be withheld, but one White House communiqué had emphasized that the "primary objective" of the talks was "the defeat of Hitlerism throughout the world." The Germans and Italians, now with the help of the Vichy French, were mounting dire new assaults on British forces. In the first few months of 1942, Japan had handed them one disastrous defeat after another in the Far East—Hong Kong and Singapore were lost, and public confidence in Churchill had been severely shaken. Both leaders were in agreement that the Allied coalition had to act with greater coordination in the struggle against the Axis powers, and the call for greater "synchronization" had filled the newspapers in London and Washington.

Despite all the hoopla about their historic alliance, Dahl knew from what he had read and heard to expect a certain amount of ambivalence, if not residual anti-British sentiment. It would be nothing compared to the entrenched isolationism that had characterized America during the so-called Phony War—as a skeptical senator had dubbed the stalemate between September 1939 and April 1940, when Hitler but did not attack for nine months—reflecting the opinion of the majority of U.S. citizens who were not yet disposed to see Hitler as a threat to democracy or to the American way of life. The American public was so determined to stay neutral that they pressured Roosevelt to remain aloof from the European conflict and vigilantly protested any assistance to the Allies as a sign that he was giving into Britain's blatant war propaganda. Political feeling was so overwhelmingly isolationist that only after France fell, and England was under siege and enduring her "darkest hour," was Roosevelt able to offer military aid to England under the guise of the Lend-Lease Act—and even then with the argument that it was vital to the defense of the hemisphere. After Pearl Harbor, America's dramatic entry into the war had brought with it a great burst of support for England, but it had faded all too quickly. Inevitably, as the weeks became months and the fighting ground on, the old doubts had returned. Some of the current bad feeling was the frustration produced by a battle without early victories, and the usual tendency in such circumstances was to blame one's allies for not doing enough.

While public anxiety over the war had weakened their ranks, there were still a great number of hard-core noninterventionists, and they remained a powerful force whose influence stretched across the American political spectrum, including such diverse pro-Nazi types as the famed pilot Charles Lindbergh and his wife, Anne (who argued that fascism was the "wave of the future"), such notable senators as Burton Wheeler and Gerald Nye (who regarded the war as just the latest bloody chapter in Europe's long and savage history), and antiwar liberals like Charles Beard, Robert Hutchins, and Chester Bowles. This disparate crew, mostly Republicans and anti–New Dealers, had organized as the America First Committee, founded back in the fall of 1940, and still strove to return their country to the old, untrammeled path of private enterprise and national ends. They took the view that the whole continent of Europe should be written off as a total loss. While the public had little sympathy for the Germans, distrust of the plundering British Empire still ran deep. Only a year ago, a commonly expressed view in conservative American newspapers was "Let God Save the King." Now, instead of being chastened, they railed against Roosevelt for tricking the American people into going to war, and they accused England of already laying postwar plans for international plunder. While beloved by the British as their best hope, Roosevelt—not to mention his wife, Eleanor, and little dog, Fala—was reportedly regarded with utter loathing by a large segment of his own country.

Dahl's brief was vague, but he knew that the British Embassy in Washington functioned more or less as Whitehall's press office, with its main focus on maintaining close diplomatic relations with the Roosevelt administration and on monitoring the shifting loyalties of the fickle American people. He would be a small cog in the embassy's propaganda apparatus, working to manufacture the sort of positive information that could counter what was thought to be most damaging to Britain and encourage maximum cooperation in the prosecution of the war. He also knew that in the ongoing effort to drum up support for the war, the British Ministry of Information in London had organized a variety of publicity campaigns, a way of hand-feeding the press, radio, wire services, and other media that influenced American public opinion. Far and away the most effective of these campaigns had focused on the heroism of the Battle of Britain pilots, who had persevered despite horrendous losses to the Luftwaffe. Churchill's famous tribute to the valiant RAF eagles—"Never in the field of human conflict was so much owed by so many to so few"—had become England's best sales pitch, urging the Americans to help "finish the job."

Dahl doubted he would be much good to his country in its public relations cause in the United States. Smart, acerbic, and impatient with ceremony, Dahl did not see himself as a natural diplomat. It was not just a question of his personal cynicism, though Churchill's rhetoric had not been much comfort when he and his fellow pilots were fighting for survival on Elevsis. There was no question in his mind that they should not have been there in the first place and had been "flung in at the deep end," totally unprepared, ill-equipped, and faced with impossible odds. It had been a colossal blunder. The enormity of the losses, the waste of life, still haunted him. Now, in his official capacity as assistant air attaché, he would be involved in the exchange of intelligence with the U.S. Army Air Force, and act as liaison between the two services—but was expected to go gently, with nothing but broad smiles and approbation, as the Americans were the "new boys," and no one wanted to strain the burgeoning friendship between the two nations.

On his first day, he reported to the British Embassy, an impressive red-brick pile that was reportedly modeled after the work of Sir Christopher Wren and cost upward of $1 million to build in the late 1920s. It was every inch the traditional English country manor—complete with an old chancery—incongruously facing Massachusetts Avenue, with a grand drawing room with mirrored walls and marble pillars and the requisite green lawns, rose gardens, and swimming pool. Dahl was assigned a small office at the Air Mission, which was located in an annex. Until permanent housing could be arranged, he was put up at the Willard, an enormous grande dame of a hotel on Pennsylvania Avenue, just two blocks from the White House, where he lived in comparative luxury after the deprivations back home. As soon as he was settled, he sent word to his mother—he dutifully wrote home every other week throughout the war, laying aside time on Saturday afternoons—and filled her in on his workplace, wonderful accommodations, and other banalities of his life in Washington. It was difficult to write without really saying anything, having been forewarned that he could not discuss his work and that embassy censors would scrutinize every piece of mail before including it in the diplomatic pouch to England. When his letters arrived at Grendon Underwood, they always bore the telltale label "Opened by the Examiner."

From the very beginning, his days were filled from morning to night with official luncheons, banquets, and receptions, as well as lectures and panels of all sorts. Boredom set in almost at once. Just as he had

feared, it was "a most unimportant, ungodly job." The embassy was full
of very serious, war-winning types who had never set foot anywhere
near to the front. As the weeks passed, he became increasingly vexed
and demoralized. In his former life, he had been admired for his ready
wit, clever turn of phrase, and the ability to talk himself into and out
of almost anything. Here in the United States he was becoming increasingly sullen and cranky. He did not even bother to hide his scorn
for the endless round of parties that composed much of official life in
Washington, and that, with America's entry into the war, had reached
a level of frenzied conviviality.

His contempt for his glad-handing duties was compounded by
what Churchill had referred to as "the inward excitement which
comes from a prolonged balancing of terrible things." Dahl could not
believe he had been cast as a cheerleader, trotted out as a handsome,
battle-scarred champion of the British fighting spirit. How many
times could he be expected to relive his experiences in North Africa
for audiences of moist-eyed congressional wives? Or sing the praises
of American airplanes' performance in flag-draped ballrooms? He was
too fresh from the field to find sympathy with the War Office's use of
the RAF's "intrepid flying men" as a propaganda tool. He felt humili-
ated at his predicament in Washington. "[I'd] just come from the war
where people were killing each other," he recalled. "I'd been flying
around, [seeing] all sorts of horrible things happening. And almost
instantly, I found myself in the middle of a cocktail mob in America.
On certain occasions, as an air attaché, I had to put on this ghastly
gold braid and tassels. The result was I became rather outspoken and
brash."

Dahl was a patriot and intensely loyal to the RAF, almost to a fault.
He was all for helping the British and American air accord but could
not help sounding off about the various hypocrisies of their dueling
propaganda agencies, which, in his view, were more often than not in

discord. It irked him, for example, that whenever an RAF raid took place within the same twenty-four hour period as a U.S. Army Air Force, strike, the British Information Service (BIS) would end up in direct competition with their American equivalent, the Office of War Information (OWI), to see which agency could get the most publicity for its respective force. Obviously, the British, who were new to the country and did not understand the complex workings of the American press system, were at a disadvantage. Similarly, he had heard that the OWI experts working in the American Embassy in London were having difficulty disseminating U.S. propaganda there and were getting little or no help from their British counterparts. Considering that they were all supposed to be pulling together, this was a situation that struck Dahl as anything but collegial, and he leaped forward to remedy the situation. When he raised this sore point in official forums, along with his suggestions as to how the situation might be improved, he managed to ruffle feathers on the both sides of the pond.

As it happened, neither country was particularly pleased to have a vocal critic of its vying propaganda efforts. Dahl knew his impertinence was not endearing him to embassy officials, but he did not much care. He could not curb his tongue when pilots were still dying in droves as a result of the Luftwaffe's renewed bombing campaign. Not that everyone found fault with his impolitic outbursts on behalf of the ordinary British fighting man. Dahl's unsparing assessment of the RAF's failures, with which he was intimately acquainted, and his frank observations about the shortcomings of their air strategy in general often got a warm reception in Washington, where many Americans had grown weary of the history-and-heroes routine of the relentless pro-British interventionists.

Dahl stood out from the other young British envoys who, for the most part, were fawning aides from the privileged class who had been dumped on the embassy's doorstep to keep them out of harm's way.

From a physical standpoint, he was pure Norwegian, with the arrogant blue eyes and imposing stature of his Viking ancestors, though he liked to boast that he was one-quarter Scottish, as his mother was descended from an illegitimate son of Sir William Wallace. He had a fine head, a high forehead, and a crown of wavy brown hair neatly parted and combed over to the right. Among his colleagues, he proudly identified himself as Norwegian rather than British, and most of his cultural references, from childhood fairy tales to favorite home-cooked meals, were rooted in his Nordic heritage. He spoke his native language fluently, as English was rarely spoken at home and as he had spent all his summer holidays from the age of four to seventeen on the islands off the coast of Oslo, where he was taught to be an intrepid sailor and adventurer in the tradition of his fearless forebears. Having survived the barbaric traditions of English boarding schools for ten years, Dahl was a part of the old-boy network without quite belonging to it; he knew its rules and rituals intimately and could partake in the hearty camaraderie while barely disguising his contempt. Despite being a fair student and star athlete—he had excelled at soccer, squash, racquets, and a fast-paced variation of handball known as "fives"—he had never quite fit in. He was always viewed by his schoolmasters with suspicion and regarded as "unpredictable" and someone "not to be trusted." He had a rebellious streak, and it was this iconoclasm that appealed to Americans. They thought they recognized in Dahl a kindred spirit, with his outrageous candor and irreverence for authority, so that those who were wary of British nobility playing at war adopted him as one of their own.

If the Americans found him refreshing, his English superiors judged him tactless, and Dahl was not surprised to learn that less than a year into the job he had managed to land himself in hot water. Conceding that he might have been impudent on occasion, Dahl apologized for his behavior and promised to toe the line. While he had taken a singularly cavalier approach to his diplomatic duties thus far, he realized he rather liked America and was not in a hurry to be sent packing. With no meaningful defense work waiting for him back in England, and no promising career path to resume when the war was over, Dahl admitted to a friend that he found himself feeling oddly rudderless. His unlikely confidant was a self-made Texas oil tycoon and publishing magnate named Charles Edward Marsh, who had moved to the capital when the war made it the most interesting place to be.

Having already made his fortune, Marsh, like many men of means, wanted to contribute to the war effort and had decided to put himself at the disposal of the government. A dedicated New Dealer, he had come to town with the idea that he could put his big money and big personality to work for the Roosevelt administration, camping out alternately at the Mayflower Hotel and at the house of the construction magnate George Brown, before purchasing a stately four-story town house at 2136 R Street in Dupont Circle. He quickly turned the elegant nineteenth-century mansion into a well-financed Democratic political salon, where various cabinet members, senators, financiers, and important journalists could count on a good meal and stimulating conversation in the news-starved town. Over time prominent New Dealers came to regard Marsh's white sandstone mansion, with its Palladian windows and Parisian-style wrought-iron grillwork, as their private clubhouse and used it as a cross between a think tank and a favorite watering hole. It had the added attraction of a side annex that was entered by a single inconspicuous door, which allowed important guests to come and go unseen. Among those who regularly passed through this discreet portal were Marsh's close friend Vice President Henry A. Wallace, Florida senator Claude Pepper, Secretary of the Treasury Henry Morgenthau, and Secretary of Commerce Jesse Jones, who was one of the wealthiest and most influential of FDR's administrators, as well as most of the major columnists, including

Drew Pearson, Walter Winchell, Walter Lippmann, and Ralph Ingersoll, editor of the crusading *PM* magazine, whose account of the Battle of Britain, *Report on England*, was a best seller. At one of these weekly gatherings, Pearson remembered Marsh introducing him to "a very vivacious, fast-talking young congressman" from Texas by the name of Lyndon B. Johnson, who the publisher had backed in his first campaign and promised was going places.

Dahl met Marsh at a party and immediately hit it off with the colorful millionaire, who was an exemplary host and an amusing and informative guide to Washington's stratified society, where new and old money, the congressional set and the diplomatic corps all jostled for recognition. As the months passed, Dahl formed the habit of dropping by Marsh's place after work for a drink, as it was just a block off Massachusetts Avenue at the foot of Embassy Row. More often than not he would linger, hoping for an invitation to dinner, as the company was good and the food far better than anything he could afford on his salary. "Charles was able to entertain on a grand level, and kept a very good staff and cook, so that during the war it was one of the best restaurants in town," recalled Creekmore Fath, a young Texas lawyer toiling in the Roosevelt administration who also frequented Marsh's table. "He entertained all sorts of Washington characters. You'd get a telephone call inviting you to dinner Wednesday, or a luncheon Friday at noon. Everybody came and traded information and gossip."

A Texan by choice rather than by birth, Marsh was a garrulous storyteller in the tradition of his adoptive state, and he and Dahl immediately fell into a good-natured rivalry that consisted mainly of trading sporting jabs about their respective homelands and telling dirty jokes at each other's expense. Passionate when it came to politics, Marsh loved an audience and would often hold forth into the wee hours on the progress of the war, the president's economic policies, the greatness of American industry, and what more he thought the

United States could be doing on the home front to secure victory. At first Dahl regarded these lively, epithet-strewn monologues as fascinating tutorials, but over time he came to realize that it was more than just talk and that the opinions the publisher expounded at night in his paneled library showed up as the next morning's editorials in one of his daily papers.

Marsh, who was actually born in Cincinnati, Ohio, had risen from the ranks as a lowly reporter to become managing editor of the *Cincinnati Post* before forming a partnership with E. S. Fentress, a business manager in the E. W. Scripps chain, on a buying spree that ended up with them owning nineteen daily newspapers in Texas, including the *Austin American* and the *Statesman*. By 1930 Marsh had merged with Eugene Pulliam, the owner of nine dailies in Oklahoma and Indiana, to form General Newspapers, Inc., which they grew into an enormous publishing empire. As the principal of several holding companies, and owner of newspaper chains that extended from Texas through the South to New England, Marsh was an active voice in American politics and an influential behind-the-scenes figure in Washington, but unlike most of the players Dahl had encountered in the nation's capital, he eschewed publicity, preferring to manipulate people and events from the privacy of his R Street study.

In 1940 he had sold all his jointly held newspapers—except for three dailies in Waco, Austin, and Port Arthur—and focused his drive and energy on fighting the Axis powers. As bombs rained down on London that winter, Marsh, working together with his friends Walter Lippmann, Senator Claude Pepper, and Ben Cohen, a member of Roosevelt's "brain trust," helped draft a plan that outlined a novel way to send military aid to Britain. At the time, Roosevelt had just won reelection, burying his Republican challenger, Wendell Willkie, by a five-million-vote margin. Churchill had come to him hat in hand, with another desperate plea for military aid, asking for ships, bombers, and munitions. The difficulty was that Britain was low on dollars, and Churchill wanted to write an IOU for the armaments—even though the Neutrality Acts demanded cash payment. In a press conference, Roosevelt responded by emphasizing Britain's plight and drawing a homely parable about a man lending his neighbor his garden hose to put out a fire. With FDR's "garden hose" endorsement, Pepper was able to get the new legislation through the Foreign Relations Committee, and after months of bitter debate it was finally passed as the Lend-Lease Act on March 11, 1941. That December Roosevelt, in one of his nationally broadcast fireside chats, declared that the United States had to become the "great arsenal of democracy," taking the country another step down the road from neutrality toward active involvement in the conflict. To the British, Lend-Lease had made all the difference, allowing them to withstand the Nazi onslaught, and they would not forget the crucial role Marsh had played in the early days of the war.

Marsh, then in his mid-fifties, was a large man in both stature and ideas and that rare individual who stood almost eye to eye with Dahl. He had a huge head and gleaming bald pate and was classically ugly in a way that was compelling. He was the sort of person of whom legends were made, and his personal life was correspondingly baroque. Marsh had fathered five children, three of whom were in their twenties, by a wife he had left behind in Texas, as well as two infants by his very young, very beautiful bride, Alice Glass. Then there was Alice's decidedly plain sister, Mary Louise, who lived with them and served as his personal secretary and ran the establishment with intimidating efficiency. Also part of this menagerie was Claudia Haines, Marsh's pretty, dark-haired typist, who had been hired by Alice because the divorced mother of two had needed a job, and Alice had taken pity on her. Dahl, no stranger to the rivalries that can develop in a household of women, made a quick study of the unusual arrangement and came to his own conclusions. The sexual tension in the air was thick enough to cut with a knife, and talk of affairs by both Charles and Alice was rampant among their friends. Ralph Ingersoll, in an unpublished memoir of Marsh, painted the indelible scene that greeted visitors to the R Street house: "Hawk-beaked Charles, the sultan in his castle, off-handedly gracious with his mini-harem in attendance."

Nothing if not grandiose, Marsh enjoyed the role of benefactor and liked to collect around him bright young men who caught his fancy. In the course of his publishing career, he had mentored a series of talented editors and writers, as well as a number of rising political stars. "Charles always had a group of young men around him, and Roald was one of them," said Fath, who numbered among Marsh's acolytes. "Roald always wore his uniform, and was very attractive and interesting, and had a rack of good stories from his years in the RAF. He was a genuine war hero, shot down and decorated, and at the same time very educated and articulate, so he was very impressive." Ingersoll, like Fath, could not help noticing how comfortable the British pilot seemed in the powerful publisher's midst, casually stretched out on the sofa with his long legs resting on the coffee table, and attributed it to "his wit and a kind of cocky British grace [that was] instantly engaging."

By the end of 1942, Dahl had become an integral part of Marsh's large, eccentric R Street household. "We all just adored him, especially my father," recalled Antoinette Marsh Haskell, who at twenty-eight was the oldest of the Marsh offspring. Along with her husband, Robert Haskell, and two brothers, Charles Jr. and John, Antoinette tried to make the lonely serviceman feel at home and invited him on weekend outings, to parties and holiday dinners. "We sort of adopted him," said Antoinette. "Roald was a real charmer when he wanted to be. He was great fun to be around. He was always doing tricks and playing crazy practical jokes, probably to cut the tension, because it was a very tense time in the world."

For Dahl, who missed his mother and sisters, the Marshes became a second family. The R Street house was his refuge. It was a place of comfort and fellowship, particularly that somber Christmas of 1942—the second since Pearl Harbor—when Dahl could have easily become engulfed in the melancholy that hung over the capital's crowded boardinghouses and the hordes of displaced servicemen and war workers. Instead, he was invited to share the Marshes' holiday feast and to admire the giant evergreen that Charles had managed to obtain despite the reported shortages caused by the lack of manpower and transportation. The tree was every bit as colossal and fabulous as its owner, and its glittering lights cheered all those in its presence, a gaudy beacon of hope amid all the uncertainty.

Fatherless from a young age, Dahl admired Charles Marsh more than any man he had ever met, and he became increasingly dependent on his advice and good opinion. Marsh was warm and generous, with an irrepressible confidence in himself and the future that exasperated his enemies and won him enduring friendships throughout his life. He was famously impulsive and dished out expensive gifts and treats for faithful colleagues without waiting for a reason or occasion. Once, when a guest admired a painting, he promptly took it off the wall and insisted she keep it as a gift. Having given himself permission to enjoy an unchecked existence, both materially and emotionally, he encouraged his young protégé to follow his example. He was an enthusiastic proponent of plunging into life with both feet, committing oneself fully, damn the consequences. He championed a sort of super-American, Whitmanesque belief in pure spirit, boundless possibility, and what he called that unshakable "bit of divine moving from the embryo to death in each of us."

It was to Marsh that Dahl increasingly turned when he wanted to escape the petty demands of embassy life, and the petty officials who were always wringing their hands over his latest remark or ill-advised stunt. Never one to follow the rules, be it at school or at the embassy, Dahl was always getting up to some kind of mischief, whether it was filching expensive cigars from his boss's office and passing them around, or sending self-aggrandizing missives to Marsh written on the thick, buff-colored British Embassy stationery and carrying the official red wax seal. His favorite pastime was lampooning the mannered style of his country's wartime representatives, particularly that of the British ambassador, the first Earl of Halifax, an old Etonian who even his erudite information officer, Isaiah Berlin, an Oxford philosopher, described as "being not of this century."

There was something about this remote, ascetic-looking man, with his withered left arm and disdainful air, that brought out the devil in Dahl. The embassy, like most British expatriate institutions, resembled nothing so much as a proper British public school and no doubt evoked unpleasant memories of the many years he had spent in those institutions and the succession of headmasters who had condoned unconscionable beatings of their young charges in the name of discipline. Dahl was not alone in feeling like he was back in school. Isaiah Berlin, who after Pearl Harbor had been seconded from the Ministry of Information to the embassy in Washington, compared the ambassador to a kind of Provost, "very grand, very vice-regal," who looked down on the junior embassy officials, to say nothing of young attachés from the various missions.

It was common knowledge that Halifax, formerly foreign secretary, had expected that he and not Churchill would succeed Neville Chamberlain as prime minister and that Churchill had sent him to America to get him out of the way. It was equally well known that as one of Chamberlain's key advisers, Halifax had advocated the doomed policy of appeasement toward the Germans and never lifted a finger to bolster Britain's defenses despite the growing threat. Moreover, Halifax was proving a liability with the Americans, who found the former viceroy of India to be the embodiment of every abominable cliché about the British aristocracy and compared him unfavorably to his predecessor, Lord Lothian, whose death in December 1940 was considered a great loss by both countries.* Only three months after assuming his post, Halifax, true to form, had managed to commit a huge diplomatic blunder by going fox hunting in the green pastures of Pennsylvania. The sight of the new British ambassador riding to the hounds with American landed gentry prompted the poet Carl Sandburg to savage him in *The Nation*, ridiculing any official representative who would go cavorting around the countryside, indulging in "conspicuous leisure," while his countrymen "were fighting a desperate war with an incalculable adversary." He noted that photographs of His Lordship on horseback did nothing for the war effort and only inspired American workingmen to ask, "Are we going to war again for the sake of a lot of English fox-hunters?" Halifax continued to come in for steady criticism from the press, and even Churchill, on his visits to Washington, had taken to excluding him from his conferences with Roosevelt.

Dahl considered Halifax a pompous fool, completely dull and devoid of humor, and took every opportunity to ridicule his obsession with blood, class, and title. Like a goodly portion of the embassy staff, the British ambassador seemed to live in the past and soldiered on in the vague hope that the future would be much the same. A wicked mimic, Dahl could not resist mocking him. He took to imitating Halifax's old-empire style, embellishing his letters with the ambassador's obsequious phrases and endowing all his American friends with exalted titles. Marsh readily joined in the fun and sent his droll replies by return mail to Dahl's embassy office, which was not without risk. His note thanking Dahl for a box of cigars, courtesy of the diplomatic bag from Havana, was addressed, "For Transmission to the King":

---

*Lothian was a Christian Scientist and refused to allow doctors to treat him when he fell ill. He died of uremic poisoning.

Your most impressive gift will be consumed in the usual way. It is only human that I add that the element of snobbery which is present in all of us will be exhaled with every puff.

You will pardon my Anglophobia.

One cigar per Sunday will be my prayer and ritual to the Union Jack.

Marsh signed the letter, "Your Obedient Servant, Charles the Bald," and included a lewd postscript: "You, of course, were courteous to the queen [Alice], but haven't you found out over there that there are many better places to take one's trousers off than the marital bed?"

Even though Dahl took the game too far, at times openly flaunting authority, his confidence and air of infallibility made him seem unassailable. "Roald could be like sand in an oyster," recalled Dahl's first wife, the actress Patricia Neal. "He seemed to feel he had the right to be awful and no one should dare counter him. Few did."

As Antoinette observed, "In a game of one-upmanship, it was hard to top Roald. He got away with a lot. He was always sarcastic, but sometimes he was very rude, and he could be cruel, and that got him into trouble."

Whether officials at the embassy eventually tripped to his prank correspondence or simply tired of his antics, Dahl came in for disciplinary action and was warned that he could be shipped back to England at a moment's notice. Aware that he was under review and that his dismissal was most likely inevitable, Dahl decided he had better take preemptive action. He began checking his options and investigating other avenues of employment. "I started nosing around a little bit," he recalled. "There were all sorts of things going on in Washington." So many British information services and press agencies had set up shop in the United States, and there were so many different bureaus, departments, and divisions—most of them a complete waste of time and energy had they not been some sort of front organizations—that there was no shortage of opportunities. Add to that the confusion of fledgling intelligence organizations, including the British-American cooperative effort recently christened the OSS, which everyone in Washington jokingly called "Oh So Secret" or "Oh So Silly." Something was bound to turn up.

"It was a very strange, chaotic time," said the writer Peter Viertel, a marine officer assigned to the OSS, who met Dahl in Washington while receiving some additional training before being sent to France to infiltrate German lines. "You couldn't tell what anyone was really doing, or who they were really working for. There were all these government agencies which had been formed, with all these different branches, full of people who were theoretically doing something for the war. You got the feeling a lot of those people were quite happy to be in those jobs, where there wasn't a lot of trouble."

It was at this unsettled moment in his life that Dahl first fastened on the idea of trying something outside normal channels. He had heard rumors about a sort of unofficial branch of the services that might be willing to take on someone like him. It was an organization that fell under the umbrella of the Secret Intelligence Service (SIS, also known as MI6). No official title had been given to this cloak-and-dagger outfit, and for that matter no prior War Cabinet approval. It was called BSC by default, after the original Baker Street address of the Special Operations Executive (SOE) in London, but the initiated preferred to think of it as a reference to Sherlock Holmes's "Baker Street Irregulars." It had been formalized as the British Security Coordination, a title created arbitrarily by the American FBI director J. Edgar Hoover, who was not raised on Arthur Conan Doyle and did not share the English enthusiasm for code names. The BSC's American headquarters were in Rockefeller Center in New York, and the shadowy figure who ran it was a wealthy Canadian industrialist turned professional saboteur by the name of William Stephenson, who had the title of director of

British Security Coordination and was head of the Secret Intelligence Service in the Western Hemisphere. Those in the know sometimes referred to him as INTREPID, after the BSC's Manhattan cable address.* "I knew who he was," recalled Dahl. "Not when I first arrived in Washington, but I very soon realized that everybody in any position of power either from the British ambassador down or on the American side knew about this extraordinary fellow."

Stephenson had been dispatched to America by Churchill after the nightmarish winter of 1940, during which Mussolini joined forces with Hitler, German bombs rained down on Britain's cities, and the enemy waited only twenty miles from their shores. As morale in Britain plummeted to its lowest point, Churchill concluded that England's only chance of survival depended on the United States' entry into the war. England had to find a way to contrive that intervention—whatever it took. America's continued isolationism would be the death of them. If the United States was to be persuaded of the utmost importance of the British cause and pushed into action, then the isolationists—the antiwar lobby, Lindbergh's America Firsters, and the Nazi-run fifth columnists—would have to be systematically undermined and eliminated. British intelligence would need a sophisticated network of agents on the ground to orchestrate the interventionist effort, and to supply propaganda that would promote fears of a direct German threat to the United States and prod the reluctant American people into supporting the war.

Dahl knew almost nothing of Stephenson or his covert operation, only that intelligence work promised another chance to serve his

*This was not standard practice, especially since Stephenson's personal designation was the number 48100, but the aptness of the code name INTREPID was apparently too good to ignore, and over time Stephenson made it his own. It has been noted that if all British officials had gone by their wartime code names, it would have had comical results: for example, Aubrey Morgan, the director of the British Information Service, would have been known as DIGESTION for the duration of the war.

country and rout the enemy, and his unquestioning readiness to do so was underscored by his recent disappointing stint as a diplomat. Although the BSC's charter was ostensibly concerned with the protection of British shipping and its vital cargoes, he would have guessed that it extended far beyond that—to include everything from small-scale sabotage and political subversion to all manner of devious activities that His Majesty's Government would prefer not to acknowledge. The British propaganda machine, in the form of the Ministry of Information, confined itself to "white," or straight, propaganda permitted in neutral or friendly countries. The BSC specialized in "black," or secret propaganda—in other words, the kind of work you did not want to get caught doing. However dodgy it sounded, if it meant that he could stay in America and make some contribution to the war effort, he wanted in. After making some discreet inquiries, Dahl quietly let it be known that he was interested in being reassigned to the intelligence service.

Before long he received word through an intermediary that his name was not unknown to them and that certain people might be interested in any information he could pass their way. "I had been contacted by one of Bill's [Stephenson] many chaps he had floating around, rather like wisps," recalled Dahl. "You never really realized they were working for him, you thought they were working for someone else, and doing another perfectly different job." While there is no record of precisely what Dahl was told, Bickham Sweet-Escott, another fresh-faced young Englishman who had been recruited by the BSC and was working in Washington when Dahl appeared on the scene, recalled that the intelligence operative who first approached him did not pull any punches. "For security reasons I can't tell you what sort of a job it would be," the agent had told him. "All I can say is that if you join us, you mustn't be afraid of forgery, and you mustn't be afraid of murder." Dahl's contact was probably similarly vague, assuring him that the skullduggery was a matter of routine and that security considerations prohibited him from saying more. In the meantime, Dahl was told he had better stay in touch.

This was the usual drill. Desperately shorthanded, the BSC recruited brains and talent where it could find them, often making only a cursory background check. They brought in friends, family members, and personable colleagues like a club voting in new members, the only qualifications being evidence of a certain confidence and imagination and the assumption of shared values. It was not easy rounding up likely candidates, as by then all the best men had already been snapped up by the older and more respectable departments. The BSC could hardly advertise their requirements, and the pressure to hire people on the spot forced them to spread a wider net than was always advisable. "This meant that recruiting could take place only by personal recommendation," Sweet-Escott explained in his wartime memoir. "In effect you were compelled to put forward the names of your own friends if you happened to know they were not usefully occupied. It was largely a matter of chance whether you got the right man for the job."

Once when they were having a hard time finding secretaries, Sweet-Escott could think of no one to recommend but his sister, Lutie, who happened to know shorthand. Just one word to the wise, and "within a week she was on her way to Cairo via the Cape and the Belgian Congo."

With his reckless sense of humor and general air of insubordination, Dahl may have been mentioned to someone on high as having the makings of an ideal informant, if for no other reason than no one so badly behaved would ever be suspected of working for British intelligence. Any one of a number of people clustered around the embassy at the time could have put his name in the hat. If there was one man who might have taken a particular interest in the enterprising airman, it was Reginald "Rex" Benson, who, in addition to his duties as military attaché and senior adviser to the ambassador, was involved in the highest levels of British security. He certainly would have taken note of Dahl's close friendship with Marsh, and the proximity to the vice president and other key cabinet figures it afforded, and might have thought it worth a try to see if the pilot could be turned into a "voluntary informer," the preferred term for spy.

Dahl had no doubt that he was auditioning for membership in a secret society and that the initiation process would be as byzantine as it was mysterious and could take months, maybe longer. It was also entirely possible that he would hear nothing. As exasperating as his situation was, he had no choice but to busy himself with his work at the Air Mission and wait. Keen to prove himself to his prospective employers, he began collecting snippets of gossip he overheard at Marsh's place. When he thought he had something particularly compelling, he would make contact and arrange a meeting: "I'd slip him a couple of bits of information which I thought might help the war effort, and him, and everything else."

The dreamer in Dahl could not help getting caught up in the romantic world of espionage and special operations. The use of code names, initials, and phrases like "our friends" and "the firm" were reminiscent of the dime-store thrillers he had read as a boy, and while the skeptic in him knew this would be no more of a game than the Greek campaign had been, the other side, the restless, starry-eyed pilot who still thought back on his days chasing German Junkers as "a grand adventure," could not resist the prospect of new escapades and excitement. He had been a gambler all his life. When he had worked for the Shell Oil Company offices in London as a trainee in 1934, he had regularly placed bets by phone on the two o'clock horse race and would sneak out of the office in late afternoon to check the results in the first evening paper. He had succeeded in beating long odds in his first tour of duty. Why not try his luck again? He had no training or experience that qualified him in any way for this duplicitous line of work, but as he later wrote, by that stage of the war "an RAF uniform with wings on the jacket was a great passport to have." It would provide all the cover he needed. And if there was one thing he had learned since coming to Washington, it was that the capital was swarming with virtuous representatives of foreign governments, and almost no one was who they pretended to be.

2

PIECE OF CAKE

Becoming a writer was pure fluke. Without being asked
to, I doubt I'd ever have thought of it.

— ROALD DAHL

SINCERE AS HE was in his desire to serve his country, Dahl's sudden enthusiasm for intelligence work was motivated more by
personal ambition than by patriotism. He had an entirely selfish reason for wanting to prolong his stay in the United States. During his
first few months in Washington, he had managed to publish a story
about his RAF experiences in a popular American magazine, and he
was rather enjoying his first taste of literary success. He was desperate to stick around a little while longer to see how it all panned out.
While he had initially undertaken the assignment as part of the British propaganda campaign, the piece had been well received, and he
had been asked to do more. It had taken him by surprise, because
back at school he had never shown any flair for writing and had been
an indifferent student at best. If he could make something of a name
for himself in America, where the hero-worshipping public was mad

for war stories, he might be able to make a go of it as a career when the fighting was over. If he returned to England, he would be just one more wounded Battle of Britain pilot, and his stories would not have anywhere near the same currency—or the same chance of finding their way into print.

Before coming to the United States, Dahl had never considered becoming a writer and had stumbled into it entirely by accident. He had been in the country only three days and was sitting in his new office at the Air Mission, staring out the window and feeling useless, when he was saved by a knock on the door. A shy, slightly built man in his forties, with thinning hair and thick, steel-rimmed glasses, advanced hesitantly into the room and introduced himself as C. S. Forester. Forester wanted to interview Dahl about his death-defying crash in the Libyan desert, which he thought might make for an exciting piece in *The Saturday Evening Post*. In a soft, apologetic voice, Forester explained that the United States had only just entered the war, and bona-fide heroes were in short supply. Dahl was that "rare bird" on this side of the Atlantic who had actually "been in combat," and his story could not fail to stir Americans.

Like many famous British authors, from H. G. Wells and Somerset Maugham to *Winnie-the-Pooh* creator A. A. Milne, Forester had been enlisted by the newly created British Information Services (BIS) to do propaganda work and write stories urging American intervention. The BIS had been established in the spring of 1941 to champion support for England in the American press and radio; it was really a catchall body for a whole range of British publicity and propaganda departments operating in the United States under the authority of the embassy in Washington. While Edward R. Murrow's coverage of the blitz for CBS News brought the war into the homes of millions of Americans and allowed them to hear the sound of the air raid sirens and drone of German bombers overhead, the BIS sought to dramatize the Nazi threat with an organized cultural propaganda campaign of its own. In some ways, Murrow's memorable broadcasts had served to point out the failure of Britain's fumbling early forays into transatlantic propaganda, which had been alternately too ham-fisted, or too highbrow, to be effective. One dismal example was a major exhibition at Manhattan's Museum of Modern Art on the theme of Britain at war, which had featured sketches of the bomb damage and works by Henry Moore, for which the Ministry of Information had pressed the celebrated poet T. S. Eliot into service. The result, called "Defense of the Islands," was a rather obscure, free-verse meditation on how history was repeating itself, and England was taking up new weapons against an old adversary. It was hardly the sort of popular fare that would fire up ordinary Americans and strengthen their resolve to defeat the Nazi menace.

To arouse American sympathy, the BIS felt that what was needed was more compulsory tear-jerkers along the lines of *Mrs. Miniver*, an enormously popular book based on a London *Times* column chronicling the hardships suffered by an upper-middle-class Englishwoman and her family. Written by Jan Struther, the book had topped the best-seller lists for weeks, and by the end of the summer of 1941 Americans were snapping up fifteen hundred copies a week. Of even more direct value to the propaganda drive was Helen MacInnes' latest thriller, *Above Suspicion,* a chilling tale of murderous Gestapo agents who hound a courageous British academic and his wife across Europe. It helped, of course, that MacInnes, one of Britain's best-selling novelists, happened to be married to the BSC agent Gilbert Highet and had intentionally tailored the plot of her book to highlight the horrors of the Third Reich.

To step up Britain's appeals to the American public and draw attention to the desperate need for aid, the BIS wanted to continue to reach a wide audience. Forester had answered their clarion call and had agreed to provide the sort of compelling human-interest stories that would dramatize the conflict and touch American hearts. In addition, these stories would showcase Britain's bravery and fighting spirit with an eye to maintaining their forces' prestige come peacetime. As Forester put it to Dahl, his brush with death might make for a rousing air force tale, with the kind of personal angle that hooked readers and made them identify with the British struggle. In any case, it was all to help the cause.

Forester was an extremely famous writer, and Dahl was somewhat flabbergasted to find him standing awkwardly on the other side of his desk. Forester had penned the hugely popular Captain Horatio Hornblower novels about navy life in the era of Admiral Nelson, which Dahl, along with most of his countrymen, had devoured. His novel *Payment Deferred* had been a hit play, and Charles Laughton had recreated his performance on the New York stage, and then again in the popular movie version. In the spring of 1940, Warner Bros. had engaged Forester to produce a screenplay of his Hornblower book that would reflect the best of British heroism. Forester had moved his family to America and after a stint in Hollywood, which he detested, had settled permanently in Berkeley, California. When war broke out, he had immediately set sail for England but was officially instructed by the British Ministry of Information to return to America and his inspirational tales rather that muck about as a stretcher-bearer in Britain. This suited Forester, who preferred to regard himself as a newspaperman who happened to write novels rather than the other way around, and he was inordinately proud of the reporting he had done during the Spanish Civil War. He took to his propaganda work with gusto and, in addition to his naval books and screenplays, cranked out a steady stream of articles about the Allied forces for both the British and American press. He frequently flew to New York, where he had an office at the British Information Service office in Rockefeller Center, and was often in Washington on wartime assignments, and kept an office at the embassy.*

Forester treated Dahl to a lavish lunch at a small, elegant French restaurant near the Mayflower Hotel and pumped him for details of his experiences in the Syrian campaign. When they sat down, he took out a small pad and pencil and laid them on the tablecloth, but between the wine and the roast duck, he managed to jot down only a few notes. Dahl, for his part, had trouble communicating his story with enough gritty realism to satisfy his listener. He kept getting bogged down in details and pointless digressions and finally offered to put some thoughts to paper and send them over later. Forester approved of the idea but urged Dahl to be as specific as possible and to rack his brains for minute observations—"detail, that's what counts in our business"—so that when it came time to fashion his scribbles into a real story, it would still have the unmistakable ring of truth. Dahl went home and spent a long evening wrestling with his memories of that doomed flight. He found that the words came more easily than expected, and he was finished by midnight. As a final flourish he tacked on the droll title "A Piece of Cake," the term pilots used to describe every maneuver regardless of how dangerous. The next day he had an embassy secretary type up his draft and sent it off to Forester without a second thought.

Ten days later Forester wrote back: "You were meant to give me notes, not a finished story. I'm bowled over. Your piece is marvelous. It is the work of a gifted writer. I didn't touch a word of it." Forester had

---

*Forester would have liked to do secret work, either for the BSC or later the OSS, but it was not to be. The closest he came was a memorable interview with Colonel Donovan, the new head of the OSS, which he described in a letter to his wife, Kathleen: "He [Donovan] was lying in bed in the St. Regis Hotel with two broken legs as the result of a car accident, and he and two regular U.S. colonels went through me and turned me inside out as if they were three doses of salt. It was interesting—obviously they were sizing me up for some mysterious purpose of their own."

sent it under Dahl's name to his agent, Harold Matson, asking that he forward it to Forester's editor at *The Saturday Evening Post* with his recommendation. The *Post* accepted it immediately and wrote back asking for more stories from the talented pilot. Forester also informed Dahl that the *Post* was paying $1,000 for his maiden effort, and enclosed a check for that amount, minus his agent's 10 percent commission.*

Like many postmortem adventure tales, Dahl's romanticized autobiographical account had only a glancing relationship with the truth. In the version he sent Forester, instead of ferrying his plane to his forward unit and crash-landing after he ran out of fuel, Dahl is pursued by an Italian patrol, and his Hurricane is hit by machine-gun fire before plummeting to earth in a ball of flame. Eager to impress his celebrated collaborator, Dahl could not resist the urge to fictionalize. He embellished freely, dressing up his desert misadventure with ground strafing, scrambling soldiers, and a trusty sidekick named Shorty. His literary license is perhaps somewhat excused by his bedridden narrator's struggle to remember exactly what had happened to him: "Slowly it all came back; not clearly and brightly at first, but a little dimly, as though by moonlight." The story unfolds in brief, vivid scenes and snatches of terse dialogue that owe a considerable debt to Ernest Hemingway, a writer Dahl much admired.

By the time the piece appeared in the August 1942 issue of *The Saturday Evening Post*, it had been packaged as a heart-pounding battle yarn, appearing under the title "Shot Down over Libya," and touted as a "factual report on Libyan air fighting" by an unnamed RAF pilot. Dahl had requested that his name be removed, citing "an old RAF custom." Adding to the anonymous pilot's allure was an editors' note explaining

---

*Dahl has told versions of this tale in many interviews, but a letter from Dahl to Matson dated May 13, 1942, lists the sale price as $300, so he may have inflated his rates over the years, but whether it was by accident or design is not clear.

that he was in the United States "for medical reasons," an allusion to yet another corrective surgery, and a neat diversionary tactic to obscure Dahl's presence as an official envoy of the British government sent to cheer on the Allies.*

"Shot Down over Libya" was just the sort of patriotic fare the British Information Services wanted to peddle to the American press, and Dahl's superiors encouraged him to do more pieces for the magazine. As a staff officer, he was required to submit everything he wrote for approval to the BIS, which deemed his action-packed tales effective propaganda. Even his correspondence with his new literary agent, Harold Matson, and various interested magazine editors was read by the British Embassy censor and bore a stamp for file references. Determined to make the most of this new opportunity and happy to have a way to earn some extra money, Dahl kept coming up with more stories about his adventures as an ace fighter. Virtually everything he wrote during this period was a mélange of personal experience and observations gleaned from fellow pilots, recreating thrilling air battles, the fear of death that strangely vanished the moment the enemy appeared, and moments of mad abandon in the midst of so much brutality. He invented dialogue with the sure hand of a novelist, not the novice that he was. When he exhausted his supply of memories, he switched to fiction, his style becoming, as he later put it, "progressively less realistic and more fantastic."

Dahl's tightly plotted battle stories proved popular and resonated with American readers who were caught up in the patriotism and fighting spirit that swept the country in its first summer of the war. He soon began getting offers from other influential American magazines, and in the months to come his short stories would appear in *Collier's*,

---

*Dahl later blamed the title and errors on the *Post's* overzealous editors. After the war, he rewrote the story with greater accuracy, restored its original title, and included it in a collection of ten war stories, *Over to You*, which was published in 1946.

Harper's, Ladies' Home Journal, and *Town and Country*, among others. "It's almost impossible to understand what an emotional time it was," he recalled. "The Americans and British against Hitler and the Nazis, [we] were fighting for a tremendous cause, I mean saving the world, literally. And emotions were running endlessly high."

Raised on stories about Norwegian trolls and wee people, Dahl decided to try his hand at a fanciful children's story about the hazards of being an RAF pilot. Called "Gremlin Lore," it was another vaguely autobiographical story about a pilot named Gus, who is happily chasing German Junkers in his Hurricane when his plane is sabotaged by a little six-inch creature bearing a large drill, who puts four neat holes in his wing and then bores straight into the engine, causing it to sputter and stop. The story introduces the reader to the existence of gremlins, the tribe of tiny mythical rogues who live amid the clouds, riding on fighter planes and bombers, and whom the RAF blamed for everything that went wrong with their aircraft, particularly crashes. The RAF had been rife with gremlin stories since the start of the war, and mentions of the bad-luck imps who annoyed RAF pilots dated back to India in the 1920s. The popular press had begun picking up oft-repeated tales of mischievous aerial pixies who hindered pilots in battle, interfering with radio transmissions, jabbing them in the back, and punching holes in their fuselage.

Aware that Disney was in the midst of making a propaganda film about military aviation called *Victory Through Air Power*, and that the strength of the Allied air forces had become a hot topic with Americans, Sidney Bernstein of the BIS sent Dahl's unpublished story to the studio on the chance that it might be a timely subject for an animated feature. Dahl's little troublemakers were a perfect fit with Disney, whose top box-office performers were tiny creatures from old folk tales—that year Dumbo led all other Disney films in gross income—and the studio was already working on the big-screen version of another British import,

Peter Pan. In the unstable and unpredictable economic climate of 1942, Disney's war films had provided a steady source of income, from aircraft identification cartoons for the army and navy to short-subject films satirizing the Nazis, including *Der Fuehrer's Face,* which was originally entitled "Donald Duck in Nuzi-Land" and dealt with Donald's exasperation with the Hitler regime. On July 13, 1942, Walt Disney cabled Dahl confirming that the gremlins had potential: "BELIEVE IT HAS POSSIBILITIES. WOULD BE INTERESTED IN SECURING THIS MATERIAL"

Disney acquired the rights to the story, with the British Air Ministry demanding final script approval, and royalties to be divided between Dahl and the RAF Benevolent Fund. Throughout that summer and early autumn, Dahl eagerly corresponded with Disney about their plans to turn his gremlin tale into a movie that would combine live action and cartoon animation, and he commented on photostats of early sketches in an attempt to help "overcome the difficulties you had in deciding what a Gremlin was like." After much back-and-forth, Dahl was delighted to hear that Disney had decided that the project should be made "one hundred percent cartoon," and he sent a quick note to Walt expressing his relief at the decision. Given the green light to make suggestions to the studio animators, Dahl could not stop himself and giddily boasted of his expertise. He presented himself as an expert "Gremlinologist," and offered to travel to the West Coast to provide an accurate physical description of "the little men"—regulation green bowler hats, and so on—"because I really do know what they look like having seen a great number of them in my time."

That fall *Newsweek, Time,* and *Life* all did stories on gremlins, tracing the origin of the name to the Old English word *greme,* meaning "to vex"—though according to some pilots, the bad-luck imps most often appeared after one too many Fremlin's, a popular brand of beer—and offering various descriptions of their appearance and jaunty attire. Rumors that the head of Disney was working on a gremlins picture and planning to travel to England to hear fairy stories firsthand caused so much excitement that the British Air Ministry was deluged with inquiries. As the London *Observer* commented: "It will seem strange indeed to the future historians who, unraveling the tale of our troubled times, discover that in the critical year 1942, a distinguished American traveled five thousand miles in order to make a film about elves; elves which, admittedly, no one has ever seen."

When gossip columns started reporting rumors of Walt Disney's impending invasion of "Gremlinland," Dahl's superiors urged him to contact the studio head and find out if he was really headed for England. Dahl queried Walt, who telegraphed the air commodore that he was unable to get away due to pressure of work, but he wrote Dahl that that was the least of his problems. The studio was getting letters from all over England and Canada written by people who claimed not only to have seen gremlins but had very fixed ideas about what they looked like. Disney had also heard from one Flight Lieutenant Douglas Bisgood, an RAF pilot who had crossed the Atlantic with Dahl, who claimed that during the two-week journey he had regaled Dahl with many of his own gremlin tales. In his letter, Bisgood made it clear he felt that he had first claim to the gremlin family names. In the meantime, the studio's research department had unearthed a number of books on the subject by British authors and was worried that they did not have exclusive rights to the gremlin legend. Disney did not want trouble. As he worried to Dahl in a letter in October: "We would want this film to be satisfactory to the RAF in every way. Our only concern is that we do not want someone to find petty faults or assume a picayunish attitude after the film is completed and thereby put us to considerable expense in making changes."

In late November, Lord Halifax consented to his assistant air attaché working on the morale-boosting picture, and Dahl was granted a short leave to go to Los Angeles. His arrival in Hollywood was noted in the gossip columns, and Leonard Lyons quoted an earnest-sounding Dahl dutifully touting the party line, saying, "We're doing this because the Gremlins are part of the RAF." Dahl spent ten days living it up as a guest of the studio, which arranged for him to stay at the Beverly Hills Hotel and provided him with a huge American car. To the twenty-six-year-old Dahl, everything about Disney's Burbank operation was big and impressive, from the sprawling black-topped studio lot to Walt's enormous office, where a stenographer took down every word uttered by the various parties present and typed them up afterward for the boss's perusal.

While he was there, Dahl succeeded in thoroughly charming both Walt and Roy Disney, particularly Walt, who, upon discovering their shared fondness for Kipling, nicknamed the lanky airman Stalky, after a British schoolboy featured in a story by the same name. Dahl persuaded both Disney brothers that it made sense to bring out an illustrated book version of the gremlins in advance of the planned movie. Following the success of an article in the December *Cosmopolitan* featuring Dahl's gremlins, accompanied by Disney's colorful illustrations, he wrote Walt urging him not to delay the book any longer, as he had already been approached by a big publishing house in England and felt certain there would be other competitors entering the field, given how "the whole subject is gaining way to such an extent now." He signed the letter, "Yours, Stalky."

Convinced that the charismatic, self-dramatizing British pilot was a good investment, Disney agreed. In April 1943 the studio joined forces with Random House, and *The Gremlins: A Royal Air Force Story by Flight Lieutenant Roald Dahl* was published to glowing reviews. The *New York Times* awarded him honors for his moral fable about the self-destructiveness of mankind and hailed the young English author's "remarkable adeptness at building up a tall tale in the American tradition." After the book's publication, Dahl was inundated with offers.

When he returned to Hollywood to confer with Disney, his visit merited a gushing mention in Hedda Hopper's column. "He was terribly pleased with the book's success," recalled Antoinette. "He got rather a big head about it, and was more arrogant than ever."

Dahl was also riding high on reports that he was working on a full-length motion picture inspired by the writings and life philosophy of Henry Wallace. The film project was conceived of by Gabriel Pascal, an English producer famous for his brilliant screen adaptations of George Bernard Shaw's *Pygmalion* and *Major Barbara*, after a chance meeting with Wallace and Dahl at Marsh's R Street house. Pascal was there with his friend and partner, Erich Maria Remarque, the author of *All Quiet on the Western Front*, one of the best pieces of reportage about the First World War. Remarque had made so much money from the book's publication that he was free to do anything he wanted, but the fame had apparently been too much for him, and he had retreated to southern France. After a long period of inactivity, Remarque had teamed up with Pascal to make an allegorical movie about the fight between "the children of light and darkness through the ages." Wallace was very interested in their notion of illustrating the principle of liberty and spent many hours in deep discussion with the pair of filmmakers. By midnight, they were so simpatico, that they began laying plans to collaborate on the film together. They spent a long weekend at Marsh's sprawling Virginia farm hammering out the details, and Dahl, with Lord Halifax's approval, was assigned the task of coming up with a rough first treatment of the script.

When the picture deal was announced in the press, Pascal explained that the ambitious project would tackle "the problems facing all humanity in the reconstruction of the post-war world" and would "carry an inspirational message to all people from an American angle." Describing Flight Lieutenant Dahl as "a great new writing talent," Pascal told reporters that the pilot-author would be handing over his draft to "two or three prominent American authors," so that the final script would bear several names. While he had given no thought to casting the central roles, he revealed that hundreds of children and youths would figure in the drama.

Marsh felt convinced that Dahl and the filmmakers were perfectly matched to their complex and provocative subject. To be sure, the cerebral vice president, an Iowa-born agronomist who had done pioneering work in developing new strains of corn and strawberries, was a singular character in American politics. A selfless and zealous reformer, he had overseen revolutionary change in the country's farm policy as secretary of agriculture, constructed a huge new bureaucracy to administer its provisions, and spouted extremely liberal, unorthodox ideas about the economy, eliminating poverty, and how to best serve the public interest. A devout Episcopalian, Wallace was also usually spiritual for a politician, and his asceticism and morality set him apart from the more urbane, secular types in Washington. He was known as a prophet who wore many hats: he lectured on science, led seminars on religion, and authored pamphlets and books on everything from world trade to economic social justice. His popularity with western farmers, along with his outspoken attacks on Nazism and the dangers of a German victory, recommended him to Roosevelt, who selected him to be his vice president in 1940. Wallace was a controversial choice at the time, and the intervening years had done nothing to endear him to conservatives in Congress.

The news that the vice president's global philosophy was going to reach the big screen made for splashy headlines in Washington and London. The tall, perpetually disheveled Wallace was beloved by many as the people's candidate and a great liberal warrior. An idealist who saw himself as an agent of change, he frequently gave speeches outlining his ideas for chartering the future of the world when peace came, and his ideas had been widely circulated in newsreels. His Republican opponents, however, regarded him as a dangerous radical and immediately dismissed the proposed film as political propaganda. It did not escape their notice that the project was to be privately financed by Charles Marsh, the Texas newspaper publisher and staunch Democrat, whose real purpose they suspected was not making a movie so much as sending a message to voters. The conservative Washington *Times-Herald* opined that while Pascal might be able to "sugar coat his story and the Wallace ideologies," it would be better if the filmmakers confined their politics to the conventional rostrums, warning that many on Capital Hill still saw red at the mention of Major Frank Capra's *Mr. Smith Goes to Washington*, which was regarded as "a libel on the staid United States Senate."

Dahl was delighted with all the attention, as well as the promise of additional film work. The whole deal had been put together with enormous haste, as Pascal had been in Washington only briefly on assignment for the Office of War Information (OWI) and had to return to London in a fortnight. He had flown back with the playwright Maxwell Anderson, whose war drama *The Eve of St. Mark* he was to direct on the London stage. The British production was being sponsored by the OWI and featured an English cast, with the exception of a few key American roles, which Pascal, with patriotic flourish, announced he would be filling with performers from U.S. Army units stationed in England. Pascal had a number of other projects on his schedule, including a long-delayed film of Paul Gallico's *The Snow Goose*, one of two pictures he owed under his United Artists contract. Before leaving Washington, he had also arranged with Halifax for Dahl to be permitted to work on a script of *The Snow Goose*, which he hoped to film in England, Canada, and the United States.

If possible, Marsh was even more excited about the project than Dahl. He was very taken with Pascal, who was born in Transylvania—he claimed to be three-eighths Hungarian, one-eighth Basque, and one-half Italian—and had an equal capacity for liquor and tall tales and told mesmerizing stories about everything from the monks of Assisi to George Bernard Shaw and Toscanini. Remarque, who was from West-phalia, Germany, was also a wonderful raconteur and told a story of being stationed in France during World War I. It was the custom of the Prussian officer in charge to hold a drinking contest each evening, with the major taking only a sip from his glass while the others were required to drain the contents. This went on all night, and every time someone fell under the table, they were wrapped up in one of the rugs and stood in the corner until everyone in the room save one was bound up in a rug. When it was down to the major and himself, the then-seventeen-year-old Remarque had dared the officer to match him glass for glass. The major finally succumbed, and Remarque had to struggle to roll him up in a rug and prop him in the corner. He told them that afterward he just sat at the table for an hour and a half before unbundling everyone.

Marsh was suitably impressed and judged Remarque to be the real thing. He was so enthusiastic about their project that in addition to putting up all the money and offering his Virginia farm as a possible lo-cation for filming, he started bombarding Dahl with suggestions. Marsh proposed bringing in his refugee friend Erich Leinsdorf, an Austrian composer and conductor with the Metropolitan Opera, to write the score. Leinsdorf had escaped Nazi Germany, and Marsh thought the perfect advance publicity for the movie would be that this ensemble of "Europeans who hate Hitler" had combined their talents to produce the movie of "The Common Man in War and Peace."

Dahl was now a very busy writer and on his way to becoming a very well-known, well-connected man about town in Washington. He fre-quently made the local society columns for being one of the luminaries at a British Embassy function or war relief fund-raiser, or for serving as one of the distinguished "patrons under 30" at special concert series for the young people in the nation's capital. He developed a wide range of contacts, becoming pals with Bernard Baruch, a millionaire and influential presidential adviser, who happened to be a bridge-playing crony of Marsh's Texan pals Jesse Jones and Will Clayton. Dahl, who could not resist any form of cards, had already joined a poker school and managed to lose his first magazine paycheck—the whole $900—to Harry Truman, a senator from Missouri.

Dahl's tales of derring-do had made him a distinctly glamorous figure. His byline was appearing in the best American magazines, and he enjoyed the same respect—even reverence—reserved for the better-known war correspondents of the day. He made friends with writers and reporters whose skill and reputation far outstripped his own modest achievements, but they accepted him as a veteran whose record of courage they admired. In time of war, the British writer Evelyn Waugh once noted, "danger justified privilege," and Dahl's recompense for having fought on the front lines was ready admission into the most vaunted circles in Washington. Creekmore Fath took him along to the White House, where he met the bright, blond Martha Gellhorn, famous for her war dispatches for *Collier's* and recent marriage to Hemingway. Gellhorn, who was obsessed with the war in Europe, was immediately interested in Dahl's RAF connections as she was always planning the next story that would get her back to the front. Her first impression of Dahl, she recalled, was of someone "very, very attractive and slightly mad," which she attributed to his "hitting the ground."

Marsh's friend Ralph Ingersoll introduced him to the playwright Lillian Hellman, an old flame who was even further to the left than he was. Hellman's current beau, the detective-story writer Dashiell Hammett, had helped launch Ingersoll's *PM*, bringing in all his New York literary pals, including such names as Heywood Broun, Dorothy Parker, Donald Ogden Stewart, and George Seldes, and earning the publication a reputation for being a Communist mouthpiece in the early days of its inception. *PM* was hardly a Stalinist front but a rather schizophrenic cross between a high-minded journal of opinion and a tabloid. It was the journalistic dream child of Ingersoll, a veteran editor of *Time*, the creator of *Life*, and the publisher Henry Luce's longtime lieutenant. When Ingersoll left the Time organization to start *PM* in 1938, one of his largest backers was Marshall Field, the department store heir, who was at the same time financing another newspaper start-up, the *Chicago Sun*. According to Marsh, who took an early interest in *PM*, the paper was losing more than a half million dollars a year and probably always would, but this was a matter of no great concern to man like Field.

Ingersoll, who made no claim of being objective—and often said there was no such thing as "objective journalism"—was one of the first editors to campaign all-out for aid to Great Britain. He frequently ranted in print about America's embarrassing "kibitzing" while London burned and was so rabid in his attacks on isolationists like Charles Lindbergh and William Randolph Hearst that it had led to rumors that he was being subsidized by that "man across the sea," i.e., Churchill. He was almost as big and loud and opinionated as Marsh himself, and over his usual liquid lunch of two martinis and black coffee, followed by a chain of mentholated cigarettes, he had fought and won the war a hundred times over. So much so that when the forty-one-year old editor was drafted into the army in July 1942, it became a cause célèbre, with Field petitioning the appeals board that he was "indispensable" in the war on the home front. In a misguided attempt to help, Marsh, without consulting Ingersoll, used his considerable influence to get him a deferment. The draft board's reversal became front page news and, embarrassed by stories denouncing him as a draft-dodger, Ingersoll enlisted in the army. He wound up earning a commission and serving on General Omar Bradley's staff and wrote a best seller about his experience. He credited Marsh with altering the course of his life and virtually revered him.

Through Marsh, Dahl also met Mrs. Ogden Reid, wife of the *Herald Tribune* publisher and very much the power behind the throne. Marsh had great admiration for Helen Reid, and the two newspaper owners were close friends and had formed their own little secret society and met from time to time to exchange information. She was very pro-British and had taken to Dahl immediately, and he often stayed with her when he was in New York. Her father-in-law, Whitelaw Reid, had been ambassador to Britain from 1905 to 1911, and in the years before her marriage she had worked as a social secretary to his wife and so had close ties to England. According to Marsh, the formidable Mrs. Whitelaw Reid had realized that her son and heir was a bit of a drunk and had engineered the marriage to her very capable assistant. Through Marsh and Mrs. Reid, Dahl got to know the *Herald Tribune's* lead columnist, Walter Lippmann, a passionate internationalist who was said to have considerable sway with policy makers. The married Lippmann had caused a local scandal by falling in love with Helen Byrne Armstrong, the wife of his best friend and fellow editor, Hamilton Fish Armstrong, who oversaw the quarterly publication *Foreign Affairs*. His divorce, followed by her divorce and their subsequent marriage, was still much whispered about among their colleagues and friends.

Dahl dined regularly with the tall, mustachioed Drew Pearson, whose infamous, gossipy "Daily Washington Merry-Go-Round" was read by everyone in town and was carried in some five hundred papers nationwide. In 1931 he and Robert Allen, then the Washington bureau chief of the *Christian Science Monitor*, had anonymously published a collection of scandalous news items about a handful of public figures in a book called *Washington Merry-Go-Round*, and although controversial it was so popular they published a sequel the following year. Pearson and Allen were unmasked and promptly fired, but by 1940 they had launched their famous syndicated column and were riding high. After Allen joined the army, Pearson soldiered on alone, making Washington politics and politicians his main beat. He was an odd duck, a tight-lipped Quaker with a quirky sense of humor, and had a house on Dumbarton Avenue that boasted a garden pool stocked with goldfish named after FDR aides, such as Harry Hopkins and Harold Ickes. He continued this tradition on his Maryland farm, where his cows were christened Cordell Hull, Henry Morgenthau, and Eleanor Roosevelt. Naturally every now and then one of the cows had to be slaughtered and would be duly devoured by Pearson and his dinner guests. He was an old-fashioned, hard-hitting muckraker, with a thick skin and cold disregard for those he angered or hurt with his disclosures, be they friend or foe. Dahl thought it far better to be his friend, and the two became regular drinking buddies and whiled away many evenings at the men's bar at the Mayflower.

Dahl also got to know Pearson's main competitor, Walter Winchell, whose column was syndicated in an astonishing one thousand newspapers, which together with his hugely popular Sunday radio show made him a force to be reckoned with. By the advent of the war, Winchell was a powerhouse widely feared because of his penchant for exposing the private lives of important public men—from mistresses and pregnancies to divorces—which gave him plenty of bargaining chips to trade for information about what was going on inside their businesses or agencies. He had morphed from a Broadway critic to a political commentator who thought nothing of weighing in on domestic and international affairs, from warning Americans that "isolation ends where it always ends—with the enemy on our doorstep," to inaugurating a regular feature called "The Winchell Column vs. the Fifth Column." A typical Winchell column would contain several dozen separate references to individuals and events, ranging from minor celebrity sightings, along the lines of spotting Marlene Dietrich at the Stork Club, his nightly hangout, to an impassioned denunciation of Nazi sympathizers or some other disreputable homegrown fascists.

While there were a number of prominent American journalists who were sympathetic to the British plight, Lippmann, Pearson, and Winchell went beyond publishing Ministry of Information handouts to actively aiding the cause whenever they could, and they were in close contact with British intelligence. Like Ingersoll, they, too, were often accused of being on the British payroll, though they had plenty of company in their surrogate form of combat. There was a long list of ink-stained crusaders who had been fighting against Hitler and Mussolini since as far back as 1933—among them Dorothy Thompson and Edmund Taylor—and who had proved helpful to the BSC in its covert campaign against isolationism and defeatism.

Dahl also met Ernest Cuneo, the affable, Falstaffian attorney and sidekick to Winchell, who was known to be a member of Roosevelt's "palace guard" and a behind-the-scenes operator bar none. A thirty-three-year-old lawyer of Italian descent, Cuneo had served as an aide to congressman and New York City mayor Fiorello La Guardia and was every bit as colorful and engaging a character as his former boss. A college football star gone to fat, he was almost as wide as he was tall and was a much-beloved figure in media circles. When Roosevelt was elected to office in 1932, Cuneo had followed his Columbia Law mentor Adolf Berle to Washington and served as the administration's troubleshooter, eventually becoming associate counsel of the Democratic National Committee. When war broke out, he added to his portfolio the duties of White House liaison officer with British Security Coordination, the OSS, the FBI, and the Departments of Justice and State.

What Dahl was only then beginning to understand was that Cuneo had such close ties to the BSC that he was considered a member of the club, had his own code name—CRUSADER—and was empowered to "feed" select British intelligence items about Nazi sympathizers and subversives to Pearson, Winchell, and other handpicked outlets. At the time, he was actually ghostwriting many of Winchell's columns and radio broadcasts, which parroted the British propaganda line of the day. For the BSC, journalists like Ingersoll, Lippmann, Pearson, Reid, and Winchell, and the facilitator Cuneo, were stealth operatives in their campaign against Britain's enemies in America. "The conduct of political warfare was entirely dependent on secrecy," states the official history of the BSC's intelligence operations. "For that reason the press and radio men with whom BSC agents maintained contact were comparable with subagents and the intermediaries with agents. They were thus regarded."

Whatever complaints embassy officials might have had with him personally, Dahl felt he was more than doing his bit for crown and country, and he was banking on his minor celebrity to stave off the threatened dismissal. In the meantime, he had taken Marsh into his confidence and explained that he was doing a little hush-hush work with an eye to getting himself transferred to intelligence. Far from being surprised, Marsh had already guessed as much and offered his assistance. "Of course, my father knew he was a spy," said Antoinette. "They talked about it and my father said, 'Look here, we're on the same team, we can help each other.'" They both wanted the same things—Britain's survival and an Allied victory—and Marsh was Machiavellian enough to think he could help Dahl while helping himself. "He got a huge kick out of it," added Antoinette. "He always said that he was a spy during the war, too." While Marsh regarded it as something of a lark and often made light of their joint espionage activities, Antoinette recalled that Dahl took the work very seriously: "Roald was a real patriot. He did it for the war effort, and he dedicated himself to it."

Marsh took Dahl under his wing and gave him the benefit of his years of experience in Washington politics. He had the veteran newspaperman's instinct for the inside scoop, nose for bull, and appetite for Capitol Hill scuttlebutt. Marsh was on a first-name basis with everyone in town who mattered, and he knew about the skeletons in their closets and the scandals in their home states. If he did not have all the answers, he knew who did, and more often than not he offered to place the call. He was an invaluable source for Dahl, a walking, talking encyclopedia of Washington life, from the stiff state dinners and senatorial committees to the "unofficial" hotel room conferences. He knew Washington was composed of tycoons, lobbyists, lawyers, deal makers, and fixers of every stripe, as well as legions of amiable young "government girls" with good legs and better memories. An inveterate memo writer who made his long-suffering secretary take down dozens of pages of dictation each day, Marsh, according to Ingersoll, would call Dahl in and debrief him, then spell out a cable for him to transmit to his bosses, saying, "I want this message to get through to 10 Downing Street right quickly and straight. Mark it urgent on your report, eyes only to your people." Then Claudia, his timid stenographer, who was always seated silently nearby and wore a perennial look of alarm on her face whenever asked to take something down, would start hammering away on her machine as he began waking up and down and dictating, still clad in silk pajamas and a brightly embroidered Chinese gown.

Occasionally, when Marsh had information he wanted to impart to Churchill that he thought was over the head of the relatively junior assistant air attaché, he would announce self-importantly that he was going to summon Isaiah Berlin, the British Embassy's brilliant, all-knowing London liaison, who communicated directly with the Foreign Office, various Whitehall departments, and the Cabinet Office. For his part, Berlin was put off by the American press baron's eccentric circumlocution—"staccato, disjointed sentences"—and overweening self-regard. Marsh "gave the impression of being powerful, not to say sinister," Berlin recalled, but he was always left feeling that there was something not quite right about him, "a screw faintly loose somewhere—and I felt rather frightened of him, as if in the presence of someone slightly unbalanced." Marsh in turn, disliked the pale, pudgy Berlin, whom he and Dahl dubbed "the White Slug."

When Dahl required specific information, Marsh instructed him to submit written questions. Typically, Marsh would respond with another memo. They communicated in this manner, trading everything from brief handwritten notes and telegrams to voluminous typed letters throughout the war. The pedagogical aspect of their relationship is evident in a short note Marsh fired off to Dahl after he took advantage of their arrangement on a recent occasion. "You woke me at four this morning, and you bumped me out of bed at five," he scolded Dahl, addressing the pilot as if he were a recalcitrant pupil. "You had an idea. You wanted to send information quickly and had been too timid to say so. Next time put the time element in mind. Time is the essence in every contract—and I think, contact." When Marsh had a lecture to impart, he would say, "Dahl, let's go for a walk," and he would be off, striding down 17th Street with his long, awkward gait, his arms swinging to and fro, holding forth on everything from a politician's potentialities to the most intimate aspects of a well-known public figure's sex life.

To help boost his standing at the embassy, Marsh arranged for Dahl to meet with important people in government and to apprise them of the RAF's accomplishments. He sent him over to see the vice president to show him photographs of the damage done by the two-ton bombs dropped by British Lancasters. The photographs, taken from 30,000 feet and blown up to a size of about six feet by four feet, were striking examples of British air power, which Dahl argued were still superior to that of the United States. Dahl used the photos as a graphic illustration of the fact that the British were now causing about two and a half times the damage to the Germans as the Germans ever did to them, largely due to the greater bomb load of their bombers. In addition, the British had found that incendiaries were fully as important as high-explosive bombs; he reported that they were dropping about one thousand pounds of incendiaries for every fifteen hundred pounds of high explosives.

Impressed, the vice president invited Dahl to sit in on his next meeting, with Major Alexander P. de Seversky of Russia, who was coming to brief him on the "airplane of the future." The famous aviation expert had crashed a bomber in 1915 and lost a leg in the process, and Dahl had read about his experiences in a recent issue of *Reader's Digest*. Disney's first feature-length war film, *Victory Through Air Power*, was based on Seversky's best-selling book by the same name, and Dahl had heard a great deal about the man and his advanced theories from Walt Disney. The major, who had been in the United States as an aeronautical engineer since the early 1920s, had developed a high-altitude pursuit plane and pushed aggressively to upgrade America's military aviation program, claiming it could not compete with the German Luftwaffe, in the process earning a reputation as a radical and a bit of a nut job. After America entered the war, Seversky's ideas on air strategy came to be regarded by many as farsighted, but he was no less controversial. The Disney movie reportedly featured his design for a long-range multigun bomber that more closely resembled a Buck Rogers science fiction fantasy than anything that existed.

A confident salesman, Seversky informed Dahl and Wallace that in his opinion the airplane of the future would probably have a range of 5,000 miles, and would be able to carry a load of 100 to 200 tons. At one point, he went so far as to imply that the United States, England, and Russia had between them all the necessary geography from which to fly the planes and "control the entire world." Wallace endeavored to bring him down to earth by explaining that he thought it would be necessary to include Latin America and China, and that it was his fervent wish that the technology did not end up in too few hands. After Seversky left, Dahl quietly advised Wallace that the British air people considered the Russian "persona non grata."

The arrival of the British foreign secretary, Anthony Eden, in March 1943 provided the perfect occasion for Marsh to aid Dahl in his intelligence work. Eden's visit was hailed as the opening of serious discussions on the part of the Allies to consider peace aims and postwar problems. On the heels of Eden's departure at the end of the month, Dahl sent Marsh a long shopping list of questions, eleven in all, clearly prompted by his superiors and drawing on his mentor's information and insight. While the first few are routine inquiries about Marsh's take on the growing opposition to Roosevelt, the upcoming 1944 election, and the Republican challenger's chances, the latter half of the questions probe more delicate issues of diplomacy, such as Roosevelt's opinion of Eden as a politician and to what extent his opinion was shared by Henry Wallace and Adolf A. Berle, the assistant secretary of state. Berle was a rising star in the administration and an important figure to the British as he served as the State Department's intelligence liaison with the White House. He was also the negotiator on the extremely sensitive problem of postwar air routes and who would have the lion's share of this huge prospective market. Dahl also asked for Marsh's nuanced assessment of Roosevelt's other top aides in terms of their character, intelligence, and efficacy. With the Yalta summit looming, the British clearly expected a showdown with Russia and wanted to pick his brain about which aides Roosevelt would be bringing to negotiate the shape of postwar Europe.

Marsh's twelve-page typed response tackled Dahl's questions in order, in each case providing a thumbnail sketch of the key players and laying out the most likely scenario in his exuberant, colloquial political shorthand. He was casually blunt: Roosevelt "is our best politician and will know how to make the people love him as they pick black beasts of isolationism"; Thomas E. Dewey, his Republican opponent, is "a liar"; and Wendell Willkie, who was running against FDR again, is "absolutely unpredictable as a politician and unreliable as a trader."

Marsh particularly warmed to the topic of Roosevelt's view of the British foreign secretary and the upcoming summit:

> *Eden is respected by Roosevelt as a good political workman who thinks post war more like he does than any other Englishman of power, but Roosevelt recognizes Churchill and not Eden is boss, so has his tongue in his cheek. Wallace believes Eden is top British mind on post war and would be invaluable in any semi-final late 1943 conference at Moscow.*
>
> *Since Berle and State expect to do the Russian preliminaries it is too early to say whether Roosevelt will select Wallace to work with Eden and Molotov at Moscow or whether he will drift with State. Berle today goes toward Russia for the first time in a public speech at Reading, Pennsylvania. . . . Berle poses as an expert on Russia in the State Department. Moscow has his number and won't have him around when the time comes. Probably Roosevelt will string him along until the time of the decision but will go into the Russian semi finals with people who can get things done and who have a good press in Moscow. It probably will be Wallace and Eden and Molotov reporting back to Roosevelt, Churchill and Stalin, unless Roosevelt is afraid of sacrificing Wallace and also afraid of offending Secretary Hull, who could veto because of his political power with Southern senators controlling Foreign Relations. . . .*
>
> *The fact that Roosevelt is believed to have consented to Russian-British agreements but refused himself to consent because of his Constitutional limitations does not mean a thing in the finals as far as Roosevelt is concerned as it is a mere finesse. He merely let the British get into the water first. He expects to get in at the proper time in the Russian bath with Stalin and then in a three-way scrubbing match with Stalin and Churchill.*

At the end of his visit, Eden extended an invitation to Berle to come to England, and Berle was eager to accept and hear them out on the problem of aviation and investment. Aside from Sumner Welles, no senior officer from the State Department had been allowed to travel outside Washington since 1940. Dahl's superiors wanted to know the likelihood that Berle would be granted permission to make the trip, and Dahl pressed Charles for his view. Marsh speculated:

> Berle may go to England if he gets the President at the right time and place which in Berle's language, is the late afternoon, alone, after the President has had a couple of Old-fashioneds and is willing to take on a couple of new ideas. Berle will spring his best ideas at the proper time and place hoping that the President will then say, "Jump on a plane for London," which is all he needs against a Hull or a Welles blockade. He is a daring young man on a flying trapeze and is willing to chance some effort to move from position number three to position number one. He is a great genius as a flatterer, is extremely industrious in reading all reports, and thus gathering a phoney reputation as a deep thinker and a perfectionist on a timetable.
>
> He may wait until Welles is sick from overwork and regretfully take his place at the "request" of Hull to the President. If Eden did not catch the true Berle I would suggest that Eden was overtired.

Dahl knew that from the BSC's perspective, his friendship with Marsh provided them with not only a unique vantage point onto the administration's thinking but also unrivaled access to FDR's left-wing vice president. Wallace was of great interest to the British because Roosevelt was not immortal—there were constant rumors that the strain of the war was taking a toll on FDR's already fragile health—and if anything should happen to him, Wallace was next in line. To Americans, Roosevelt's health was practically an article of faith, and as Dahl discovered, even mentioning the subject in passing was considered tasteless beyond description. His superiors, however, were practically paranoid about the conspiracy of silence surrounding FDR's condition. If he caught a cold, they wanted to know about it. Wallace's firm identification with the causes of social justice at home and abroad was also cause for worry. He was perenially trying to invest the war with a moral purpose and warned that if the nations returned to the status quo when it was over, it would have been a failure. He was also strenuously opposed to imperialism and given to making critical comments about England's relations with India that could be interpreted as anti-British and which did not sit well with London.

Unbeknownst to Dahl at the time, the head of SIS, Stewart Graham Menzies—always discreetly referred to as "C" in government circles outside the organization—regarded Wallace as "that menace," a man who had spent years under the spell of Nicholas Konstantin Roerich, a Russian guru and charlatan who was suspected of being a Communist agent. Among a long list of questionable activities, Roerich had been agitating Tibetans against the British Indian empire. Wallace eventually broke with Roerich but not before their association made headlines suggesting that Wallace dabbled in the occult sciences, which put a permanent black mark by his name.

It was difficult to know exactly what to make of the vice president, and the British were not alone in thinking so. It was safe to say that a good portion of the American public regarded his mystical worldview with suspicion bordering on contempt. Wallace was a singularly divisive figure: his vehement detractors believed his extraordinary personal quests for enlightenment over the years qualified him as a crackpot, while others defended him as a "gentleman and a scholar" and the champion of all that was decent and progressive. Even Lippmann, who was a close personal friend, thought Wallace was unsuited to be president, believing there was too great a risk that under pressure he could go "crazy."

Despite his mystical bent, Wallace had earned a reputation as an energetic idea man as head of the Department of Agriculture and then as vice president, and his early and unwavering support for Roosevelt's policy of international collective security and national defense won him the president's loyalty. When the country mobilized for war, Roosevelt rewarded Wallace by appointing him to a number of powerful positions: as a member of his Top Policy Group; as chairman of the Supply Priorities and Allocations Board; and as chairman of the Board of Economic Warfare. As the only scientist in FDR's cabinet, he also led the top-secret committee that oversaw the military research project on atomic weapons, and made the recommendation to proceed with the development of the atom bomb. James Reston of the *New York Times*, who went so far as to dub him the "Assistant President," opined: "Henry Wallace is now the administration's head man on Capitol Hill, its defense chief, economic boss and No. 1 postwar planner." And beyond that, he was someone the British wanted watched.

At the time, Dahl had no idea to what extent he was toying with a stick of wartime dynamite. He was involved in such an elaborate and enjoyable game of cat and mouse with Marsh, who was proffering all manner of politicians and diplomats and policy makers for his entertainment, that it must have all seemed like great sport. Moreover Marsh was so ardently pro-Churchill, he appeared wholly unconcerned about the information that might pass through his hands to the British. To Ralph Ingersoll, who watched their relationship progress (though he was not aware of Dahl's BSC connections until after the war), Marsh's preoccupation with Dahl was matched only by the latter's with the former, so that at times it was difficult to tell who was cultivating whom. "With no source as frank and direct,

Roald was both fascinated and amused," observed Ingersoll. "He [Dahl] and his bosses both knew the authenticity of Charles's sources and respected his sincerity and intelligence—though were no doubt often confused by the erratic intensity—and originality always close to whimsicality."

3

ENTHUSIASTIC AMATEURS

He did not make the psychological mistake of swearing me to secrecy. He never mentioned secrecy at all. That impressed me, because at that time I was perfectly aware that whatever his exact occupation was, it was very secret indeed.

— NOËL COWARD, *Future Indefinite*

AFTER HE BEGAN freelancing for British security coordination, Dahl became thoroughly entranced with William Stephenson, who he had come to think of as "this mythical, magical name in New York." Reportedly known to only a handful of the thousands of agents in his employ, Stephenson was the kind of cloaked figure who gave rise to wildly disparate rumors and, far from discouraging them, planted many of the most misleading stories himself, partly to enhance his mystery and power and partly because the miasma of conflicting reports helped to protect his anonymity. He was the brains behind the British Security Coordination, the complex secret intelligence, counterintelligence, and black propaganda operation that Churchill had charged him with developing in the United States more or less from scratch in the first year of the war, when American intervention had been anything but certain. Dahl imagined him to be a silent, unknown creature "hiding in the back of a dark room somewhere" and found himself irresistibly drawn to the remarkable mind and charismatic personality that allowed him to spin such an elaborate web of intrigue.

Dahl was always attracted to larger-than-life personalities and grand characters, and since coming to Washington he had met more than his share. He was enormously impressed by the worldly Marsh and his intimate grasp of the inner workings of American political power and influence. And yet something about the danger and excitement surrounding Stephenson, a tension that was almost palpable, was more directly connected to the charged atmosphere of the period. There was no denying the mystique of this secret warrior. Even before he took charge of the BSC, the forty-six-year-old Canadian had managed to achieve almost legendary status—amateur boxing champion, decorated World War I flying ace, self-made millionaire by the age of thirty.

By all accounts, Stephenson had survived a Dickensian childhood in the frozen heart of western Canada and at nineteen, eager for action, had enlisted in the light infantry.* He was fighting in the trenches of France when he was felled by a serious gas attack that put him in the hospital in England for months. Instead of opting for an honorable

---

*A first-class storyteller, Stephenson began fashioning a new identity for himself long before his spying days and lied about his past in countless interviews and to two successive biographers. The records indicate that he was born in Winnipeg in 1896 to an impoverished immigrant Icelandic family, and when his father, a day laborer, died, leaving behind a widow with three small children, William was given away to relatives who could afford to raise him. He was never formally adopted, but his name was changed from William Samuel Clouston to William Samuel Stephenson, a fact that was revealed years after his death by the Canadian reporter Bill Macdonald and became the basis of his revisionist history entitled, *The True Intrepid: Sir William Stephenson and the Unknown Agents.*

discharge, he applied to flight school, and after nine months of training at a Royal Flying Corps facility near Denham, he quickly made a name for himself with the RAF's 73 Squadron. He was said to be a brilliant fighter pilot, reportedly shooting down anywhere from twelve to twenty-six German planes. According to one anecdote, when his Sopwith Camel was damaged by enemy fire during a battle, he managed to land the out-of-control plane and, "mad as hops," jumped into another machine and took out two more Germans. Dahl could not have helped but be impressed by his record: he was awarded Britain's Military Cross and the Distinguished Flying Cross, as well as France's Legion of Honor and Croix de Guerre with palm. There were stories that when he finally crashed and was captured by the Germans, he organized a daring escape, carrying with him a can opener poached from the POW camp—which he promptly patented and turned into a commercial success.

Although he had left school after the sixth grade to earn a living, Stephenson had a natural technical aptitude, and while in the service he learned everything he could about airplane design, internal combustion engines, navigation, and wireless communication. When the armistice came, he returned to Canada with the twin-handled German can opener he dubbed the Kleen Kut and launched a career in manufacturing and sales. After some initial success, the new company floundered, and Stephenson hightailed it out of Winnipeg after filing for bankruptcy, leaving a string of debts in his wake. Convinced that some of the emerging technologies held out great promise for the future, the budding entrepreneur headed for England and invested what little capital he had left in two nascent British electronics firms, General Radio Company and Cox Cavendish Electrical Company. His instincts proved correct, and in a matter of months the self-taught tinkerer had teamed up with a leading research scientist named T. Thorne Baker to perfect an apparatus that could transmit images by wireless. Their pioneering new device transmitted photographs suitable for newspaper reproduction, and Stephenson was in on the ground floor of an immensely profitable new business.

Coupling his technical capabilities with a zeal for marketing, Stephenson capitalized on the boom in commercial electronics and made his first fortune selling cheap radio sets to a public enthralled by the sound of the BBC. He arrived on the scene at the moment when new technologies, which had been in development since World War I, would revolutionize communications, and he had the foresight to recognize many of the new forms it would take. He realized that the same technology used to reproduce a still picture could be used to broadcast a moving picture—by increasing the rate of transmission to the time necessary for persistence of vision—and worked at experiments that demonstrated that broadcasting moving images would soon be feasible. Eager to expand into new areas and attract overseas investors, he traveled to America, where he investigated the possibilities of recorded sound and "talking pictures" and immediately spotted the enormous potential in mass entertainment.

Throughout the 1930s, Stephenson expanded his wealth and holdings, becoming partners and friends with some of Europe's most influential figures in finance, industry, publishing, and government. His main business office, in St. James's Street, off Piccadilly, was known as a meeting place for some of the best brains on either side of the Atlantic. He had a gift for commerce: a small holding company he formed with one associate ended up attracting so many wealthy partners that by 1930 it had swelled to become British Pacific Trust, a worldwide investment company, with Stephenson installed as chairman. He poured money into the burgeoning movie business and started Sound City, one of England's first major film production companies, home to Shepparton Studios, where in 1934 Alexander Korda, who became a close friend, was shooting *Saunders of the River*. He followed up on his early interest in aviation by buying General Aircraft Limited, and that same year a plane designed and built by his firm won the King's Cup air race. Among the dozen or more companies he had accumulated was Earls Court Grounds Ltd., which built what was then the world's largest stadium and exhibition hall in London; Alpha Cement, one of Britain's largest cement companies; and the Pressed Steel Company, which manufactured 90 percent of the car bodies for British firms such as Austin, Hillman, Humber, and Morris.

During this hectic period between the wars, Stephenson acquired the habit of passing along information he had gathered in the course of his travels to various friends in positions of influence, many of whom had ties to government and the intelligence service. He would consult with his friend Charles Hambro, the wealthy London financier, who, in addition to being a director of Hambro's and the Bank of England, was chairman of the Great Western Railway Company and did part-time service at the Ministry of Shipping and the Ministry of Economic Warfare. What began as a way of comparing notes with concerned colleagues gradually evolved into more of a watchdog role by 1933, as Hitler became chancellor of the new Germany, fascism swept over Italy, and tensions escalated throughout Europe.

On one of his frequent buying trips for Pressed Steel, Stephenson discovered that Germany had greatly increased rate of steel production and that virtually all of it was earmarked for the manufacture of armaments. When he returned to London, he reported the flagrant violation of the Treaty of Versailles to friends in government, and word of his findings filtered back to Churchill. Stephenson soon found himself drawn into the former First Lord of the Admiralty's circle of secret advisers, a league of like-minded activists who toiled in every sector of government from the Foreign Office to the Ministry of Defense and who depended on Churchill to be their voice in Parliament and sound the alarm about Germany's renewed belligerence. Out of favor and out of power, Churchill had no access to official documents and had to rely on networks and inside intelligence to provide fodder for his newspaper columns, which railed against a government "lost in a pacifist dream."

Stephenson began working for Churchill's so-called Z organization, along with his friends Korda and Hambro. He monitored German rearmament and regularly funneled information about steel production in the Ruhr, surreptitiously copying balance sheets that he was able to obtain through his myriad business contacts. He documented other examples of the German military buildup and met with German aviation officials who were interested in his prize-winning airplane; he gleaned information about the Nazi war machine and blitzkrieg strategy of attack. In 1936 he turned up the chilling statistic that Germany was spending in excess of 800 million pounds on military expenditures, including preparedness measures such as fortifying strategic roads. Using his companies as a front, Stephenson collected evidence of how Germany was disguising its rearmament, revealing how companies manufacturing hairpins were also turning out howitzers, and how tank designs were hidden among seemingly innocent blueprints for tractors. He was bold enough to attempt to implement some of Churchill's more ambitious early countermeasures against the Germans, including a scheme to sabotage Swedish iron-ore transports to Germany that was compromised when details of the plan were leaked, as well as a plan to hire a sniper to assassinate Hitler that was vetoed by Lord Halifax, then Britain's foreign secretary. With little or no guidance, Stephenson acquired his only training in espionage on the run, compensating for his lack of experience with hubris and sheer ingenuity—never hesitating to make up his own rules as circumstances required.

From Dahl's perspective, Churchill could not have picked a more determined, wily operator than Bill Stephenson to head up his vast covert spy network in North America. His résumé was a virtual study in self-invention, courage, and inspired opportunism. The boyhood desire for heroes dies hard, and there is nothing like war to rekindle youthful visions of daring leaders and the romantic admiration for men of action. Dahl had always been something of an outsider all his life, an aloof and sharp-eyed observer of human foibles, but Stephenson was very much on the inside, thoroughly committed and coldly compelling. He awakened in Dahl a sense of loyalty and commitment— that higher plane of feeling that he craved since being grounded. "He [Stephenson] had such immense capabilities," recalled Dahl. "Before the war, he worked hard, he played around with his businesses and his scientific things, he coupled them up and made a fortune with apparently no trouble at all. But when the war came, he was really put to it by Churchill, and then he went to full stretch."

At this stage, Dahl still had only an inkling of the BSC chief's ferocious dedication and singleness of purpose. It was many war months before he would meet Stephenson, become his friend, and begin to learn about the extraordinary lengths the Canadian had gone to in order to help Churchill manipulate America into the war. From the moment Churchill was restored to his old seat at the Admiralty in September 1939, after Germany's attack on Poland pushed England to declare war, one of his first orders of business was to strengthen Britain's intelligence capabilities. Shortly after returning to the government, he created the Special Operations Executive (SOE), a top-secret branch designed to stimulate and supply sabotage and subversion behind enemy lines in Nazi-occupied countries, stir up riots and disorder that would weaken Germany's stranglehold on the Continent, and "set Europe ablaze." At the same time, Churchill knew that the real key to victory lay to the west, that American participation in the war was Britain's most important single objective. To that end, he asked Stephenson to undertake a secret mission to Washington aimed at improving Anglo-American cooperation, which would hopefully lay the foundation for the step-by-step process of securing U.S. assistance in the war effort.

Traveling under his usual cover as a Canadian businessman, Stephenson flew to Canada on a military plane and arrived in Washington on April 2, 1940. His orders were to gain the confidence of J. Edgar Hoover, the director of the Federal Bureau of Investigation, and "to establish relations on the highest possible level" between the two countries' intelligence agencies. Before departing, Stephenson wrote to his old army buddy Gene Tunney, the burly American heavyweight boxer whom he had met in France during the First World War and who had since become a boxing legend. Aware that Tunney and Hoover knew each other, he asked his old friend to help arrange a meeting. Stephenson, who had included a sealed letter to be forwarded on his behalf, explained that this was a confidential undertaking and that not even the British ambassador would be involved. "Sir William did not want to make an official approach through well-placed English or American friends," recalled Tunney. "He wanted to do so quietly with no fanfare."

Hoover agreed to see Stephenson the following day, promising to make him his first appointment. A dour-faced former lawyer and criminologist, Hoover listened to the British proposal, then firmly declared his opposition to any cooperation between the SIS and the FBI on the grounds that it infringed on the Neutrality Acts. He made it clear he would not consider sanctioning any liaison with the British without a direct order from the White House. He had no reason to welcome a foreign intelligence agency onto his turf, and the political no-man's-land between the SIS and the FBI promised to be nothing but trouble. Stephenson succeeded in making enough of an impression on Hoover that he allowed that if the president could be persuaded to sign off on such a collaboration, it would be conducted personally by himself and Stephenson, no one else, and no other government agency was to be informed.

During his brief sojourn in America, Stephenson made a point of seeking out another old associate, the New York millionaire Vincent Astor, Roosevelt's childhood friend and now intelligence chief. Astor was a member of the old Anglo-American fraternity and a founding member of the Room and the Walrus Club, two bodies favored by well-connected Wall Street financiers who liked to be well informed on the movement of money and about its corrolary, covert intelligence. Astor had a long-standing relationship with the SIS. He agreed to take up Stephenson's cause, insisted on putting him up at his "broken-down boarding house"—the St. Regis Hotel on Park Avenue—and briefed Roosevelt on his mission. According to Kim Philby,* who joined the SIS in 1940 and was nothing if not a keen observer of the various players, "A true top-level operator, Stephenson was not used to fooling around at the lower levels. His achievement was to stimulate the interest of Roosevelt himself, and to make quite sure the President knew that Stephenson and his backers, among whom were SOE and MI5 as well as SIS, had a lot to offer."

On his return to London, Stephenson argued in favor of forming a much broader intelligence and security system than had hitherto existed to assist with the war. After hearing his report, Churchill appointed him the new head of British secret operations in the United States. He would replace Sir James Francis Paget, a debonair and socially well-connected officer. The time had passed for gentlemanly agents and their tried-and-true methods. The pressure of war now demanded that they do far more in the field than the collection of enemy intelligence, and this necessitated a changing of the guard. The SIS would have to rise to a new level to defeat the Nazis. Churchill agreed with Stephenson that the only truly effective form of intelligence was counterintelligence, and to carry out this work they needed new blood—dynamic and innovative men who could confront the challenges ahead with new ideas, organizations, and action.

Stephenson was a master of subversive technology, ruthless in his

---

*He was later revealed to be a Soviet double agent and the ringleader of the legendary Cambridge spies.

dedication, who understood that in order to drag the reluctant American people into the war, it would be necessary to engage in all-out political warfare. He was at heart a bandit, who could be counted on to execute difficult orders that might give the best-schooled officers pause. Churchill also recognized that as a North American industrialist—who spoke with almost no trace of an accent—Stephenson would have a far easier time persuading the Americans, who sometimes resented the plummy tones of British government ministers. Moreover, Stephenson's widespread connections in the financial community could prove extremely useful, especially as his people would be thin on the ground for the first few months. "Realizing what a task he was faced with, and knowing Stephenson, as he did very well, he picked the right man," recalled Colonel Charles (Dick) Ellis,* a highly experienced intelligence officer whom Stephenson chose to be his second in New York. "He had a sort of fox terrier character, and if he undertook something, he would carry it through."

Churchill's powerful spymaster, Stewart Menzies, took a dim view of the appointment. He objected to Stephenson both as an unprincipled outsider and as an independent operator who seemed to feel he was answerable to no one. Menzies was Stephenson's opposite in almost every respect. Groomed for the job almost from birth, he was an upper-class product of Eton, who had begun his long SIS career as head of counterespionage in France in his early twenties. He had spent the entirety of his adult life in the secret service of the state. While the enterprising Canadian's industrial and economic information had been appreciated, Menzies disliked his methods and the brash vulgarity of his style. He cautioned Churchill that it would be unwise to entrust a job that was

---

*Ironically, Ellis, who had impeccable credentials, was later suspected of having sold secrets to both the Russians and the Germans. During a "hostile" interrogation by MI6, he reportedly confessed to Nazi espionage.

so delicate, and of such ultimate importance to the country, to someone who had no background in military intelligence or diplomacy and was so far removed from the halls of the SIS and the Foreign Office, the pool from which senior field personnel were normally recruited.

Stephenson had formed an equally unfavorable opinion of Menzies and the cumbersome, rigid bureaucracy he oversaw. As a social upstart from the backwoods of Canada, he chafed under "C"'s aristocratic authority and had little time for his cherished old-boy network. Accustomed to a high degree of freedom, he also balked at the idea that he would have to receive his directives from Menzies and "that gang at Broadway," a derisive reference to SIS's London headquarters at 52 Broadway. He asked Churchill for time to consider the appointment, to be certain this was the best way to serve his country. He conferred with a great number of colleagues, both old and new, pushing to sweep aside the "thumb-twiddlers and military dinosaurs" and make way for new methods of warfare and more aggressive tactics.

In the end, it was Hitler who would decide his course of action. Early on the morning of May 10, Germany's armies marched into Holland and Belgium. Later that same day, Chamberlain resigned, and Churchill was summoned to Buckingham Palace and asked to assume leadership of the wartime government. In his first day as prime minister, Churchill totally reorganized the government, installing a list of new cabinet ministers he hoped would reinvigorate the war effort. He was adamant that Stephenson go to New York, and his wishes prevailed.* As director of

---

*Stephenson always maintained that Churchill gave him his orders on May 10, in his old rooms at the Admiralty because he had not yet moved into 10 Downing Street. As a number of scholars have subsequently noted, however, Churchill's movements on that historic day have been documented in detail, and it is extremely doubtful that the two men came into contact. While it appears likely that Stephenson was mistaken about the exact date of their meeting, this discrepancy, among others, has become a source of endless controversy and has led some critics to question his basic credibility.

British Security Coordination, Stephenson's assignment, as set down in the official history of the BSC, was "to do all that was not being done, and could not be done by overt means, to assure sufficient aid for Britain and eventually to bring America into the war."

Stephenson made another quick, flying trip to Washington at the end of the month, reportedly making a surreptitious call on the president at the White House. While it is less than clear just how and when Stephenson's liaison with Roosevelt was effected, Robert Sherwood, FDR's speechwriter, in one of the more reliable statements about the behind-the-scenes machinations during this period, wrote: "Six months before the United States entered the war . . . there was, by Roosevelt's order and despite State Department qualms, effectively close cooperation between J. Edgar Hoover and the F.B.I. and British security services under the direction of the quiet Canadian, William Stephenson." That Roosevelt would agree to something that ran counter to his country's own policy and flirted with the idea of a secret sphere of war provided the tacit permission that Stephenson needed to begin his mission. Roosevelt's dedication to the anti-Nazi cause was such that it drove him to risk impeachment by taking steps to aid England's survival, according to the official history of the BSC, even to the point of allowing Sherwood to show important foreign policy speeches to Stephenson before they were delivered.

Traveling under the standard diplomatic cover of "passport control officer," Stephenson arrived in New York for the second time on Friday, June 21, 1940. This time he was accompanied by his wife, Mary French Simmons, the pretty, soft-spoken daughter of a rich tobacco exporter whom he had married in 1924, after falling in love with her on the voyage back from his first business trip to the United States. Before disembarking from the SS *Britannic*, the couple filled out immigration forms listing their address as the Waldorf-Astoria. In the blank corresponding to the purpose and length of their intended stay, Stephenson scrawled "indefinite."

Despite what he wrote on the immigration forms, Stephenson and his wife put up at Vincent Astor's hotel, the St. Regis, eventually taking a spacious apartment in the Dorset House, a luxury building overlooking the East River. Appalled to discover that his predecessor had worked out of a small room in the British Consulate that was both "cramped and depressing," not to mention all the way downtown in the Cunard Building, Stephenson made it clear from the start that he needed something considerably larger and more centrally located for the complex underground apparatus he envisioned. He worked temporarily out of a suite at the Hampshire House, on the south side of Central Park, before settling on a large suite of offices on the thirty-sixth floor of the International Building in Rockefeller Center, at 630 Fifth Avenue, in midtown Manhattan. Stephenson managed to rent the place for a negligible sum from the owner, Nelson Rockefeller, who, like Astor, was an ardent Anglophile and fellow member of the Walrus Club. For the same reason, a British intelligence front group, Fight for Freedom, was housed on the twenty-second floor of the same building, along with a number of other British propaganda agencies. That Rockefeller Center also happened to include the famous RCA tower, home to NBC, and was a stone's throw from CBS and a slew of other major news organizations, was an added bonus.

In less than six months, Stephenson totally rewrote his job description and extended his influence to include the Security Division, Naval Intelligence Division, and Special Operations Executive (SOE)—which covered censorship, codes and ciphers, security, and communication—and was soon running nine distinct secret organizations in the United States and throughout North and South America, controlling what Hoover complained was an army of British secret agents. Stephenson had extraordinary power and license to direct his organization as he saw fit, deploying the organs of subversion, propaganda, and political warfare. His first order of business, according to Sherwood, was the "detection and frustration of espionage and sabotage activities in the Western Hemisphere by agents of Germany, Italy and Japan, and also of Vichy France." Initially, Stephenson was supposed to concentrate his efforts on enlarging American material aid to Britain, and on tightening security at the ports, railroads, and storage areas to protect British shipments from American factories, but he wasted no time engaging in offensive, as well as defensive, operations against the enemy.

His primary directive, coming straight from the lips of the PM, was that American participation in the war had to be secured. It was the single most important objective for Britain. Defeating Nazism was the surest route, the only route, to victory. The BSC agent John Pepper, a good-looking young businessman who had worked for Stephenson's London corporation and accompanied him to New York, clearly outlined their mission to a potential new recruit named Betty Thorpe:[*]

> Our best information is that the forces of isolationism, a front here for Nazism and Fascism, is gaining, not losing ground. . . . We feel there is German money and German direction behind the America First movement, though many of its followers may not know it and would in fact be shocked to know it. If we can pin a Nazi contact or Nazi money on the isolationists, they will lose many of their followers. It might be the deciding factor in America's entry in the war, if the American public knew the truth.

One of Stephenson's first priorities when he assumed control of the BSC was to spread propaganda designed to strengthen the interventionist cause and undermine the isolationists. Since the beginning of

---

[*]Thorpe worked for Stephenson under the code name CYNTHIA and achieved postwar fame as the beautiful American debutante-turned-spy who helped steal crucial naval ciphers from the Vichy French.

the European war, the British ambassador, Lord Lothian, had repeatedly voiced his concern over the strong isolationist sentiment in the United States and warned that nine in ten Americans were determined to keep their country out of the war. A BSC survey done in 1941 found that nearly one million Americans were members of isolationist organizations such as America First, which had as many as seven hundred chapters across the country; some, like the American Nazi Party, were committed to aiding the Axis powers. While most Americans hoped for Allied victory, far fewer believed that providing military support to Britain was necessary to achieve it, and they were reluctant to become involved because of their memories of World War I. As a consequence, the Lend-Lease Act was hotly contested for months and was barely passed by a bitterly divided Congress.

To sway public opinion in favor of aid to Britain, Stephenson declared a covert war on the isolationists. He aggressively propelled the BSC into a vast array of aggressive new initiatives, from producing propaganda that portrayed Germany as an enemy of democracy and capitalism and a Nazi victory as a "threat to the American way of life," to monitoring and reporting on isolationist groups and harassing and publicly humiliating their leaders. When Senator Gerald Nye gave an anti-British speech in Boston in September 1941, the BSC littered the area with handbills accusing him of being an appeaser and "Nazi lover." After Representative Hamilton Fish gave a speech criticizing the interventionists, he was presented with a card that read, "Der Fuhrer thanks you for your loyalty," just as the pool of photographers began snapping photos. Not all of the BSC's ploys succeeded. An attempt to disrupt one of Lindbergh's America First rallies at Madison Square Garden backfired when counterfeit tickets, created by the BSC with the idea that his fans would be turned away in droves, ended up only further packing the hall. As a consequence the pro-German flying ace ended up preaching his pacifist doctrines to an enthusiastic audience of 20,000, with almost as many cheering for him on the streets outside.

To shake Americans out of their complacency, the BSC went to fantastic lengths. They even hired the Hungarian astrologer Louis de Wohl, whose prognostications had once caught the fancy of the Führer himself, to prophesy Hitler's imminent doom and undermine public confidence in the invincibility of the Nazis. Stephenson staged a press conference on August 6, 1941, at which the astrologer unveiled his predictions to the astonished reporters: Hitler's horoscope showed that his fall was certain. Stephenson arranged for de Wohl's revelations to become regular tabloid fodder over the next several months and saw to it that his forecasts were echoed by shamans in other parts of the world, including an eminent Egyptian astrologer in Cairo and a Nigerian priest in a remote village. Stephenson even went the extra mile, making sure that one of de Wohl's prophecies—that an ally of Hitler's would soon go mad—was fulfilled ten days later, when a French naval officer who had escaped from Martinique reported that the island's Vichy French governor had gone insane. With his fateful vision legitimized, the newly celebrated "astro-philosopher," as the papers dubbed him, toured the country, declaring Hitler's coming defeat at meetings, over the air, and in widely syndicated newspaper columns. According to the BSC history, the British found the Americans surprisingly easy to manipulate: "It is unlikely that any propagandist would seriously attempt to influence politically the people of England, say, or France through the medium of astrological predictions. Yet in the United States this was done with effective if limited results."

Running a large intercontinental intelligence network required building up a significant staff, and new personnel were recruited from Canada, England, and the United States. Stephenson's BSC agents were an unorthodox group, but then it was unconventional duty. They were, to his mind, insurgents, fighting a guerrilla action in a foreign country. He recruited people from every walk of life and favored enthusiastic amateurs, whose names and faces were unknown to the Gestapo and other enemy intelligence agencies, and had no ties to the British SIS. They were hired for their background, education, and originality—any formal training in the tradecraft of spying was secondary and came later, if at all. They included all sorts, from Dick Ellis, the professional intelligence officer Stephenson had brought from London to be his deputy; to Louis Franck, who was in charge of liaison with the Americans on technical matters such as the manufacture of radio equipment and other devices, as well as the management of the newly founded sabotage-training school in Canada, among other things; and Connop Guthrie, an Englishman with extensive experience in shipping who led the industrial security division. Among the British businessmen and financiers who handled key executive jobs were Richard Coit, who served as propaganda chief; John Pepper, who became intelligence chief; and Bickham Sweet-Escott.

Then there was the special operations section, a particularly learned group, among them Bill Deakin, a professor; Freddie Ayes, a philosopher; and Gilbert Highet, a classical scholar. There was Alec Halpern, an omniscient White Russian, nicknamed Monsieur le President, whose main function was to put feelers out to the different ethnic communities in the United States to assess their sympathy with Britain, as well as to find and recruit agents of Greek, Yugoslav, Bulgarian, Rumanian, or Hungarian extraction who might be of help in special work in Europe and Asia. Because of the diversity of languages involved in interrogations and examinations of documents, he also hired a small staff of linguists. The BSC cleverly tailored its messages to appeal to particular ethnic groups, targeting Catholics by spreading stories of Nazi desecration of churches, dispatching Irish agents to organize a network called the Irish American Defense Association, and persuading the journalist Max Ascoli to make inroads into the Italian-American community through the Mazzini Society.

These agents were supported in their efforts by a galaxy of creative talent such as the filmmakers Alexander and Zoltán Korda, who made pro-British propaganda films about their soldiers' romantically danger-ous exploits; and the magician Oskar Maskelyne, who was brought in specifically to create an illusory army to mislead and confuse the Germans. The composer Eric Maschwitz was made head of the BSC's documentary warfare division, known as Station M, tasked with forg-ing and fabricating wartime documents. There were also a number of Mata Hari types, such as Betty Thorpe, attractive young women in well-placed embassy jobs or exalted social circles who were in a posi-tion to hear important information, carry messages, and on occasion pilfer documents. For the same reason, Stephenson also sometimes re-cruited celebrities as couriers. Noël Coward and Leslie Howard were among those assigned tasks of a glamorously dangerous nature.[*]

Coward, famous for his plays *Fallen Angels*, *Hay Fever*, and *Private Lives*, was offered a job by Stephenson in the summer of 1940, after a clandestine meeting in an absurdly feminine chintz-covered room at the Hampshire House. "He was small, quietly affable, and talked very little," recalled Coward. "He gave me two strong Cuba Libres one after another, and waited politely for me to talk a great deal. I obliged, up to a point, and was asked to return a few evenings later." Coward had met Stephenson once before, very briefly, in London when he

---

[*]Howard was reportedly running an errand for the BSC when his plane from Lisbon was shot down by the Germans in 1943 over the Bay of Biscay. Eight German Ju-88s attacked the DC-3 passenger flight, which was not in a designated war zone at the time. Several in-depth accounts of the incident have concluded that the Germans were well aware of Howard's intelligence work and deliberately targeted his flight with the idea that the death of the popular entertainer and outspoken patriot would hurt British morale.

was first recruited. He had gone St. Ermin's Hotel on Caxton Street, the original headquarters of the SOE before they moved to 64 Baker Street, to meet "a contact" in the foyer. "I waited in this squalid place and eventually a man said, 'Follow me,'" he recalled. "He wheeled me round and into an elevator. It was only labeled to go up three floors. To my absolute astonishment it went to the fourth floor. An immense fellow guarded the place, all scrunched up inside a porter's uniform. Well, this was the Special Operations Executive. What we later called the Baker Street Irregulars. Some chap was saying that President Roosevelt wanted us to do his fighting." Stephenson was present but kept to the background and was "very calm, with those sort of hooded eyes watching everything."

This was not Coward's first foray into intelligence work. When war broke out, he had undertaken a mission for the SIS to set up a propaganda bureau in Paris, and his celebrity, busy theatrical schedule, and international travel had also made him useful to the Ministry of Information, which tapped him to do propaganda work in America. Coward expressed his desire to do something more for his country's cause—a planned mission to do anti-Nazi work in South America had been called off at the last minute—and Stephenson assured the would-be spy that he could be of considerable service to the BSC and would be asked to undertake espionage assignments that required a delicate touch. In the meantime, his work for British War Relief in America would provide him with a reason to tour the country and "talk up" support for the Allies. "I was to go as an entertainer with an accompanist and sing my songs and on the side doing something rather hush-hush," Coward wrote in his diary. "He saw where my celebrity value would be useful and he seemed to think I ought to be as flamboyant as possible, which was very smart of him. My disguise would be my own reputation as a bit of an idiot . . . merry playboy. It was very disarming. Very clever of him."

By all accounts, Stephenson was the magnetic core around which these myriad stars rotated. A workaholic, he had almost no life outside the section, remaining largely anonymous and invisible in the city. No one seeing this short, square, sagacious-looking man in the elevator would have mistaken him for anything but a businessman, albeit one who kept very long hours. It was not unusual for him to work until midnight and to be back at his desk by dawn. As one BSC subordinate recalled, "It took eleven secretaries to keep up with him." He rarely left the building unless it was to liaise with British and American intelligence in Washington, and more often than not people were expected to make the trip up to New York to be briefed. To facilitate communications between New York and the Washington office, Stephenson had installed a state-of-the-art teleprinter, known as the Telekrypton ciphering machine, or TK, which instantaneously coded or decoded the messages passed between the two bureaus.

When Ian Fleming met the BSC director the following spring, while on an assignment for British Naval Intelligence, he knew at once that he was in the presence of an extraordinary individual—a very tough, very rich, single-minded patriot, and "a man of few words." Fleming was completely captivated by Stephenson's elaborate setup and the vast array of sophisticated equipment he had accumulated, particularly the mechanical ciphering machines. Drawing on his background in radio and electronics, Stephenson had made improving the communications division one of his priorities, and he boasted it was "by far the largest of its type in operation." Fleming, who was fascinated by gadgets of all kinds, carried a small commando knife with him on most foreign assignments, along with a trick fountain pen that ejected a cloud of tear gas when the clip was pressed. In Stephenson, he had finally found someone whose passion for sophisticated weaponry surpassed even his own, and his frank admiration led to a quick rapport and a rapidly developing friendship. Within a short time of their meeting, Fleming came to regard the Canadian as "one of the great secret agents" and a man who had "the quality of making anyone ready to follow him to the ends of the earth." A mere commander and a comparative newcomer to the intelligence world, Fleming was self-conscious about his late start. He had failed the Foreign Office exam and was anxious to prove himself. He had also lost his father early in life—he was nine when Robert Fleming was killed in the First World War—and looked up to the BSC chief as a role model and mentor.

Until the spring of 1939, Fleming had been happily employed as a stockbroker in the old London firm of Rowe and Pitman, when he had been invited to a luncheon with Rear Admiral John Godfrey, the newly appointed director of Naval Intelligence, and informed that he had been appointed a lieutenant in the Royal Naval Volunteer Reserve, and that his duty from then on lay in serving as the admiral's personal assistant. He most likely owed his sudden career change to his older brother, Peter Fleming, a well-known explorer and author who had already been recruited by the SOE because of his extensive travels in and knowledge of the Middle East. Aged thirty-two and thirty-one respectively, the Fleming brothers were considered too old and inexperienced for frontline commands, but their Eton education and facility with languages singled them out as agent material. In the small, interlocking establishment circles at Whitehall and the City, the Fleming name was known. It did not hurt that Ian had done a stint at the Reuters news service, where he had volunteered to take on a little espionage assignment in the Soviet Union, and in the process earned a reputation as a fellow who could think on his feet.

Ian was tall and strikingly handsome, with blue eyes, thick brown hair, and a long nose that was somehow more attractive for having been broken. He was so impossibly clean-cut and square-jawed that when he reported to the Ministry of Defense in his blue serge uniform, he was promptly dubbed "the chocolate sailor" by an envious colleague.

While his operational experience was limited to one brief mission in France, he was an extremely energetic and efficient administrator, becoming the chief contact between the Admiralty and the SOE. He also turned out to be highly imaginative when it came to devising espionage schemes, and while most of his proposals were too far-fetched to be practical, some were just crazy enough to be worth trying. One bright idea that got provisional approval before being scrapped was a detailed plan to capture German codebooks—of great value to the cryptographers—which involved staging a dummy crash of a Luftwaffe plane, which in theory would lure in one of the high-speed German launches patrolling the Channel and allow a team of saboteurs to overpower the crew before they realized it was a trap.

Fleming knew from his access to eyes-only documents that Stephenson, by carefully nurturing his unofficial relationship with the FBI, had already rendered "innumerable services to the Royal Navy that could not have been asked for, let alone executed, through normal channels." On that first trip to the United States in May 1941, Fleming had accompanied Admiral Godfrey on a covert mission to Washington aimed at strengthening the ties between the British Admiralty and U.S. Naval Intelligence. It was, in essence, an attempt to initiate the same backstairs dialogue Stephenson had so successfully established with the Americans. They never had a chance. After listening to their exposé of security problems "with the air of doing [him] a favor," Hoover made it clear he had no interest in accommodating the British any further and politely but firmly showed them the door. "Hoover had his channels with Bill Stephenson," recalled Fleming, "and his common-sense, legalistic mind told him it would be unwise to open separate channels with us."

Godfrey's snubbed overture to Hoover had served only to highlight British intelligence's frustration with the clumsy, one-sided arrangement, in which all of their useful information and requests for action had to be transmitted through the FBI. Increasingly touchy about incursions on his turf, Hoover had become close-fisted and combative, and in the absence of an American counterpart to the SOE, there was no other authority the British could turn to for assistance. The FBI had been created under the New Deal to fight crime, and while Hoover had added counterespionage to his roster of responsibilities, the FBI made no organized effort to collect secret intelligence from friendly and neutral countries, to say nothing of the enemy. The U.S. Army's Signal Intelligence Service was an outdated and understaffed organization, a relic of the First World War and the prevailing isolationism that followed in its wake. As a result, the Roosevelt administration was poorly informed, and almost entirely dependant on tip-offs from its embassies and service attaches abroad, and the kindness of its allies. Vincent Astor, in his waning days as the president's intelligence adviser, reported the British complaints to the president and lamented the bureaucratic delays and lost opportunities: "It is certainly a bit difficult to conduct an effective blitzkrieg of our own against malefactors when information becomes stymied in department files for six weeks."

Prescient as ever, Stephenson had been arguing for the creation of an American secret service organization, to be headed by someone sympathetic to the British government—or, more to the point, someone with whom he could work—and had been assiduously pushing his own candidate to run the new agency. Colonel William Donovan was a prominent attorney and Columbia Law School classmate of Roosevelt's, an irresistible Irishman with a forceful personality and immense charm, who had already run for office several times as a Republican. He had won a jacket full of medals in World War I, ended up as commander of the legendary "Fighting 69th," and was affectionately known to the press as "Wild Bill." Donovan, at the request of the president, had traveled to London in July 1940 on a fact-finding mission to survey fifth column activity in England. His "real object," however, was to assess the state of the British defenses, as well as the underlying morale, with an eye to collecting as much information as possible in the event America entered the war: Would England fight on at all costs or, as the defeatist ambassador Joseph Kennedy kept warning Washington, would the country surrender in a matter of months? Stephenson, aware of the importance of his visit, had arranged for the American lawyer to meet with everyone who could help his inquiries, including an interview with Churchill.* Donovan found the British still full of grit and determination and in turn assured them that he was an experienced and influential adviser on whom they could rely. Acting as a middleman, Donovan reported back to Washington that England could hold out, and in December he returned to London with Stephenson for another round of talks about Britain's urgent need for supplies and military support, with destroyers topping the list.

Throughout that autumn, the two men were in regular contact as they evaluated the British prospects, the imminence of the Nazi assault, and a German fifth column that they believed threatened not only Europe but the whole Western Hemisphere, which Donovan

---

*The Americans and British are still arguing about who deserves the most credit for the creation of the OSS. Years later, Stephenson claimed to have had a hand in orchestrating Donovan's mission, which was decisive in paving the way for the formation of the agency. In his book *Wild Bill and Intrepid*, author Thomas Troy, a retired CIA staff officer and historian, argues that the preponderance of evidence suggests that the initiative for Donovan's trip came from Secretary of the Navy Frank Knox. He makes the case that there is little evidence to support Stephenson's additional claims that he accompanied Donovan on that trip and that they were old friends. As Troy writes, Stephenson, who was recalling these events in his retirement, and after a debilitating stroke, in all likelihood "read history backwards. He was to develop such a close and mutually fruitful collaboration with Donovan, was to make so many Atlantic crossings with him . . . that it is quite probable he unconsciously pushed the line of collaboration back to the beginning of the trip, transforming, in the process, 'advance knowledge' into the conception of it."

proceeded to describe in a series of articles that ran in newspapers across the country. Both men pressed hard at the highest levels, for the badly needed supplies and lobbied tirelessly for the destroyers-for-bases agreement that ultimately provided England with fifty-four aging destroyers at a time when they were desperate for combat escorts to protect their convoys from U-boats. In the months that followed, Stephenson continued to cultivate Donovan, who had already proven his value and promised to be of great importance to him in the future, not only as a personable and vigorous figure close to the administration but as someone who had earned the trust and gratitude of the British government. If Stephenson had not yet fully conceived of the kind of sister organization the BSC required to function more efficiently in America, he was astute enough to identify the man he wanted to lead it early on. To make sure Donovan remained the front-runner, Stephenson exerted his influence on both sides of the pond and later admitted that some in the old-school circles of the SIS would have been horrified to learn the extent to which he was "supplying our friend with secret information to build up his candidacy for the position I wanted to see him achieve here."

On June 18, 1941, Stephenson got his way, and Roosevelt appointed Donovan to the newly created office of coordinator of information (COI), acting as an adviser to the president on all matters concerned with intelligence, propaganda, and special operations. It was a huge assignment, and it was almost impossible to expect Donovan to be able to come up with a complete outline for the wartime organization at once. Stephenson offered Donovan his help in getting the new agency off the ground and "pressed his view" that it should be patterned after his own organization. Donovan, for his part, acknowledged Stephenson's role as "the earliest collaborator with and chief supporter of the early movement" to expand the country's secret activities, "whose early discussions with the Coordinator were largely instrumental in bringing about a clearer conception of the need for a properly coordinated American intelligence service."

During this same period, Admiral Godfrey, who had befriended Donovan during his recent trip to London, was staying at his house in Washington and finding all his efforts to coordinate the two countries' intelligence services frustrated at every turn, until Stephenson advised him that his host might be the answer to all their problems and that he was on the point of having him installed in power. To cut through red tape and speed up the process, Stephenson then maneuvered to have Sir William Wiseman, the SIS's man in New York during World War I and one-time liaison to President Woodrow Wilson, explain the British Admiralty's predicament to Roosevelt. This was done during a dinner party at the home of Roosevelt friends on Long Island. The result, Godfrey recalled, was that three weeks later Donovan received "$3,000,000 to play with as head of a new department."

Having done what he could, Godfrey returned to England alone, leaving Fleming behind with instructions to do everything within his power to help establish the joint intelligence machinery. Godfrey approved of Fleming's friendship with "Little Bill" (Stephenson) and "Big Bill" (Donovan) and thought that the more his assistant could learn about their ally's point of view, the more he could do to improve their relations. "Ian got on well with the Americans," recalled Godfrey, and "operating on a slightly different plane to mine, he was able to discover how that land lay and warn me of the pitfalls." His energy and flair also appealed to Donovan, who found the young commander far more amenable and productive than the more deliberate, slow-moving admiral. "Fleming suffered not at all from Very Senior Officer Veneration," observed Donald MacLachlan, a colleague in naval intelligence. "He was ready—indeed, more ready than Godfrey himself—to stand up for a case against a Vice-Chief of Naval Staff or Director of Plans. This easy confidence made him very effective in defense of the DNI's side-shows, some of which were to expand famously and create all kinds of unfamiliar problems for the Admiralty's civil servants."

Fleming thought Donovan a "splendid American" and was eager to help him in any way he could. Over a period of several days, he worked with him while staying at Donovan's Georgetown residence, drafting what he later described as the "original charter of the OSS," as well as a second document he called "my memorandum to Bill on how to create an American Secret Service." While neither of these memos fully qualified as "the cornerstone of the future OSS," as Fleming later claimed, they comprised a thoughtful, practical outline of the kind of wartime organization the Americans needed, informed by the British service's century of experience.

Ivar Bryce, Fleming's Eton classmate and closest friend, recalled Fleming telling him that he wrote the charter out in longhand, "as a sort of imaginary exercise describing in detail all the arrangements necessary for financing, paying, organizing, controlling and training a secret service in a country that had never had one before. And it included a mass of practical detail on how much use could be made of diplomatic sources of intelligence, how agents could be run in the field, how records could be kept, and how liaison could be established with other governments." Fleming even sketched his notion of the ideal American intelligence officer: "[He] must have trained powers of observation, analysis and evaluation; absolute discretion, sobriety, devotion to duty; language and wide experience; and be aged about 40 to 50." Donovan greatly appreciated Fleming's advice and before he left Washington presented him with him a small souvenir—a .38 Colt Police Positive revolver with the inscription "For Special Services." Fleming would later imply he received the gun as a reward for far more dangerous work than being a pen pusher.

It took only a word from Fleming, and Bryce, a wealthy playboy from a good family, found himself working for Stephenson in New

York, after what he later recalled as a remarkably short interview at the Westbury Hotel. The man who vetted him, and subsequently became his immediate superior, was Dick Coit—known affectionately to his staff as Coitus Interruptus—"a cherubic sixty-year-old" with a pink face and fiery disposition who helped oversee the BSC's Special Operations Section. As Bryce would later write in a book of reminiscences of his adventures with Fleming, Coit told him the BSC could use someone like him, "if you are willing to follow any orders, and accept whatever happens to you, and on no account ever to reveal the smallest detail concerning your work." Bryce then signed the Official Secrets Act, "a terrifying document," and swore "total and blind and everlasting obedience."

As he had joined around the time when the BSC was taking over the SOE's responsibilities for Latin America, Bryce spent the first few months working in what he said felt like "an export office," sitting behind an accountant's desk and dealing with dreary commercial and cultural matters in Venezuela, Brazil, Cuba, Colombia, and Peru. His first real assignment was to help find and train "bodies," the term for agents, that the SOE needed to carry out risky missions to disrupt Nazi and anti-Allied activities in the area. The Latin countries were honeycombed with German organizations such as Auslands Deutsch, and the Reich had even gone so far as to establish some secret military training camps in the continent's interior. At the time, it had seemed probable that the Germans would invade South America using the Vichy French territory of Senegal as a staging area. Given the scant opposition in the area, military strategists estimated that the German conquest of the continent would take less than a month. With that threat in mind, Stephenson thought it was worth trying to mount at least a skeleton resistance force. Of the twenty young men whom Bryce managed to recruit in Latin America for the BSC's operation, more than half were rejected for one reason or another. Of the small pool who eventually passed muster, only a handful successfully completed their hair-raising missions and returned home safely. Most of those who were caught were tortured, then shot. One, a young Dutch friend from Brazil named Jan van Schelle, was reported killed. He had parachuted into Holland after his underground operation was exposed and had the misfortune to put down among a reception party of Gestapo agents. Bryce felt "the dreadful responsibility" of selecting these candidates given the catastrophes that might befall them. His friend had enjoyed a happy and useful life in Brazil, and it was he "who suggested to him what he might exchange it for."*

The BSC's anti-Nazi underground was from the start "a shoe-string operation," and relatively little had been accomplished by the spring of 1942 when Hoover moved to rein in Stephenson's activities and ordered him to curtail their defensive efforts in the southern republics. Hoover, Bryce noted, was a man for whom "jealousies and petty rivalries meant more than great causes." Although the FBI director was "on good terms" with Stephenson, "he was immensely touchy at the thought of any British interference in what he regarded as 'his territory.'" In March, Bryce alerted Lippmann to the gravity of the situation: "If you felt at all inclined to write anything about the danger to S. America, I could give you any number of facts which have never been published, but which my friends here would like to see judiciously made public, at this point."

Still preoccupied with Nazi designs on Latin America, Bryce, holed up in his BSC office, took to sketching worst-case scenarios on his blotter showing what the area would look like if forced to submit to

---

*A later investigation revealed that von Schelle was captured by the Germans as part of Operation Nordpol and reportedly was made an unwitting accomplice to their plan to penetrate a major SOE network in France. He survived the war and ultimately returned to Brazil. Bryce was never informed of the results of the SOE investigation and went to his grave still burdened by his part in his friend's death.

Nazi rule. There would be the inevitable rearrangement of national borders, with Nazi-oriented governments probably gaining territories, while some homelands might be totally eradicated. In his trial maps, he imagined what would happen if Hitler got his way, and drew a logical extension of the idea: "The obvious aggrandizement of Paraguay, the land-locked and poverty-stricken but immensely militaristic kingdom of the great German dictator Stroessner, would of course be enlarged: a great corridor to the Pacific, at the expense of Chile, Paraguay's old enemy. The abolition of Uruguay, the Switzerland of South America."

According to Bryce, after looking over his sketches, it occurred to Stephenson to try to pull a fast one and plant a fake map in a known German safe house on the southern coast of Cuba, where Nazi agents stored radio equipment used for signaling U-boats in the area. Stephenson then planned to tip the FBI, which would promptly raid the Nazi outpost and fall upon "a monster prize." Bryce could only speculate on the immense value of such a find, especially when it came to sounding the alarm in America, which still felt safely removed from the Nazi threat: "Were a German map of this kind to be discovered or captured from enemy hands and publicized among the good neighbors themselves, and above all among the 'America Firsters' with their belief that America could get along with Hitler, what a commotion would be caused."

One of Bryce's trial maps was immediately given over to Station M, the BSC's technical facilities in Canada, where Eric Maschwitz ran a chemical laboratory and photograph studio, and had the ability to fabricate images, such as atrocity pictures, and to "reprint faultlessly the imprint of any typewriter on earth." Forty-eight hours later Maschwitz and his team of experts had created an authentic-looking German map, slightly worn and discolored from frequent use, which, Bryce marveled, even "the Reich's chief mapmakers for the German High Command would be prepared to swear was made by them."

On this occasion, Stephenson may have outdone himself, passing the forgery on to Donovan, who gave it to Roosevelt. On March 11, 1941, the president made a dramatic announcement during his Navy Day radio address, revealing that he had proof that Hitler's plans for conquest extended across the Atlantic Ocean. "I have in my possession a secret map," he solemnly intoned, "made in Germany by Hitler's government—by the planners of the new world. It is a map of South America and a part of Central America as Hitler proposes to reorganize it." Roosevelt went on to describe the principal features of the map, including the Panama Canal, "our great life line," and Germany's plan to carve the region up into five vassal states. "That map, my friends, makes clear the Nazi design not only against South America but against the United States as well." Bryce's map, which had been produced rather than procured by the BSC, was held up to the nation as one of the "grim truths" of Hitler's future plans and demanded a response. Americans, Roosevelt declared, were "pledged to pull our oar in the destruction of Hitlerism."

From the BSC's point of view, the map was a daring gambit that resulted in a propaganda coup. As expected, the German government responded to Roosevelt's radio broadcast by angrily denouncing the document as a fraud. The Italian government immediately demanded that unless the president published the map within twenty-four hours, Roosevelt would acquire "a sky-high reputation as a forger." Their furious protests only served to make the phony document appear more real. At a press conference the following day, FDR declined to make his "secret map" available, assuring reporters that it came from "a source that is undoubtedly reliable." Bryce, who was sure the president's speech was inspired by his invention, was amazed by the impact of the broadcast. "The item was made full use of by the media," he recalled, "and gave distasteful but unanswerable food for thought to the many who believed that European wars could have no influence on the inhabitants of the Western Hemisphere."

While the map's true origin was not discovered at the time, Adolf Berle strongly suspected that Stephenson and his boys were behind it. Another document cited by Roosevelt in the same speech, supposedly detailing a Nazi plan to abolish all the world's religions, seemed equally spurious. Berle knew that the BSC specialized in manufacturing fake documents, and the written proof outlining German plans for world domination struck Berle as a bit too convenient. In a memorandum forwarded to Cordell Hull, Berle warned that Americans should be "on our guard" against these "false scares" concocted by the British. Only a month earlier, Berle had written a detailed memorandum enumerating the potential dangers of the British operation being run by the "security co-ordinator" Mr. William S. Stephenson, arguing that it was developing into "a full size secret police and intelligence service" and was supported by shadow force of "regularly employed secret agents and a much larger number of informers, etc."

Looking ahead, Berle worried that in any number of conceivable wartime scenarios—if Britain fell to the Germans, and they were faced with a new hostile occupation government; or some mission went wrong and their activities were exposed—this unofficial band of spies could prove a real liability. "I have good reason to believe that a good many things done are probably in violation of the espionage acts," he warned, adding with lawyerly caution, "We should be on very dubious grounds if we have not taken appropriate steps." When he learned that Stephenson had succeeded in having his position in the United States formalized as director of security coordination, Berle was not pleased: "It's a bad title—& worse to talk about. I would shut up and watch it." In the months that followed, Berle grew increasingly hostile toward the BSC's interference on American soil and began leading the effort, with Hoover's quiet encouragement, to discontinue the British spy unit.

Despite these turf battles with American authorities, the BSC continued its special operations. Over the spring and summer of 1941, Fleming was afforded a rare glimpse into the hidden workings of the organization, with Stephenson acting as his personal tour guide in its subterranean labyrinths. Before returning to London, Fleming was permitted to observe an active operation and was a spectator at a BSC-staged break-in at the Japanese consul general's office, conveniently located on the thirty-fourth floor in Rockefeller Center. In the course of a single night, Stephenson's men gained entry with the help of the janitor and managed to crack the safe and make microfilm copies of the codebooks, which contained ciphers the Japanese had been using to transmit messages to Tokyo by short-wave radio. Before morning, everything in the safe was returned to its exact place, and there was no sign they had ever been there. Fleming would never forget the episode, filing it away as one of the more thrilling adventures of his wartime service, though he knew full well that Stephenson considered it strictly routine.*

Stephenson allowed Fleming privileges far above his rank. He invited him to his penthouse, which for all practical purposes was a safe house, where he held court in an elegant two-storied drawing room with an enormous fireplace and regularly gathered the grand and near-grand of the British High Command. Among those who could be found there, at various times, were General Lord Ismay, the prime minister's defense chief of staff; Major General Sir Colin Gubbins, chief of the Special Operations Executive; Lord Beaverbrook; and many others. It was there that he introduced Fleming to the handful of figures in his inner circle, including Ernest Cuneo, Donovan's personal liaison

---

*Fleming's first novel, *Casino Royale,* published in 1953, contains a highly exaggerated reference to the mission—in which James Bond shoots a Japanese cipher expert at Rockefeller Center—as the first of two dangerous assignments that earned Bond his double-0 classification.

between British intelligence, the White House, and the FBI. It was at a party at Stephenson's that Cuneo observed the young naval attaché's "all but blind adoration" for the quiet Canadian, noting that it was evident even then that "William was one of the very few firm and brilliant stars in the heavens of Ian Fleming."

Fleming immediately engaged Cuneo in a typical Anglo-American exchange, characterized by a spirited verbal sparring that gave the British an opportunity to test the ground and take the measure of their opposite numbers. According to Cuneo, most of their wartime conversations, even on the gravest matters, were carried on in this manner, with a combination of sporty bravado and slightly patronizing maliciousness, "all against an atmosphere of merriest and warmest friendship." There, in the soft gloom wreathed with the smoke of their cigarettes, they traded secrets vital to the security of their agents, operations, and troops on land and sea. It was a game, but there was a war on, and as played by these calculating men, it was for keeps. To Cuneo, who negotiated Stephenson's Dorset drawing room as gingerly as a debutante at a spring ball, it all went to prove the old Shaw adage that America and England were two countries "separated by a common language."

A latecomer to the club, Dahl, like Fleming and Bryce, was destined to become another of Stephenson's trusted subordinates—one of his "special boys"—held in reserve and carefully groomed until needed. They were the BSC's blue-eyed social butterflies, meant to use their charm and guile to feel out what the other side was thinking, convey messages between principals without creating any unnecessary awkwardness, and in general help smooth the way. In the ancient art of diplomacy, the go-between always played an important role. "Bill knew this very well," said Dahl. "That's why he planted fellows like me."

4

SPECIAL RELATIONSHIPS

He's a killer with women.

—Patricia Neal

Dahl was making a name for himself as a writer, enjoying an eventful and productive war, and having by his own account "a roaring time." Washington's bustling, affluent society seemed largely unaffected by wartime restrictions, and he happily drank, dined, and hobnobbed away his evenings. All the luxuries that had long since disappeared from shelves back home were easily procurable. There was fresh fruit and steaks, and champagne was plentiful. He was untroubled by the inconveniences that irked local residents, whether it was the overcrowding caused by the influx of government workers, the shortage of accommodations, or the long lines at the lunchrooms and cafeterias. The complainants did not have his memories of RAF canteens, horrendous chow, and hard bunks. They could not share his simple pleasure, after finally gaining a counter stool, of digging into a plate of bacon and eggs. Even when beer was rationed, he was perfectly content to roam from bar to bar in the quaint cobblestoned district, wandering home late at night under the dimmed streetlights— one of the few visible signs of belt-tightening in the capital—that gave off the faint amber glow of a flashlight with a dying battery.

He was comfortably ensconced in a small Georgetown house at 1610 34th Street, which was sandwiched in a row of faded-brick Federal-style buildings on a narrow tree-lined street. The two-story building, which had three separate though otherwise identical entrances, had seen better days, and he shared his sliver with a Lieutenant Richard Miles, an assistant naval attaché at the embassy. Miles had been sent to Washington by the British Information Service and was a delegate to the International Student Service Assembly. He had been badly wounded in action and had required surgery to have one ear reattached. The operation had left him with a long scar, though it did not make him any less attractive—or appealing to the ladies. In a town woefully short of men since the war began, the two eligible young officers were in great demand and never lacked for invitations. "They were having a ball," recalled Antoinette. "They were big British war heroes, you know, the toast of town. And Roald was a very good flirt. Girls were crazy about him. He had all the hostesses eating out of his hand. The ambassador sent him to the parties to see how things were going, and sound people out."

With the playgrounds of Europe closed to tourists, moneyed society was forced to stay home, and Washington was brimming with wealthy dowagers and their bored, unmarried daughters. They took houses in Georgetown or large estates in Bethesda, hired social secretaries and huge staffs, and devoted themselves to throwing what the *Washington Post*'s gossip columnist Hope Ridings Miller dubbed "parties for a purpose"—for they also serve who only stand and pass the punch. Socialites, busy planning their wardrobes and weekly soirées, frantically sent messengers around town with their calling cards and complained of the agonizing pressures of aiding the war effort. Capital society was the American court, complete with its own courtiers, pretenders to the throne, and inevitable hangers-on. In a city where position mattered more than personality, even the most soporific government official counted as "somebody," and the humblest embassy attaché—such as Dahl himself, who at home might be considered only marginally acceptable—rated a mention in the Social Register. Guest lists centered on the White House, Congress, the State Department, and foreign embassies, and a surprising amount of business, along with more intimate transactions, was negotiated across the dinner table.

Washington was still a small, provincial southern town in many respects, and the men who ran the government moved with ease and confidence from the capital's conference rooms to the drawing rooms of prominent figures who lived nearby. From the start of the war, the city's leading social powers had been uncorking champagne and spooning caviar in an effort to lure the eminent men from finance, industry, science, and academe who had descended on Washington to take up government posts. These "dollar-a-year men" ran virtually every wartime agency and were highly desirable game in a town populated with determined climbers of one kind of another. Potomac matrons, old and new money alike, competed to see who could corner more of these important targets, and there were all sorts of stories about the lobbying and scheming that went on to secure the most coveted RSVPs. Marsh considered some of these high-profile ladies to be little more than low-grade "racketeers." After a weekend in New York, where he kept an apartment in the Hotel St. Moritz, he came back ranting about Elsa Maxwell, the original "hostess with the mostest," and told Dahl she was in fact "paid to throw parties" and took a 10 percent commission. La Maxwell was a successful former actress, composer, and syndicated columnist who hosted a weekly radio show called, of all things, *Party Line*, in which she dispensed quantities of mindless fluff along with the occasional political insight. Based on her dubious claim to fame, she had become a preeminent Republican party-giver and had staged two well-attended events in honor of Wendell Willkie, with the bills reportedly footed by wealthy New York backers. Marsh was fit to be tied.

To these patriotic ladies, Dahl, with his conspicuous charm and reputation as a rising literary star, was a much sought-after guest. They commented on his lanky good looks, comparing him flatteringly to Henry Fonda and Gary Cooper. Dahl basked in their fawning attentions. He played the innocent abroad, allowing himself to be courted by rich older women, and did his best to keep them entertained with tales of his escapades in Hollywood. A gifted conversationalist, he related to everyone he talked to in a direct, personal way, remembering names and special interests. As Susan Mary (Mrs. William) Patten drily observed in a letter to her friend* Joseph Alsop, the *New York Herald Tribune* columnist who had enlisted in the navy and was stationed in China, "Dahl, an R.A.F. man whom you may have met here—is a dark broody creature who invented the gremlims [sic] and has done some other writing and is much loved by the ladies. . . ."

In his brief time at the British Embassy, Dahl had managed to become a favorite with the hard-partying Washington press corps, a development that seemed to please both sets of bosses—official and unofficial. From the embassy's point of view, the newspaper publishers, along with the editors and journalists in their employ, had unparalleled power to mobilize public opinion, and it was useful to gauge their sympathies and, whenever possible, influence them toward support of Britain and the war.

Dahl's BSC contact shared this view but indicated that any insight

---

*After the death of her husband in 1960, she married Joe Alsop, fully aware that he was gay, and became a formidable Washington hostess in her own right.

that could be gleaned from prominent members of the press about internal American politics—especially the privately expressed views of the president, say, or any of his cabinet members or close advisers—would be of great value in certain high offices in London.

Newspapermen generally know much more than they print, and the BSC regarded them as a prolific source of intelligence: "The truth is that the majority of American politicians, not excluding Cabinet ministers, are willing to supply influential members of the press with 'inside' information in return for favorable publicity," the official history states. "Such information is, of course, usually handed out under pledge of secrecy—to be used as 'background material' and not for publication. But it is given out nonetheless," and, as the BSC had discovered, it contained "much material of political interest" as well as "secrets of vital importance."

All Dahl had to do was keep up a cheerful front and eavesdrop his way though the yawning Sunday breakfasts, hunt breakfasts, luncheons, teas, tea dances, innumerable drinks parties, banquets, and not infrequent balls. Incredibly, Washingtonians could squeeze three or more of these events into a single day. He was to listen to what was being said, chat up the politicians and policy makers he met along the way, and obtain as much firsthand information as possible on their attitude toward Britain and U.S. participation in the war. He was to be as engaging as possible, a bright and breezy presence at table, and encourage confidences from those in the know. An attentive dinner partner could always pluck, from among all the war talk and congressional scuttlebutt, the occasional pearl.

As far as doing any actual work along the lines of counterespionage, all that it actually entailed was keeping a watchful eye on Britain's enemies in the capital, principally the leading isolationists, who agitated against the crumbling empire, funded influential pro-German organizations such as the America First Committee and the German American Bund, and in some cases continued to do business with Germany on the basis that the Third Reich would soon dominate all of Europe. Dahl was to keep track of various conservative politicians and journalists who sympathized with these front groups and the lunatic isolationist fringe, monitor where they went and who their friends were, and ponder ways they might be publicly embarrassed and discredited. There were a variety of ways of attacking isolationists and Nazi sympathizers. If, for example, their unsavory past were to come to light or salacious rumors of an affair wound up in the gossip columns, that might serve to undermine an individual's prestige and influence. He was also expected to help spread disinformation, a nifty wartime euphemism for deliberately supplying false statements in aid of a higher truth. These might be pure invention or based an half-truths culled from intercepted letters and secretly opened diplomatic mail. The British had found that their efforts at disinformation were often most effective when promulgated on the cocktail circuit. A lie repeated often enough by important public people soon took on the ring of truth.

Of course, Dahl's efforts were merely a drop in the bucket. For large-scale whispering campaigns, the BSC maintained an organization known as the Rumor Factory, which dated back to 1941 and was directed from the New York headquarters. Its purpose was to make sure misleading stories were spread through many different channels—from established newspaper and radio figures to special commercial and diplomatic contacts—and on many different social, professional, and economic levels. The BSC took this form of political warfare very seriously, and the official history lists the key rules its representatives were expected to observe:

1. A good rumour should never be traceable to its source.
2. A rumour should be of the kind which is likely to gain in the telling.

3. Particular rumours should be designed to appeal to particular groups (i.e., Catholics, or ethnic groups such as Czechs, Poles, etc.)

4. A particular rumour should have a specific purpose.

5. Rumours are most effective if they can be originated in several different places simultaneously and in such a way that they shuttle back and forth, which each new report apparently confirming previous ones.

At times it was difficult to distinguish between work and play. Dahl took distinct pleasure in wooing some of Washington's most influential women, including Mrs. Eleanor Patterson, the wealthy, divorced publisher of the *Washington Times-Herald,* a conservative paper that had the largest circulation in the city. A member of the Chicago Medill Patterson family, she had a stake in the New York *Daily News,* owned and published by her brother, Joseph Patterson, and the *Chicago Tribune,* owned by her cousin Robert McCormick. In the year leading up to America's entry into the war, the press had been sharply divided over whether the country should intervene; the East Coast establishment remained faithful to Britain—including *New York Times* publisher A. H. Sulzberger, *New York Post* publisher George Backer, and Ogden Reid's *Herald Tribune*—while Patterson and the owners of the Roosevelt-hating Hearst papers vigorously opposed any involvement in the war. They hammered home the isolationist view—"Let 'em get on with it. It's none of our business"—in the pages of their newspapers and seemed determined to regard America's eventual entry into the war as proof that their great country was once again being forced to pull England's chestnuts out of the fire.

Cissie, as Mrs. Patterson was known to everyone, occupied a marble palace on Dupont Circle, never missed an important party, and freely indulged in Washington's favorite indoor sport—gossip. She was so devoted to the doings of the cave dwellers (the term for wealthy high-ranking natives) that she significantly expanded the society section in the *Times-Herald* and hired blue bloods at high salaries to cover capital dinner parties. The society pages quickly became a must-read with everyone from ambassadors to parlor maids, giving her paper the largest circulation and inspiring rival publishers to begin allocating more column inches to dinners and teas. As the British Embassy's formal affairs invariably outdid all the others in pomp and circumstance—from the gold-crested invitations to the scarlet-liveried footmen in breeches and white gloves—they were a staple of her gossip pages. Despite being a grandmother, Cissie was tall and very slender and enjoyed flaunting her girlish figure. Dahl, who loathed her on sight, rather enjoyed collecting dirt on her. "She absolutely hated Roosevelt," recalled Antoinette, "and it was his job to spy on people like her."

Then there was Evalyn Walsh McLean, the flamboyant hostess whose popular Sunday-night dinners, complete with dance orchestras, previews of first-run movies, and a hundred or more well-heeled guests, were legendary in wartime Washington. She always appeared dressed to the teeth, topped off by her trademark oversize round glasses, which gave her an owlish appearance. She never received her guests without the enormous 92 1/2-carat Hope diamond dangling from a gleaming chain around her neck, jokingly warning onlookers, "Don't touch it, bad luck you know," referring to the jewel's well-documented history of bringing misfortune to those who came into its possession. Like her close friend Cissie Patterson, she was conservative, rabidly anti-Roosevelt, and had loudly protested America's entry into the war. She thought Roosevelt was an irresponsible reformer with a mania for power and that he had a poorly dressed wife who had no idea how to behave in politics or private life.

McLean's parties were famous for attracting an interesting cross-section of the power elite, in part because her guest lists were regularly reprinted in the "Town Talk" section of the *Washington Post*, and in part because Friendship—her palatial Massachusetts Avenue manor house complete with ballroom, theater, ornate gardens, golf course, greenhouses, and stables—had earned a reputation for being a gathering place of fifth columnists, appeasers, apologists for Hitler, right-wing Republicans, and Roosevelt-haters. President Roosevelt once went so far as to compare her crowd to Britain's "Cliveden set," a privileged circle of anti-Semites and Hitler admirers who had frequented Nancy Astor's Buckinghamshire house, Cliveden. McLean viewed the presidential snub as a badge of honor, particularly as FDR also slammed her pal Cissie Patterson as a social "parasite" who was more interested in tea-partying than helping the war effort. The controversy only served to make her gatherings more newsworthy. The *Washington Post* took to sending a reporter by most Sunday nights to take down all the license plates and published them in the morning paper.

Evalyn Walsh McLean's father had discovered gold in Colorado and had left her a huge fortune. With more money than sense, she married a bounder by the name of Edward (Ned) Beale McLean, and after two decades of headlines covering his incredible indulgences and debauchery, she filed for divorce. Before the papers were finalized, Ned McLean descended into an alcoholic stupor, and she had him committed to a mental institution in Towson, Maryland, where he insisted to the end that he was a German spy and a double agent. Widowed in 1941 at the age of fifty, Evalyn dedicated herself to regaining her lost stature and reputation. Perhaps realizing that her aristocratic way of life was in poor taste now that American boys were dying by the thousands, she negotiated a deal with the government to donate the historic Friendship mansion and fifty-seven acres of the seventy-five-acre holding to provide housing for defense workers. She even had the estate's massive wrought-iron gates melted down to make armaments. Before she surrendered the family seat, she threw a sumptuous wedding for her fourth child and only daughter, Evie, who married

Robert Rice Reynolds, a much older second-term Democratic senator from North Carolina and a well-known Anglophobe and isolationist. Washington's most indomitable hostess then relocated to the red-brick ghetto of Georgetown, where she kept up her lavish level of entertaining at Friendship II, a hastily acquired twenty-room town house at Wisconsin and R Street, even though it meant enclosing the balcony and putting tables on the patio to accommodate her large parties.

Drawn by the glamour and good food, New Dealers and foreign diplomats overlooked her politics and flocked to the parties, where she was known to seat interventionists and isolationists side by side. McLean avidly sought out a brilliant, eclectic group for her sparkling soirées, collecting admirals, senators, judges, journalists, famous writers, and Hollywood stars to adorn her tables. She regarded Dahl, an unencumbered male, as a prized new addition, and made the dashing RAF pilot a regular at her "Sunday nights." It didn't hurt that he often escorted British dignitaries when they came through Washington and would offer to bring along the likes of Noël Coward as an extra man. Little did she realize that both Dahl and Coward had been contracted to do second-story work for the BSC and were scribbling notes on the backs of matchbooks and dinner napkins. Dahl would report back to the BSC on all those in attendance, which at one fete included such VIPs as Lord Halifax, Assistant Secretary of State Adolf Berle and his wife, Colonel Byron Foy and his wife, the former U.S. ambassador to Japan Joseph Clark, the magazine publisher William Ziff, Herbert Hoover and his pal Gene Tunney, now a commander in the navy, three Supreme Court justices, seven senators, a couple of representatives, and assorted members of the diplomatic corps. Naturally Frank Waldrop, the hard-line isolationist who was managing editor of the *Times-Herald* and author of its anti-Roosevelt editorials, and his boss, Cissie Patterson, were present.

Also to be found at most of her parties was her conservative son-in-law, Senator Reynolds, who had modified his views since Pearl Harbor—after initially blaming the December 7 attack on the British—and distanced himself from the ultranationalist, fascist, and anti-Semitic organizations he had aligned himself with in the early days of the war. Back in 1939 Reynolds had founded the Vindicators Association, which disseminated its poisonous ideas in a publication, the *American Vindicator*, that was often sold at German American Bund rallies. He furthered his reputation for being pro-Nazi and anti-British by associating with such demagogues as Gerald K. Smith, an infamous American fascist, and Father Charles Coughlin, an anti-Semitic radio priest, accusing the president of leading the country into war, and voting against the Lend-Lease Act as well as most of FDR's aid-to-Britain policies. After war was declared, he disbanded the Vindicators Association and became fiercely promilitary, advocating national unity, the purchase of war bonds, the internment of Japanese-Americans, and renewal of Lend-Lease. Despite his bitter opposition to FDR's foreign policy, he became the powerful chairman of the Military Affairs Committee, and the British, who trusted him about as far as they could throw him, monitored his every move.

At one of McLean's seated dinners, Dahl caused quite a scene when he found himself across from Waldrup, who along with labor leader John L. Lewis were the evening's honored guests. Seated nearby was Lieutenant Winston Frost, a naval hero just back from the Pacific, lending their end of the table a distinguished military air. Quite forgetting himself, Dahl confronted Waldrop. "Just why are you trying to create friction between the British and American governments? First will you answer yes or no, are you?" he demanded. "Yes, I am," Waldrup answered immediately. "So is Goebbels, carry on," retorted Dahl. "I am against the British now, yesterday, and tomorrow," Waldrup continued more heatedly, "I am for America first, last, and all the time. I am afraid of the British. They are clever and I don't want any more of this

'Winnie' and 'Franklin.'" Dahl snapped: "So says Hitler. Carry on." The silence around the table was deafening.

Dahl invited Lewis to join the fray, but he preferred to remain silent, staring uncomfortably into his demitasse cup. Apparently unable to stand it a minute longer, Frost unleashed a ten-minute tirade against Waldrup: "Do you realize that if you were in the South Pacific today there are boys in the U.S. Eighth Air Force who would tear you limb from limb for the things you write?" Waldrup muttered, "Well, I guess I won't go to England." After dinner was cleared, Frost continued his frontal assault, pinning John Lewis into a corner until he was finally rescued and mollified by the hostess's daughter-in-law.*

Far from ruining the evening, Dahl discovered that his unschooled-puppy routine, running ragged over the rules of decorum and pissing all over an important guest, pleased his hostess no end. Evalyn Walsh McLean considered these little contretemps the key to a successful gathering, especially as it guaranteed that her party would be discussed in discerning circles for days afterward. When it came time for her guests to leave, she bid Dahl good night, adding gaily, "Be sure and come back at your regular time next Sunday. We won't count this one." Then, holding out the necklace with its large blue gem in her habitual, dramatic parting gesture, she declared, "Look, here is the Hope diamond! Look at it. And you *will* come again, won't you, and I *will* see you again next Sunday, won't I?" As he bowed his way out the door, Dahl offered, "Do you want me to wear it for good luck until next Sunday?"

Marsh had no appetite for McLean's nonstop revelries and considered her a drunk and a fool. He questioned why anyone in their right mind bothered with the woman. While Dahl conceded that

---

*Dahl related this amusing dinner anecdote, and the subsequent dish on Evalyn Walsh McLean, to Marsh, who had the verbal report typed up in memo form and passed it on to the vice president for his perusal, under the sardonic heading: "SOCIAL NOTE—ATTENTION MRS. WALLACE."

McLean was an exhibitionist and often "tipsy," he respected the way she had thrown herself into relief work, volunteering at veterans' hospitals and opening her home to wounded soldiers. Dahl maintained that McLean, far from being a bubble-headed pleasure-seeker, had "a brain" and knew what she was about. "Her basic thought is anti-Communism," he advised Marsh, noting that she was part of a growing clique who believed that Russia was the real enemy and who warned one and all that "Stalin is ten times as dangerous as Hitler."

On more than one occasion, she had told Wallace just exactly what she thought of him for "being so friendly to the Russians." One night when he came to dinner, she asked him: "Now, Mr. Vice President, suppose you were in a barroom brawl and got rescued by a barroom bum. He might have saved your life. But would you take him home and let him share your home with your daughter and wife?" Dahl told Marsh he thought her fixation with the Hope diamond was that it symbolized private property, which she believed Roosevelt, the war, and the Russians all endangered. While he disliked the fact that she catered to "two of the biggest anti-British baiters in town" (Waldrup and Patterson), this objection was outweighed by larger concerns. "She runs a good saloon," he told Marsh matter-of-factly, "and there are lots of folks to see and that's my business."

Less than two weeks later Dahl was invited to another lavish dinner at Friendship, this one a seated affair for sixty guests. He soon found himself up to his neck in anti-Russian talk. At the end of the night, when the British air attaché finally made to leave, Mrs. McLean drew him to one side and asked to see him again, so eager was she to sponsor and instruct the tall, talented, delightful flier. "Come back Friday night for an intimate little talk," she whispered in his ear. "I want to get you straight. You are a presentable young man. I know some people who may control your future."

Dahl, whose confident sexuality only added to the powerful effect of his intellect, "cut quite a local swath," as a young Katharine Graham pointed out in the course of promoting one of his new stories in her *Post* column, "The Magazine Rack." Graham, whose husband, Philip Graham, had just recently taken over the *Post* from her father, Eugene Meyer, was very much part of the social swim, and Dahl saw her often at the parties of bright young New Dealers in Washington. "Girls just fell at Roald's feet," confirmed Antoinette Marsh. "I think he slept with everybody on the East and West Coasts that had more than fifty thousand dollars a year." At the time, it seemed that almost no one was immune to his charms, an impression that was reinforced when Dahl turned up at the R Street house one night with "Eisenhower's girlfriend" on his arm. "There was a parade of women," said Antoinette, adding, "I think he liked to show them off to my father."

As his popularity grew, Dahl became more arrogant. He had discovered that nothing was so persuasive to a woman as a man in uniform, especially against the backdrop of ever-present danger and imminent separation. Dahl had no qualms about laying claim to the perks of war and took to bragging about his many conquests to Creekmore Fath, who was convinced his friend was "one of the biggest cocksmen in Washington." Fath remembered Dahl proudly showing off various trinkets bestowed upon him by his many admirers as tokens of their affection. The most famous of these was Millicent Rogers, the Standard Oil heiress, a former model and fashion plate, who presented Dahl with a Tiffany gold key to her front door, along with a gold cigarette case and lighter. Extravagant, and extravagantly beautiful, she was notoriously frisky, and her love life had been making headlines for years. At nineteen, she had defied her parents and eloped with a dissipated Austrian count, surfacing some weeks later in Paris pregnant with his child. Count Ludwig Salm von Hoogstraten, an internationally known tennis player who was descended from an aristocratic European family that had lost all its money in the last war, held out for a huge settlement. Rogers' father paid off the penniless fortune-hunter and forced her to return home, so her baby would be born in New York. Immediately after the divorce, she became engaged to the Argentine playboy and sportsman Arturo Peralta-Ramos and produced another two sons. She followed up with another divorce and another marriage, this time to a square-jawed Wall Street banker named Ronald Bush Balcom.

Forty-one and freshly divorced when she met Dahl, she was independent and adventurous and inclined to similar men. Dahl found her intoxicating: wide-set blue eyes, high cheekbones, and alabaster skin framed by soft shining hair in a pageboy cut. She was intelligent, with a quick wit and well-developed gift for mimicry that made her quite devastating at parties, and the best company. More than anything it was her forceful personality and originality that distinguished her from other society women. She dressed with enormous flair, in creations of the greatest couturiers of the day, from Mainbocher and Schiaparelli to Charles James, remaking their clothes to complement her long frame and paring them with dramatic twenty-four-carat gold jewelry of her own design, so that no one who saw her would ever forget it. She favored attention-getting costumes, appearing one day as a Tyrolean peasant, in a dirndl and matching hat, and the next as Marie Antoinette, swathed in yards of silk taffeta.

Raised on sprawling estates in Southampton and Palm Beach, as well as a succession of rented European castles, Rogers lived in an eighteenth-century manor in Tidewater, Virginia, that more closely resembled a museum than a home. Dahl, who thanks to Marsh was fast developing a taste for the finer things in life, was bowled over by her collection of art, which included treasures from all over the world, including Empire and Biedermeier furniture rescued from her Arlberg chalet and a trove of modern French paintings. Inspired by her eclectic finds, from the group of antique clocks to a cluster of superb drawings by Watteau, Fragonard, and Boucher, Dahl vowed that as soon as he had enough put away, he would begin buying paintings for a modest collection of his own. Rogers' house was a jewel box, crammed full of furniture and objects she had picked up along the way from her marriages and many travels, but every piece told a story, and taken together they added up to something more and seemed to him evidence of a life well lived.

Rogers rarely stayed in one place for long and flitted between several grand residences, including a sumptuous town house on Manhattan's East 66th Street. She spent much of her time in New York, where she chaired the Medical and Surgical Relief Committee, a relief organization she founded in 1940 to send medical supplies to England and the war zones of Allied nations. Beginning with six New York doctors, she raised over a million dollars and expanded her organization until it was nationwide, with more than four hundred volunteer doctors and two hundred nurses from hospitals and pharmaceutical companies all over the country, working to send drugs, vitamins, first aid kits, and surgical instruments to those in need all over the world. She also invited shell-shocked navy pilots to stay at her home in Virginia, inviting four at a time, believing that the beautiful surroundings would help with their rehabilitation. Although earnest about her work, she had a delicate constitution and a short attention span. She had no interest in marrying again but, spoiled and willful, demanded her lovers to be at her beck and call. It did not take long for Dahl to discover that she could be temperamental and controlling. She played musical chairs with men and seemed to have secret lovers tucked away in every European capital. An incorrigible flirt himself, Dahl was not particularly disturbed. He enjoyed being a part of her swell crowd and made the most of it.

When he had exhausted the city's supply of heiresses, Dahl chased actresses. For a time, he dated the young English actress Leonora Corbett, who had made a name for herself on the London stage in such plays as *Lady in Waiting* with Robert Donat and *Other People's Lives* with Maurice Evans. During the air raids in London in 1940, she had bravely stayed in the city to perform *Under Your Hat* and entertained the troops at British military camps. She was playing her first role in America, starring in a Broadway production of *Blithe Spirit*, and Dahl went to New York as often as he could to see her. Corbett was sensible enough to break it off with Dahl and soon thereafter became engaged to a vice president of NBC.

Dahl's superiors watched his rake's progress with grudging admiration. A certain amount of hanky-panky was condoned, especially when it was for a good cause. Down through the ages, royal courts had relied on pillow talk to discover which way the king was leaning, and the British Embassy was not above resorting to that time-honored tradition. At the next embassy dinner, Dahl was intentionally seated next to the glamorous blond Clare Boothe Luce, the new Republican congresswoman from Connecticut, who was married to Henry Luce, the powerful *Time* and *Life* publisher, though he was rarely seen at her side after she took office. They had been married almost ten years by then, at about the time indifference often sets in, and it was said that her Victorian-era husband preferred the quiet comforts of his country estate, while she liked to entertain company in her Washington hotel suite. As expected, she immediately latched onto Dahl and monopolized his attention throughout the evening and, from all reports, well beyond that. "She went for Roald because he was handsome, available, and a good dinner companion," said Fath, who shrugged off the wartime fling as "just one of those things."

There was nothing casual about the British authorities' interest in Mrs. Luce, however. By 1943 both Luces were in disrepute for their antiempire attitudes and frequent attacks on Churchill and were on a list of "enemies" who were considered a threat to the British Empire. Their recent articles about British India, portraying the colonial record as one of brutal oppression, had only fueled the hostilities. As Rex Benson, Halifax's confidential adviser, noted in his diary: "She is a clever hard-boiled ambitious young lady backed by a wrong-thinking husband for whom success as a big newspaper man & money has & probably is still the main object of living. The less these two practise the art of statesmanship the better." According to Marsh, at a dinner given by Mrs. Ogden Reid some two years earlier, Mrs. Luce had voiced her violent opposition to Roosevelt, saying that she distrusted him so utterly that she could never be for anything he was for, no matter what it was, including Lend-Lease. Her position was so extreme that even Wendell Willkie had reproached her. Shocked that anyone so fragile and lovely looking could be so venomous, he had murmured, "Clare, you just can't be that way."

With an actress's talent for publicity and playwright's flair for polished invective, Mrs. Luce had been making a real nuisance of herself. She had toured Europe alone for five weeks in 1940 and written up her personal observations as a book entitled *Europe in Spring*—Dorothy Parker famously called her review "All Clare on the Western Front"—which immediately became a best seller and validated her as an expert on the war. Both she and her husband had campaigned vigorously for Willkie, the Indiana dark horse Republican candidate for president that year, and propelled by her acid tongue, Mrs. Luce had become a political force. Not only did she get herself elected to Congress in 1942, she had managed to snag a seat on the House Military Affairs Committee.

In her maiden speech on February 9, 1943, she attacked Vice President Wallace, who was advocating postwar freedom of the skies and coined an infamous put-down to dismiss his ideas: "But much of what Mr. Wallace calls his global thinking is, no matter how you slice it, globaloney. Mr. Wallace's warp of sense and his woof of *non*sense is a very tricky cloth out of which to cut the pattern of a postwar world."

She proceeded to ridicule an article Wallace had written in that month's edition of *American Magazine*, entitled "What We Will Get Out of the War," in which he called for the establishment of a United Nations authority to control "a network of globe-girdling airways," and the internationalization of all airports. In the same way that the advent of railways had opened up the western frontier in America, Wallace believed the new age of air travel promised to unlock the vast resources of the undeveloped regions of the world, including Asia, Africa, and South America. Transatlantic air travel would open new outlets for trade and new opportunities for industry, and it would create an enormous market for aircraft manufacturing and air transport on a worldwide scale. For the sake of the advancement of aviation, and all that it could do for the world's economies, he opposed carving up the skies into "spheres of influence," as many private interests desired. "Freedom of the air," he wrote, "means to the world of the future what freedom of the sea meant to the world of the past."

In her thirty-minute address "America's Destiny in the Air," Mrs. Luce argued that Wallace's acceptance of the doctrine of "freedom of the air" was as woolly headed as most of his philosophy and would mean surrendering strategic control of the skies to Britain in some misguided plea for "internationalization." Practically speaking, it amounted to cutting the throat of America's own air industry. Not only would it give the semi-government-owned British Imperial Airways free access to U.S. airports but also would Britain them to expand its air routes using the very Lend-Lease planes America had sent its ally in its hour of need. It was already clear to far-thinking people that as soon as the armistice came, there would be a race between the Americans and the British for control of the strategic air routes and bases of the world. Inevitably the victors of this war would divide the spoils, in this case the "new frontiers" opened up by the airplane. "The future of every nation in the air today is being given shape inexorably by military and civilian policies now being practiced in the very middle of a great war," she declared theatrically. The best way to keep out of another war was to maintain the policy of "air sovereignty"—the system in place before the war, by which each nation denied the airplanes of other nations the right to fly over its airspace save by special permission or treaty—and to keep "America on wings all over the world."

All the American press caught was the term "globaloney" being hurled at the vice president like a cream pie in the face. The speech created quite a stir. The House chamber was usually fairly empty in the late afternoon hour when she delivered her address, but curiosity about the ravishing blond legislator had brought the members out in force. When she drew blood with her opening remarks, the gentle-woman from Connecticut made herself infamous on the Hill. The Washington press had a field day, as did the cartoonists. Walter Lippmann advised Isaiah Berlin not to attach too much importance to Mrs. Luce's speech, and said that the current joke in congressional circles was that there had been much "clarification of loose thinking." At the same time Wallace's lofty ideals and admirable intentions garnered worldwide attention, and he ultimately included the address in a collection, entitled *Democracy Reborn*.

This was not the first time Wallace and the Luces had crossed swords. Clare's jealous nationalist position was perfectly in keeping with her husband's dogma of postwar American hegemony first outlined in "The American Century," a *Life* editorial published in 1941, in which he explained that intervention would allow America to wrest strategic control of the war from Britain and enable the nation "to exert upon the world the full impact of our influence, for such purposes as we see fit, and by such means as we see fit." Luce was aiming at another American Manifest Destiny, in the form of postwar domination of the world by U.S. industry. Wallace had found the *Life* editorial's tone objectionable and had delivered a strongly worded rebuttal: "Some have spoken of the 'American Century,'" he wrote. "I say that the century on which we are entering—the century which will come out of this war—can and must be the century of the common man."

The British had also been deeply shocked by Henry Luce's strident call upon the American people "to assume leadership of the world," particularly as it implied the denouement of the British Empire. Now his wife's shrill cry for "air imperialism" was cause for fresh alarm. They registered Mrs. Luce's threatening tone, as they had for some time been pressing the United States for internationalization of air bases, some of which had become vital crossroads of the sky and were key to the future of their foreign trade. She was effectively resisting any of the proposed measures that might limit the possible future expansion of American airways.

Long before Congresswoman Luce panned the British air routes, the Air Ministry and Foreign Office had warned of a bleak future for British carriers. "All bets are off at the end of the war," Harold Balfour, the British undersecretary for air, had told the House of Commons in December 1942. According to the existing agreements under which the Lend-Lease bases had been built on British territories—extending all the way from Newfoundland to Bermuda, across central Africa, as well as in the Pacific—six months after the war was over, they would be closed to British use. Pan Am was already flying to more than sixty countries, and the Americans would inevitably demand continued use of the bases they had constructed at great expense, estimated at roughly one billion dollars. The Americans had more money, and more modern aircraft. Making matters worse, in recent years the British had all but abandoned manufacturing transport planes in order to focus on the production of military machines, and at the end of the war they would not have a single modern passenger plane in production.

In her inimitable way, Clare Boothe Luce had touched a nerve. The British government urgently needed to negotiate an equitable settlement with the United States or else lose the lucrative new market in transatlantic trade and travel. If they did not act soon, the air controversy could become potentially explosive, even in a time of war. "Otherwise there will be friction," predicted the Honorable W.R.D. Perkins, Conservative member of Parliament, during a speech in late 1942, "and we might even have *another Boston tea party*."

Adding insult to injury, two days after the congresswoman's fiery address, Drew Pearson reported in his "Merry-Go-Round" column that the State Department had cleared her speech and, while not objecting to any of her criticisms of the British, had blue-penciled some of her caustic remarks about Russia. Isaiah Berlin duly relayed Mrs. Luce's remarks and the Pearson column to London in the "Weekly Political Summary," his brilliant press and opinion surveys for the Foreign Office, which were a favorite of Churchill's, even though they were always signed and sent out under Halifax's name. Mrs. Luce had succeeded "in stirring up strife among the allies," Berlin reported, adding as an aside that "globaloney" was "a catchword already being ridden to death by the isolationist press." The air negotiations promised to be an ongoing source of turbulence and were something the War Cabinet would need to consider. In the meantime, young Dahl was instructed to romance Clare, who was thirteen years his senior, to see if, with the right kind of encouragement, she could warm to the British position.

Dahl complained to Fath that he had received some pretty steep orders in his time, but this topped them all. According to Fath, Dahl groaned: "I am all fucked out. That goddam woman has absolutely screwed me from one end of the room to another for three goddam nights." Dahl claimed he had gone back to the ambassador that morning and attempted to plead his case: "'You know it's a great assignment, but I just can't go on . . .' And the Ambassador said, 'Roald, did you see the Charles Laughton movie of Henry VIII?'" When Dahl said yes, Halifax continued: "' Well, do you remember the scene with Henry going into the bedroom with Anne of Cleves, and he turns and says, "the things I've done for England"? Well, that's what you've got to do.'"

"She was something else," recalled Antoinette Marsh. "Roald would talk about her, but I think he was always careful not to say too much, at least not in front of me. But I knew he had slept with her, which interested me because she was much older than him."

All this time, Dahl had been biding his time at the embassy, doing as he was told like a good boy, when "a lucky stroke" came his way. It was an ordinary night in June, and he was dining at Marsh's R Street mansion, as was his custom. When he arrived, Marsh tossed a sheaf of papers into his lap and said, "You're a flying chap, what do you think of that?" Marsh asked him to take the papers to his study and peruse them carefully, and Dahl obliged. As soon as he cast his eyes down the first page, however, he realized it was "an immensely secret cabinet document." From what he could tell, it was an outline of postwar plans for civil aviation, and while the Allies were busy fighting, it appeared that America was plotting to steal the march on everyone. "I thought, my goodness, I've got to do something about this," Dahl recalled. "This would make them rock back at home."

Marsh had given him a draft of a pamphlet written by his close friend Henry Wallace. Entitled "Our Job in the Pacific," it summarized the vice president's postwar goals, among them international control of the airways, economic assistance for the industrial development of Asia, and the demilitarization of Japan. Wallace was also in favor of "the emancipation of colonial subjects" in the British Empire, including India, Burma, and Malaya. Dahl could feel his "hair stand on end." Dahl immediately realized the document's importance, and knowing that his superiors would want to see it, he excused himself saying that he was going to finish reading it downstairs. He quickly phoned his

BSC contact, explained the urgency of the situation, and convinced him to meet him on the corner as soon as possible. The agent knew something was up and materialized on the street in front of Marsh's house in a matter of minutes.

Dahl sneaked out of the house and handed the document through his car window, warning his partner in crime to be back in half an hour or there would be hell to pay. "He flashed off," recalled Dahl, "and I'm around downstairs, near the lavatory door, and if the chap upstairs had come down looking for me saying, 'have you finished reading it?' then I'd of been in the lavatory you see, saying 'I'm sorry I'm caught short.'" As it turned out, the agent went straight to the BSC's Washington offices to make copies and made it back within the allotted time. Dahl nipped back out, collected the paper, and no one was the wiser.

Dahl returned the as-yet-unpublished paper to Marsh "without comment," but he knew even then that copies were on their way to Bill Stephenson, then to "C," and finally to Churchill. He was later told that the document created "a bit of a stir" in New York and again when it reached London. Churchill reportedly "could hardly believe what he was reading." Wallace's proposal contained much of the same material Clare Boothe Luce had referred to in her controversial speech a few months earlier, and it spelled out the American government's postwar plans for civil aviation and how "people like Adolf Berle were conspiring with Pan Am to take over the commercial aviation of the entire world after the war was over," a suggestion that, coupled with the liquidation of the British Empire, inspired Churchill "to cataclysms of wrath."

The incident only intensified British suspicion of Wallace, already high due to his performance during Churchill's visit to America that May, his third since the start of the war. After a pleasant weekend at "Shangri-la," FDR's term for his presidential retreat in Maryland, Churchill's mood quickly deteriorated as the British and American talks deadlocked on the issue of invading Italy. Churchill had crossed the Atlantic firm in his resolve to obtain Roosevelt's commitment to take action against Italy and contain German forces. After several tense days of debate, a compromise was reached, but Churchill left in a dark mood. He had not been cheered by the vice president's open criticism of his notion of "Anglo-Saxon superiority," which Wallace had argued might be offensive to many nations of the world, not to mention many Americans.

As Wallace himself wrote in his diary on May 25, "Charley Marsh told me that it had just come to him [presumably via Dahl] during the last few days that the British had their fingers crossed so far as I was concerned.

> *Apparently my frank talking with Churchill at the Saturday and Monday luncheons has caused the British to reach the conclusion that I am not playing their game of arranging matters so that the Anglo-Saxons will rule the world. Frankly I am glad to know where they stand and that they know where I stand. I am sure that the 200 million Anglo-Saxons in the United States, England, Canada, Australia, New Zealand and South Africa are not enough to run the world and that if we try it in the spirit which seems to be animating Churchill, there will be serious trouble ahead. I am quite sure, in spite of all his protestations to the contrary, that Churchill is capable of working with Russia to double-cross the United States, and with the United States to double-cross Russia.*

It was "the Wallace affair" that finally brought Dahl to Stephenson's direct attention. While it had resulted in a major embarrassment for the vice president, Dahl's unseen bosses at the BSC regarded it as a feather in his cap. Stephenson had reportedly inquired as to how the purloined pamphlet had fallen into their hands, and when told by his henchmen that they had had it from "some chap in Washington," he had asked, "Who?" Impressed by Dahl's quick thinking, Stephenson began to formulate his own plans for the young pilot's future.

For Dahl, the whole business had been unbelievably thrilling and not a little traumatic. He knew fallout from the controversial pamphlet would continue to make itself felt in British officialdom and had already strained relations in Washington. Having completely exaggerated the affair's importance in his own mind, Dahl was convinced it could have serious long-term repercussions. He worried about how the British objections to the vice president would make themselves felt and what sort of pressure might be brought to bear by the BSC. He had begun to understand that Stephenson "could be very devious" and often acted indirectly through others—whether it was through Beaverbrook or someone else—to achieve a desired result.

Despite his misgivings, Dahl found himself in the awkward position of not being able to fully confide in Marsh. By now, he was used to heading straight to the R Street house to boast about his eavesdropping escapades and close shaves, but in this case he dared not disclose his underhanded activities. He may even have suffered a twinge of guilt about his shabby treatment of his mentor's close friend. He genuinely liked and respected Wallace and would later observe that he was "a lovely man, but too innocent and idealistic for the world." Marsh, oblivious to any double-dealing, treated Dahl's apparent state of anxiety with humorous indulgence. Aware that his high-spirited young friend had fallen afoul of embassy officials and was endeavoring to make a fresh start with British intelligence, Marsh sent Dahl a long, fatherly letter in late June lecturing him on the difficult choices that lay ahead:

> *You have shown on several occasions that you truly wish the best for all in the medium of Air which you serve.*
>
> *You have weight on your spirit. Your duty to your country as an ad-*

vocate is one weight. The demands of superiors and colleagues which do not coincide with your judgment or your spirit is another. . . .

To this date you have approached life with great sensitiveness. Not to hurt people is the first impulse of a generous and sensitive soul. But in the conscious being of not hurting—of not being cruel—comes the complexity of life. It is here that the spirit is bound by weights and conflicts.

Adopting the fervent tone he reserved for his philosophical discourses on the flourishing soul, Marsh advised Dahl to chart an independent course and cease "measuring and weighing his actions according to the demands of others," a reference not only to his immediate superiors but also the conspiracy of women back in England—his mother and four sisters—who despite being separated by an ocean still had him on a very short leash. Marsh believed that only by heeding his own instincts could Dahl free himself to find his true calling:

You have had the wisdom already to refuse to tie yourself to a personal ambition such as becoming a member of Parliament. Another side of you tells you that you are twenty-seven [he was still twenty-six]; that the future is uncertain; that you have certain responsibilities of family and country. And I say the first thing is to get the weight off the soul. Look clearly . . . into the future. When you may do this serenely the first question that will come to you is "What do I most want to do in life." You will be surprised that the answer will write itself. . . . The truth of what to do then comes. It is somewhere in this process that I may be of service to you.

Pledging his understanding and support, Marsh added portentously, "Any time—any place—where you wish me alone in friendship to hear, you will as a right of yours and as a pleasure of mine, make use of me." In the months to come, Dahl would do just that.

5

BUFFERS

I would do my best to appear calm and chatty, though
actually I was trembling at the realization that the
most powerful man in the world was telling me these
mighty secrets.

—ROALD DAHL, "Lucky Break"

ANOTHER "RATHER LUCKY THING" happened to Dahl that spring. As
his *Gremlins* fame increased, his name caught the eye of Eleanor
Roosevelt, who had just finished reading the little illustrated Disney
book to her grandchildren. She had been enchanted by the tale and
on learning that Dahl was in Washington saw to it that he was invited
to dinner with her and the president at the White House. Dahl found
the First Lady to be surprisingly charming and kind and completely
devoid of the condescension one might expect from someone of her
station. With his elegant manners and winning sense of humor, he
quickly set about ingratiating himself with the president's wife, sending her a signed copy of his book and on another occasion a toy widget,
one of the gremlin figurines created by the Disney marketing division,

which had recently enjoyed great success with its new line of Mickey Mouse dolls. As it happened, his roommate, Richard Miles, was also on friendly terms with Mrs. Roosevelt, and Dahl accompanied him to White House functions hoping to see her again. At the end of May, Eleanor Roosevelt wrote Dahl gratefully acknowledging the book he had sent, which she considered "delightful," and expressing her hope that he and his friend Lieutenant Miles would "come in soon" for another visit. As Dahl later boasted, Mrs. Roosevelt "took a liking to the young RAF fighter pilot who had been shot down and rather badly burned." He was soon rewarded with a second invitation to the White House. "So I went to dinner there," he recalled, "and I went to dinner again, and again, and FDR was always there and a bunch of other people."

In the weeks that followed, Dahl kept up a warm correspondence with Eleanor Roosevelt. He further endeared himself to the First Lady when he managed, working through embassy channels, to track down a photograph of her second oldest son, Elliott, who was a colonel in the army air forces stationed in Malta. Elliott had originally been assigned as an air intelligence officer but had been determined to fly combat missions and had signed waivers allowing him to do so despite less-than-perfect eyesight. He had flown photographic reconnaissance missions in unarmed planes over Europe, repeatedly taking heavy fire and, according to press reports, had demonstrated great bravery. By then all four of the Roosevelt boys were in the service, and the First Lady told Dahl she missed them and worried about their safety. Franklin and John were in the navy, and James was in the marines. A house once filled with loud boys seemed very quiet and empty in their absence. Shortly after writing to thank Dahl for "the excellent photograph," Eleanor extended an invitation to the young pilot and his friend to spend the July Fourth weekend with her and her husband at the Roosevelt family retreat, Hyde Park.

Dahl, with roommate Miles in tow, made the long train trip to Poughkeepsie, with the Hudson River on their left the whole way, their palms sweaty at the prospect of a weekend spent in the company of the president and the First Lady. They were met at the station by Schaeffer, Mrs. Roosevelt's chauffeur of some twenty-four years, and taken to Val-Kill Cottage, a large, beautiful fieldstone building that FDR, at Eleanor's request, had built as a private refuge for her and her friends. It was where she and her personal secretary, Malvina "Tommy" Thompson, now resided and where Dahl and Miles would also be staying. Tommy Thompson had long ago ceased to function merely as Eleanor's assistant and had become her close friend and constant companion. A divorced former teacher, she had joined the Roosevelts' staff back when FDR was governor of New York and proceeded to make herself indispensable. She handled all the First Lady's correspondence, and it was to her that Dahl had written his tentative advances, asking her to pass his note on to the First Lady.

During the drive, Schaeffer also informed them that the president was up at the Big House with Crown Princess Martha of Norway, along with her lady in waiting and three children. Dahl knew the princess and her family had been in exile since the Nazi invasion in the spring of 1940 and had accepted Roosevelt's offer of asylum. They were riding out the war in Washington and had taken up residence at Pook's Hill, a large estate near Bethesda, Maryland. He also knew that her husband, Prince Olav, along with his father, King Haakon VII, had remained behind in England to oversee the Norwegian war effort and that her extended visits to Hyde Park and the White House had led to speculation about a romantic relationship between the very attractive, charming princess and the president. It all promised to make for a diverting weekend.

When Dahl and Miles arrived at the cottage, Mrs. Roosevelt was standing at the door to greet them. After showing them to their rooms so they could freshen up, she told them to come out to "Tommy's porch" for a drink when they were ready. By the time they joined the rest of the company, she and Tommy were dishing out martinis to Eleanor's aunt, Mrs. Maude Gray, a thin, gray-haired old woman who was the wife of the American minister in Dublin, and her niece. Dahl remembered the young lady, and her shapely figure, from a previous meeting in Washington. They all sat down to a pleasant supper, and later in the evening Mrs. Roosevelt read aloud selections from Stephen Vincent Benet's "John Brown's Body," during which he dozed off.

Saturday morning was jump-started by a phone call from Henry Morgenthau, the secretary of the treasury, asking to speak to Mrs. Roosevelt, his loud, querulous voice bellowing through the receiver. Dahl had to hastily pull on his pants and go in search of the First Lady, whom he located in the kitchen making toast. She later told Dahl that Morgenthau had been somewhat taken aback at being told by a sleepy Englishman that "she was not in his bedroom." After breakfast, they went for a swim in the pool, which Mrs. Roosevelt had installed next to the cottage for her children. She was not a great swimmer but executed some competent dives off the springboard.

Dahl was surprised to find that the Roosevelt compound had a much more rustic, informal atmosphere than he had imagined. At lunch, Mrs. Roosevelt entertained them with a picnic in the garden, and the crown princess was there with her young children, Prince Harald and his two sisters, Princesses Astrid and Ragnhild, who were frolicking on the grass. Dahl and Miles roughhoused with the young royals, and when Dahl noticed that a piece of glass was chipped from the rim of the Coca-Cola bottle that Prince Harald was holding, he told him with a perfectly straight face that the president had eaten it. The future king of Norway was not at all sure he believed it and promptly went to check with the president. Roosevelt said of course he ate glass every evening, it made him "sharp." Dahl entered into a competition with the crown princess to see who was better at tying a blade of grass into a knot with their tongue. She was indeed attractive, with dark hair, bright eyes, and a good figure. She also proved surprisingly adept at the game, quickly coaxing the sliver of green to do her bidding. Eventually Morgenthau showed up, and after some polite chitchat Dahl attempted to steer their conversation around to the subject of postwar civil aviation, which was a hot topic at the moment. Morgenthau did not seem to be well informed and expressed surprise when Dahl told him that Berle was in charge of the negotiations.

At three o'clock, the picnic broke up. Dahl, transfixed, watched as the president was hoisted out of his wheelchair and into the driver's seat of his car by the burly men in his Secret Service detail. Roosevelt had a magnificent old Ford that had been specially fitted with hand controls in place of pedals because of his paralyzed legs, so the throttle and clutch were operated by squeezing various levers. With the crown princess beside him, Roosevelt took off, driving furiously, the old Ford bouncing over the grass, and all the bodyguards, who had stationed themselves throughout the woods during lunch, leaped into their cars and took off after him.

In the late afternoon, they drove to the Roosevelt Library, which included a museum filled with official mementos and gifts, including a large gold crown from the sultan of Morocco that Roosevelt confided he had valued and was worth only about five hundred dollars. They attended a concert for the troops who were guarding the estate, and Dahl sat next to the president in the front row. As soon as it was over, Roosevelt announced it was the "children's hour," his quaint term for cocktails, and they all went up to the Big House and congregated in his study, where he began expertly mixing martinis from an impressive array of bar equipment. The Roosevelts' oldest son, Jimmy, who had contracted a severe case of malaria in the Pacific and had been sent back to the United States to recuperate, joined them, along with his wife and several other members of the large, extended Roosevelt family. At one point, Richard Miles turned to the president and asked what Dahl considered a shockingly inappropriate question: "You must be pretty tired?" The president replied in the affirmative. "I have had four dispatches from Winston today," he told them. "One only a few minutes ago, and I have replied to each one of them. That is the equivalent to writing four full pages of newspaper articles."

Dahl found that he got along well with the president, who spoke to his guests in a disarmingly warm manner, appreciated a good joke, and seemed to be thoroughly admirable and decent, if not exactly awe-inspiring. "He did not 'glamor' me as I expected he would," Dahl told Marsh later. "His great genius seems to me to be his colossal memory and egotistical drive." In part, this may have been because the white-haired, sixty-one-year-old Roosevelt struck him as being "the most tired man" he had ever seen, though he seemed perfectly at ease among his guests and appeared to be enjoying himself.

After dinner, Dahl and Miles returned to the cottage with Mrs. Roosevelt in her open Buick. As they drove back to Val-Kill, Dahl took note of the elaborate security precautions at the presidential retreat. There were Secret Service agents at every gate, and at every corner there was a telephone box. As soon as they left the Big House, a guard called down to the nearest box along the line that "Mrs. R. was on the way," and the message was relayed from box to box all along the route until they reached their final destination. They stayed up talking for quite a while, and Dahl again attempted to explore the subject of postwar civil aviation. Mrs. Roosevelt remembered hearing the president hold forth on the subject after Major General Harold George had raised the same issue. She said the president had replied "with a wave of the hand" that the whole matter seemed "quite simple" and went on to explain that there should be free use of aerodromes in all countries, by all countries, but that foreign nations should not be allowed to operate as internal carriers between ports in other countries—by which she meant the right of cabotage. Dahl was duly impressed.

Sunday morning was spent reading the papers, swimming in the pool, and playing badminton with Miles. Mrs. Roosevelt did some paperwork and made a number of calls. Dahl noticed that when she phoned up to the Big House, she asked to speak to the president, adding somewhat tentatively, "but only if he is not busy, I do not want to bother him." The president took the call.

At Sunday lunch, Roosevelt looked rested and was in much better form than the day before and presided over a large table of fifteen, including Princess Martha, regaling them with morbid tales about headless bodies in the Roosevelt family vault. He laughed uproariously at his own stories—including one about a dead man's stinking body pickled in a barrel of rum—and ignored the look of distaste with which the women viewed their fish chowder. When the meal was over, FDR suggested they go to his retreat, Hilltop Cottage, farther up in the woods, and Dahl watched as he was again wheeled to his car and lifted into the driver's seat. The minute he was behind the wheel, he impatiently waved everyone away and tore off down the road, his phalanx of bodyguards in hot pursuit, with his son, Dahl, and Miles trailing behind in a third vehicle. Jimmy Roosevelt later confided that his father always drove too fast and "took delight in trying to leave his bodyguards behind," though he never succeeded in losing them altogether. The president took his car out every day when he was at Hyde Park and would go whizzing around the narrow country lanes with the guards giving chase. It was one of his favorite games and apparently gave him an enormous amount of pleasure.

As the rest of their party had opted to walk, Dahl and the president were among the first to arrive and had a chance for a long chat on the veranda, during which FDR asked a lot of pointed questions about German pilots. Dahl knew not to bring up politics because he had heard Roosevelt say earlier in the day that the thing he liked best about his country weekends was that he did not have to spend his time continually answering questions about affairs of state. Just as an experiment, he dropped Marsh's name. The president replied amiably that he knew the newspaper publisher and agreed with Dahl that he was "a very nice man."

After a pleasant interval, it was decided they should visit Miss Sara Delano, an aged cousin who, they were forewarned, was quite a character. The whole party piled back into their cars and, with the president and Princess Martha leading the way, drove a goodly distance on the main road to her home in a neighboring village. Miss Delano turned out to be an attractive woman of sixty who looked closer to forty, had purple hair, wore trousers, and owned thirty red setters. She made them all very stiff drinks and handed the president a Tom Collins with three hefty measures of gin.

Miles, his tongue loosened by all the alcohol, managed to be totally inappropriate again and asked the president what he thought of Churchill as a postwar premier. The president gave him only two good years after the war had finished. The conversation drifted to Roosevelt's own political problems, and he conceded that Americans were growing restless and had seen too much of him over the last ten years and "would do anything for a change." If they got the change they wanted, he bet the next fellow would barely be getting started before voters would be shouting and yelling to go back to what they had before. They moved on to a discussion of the Republican candidates. Roosevelt had a grudging admiration for Willkie and made it clear he was the only one of the lot he could envision in the office. By the time they decided to head home, it was raining, and the president opted to make the return journey in one of the closed cars. This left Jimmy to operate FDR's peculiar contraption with no pedals, with Dahl and Miles for passengers, so that the trip back was a memorable one. They said good night to the president at the Big House and returned to the cottage for supper with Mrs. Roosevelt and other members of the family.

By the end of the visit, Dahl found himself more impressed with the homely First Lady than with her husband. As he later told Marsh, she was no fool and wrote every word of her "My Day" column herself. She had strong opinions and could be surprisingly candid, particularly about anyone she disliked. When he had asked what she thought of Adolf Berle, she had made a face that left no doubt as to how she felt. The Roosevelts clearly had a complex relationship, but Eleanor had worked out an arrangement in which she played the role of a super-secretary, screening calls, deciding who would get in to see the president and who would not, and discussing issues with advisers like Morgenthau. Dahl estimated she shouldered "about ten percent" of her husband's workload. "The President's attitude toward her is that she is good help," he told Marsh. "She is very aware of his moods and 'plays' him very effectively. She has found out how to have a minimum of conflict." He found it interesting that before he left, she had taken the trouble to reassure him that the president was not unduly worried about the election problems on the home front, adding that he was "too old a hand" for that. His policy, she explained, was "to sit back and let everyone talk themselves to a standstill." Dahl thought it was as good a description as any of what he had witnessed over the weekend.

After Sunday-night supper, Dahl left to catch a late train to New York, where he had business to attend to. As Monday was the Fourth of July, Miles opted to stay on another night. Schaeffer deposited Dahl at the station, but he ended up having to borrow twenty-five dollars from the driver after discovering he had left all his money on the dressing-room table at the cottage. Despite his initial nervousness, it had been a marvelous weekend. It had been a relief just to escape the sticky heat and humidity—which was nothing unusual as Washington summers go, but to the British it was nothing short of oppressive. Dahl's embassy colleagues had taken to fanning themselves limply in the corridors and complaining that they deserved "tropical post pay." By comparison, Hyde Park, situated on a bluff overlooking the Hudson and surrounded by hundreds of acres of dense forest and shady walks, was, Dahl wrote Eleanor appreciatively, "like diving into the sea from the middle of Connecticut Avenue and not coming up for two days." A few days later Mrs. Roosevelt's reply arrived in the mail: "Miss Thompson and I appreciate your letter and are so glad you enjoyed the weekend. I hope very much you can find the time to come again."

Dahl considered the weekend to have been a great success. Over the three days, he had also found time to curry favor with Princess Martha. She and the children were headed to Long Island for the summer, and before he left she had told him to phone her the next time he was in New York. Her number was listed under the false name "Mrs. Aubert." Dahl was astute enough, however, to devote his flattering, earnest attention to the First Lady. He spent a good deal of time talking to her faithful companion, Tommy, and although a stout, no-nonsense woman in her late forties, she had a quick, dry wit, and they got along famously. In his thank-you letter, addressed to "My Dear Mrs. Roosevelt," Dahl promised to send along the information about mothers of Eagle Squadron boys that she had requested, and he went out of his way to express his great esteem for "Miss Thompson." More invitations soon followed.

As soon as he got back to Washington, Dahl prepared an exquisitely detailed twelve-page report of his stay at the presidential retreat for the BSC, filing it under the businesslike heading, "Visit to Hyde Park, July 2nd to 4th." In it he faithfully recorded all of Roosevelt's statements about Churchill, FDR's recollections of various conversations between himself and the prime minister, his reflections immediately after the destroyer-for-bases deal, and on and on. Dahl made a copy of his report and gave it to Marsh. On July 6, over drinks at the R Street house, Dahl also gave Marsh the benefit of his personal impressions and speculations, following up on a few points he apparently felt were too scandalous to put down on paper.*

He told a skeptical Marsh that he believed the president would "like to quit," adding "I think it is 50-50 that he will if the war or anything else does not suit him. He certainly has not made up his mind finally."

As for the perennial rumors of a royal liaison between the princess and the president, Dahl was inclined to think that all the smoke indicated a real fire. "The Crown Princess never left the President for one minute," he said. "She always called him 'Sir,' and rode with him right in the front seat and sat every meal at his side." Of course, Dahl noted, this was only right and proper as she was royalty. While some of this could be put down to protocol, in his opinion "there was more to it than that." Dahl believed that Roosevelt personally made sure that the lovely Norwegian was always by his side. "The President simply saw to it that it was done that way," he said, adding, "The Crown Princess is a very high class lady. The President has it in his mind that he would like to sleep with her."

Most important, Dahl came away convinced that Roosevelt was "entirely under the influence of Churchill." The president seemed to have the prime minister very much in mind. "He speaks of him constantly," reported Dahl. "It is 'What will Winnie do?' and 'What will he say?' and 'I communicated with Winnie four times today.'" Marsh later noted that "the British eyewitness" watching FDR was most positive on this point: "I am certain that Roosevelt is under the spell of Churchill," Dahl hold him. "You can't be fooled by an act. Roosevelt was consistently affectionate whenever he said the name 'Winston' and the name was constantly in the conversation."

---

*Dahl's verbatim observations, filed under "Comments of a week-end reporter—Hyde Park," were transcribed and preserved for posterity by Marsh's secretary.

The following morning, after mulling over Dahl's "private report" of his visit to Hyde Park, Marsh reflected on the RAF pilot's scrupulous honesty in a memo he dictated for his own files, concluding, "He is truthful. I judge this from two items in the report itself:

He [Dahl] wanted to know if his friend Marsh was plus or minus with the President, so spoke of his country home simply to bring Marsh in. The fact that he put this in the report shows he left nothing out.

The fact that he reported all details of his friend Richard's [Miles] actions shows that he is both truthful and pitiless.

Marsh also found it significant that Dahl had raised the subject of the vice president with Mrs. Roosevelt, knowing full well that he was working hard to keep his man Wallace on the ticket for FDR's fourth term:

The name of Wallace came up with Mrs. Roosevelt while she was discussing a group of other persons, as she was speaking somewhat disparagingly of them. Dahl said: "What about Vice President Wallace?" Her approximate reply was: "He is not in their class." When Dahl asked what she meant, he said, "She meant that Wallace had a standing as a person so much higher than them that she did not class them together."

At the end of Dahl's verbal report, Marsh scribbled a note: "This young observer does not know that the President is a genius of shift and that if Stalin-Roosevelt becomes decisively important to Roosevelt, he will not be under any Churchill spell." He added, "Remember a country squire at this moment is enjoying hugely the friendship of a queen-to-be." Then he packaged up both reports and passed them on to Wallace. Someone—whether it was Marsh, Wallace, or a blushing secretary is unclear—scratched out the line about the president sleeping with the princess before consigning the report to the filing cabinet.

In Marsh's eyes, the fact that Dahl had voluntarily undertaken a little high-level snooping on his behalf was evidence that his friend was indeed a loyal spy. Only in the upside-down world of espionage, where things tended to happen for the least logical of reasons, could he have convinced himself that this was the case. Dahl, who thought Marsh was in his own way "as naïve as Wallace," happily made use of his personal association with both men. In this complex web of relationships and layered obligations, his allegiance to Marsh took precedence. For the most part, Dahl occupied the ambiguous role of informer without suffering any undue torment about a divided life or the perils of commitment. He was not without scruples, but winning the war took precedence over all other considerations. Moreover, his friendship with Marsh rested on profound admiration, affection, and absolute trust. Similarly, despite knowing that Dahl was a British agent who considered everything he saw or heard as fair game for his weekly intelligence summaries, and might betray the confidence of friend and foe at the drop of a hat, Marsh's faith in and fondness for his young protégé never wavered. Despite its inherent absurdity, their partnership continued to thrive.

As a frequent guest at the White House and Hyde Park, Dahl soon won the confidence of the president and reported back to his superiors on their tête-à-têtes. He found opportunities to be alone with FDR, and during these unguarded moments they would engage in idle gossip, and the president would sometimes comment in passing on the bombing offensive in Germany or a new plan to sink U-boats. "I remember once walking into FDR's little side room before lunch at Hyde Park on a Sunday morning, and he was making the martinis, as he always did, and he looked up at me. I was literally nobody to him, I was a friend of Eleanor's. And he said, 'I've just had a very interesting cable from Winston.'" It was Roosevelt's way of letting Dahl know that he was aware that he was reporting back to British intelligence, and that part of the game was that neither of them acknowledged what the other was up to. On occasion, the president might drop a hint in order "to prepare London" about which way he was leaning on a particular issue. Dahl came away with the impression that FDR's aim was not to divulge secrets so much as to try to prevent the serious divergences that often threatened to develop between their two countries.

This cozy arrangement enabled Dahl to become a back-channel conduit of information. The president and Churchill were, through one means or another, in constant conversation during the war and did not necessarily rely on official liaison. In fact, because Halifax was regarded as a weak link, they used Harry Hopkins to such an extent that both the ambassador and the secretary of state had their noses permanently out of joint. Hardly a seasoned diplomat, Dahl was just one of many nimble young men who happened to be in the right place at the right time and were recruited to serve as intermediaries, "buffers" in the language of the trade, to establish an area of what Cuneo called "discreet indiscreet conversations."

It went without saying that this unofficial exchange of views could be far more frank than anything that could take place at the official level, and that according to the diplomatic fiction adhered to by both sides, the official services knew nothing about it. "My job really was to try to oil the wheels between the British and the American war effort, and they were often pretty rusty and creaky," recalled Dahl. "I started going out and staying weekends at Hyde Park, and up there, of course, there were always Roosevelts, and people like Henry Morgenthau, and a lot of other cabinet ministers. . . . I was able to ask these fellows some quite pointed questions and get quite equally pointed replies from them which they would never have given to the ambassador or anyone like that. For instance, there might have been something going on between Churchill and Roosevelt inside the war effort, the second front, or the landing in Southern France, or the Mediterranean, which Winston wanted and FDR didn't. And I could ask FDR what he felt about it over lunch and he would tell me quite openly, you see. Far more so I think than he would have told Winston in a cable."

Dahl would immediately pass on everything he heard to the BSC. By then, Stephenson's domestic network of undercover spies and contacts was well established, with bureaus in most large American cities. He oversaw a sprawling, highly mechanized intelligence empire that had expanded to two floors of the International Building in Rockefeller Center, employed more than a thousand men and women—and nearly twice that number in Canada and Latin America—and occupied office space, studios, and hotel rooms scattered around New York and Washington. The long debate over Donovan's domain had finally been settled, and the COI had been renamed the Office of Strategic Services (OSS), and a branch in New York, under Allen Dulles, had been established a floor above the BSC in Rockefeller Center. "With unstinted and constant generosity, Stephenson lent his most trusted subordinates to assist," said David Bruce, the highly regarded OSS officer who later became American ambassador in London. "Clothed in clandestinity, [they] provided an essential complement to military and political measures through covert means."

Roosevelt relied on Stephenson and his "trusted subordinates" to maintain this back channel for his secret dealings with Churchill. This arrangement afforded him much greater latitude, as well as a certain freedom from supervision by the nervous nellies and watchful old-school diplomats who infested the OSS in its early days. For everyone's protection, it made sense to keep Dahl at arm's length. It suited Stephenson for the air attaché to consider himself an outside agent, reporting to the BSC's contacts in Washington rather than to the inner sanctum in New York. "You never spoke directly to him [Stephenson],"

Dahl recalled. "You told someone else, and someone else told someone else, and then they told Bill." Stephenson would, in turn, pass on any valuable information to London, and to Churchill.

Dahl was persuaded that every little bit helped: "Although it was in a way bleeding information on the highest level from the Americans, he was doing it not for nefarious purposes but for the war effort." As Robert Sherwood, the well-known American dramatist who did propaganda work for Donovan during this period, later admitted: "If the isolationists had known the full extent of the secret alliance between the U.S. and Britain, their demands for the President's impeachment would have rumbled like thunder across the land."

Stephenson must have congratulated himself on his choice of the enthusiastic young airman, whose entrée with the Roosevelts could not have begun more innocently and who could now be exploited for Stephenson's own ends. The BSC director belonged to the new school of intelligence chiefs who believed writers and intellectuals often made for the best and subtlest agents, and Dahl was turning out to be something of a find. He was a natural choice for their kind of work. He had a writer's ear for the telling phrase and a talent for asking questions without appearing overly inquisitive. As a pilot and author, he also had legitimate cover, which was always the best kind. Dahl had maneuvered—or stumbled—into the role expected of him and was perfectly positioned to extend the BSC's network of well-placed Washington sources.

From Dahl's perspective, there did not seem to be anything terribly dangerous about what he was doing. It was not as though he was ransacking offices and rifling through diplomatic bags. He was simply a purveyor of information. The stuff he was passing along was useful, important even, but not vital. Whether or not his information would be exploited, or lead to any subsequent "action," was determined by his masters in New York and in London. He had to watch his step, of course. The Monroe Doctrine made the BSC's activities unpopular, and a mistake would prompt all sorts of embarrassing public questions, press scrutiny, and political controversy, which was the last thing a furtive organization wanted. Berle, a hard-charging forty-four-year-old Harvard lawyer, was already complaining about "the very considerable espionage" that the British were carrying on within the United States and would seize on any excuse to start another row about why they had been granted "free rein" in the first place. Strictly speaking, however, most of the stuff he was trafficking in was material that he was more or less entitled to know as an embassy attaché. If he was caught with notes—say, a report on the administration's postwar air policies or even a file on American security arrangements—it would not really prove anything. A lot of what passed for espionage in those days could be described as enterprising reporting. Dahl was assured that he had nothing to worry about. As Stephenson was fond of saying, "That's why our side has agents; the enemy has spies."

6

ONE LONG LOAF

The army had a saying that bread is the staff of life and
that the life of the staff is one long loaf.

—BICKHAM SWEET-ESCOTT, *Baker Street Irregular*

BY THE SUMMER of 1943, the focus of Dahl's secret work in Washington consisted of staying close to Marsh and Wallace, and keeping "pretty careful tabs on his [the vice president's] Communistic leanings and his friends in those quarters," and reporting back to Stephenson. The official history makes frequent reference to Dahl's undercover assignment as the "BSC officer in Washington" who was "in frequent consultation with Wallace." It was not difficult for Dahl to keep track of their movements, as all three men were close friends and saw one another often. The vice president had become rather fond of the long-limbed British airman, in part because of his striking resemblance to his youngest son, Robert, who was in the army. Dahl and Wallace had much in common, sharing a dry sense of humor, a lively curiosity about the world, and a playful eccentricity that occasionally got them into trouble. They were both vigorous men—

intellectually and physically—and enjoyed testing each other's prowess in conversation as much as on the tennis court, where they both excelled. After their morning game, they often walked downtown to work together, their matching long strides perfectly in sync, boisterously debating who had had the better backhand. They were also daily visitors to Marsh's R Street home, and though Wallace was more stiff-necked than Dahl, both reveled in the rowdy publisher's high-spirited, profane company. "Henry Wallace was dropping in literally every afternoon for a chat," recalled Dahl, who became accustomed to finding him with Marsh in the oak-paneled library, club chairs drawn close together. "He was a man without rudder and Charles gave him a lot of rudder. Of course, Marsh loved it because he got a bit of gossip and he felt closer to FDR."

Meanwhile Dahl, always a quick study, had taken to intelligence work like a duck to water. His natural talents equipped him perfectly for his new profession, and all through the summer months he worked on cultivating sources and applying his skills to further establish himself in the key situation in which he had landed. Marsh had tutored Dahl in the beat reporter's trick of extracting information, stockpiling titillating gossip items to peddle later, and rewarding reliable informants in whatever currency they valued most. One of Dahl's best sources of information from inside the White House was Marsh's old pal Drew Pearson. "He had a direct pipeline to the cabinet," Dahl recalled. "In fact he had a cabinet minister [member] in the palm of his hand. So after every cabinet meeting of course Drew got a full report." (The BSC history indicates that Pearson relied on three cabinet members: Ickes, Morgenthau, and Francis Biddle.) In due course they struck a deal. "We became very good friends and we exchanged information openly," said Dahl. "We told each other that there we were, and that's what we wanted. He wanted it for his column, and he knew I wanted it for other reasons."

Pearson kept extensive records of the misdemeanors, both large and small, of administration figures, and according to the BSC history, he "was adroit at hinting that he would not use the information if they made a point of telling him now and again what was going on in their departments":

> He was said to have in his possession an affidavit, signed by someone in a position to vouch for Sumner Welles's alleged homosexual activities. Whether or not this was true, it seemed strangely inappropriate to observe the suave and snobbish Welles making frequent visits to Pearson's house, in order to keep him au fait with events.

The results of this technique were deemed "highly satisfactory" by Stephenson, who "gave instructions that Pearson should be cultivated as a potential source of important intelligence." Without identifying Dahl by name, the report goes on to state that "a BSC officer in Washington spent many months gaining Pearson's confidence, and by the middle of 1943 the acquaintance had begun to produce solid results in the form of reports on, *inter alia*, political changes, the President's intentions and the views of high naval and military officials. The friendship grew closer until, early in 1944, the BSC officer was 'regarded as one of the family.'"*

Dahl's barter system with Pearson was simple. His BSC contacts would supply him with "good, fairly safe" Whitehall items about the war effort, which, from Pearson's point of view, was "quite interesting, exciting stuff." With Stephenson's blessings, Dahl would swap it for

---

*It seems likely that Dahl, as one of the authors of the official history, wrote the section on Pearson himself, particularly as it contains many vivid passages that stand out from the rest of the report, and details a number of incidents that Dahl was personally involved in and that he later recounted in an interview with the CBC.

what he thought was far more interesting and exciting stuff in return. "For all I know he may have been [doing] exactly the same thing to me, and was told what he could tell me, and feed to the British," said Dahl. "But I don't think so, and I don't think Bill [Stephenson] thought so either."

Marsh was of particular value when it came to deconstructing Washington gossip and assessing it in the context of the delicate intricacies of government and press machinery. Time and again, when Dahl's superiors wanted to sound out Marsh on some new incident, they would dispatch the air attaché to confer privately with his well-informed friend. Dahl, having consulted Marsh, would invariably return with the goods. So when a senior British official became involved in a bizarre melodrama involving a chief administration figure who had become the target of scandalous gossip, Dahl naturally asked Marsh if there was anything that could be done about the rumors, which were given wide publicity.

The trouble started with Harry Hopkins' marriage to his third wife, Louise Macy, which took place at the White House on July 27, 1942, with the president acting as best man. Hopkins, who was dogged by controversy even in the best of times, returned from his honeymoon to find himself the subject of an outrageous story claiming he had been treated to a two-week holiday aboard the yacht *My Kay IV*, which had been commandeered for naval use but was delayed so that he and his bride could cruise the Great Lakes, all at taxpayer expense. The newlyweds had in fact spent a quiet honeymoon on a Vermont farm, and Hopkins had been back at work exactly eleven days after the wedding. No matter how vehemently the White House denied it, and despite an FBI investigation, the damaging rumor continued to circulate around Washington for many months. Hopkins was still consulting lawyers as to whether he had any legal recourse when he was hit by another smear. The embarrassing item, which first appeared in the *Times-Herald* in January 1943, reported that the vastly wealthy and controversial British press baron Lord Beaverbrook, aka Max Aitken, had presented Hopkins' bride with "a parure of emeralds" as a wedding gift, creating the appearance that the British had offered a bribe to the wife of the president's top aide. (Apparently no one knew precisely what a "parure" was, so the gift was alternately described as a necklace, a bracelet, earrings, and a tiara, when in fact it would have been the whole ensemble.) Beaverbrook's emeralds were said to be a token of appreciation for Hopkins' role in dispensing the multibillion-dollar Lend-Lease program on which Britain so depended.

The story, following in the wake of the *My Kay IV* rumors, created a sensation. The White House ridiculed the "malicious rumors now being published by certain newspapers hostile to the government" but did not issue a clear denial. Mrs. Hopkins repudiated the idea of a British payoff and told the press, "I don't even own one emerald. It's a lie." Beaverbrook declared, "It's all nonsense. The story is a fabrication from first to last, but the Germans will like it." Despite being roundly denied by both parties, the story took on a life of its own and continued to reverberate around Washington. Isaiah Berlin worried in his weekly summary that the story "is still circulating and many old lies are bound to be dragged out once more." The British wanted to know the identity of the smearer and to put an end to the adverse publicity. The scurrilous story was being revived again, this time in Pearson's "Merry-Go-Round" column, on the eve of the new Lend-Lease appropriation, at a time when the bill's American critics were looking for ways to discredit British administrators and their handling of Lend-Lease funds.

As Dahl predicted, Marsh was not only able to identify the likely source of the item but elaborated at length on his ulterior motives in leaking it. It was Marsh's contention that Pearson's story—which included such damning details as a description of the Beaverbrook gift (an emerald bracelet) and its value (half a million dollars)—originated with Bernard Baruch because he was "out to get Hopkins and get him fast." This Marsh had straight from his pal Lyndon Johnson. The tall, white-haired Baruch looked like a pillar of rectitude and liked to pass himself off as a behind-the-scenes player, always willing to remain the adviser and never the administration star. Marsh told Dahl not to believe it. He shared Dorothy Parker's view to the effect that there were two things one could never figure out—the theory of the zipper and the precise function of Bernard Baruch. Marsh believed "old Barney" lusted for power and probably planted the smear about the priceless bauble in hopes of further tarnishing Hopkins' reputation and removing him as the leader of Roosevelt's brain trust.*

Inasmuch as the president liked to read the "Merry-Go-Round," one of the best ways to influence FDR's mind was through the column, and Baruch knew this better than anyone. Furthermore, Marsh had it on good authority that most of the administration scoops in "Merry-Go-Round" came via South Carolina senator Jimmy Byrnes to Barney Baruch to *New York World* editor Herbert Swope to Pearson. Byrnes, according to Marsh, was a "tool" of Baruch's and knew how he felt about Hopkins. Swope was "crooked" and also planted stories in the press for his buddy Baruch. All this Dahl piped back to the BSC, while noting that Marsh hated Baruch beyond all reason and generally sought to discredit him whenever possible.

For all that Dahl found Marsh useful for practical purposes, Marsh made equal and opposite use of his protégé. As a coconspirator, he expected payment in kind—his intelligence in exchange for British intelligence. At the end of each day, Dahl would stroll into the R Street house loaded for bear, and Marsh would pump him for all the "high-

---

*Although the matter was never publicly resolved, Marsh was right. In his memoir the *Chicago Tribune* reporter Walter Trohan revealed that Baruch was his source but had "stretched the story a bit." Beaverbrook's emeralds were in fact diamonds, in the form of antique clips, and the family heirlooms were worth several thousand dollars.

level stuff" from the embassy, as well as everything Pearson had leaked after the cabinet meeting. Similarly, after Dahl's visits to the White House or Hyde Park, Marsh would bombard him with questions: "What does he [Roosevelt] look like? What did he and so-and-so talk about? . . . Is his health okay? . . . Did they bring up the new appointment?" Dahl would supply the salient details, delivering entertaining monologues or humorous typed reports that resembled short stories, complete with characters, scenes, and dialogue. Marsh was never less than a rapt audience. "He would be fascinated," recalled Dahl. "That was meat and drink to him."

The Texas publisher marveled at the ease with which the young pilot had landed himself in the catbird seat. He envied Dahl his friendship with the Roosevelts and the weekend forays to Hyde Park, a level of intimacy that Marsh had never managed to achieve. Marsh's publishing empire had earned him a reputation as a kingmaker in Texas politics, but he had never been able to quite duplicate that role in Washington. A millionaire many times over, Marsh felt a nagging guilt at having been just old enough to avoid military service during World War I, opting instead to stay home and advance his career while other men did their duty. He was determined that in this war, he would repay the debt he felt he owed his country. It was a constant source of frustration to him that despite his many contributions, he had never been able to crack Roosevelt's inner circle, the vaunted "palace guard."

What made it all the more galling was that Marsh had been lobbying for a job as far back as the summer of 1932, when he first met FDR's mother, Sara Delano Roosevelt, when Franklin was governor of New York and the Democratic nominee for president. Marsh had been introduced to her by Colonel Edward M. House, an ingratiating, English-educated Texan, who was then among the most influential men in Democratic politics and had served as President Woodrow Wilson's closest adviser. Marsh looked up to House as a mentor and curried favor with the elder statesman by supplying him with political insights he had gathered from his editors and publishers around the country, which House passed on to Sara Roosevelt, who was intimately involved in her son's campaign and controlled the purse strings. Shortly before the election, Marsh, taking his cue from House, had written directly to FDR, clearly hoping for some sort of recognition in due course:

> *Dear Governor:*
> *I have never congratulated an elected candidate because I had no wish to clutter his mail. This is merely to let you know that during the next four years: 1) I shall not recommend any man for your office. 2) I shall attempt to do anything that you may ask me to provided there is no personal publicity involved and no salary.*

On the morning of March 4, 1933, the day Roosevelt was sworn into office, Marsh penned a laudatory front-page editorial in the *Austin American-Statesman,* an obstinate show of support given the fact that Texas' press was overwhelmingly united against FDR's New Deal politics. Marsh wrote:

> *Men do not make times. Conditions make men. The man who took the oath as president of the United States today has the honesty and clearness of mind which must be the basis—the foundation—of a spirituality that was Wilson's, of a practical clearness of application that was Lincoln's.*

Roosevelt never responded to Marsh's overtures. Marsh, who eventually became an adviser and friend to Sara Roosevelt and visited her several times at Hyde Park with his daughter, Antoinette, when she was attending college nearby at Vassar, recognized that FDR probably dismissed him and House as belonging to his mother's generation and the old wing of the party. It was also possible that FDR knew they had served as Sara Roosevelt's financial advisers and blamed them for his mother's tightfistedness, and for turning down his request for more funds when he was in need. Early on Marsh had hoped FDR would award him with an official post and lamented that he had been in line for the ambassadorship to Hungary before the Nazi invasion of eastern Europe. Instead, he watched as FDR drafted dozens of industrial executives from the other side of the aisle—many of whom had bitterly opposed his liberal policies—to head up wartime agencies. As the months passed and no appointment materialized, Marsh had to content himself with serving the country the only way he could, by putting his investigative skills to work gathering information on a broad spectrum of economic, industrial, and political fronts and making it available to those in power. "He and Roosevelt did not get along personally, I think their egos clashed," observed Antoinette. "But Roosevelt used him, and Dad was for him all the way."

Marsh always claimed that he had no interest in socializing with FDR because he was so insincere and that listening to him made him "positively sick to his stomach." Dahl suspected his sour attitude stemmed from years of feeling snubbed by the Democratic leader, and he occasionally suggested ways the publisher could make overtures of friendship that might be well received. Whatever Marsh's personal feelings, they did not interfere with his admiration of the president as a leader. As Wallace noted in his diary, "According to Charles, Roosevelt is the most skillful politician this country has ever had. Charles has absolutely no respect for Roosevelt as a man but as a politician he thinks Roosevelt has remarkable ability and that he is great asset for the world, that he has done great good and probably will do even greater good."

When Wallace assumed the vice presidency in 1941, swept in when FDR was elected to a third term, Marsh saw his chance. Taking his cue from Colonel House, Marsh positioned himself as Wallace's shadow adviser, becoming his minister without portfolio, inundating him with memos, reports, and suggestions, writing drafts of speeches, and conferring with him several times a day. Marsh was always at his best at these informal, feet-up sessions, and Wallace, who never took much interest in the minutiae of Washington politics, was all too happy to leave the nuts-and-bolts analysis to him. To commemorate his ascendance, Marsh commissioned a large oil portrait of himself, labeled it "the Preceptor" (a reference to a running gag between him and Dahl that had to do with a California religious cult run by a "master of mental-physics" who called himself the Preceptor), and hung it over the mantelpiece of the R Street house. Dahl took to calling Marsh by the painting's title and occasionally addressed his letters "Dear Preceptor."

If his White House access extended no further than the vice president's office, Marsh would make the most of it. "He always wanted to be great manipulator behind the scenes," said Welly Hopkins, a Texas legislator who first met Marsh when he was in the Texas House of Representatives and later saw a lot of him in Washington while working as a special assistant to the U.S. attorney general. "He had grandiose ideas. He would have liked to have been a little William Randolph Hearst, because he got into very much of a newspaper broker position. He bought and sold newspapers all over the United States." According to Hopkins, Marsh's biggest problem was that he could be extremely difficult, to the point of being abrasive. "He could be rude at times because of his over-weening ego. Charlie Marsh, to himself, would think he could do anything, get anything done that he wanted done. He was a very forceful fellow, and to some people very persuasive."

By June 1943 Dahl could almost always find Marsh and Wallace together in the late afternoons, huddled down in "the cooler," the air-conditioned conference room on the first floor of Marsh's town house, plotting the vice president's future. When he interrupted them one muggy evening in June, they were in deep discussion about a recent report in Pearson's "Merry-Go-Round" column that Harry Hopkins was working to secure Roosevelt a fourth term but was against Wallace as his running mate for a second term because it might cost them votes. After the item appeared, Hopkins had personally reassured Wallace that there was no truth in it, but neither Marsh or Wallace was confident he could be trusted. They were constantly trying to gauge every nuance of the president's attitude toward his vice president, and the way it manifested itself in the various statements and actions of members of his brain trust.

While Wallace respected Marsh's judgment, consulted him on a wide range of matters, and seemed to rely on him heavily at times, his journal entries make it clear that he took much of what the bombastic publisher said with a grain of salt. After a dinner party given by Sir John Orr, the well-known Scottish scientist and politician, in which Charles proceeded to totally monopolize the discussion, holding forth at length on why a fellow like Hitler had to blow up or subside, Wallace noted in his diary: "As I listened to his [Marsh's] conversation, I could not help thinking that perhaps he himself was an illustration of what he was expounding."

By late summer, when the heat drove away most of society and nothing much was happening in the capital, Dahl began spending his free time at Marsh's vast eight-hundred-acre Virginia estate, Longlea, located in the foothills of the Blue Ridge Mountains. The eighteenth-century English-style manor house, modeled on a mansion with a similar name Marsh had spotted on a visit to Scotland, was Charles's gift to his young mistress, Alice Glass. He had bought the land in 1932 and spent four years and a small fortune building the rambling stone mansion, with its many bedrooms and broad, hundred-foot-long flagstone terrace, which ran the length of the house and was bordered by a low stone parapet, beyond which the land dropped off steeply to reveal a scenic bend in the Hazel River. Here, in the heart of Virginia hunt country, sixty miles outside Washington, Marsh set up his bride-to-be in great style, giving her free rein over the design and decoration of their palatial new home. She hired the New York decorator Benno de Terey, a handsome Hungarian known for his exquisite taste, and filled the interior rooms with sumptuous furnishings. The magnificent drawing room boasted an eighteenth-century Aubusson carpet, an enormous crystal chandelier, a Monet landscape, and at the far end of the room, a gilded Chinese Chippendale mirror hung over the mantelpiece. A grand piano stood in the bay window facing the terrace, framed by rich brown and gold damask curtains. The room was painted the palest blue, and every piece of furniture was upholstered in pure white. It was so ornate and forbidding that Marsh preferred to retreat to the mahogany-paneled library, with its large, inviting fireplace, bright Persian rug depicting a hunting scene, and Chinese opium table piled high with the day's papers.

Dahl thought it by far the finest house he had seen in America. He would always remember the long winding drive that led up to the house, allowing a first fleeting glimpse of the blue slate roof and great chimneys that rose above the rolling hills. The approach was long and winding and cut through the woods and across green meadows that seemed to stretch for miles and were empty save for a herd of Black Angus cows. Longlea was a working farm. A half mile down the hill from the main house was the manager's cottage, stables for Alice's horses, a barn for the milk cows, and a poultry yard stocked with chickens, turkeys, ducks, guineas, and some ferocious hissing geese. There was a vegetable garden, a cutting garden, and a strawberry patch. All this was overseen by Marsh's very correct Bavarian butler, Rudolf Kolinger, a former cavalry officer who had served the kaiser and who dictated menus to the chef, stocked the wine cellar, ran the staff of twenty black servants, mixed the drinks, and waited on table in the tradition of great country houses on the Continent.

Longlea had everything required to entertain on a grand scale, which Charles and Alice did constantly, hosting lavish weekend parties for all their new Washington friends and old Texas chums. Marsh believed in patronage, and beyond wanting to consolidate his power and influence in government, he built a house that would attract artists and musicians and writers. He sought to surround himself with a lively, sophisticated court, and his frequent guests included Vice President Wallace and his advisers; Welly Hopkins and Harold Young, a hearty back-slapping Texas politico; Lyndon Johnson, and Lady Bird; Beanie Baldwin, head of the liberal Political Action Committee and his aide, Palmer Weber; the wealthy Brown brothers of the Brown and Root construction company; the musicians Erich Leinsdorf and Zadel Skolovsky; the Randolph Scotts; as well as assorted cabinet officials, academics, writers, and journalists.

Charles also believed in pleasure and urged his friends to indulge their sybaritic natures. Guests would spend leisurely days relaxing by the pool, sunning, swimming, or playing tennis. There were all the pastimes of landed gentry, including fishing, shooting, and riding. Alice often went for morning rides and occasionally organized a hunt—known as the Hazelmere Hunt after the river—leading a small party of friends in a fast gallop across the soft green hills. She was a superb horsewoman and, Texas country girl that she was, an excellent shot. She had a skeet shoot installed on the high bluff overlooking the river and picked the spinning clay disks out of the sky with deadly precision. In warm weather, the outdoor terrace, with its breathtaking view of the mountains, became the center of activity. It was an idyllic spot, framed by flowering trees, mimosa, and a rose garden, and in the evenings their perfumed scent hung heavily in the air. Alice had ordered thousands of daffodils to be planted from the stone balustrade down to the cliff's edge, so that in spring it was a blazing carpet of yellow. Breakfast and lunch were served outside, as well as cocktails, which were on offer morning, noon, and night. A bottle of champagne was always open. At Longlea, dinners were a very formal affair and were served in the elegant dining room with its long mahogany table, laden with gleaming crystal and silver, and rows of ribbon-backed Hepplewhite chairs. Alice loved to dress up and dazzled in the latest evening gowns, while Marsh, with his sculpted profile and gleaming pate, looked almost regal in his Fortuny smoking jackets. "Alice was a beautiful and charming hostess, very out-going and friendly, and interested in everything that was going on in Washington and the war," recalled Creekmore Fath, who looked forward to the glamorous weekends. "It was an amazing time, and an amazing house, and Charles made it all very entertaining."

To Erich Leinsdorf, "People like Charles and Alice [were] the best in any country under any circumstances." The Marshes had first be-friended the young concert pianist at the Salzburg Music Festival dur-ing one of their many sojourns to Europe during the early years of their affair. He had played at their private villa in St. Gilgen on the Wolfgan-gesee, and afterward Alice, who was very much taken with the gifted twenty-five-year-old, had awarded him pride of place next to her at dinner and later invited him to come visit them in Virginia. Leinsdorf, who by his own account was lucky "to conduct his way out" of Nazi-swamped Austria by getting himself invited to lead the 1937 season of New York Metropolitan Opera, remembered Longlea as something out of a dream. "There was a constant stream of guests," he wrote in his memoir. "The accents were new, the lavish and easy life with martinis served at eleven in the morning was new, my room with its elegant antique furnishings was new. . . . I just sat goggle-eyed."

Longlea was a showplace, designed to display Marsh's most exqui-site acquisition, and Alice, like the house, did not disappoint. Almost six foot in her bare feet, she was slim, graceful, and startlingly beauti-ful, with delicate features, wide-set blue eyes, and strawberry-blond hair that cascaded past her shoulders. When she descended Longlea's dark, oak-paneled staircase, a hush would fall over the hall as all the assembled guests turned to stare. The noted New York society photographer Arnold Genthe, who was hired to take her portrait and was known for taking the famous picture of Greta Garbo that first piqued Hollywood's interest, maintained that Alice was the most stunning woman he had ever seen. He was so besotted—by the queen and her palace—that he asked her to scatter his ashes on the grounds when he died.

If there was one thing Alice knew, it was how to make a lasting impression. The first time Charles Marsh saw her, she was stark naked, a pale, shimmering goddess rising unexpectedly from the mists of his Austin swimming pool. Marsh was then in his midforties and still made his home in the Texas capital, where he was a prince of the city and one of the most powerful men in the state with his string of fifty newspapers and a fortune that included oil wells and large tracts of real estate. He lived in the proverbial big house on the hill, an immense Tudor mansion in the exclusive district of Enfield, which had a commanding view of town and boasted one of the first private swimming pools in the area. With Leona, his wife of twenty years, and their three children away for an extended stay at their summer home on Cape Cod, he had been feeling bored and lonely and on a whim had decided to throw a party and open his home to Austin's elite. At two A.M., after the last of his many guests had said good night, Marsh had wandered back outside to enjoy a cigar in the early morning cool when, as he later recounted the episode to Ingersoll, he was stopped in his tracks by the sight of a bold young girl emerging from the water, "her long blond hair flowing among her fresh young breasts."

Alice was not yet twenty. Intelligent and ambitious, she had fled the small Texas town of Marlin, where her father was the bank president, for the excitement of the capital city. She was working as a secretary in the state legislature and already had a long line of suitors when she entered Marsh's life in the summer of 1931. The morning after the pool escapade, a smitten Marsh reportedly rolled over in bed and announced to Alice, "You are not for Austin, Texas, little girl." Always one for rearranging people's lives and underwriting their futures, he offered to send her to New York, where she could attend college and complete her education. Within weeks, Alice was installed at the Barbizon Hotel in Manhattan, and Marsh, who had left his wife and Austin with little more than his slippers, was a frequent visitor. By the fourth year of their affair, he had bought her an apartment on Central Park South and was enjoying a new life in New York when she announced she was pregnant.

Marsh was determined to marry Alice, but it was easier said than done. Leona took a dim view of divorce and announced her determination to fight it tooth and nail. She engaged an ex-governor of Texas as her lawyer to persuade Charles to change his mind. Failing that, she warned she would file suit against him for violation of the Mann Act: Alice was most definitely a minor when Marsh first set her up in New York and had been transported across state lines with "immoral purposes" in mind. When Marsh met with Leona's team of lawyers, he told Ingersoll, he called their bluff, telling them that when they had him in court, he was prepared to testify before a jury of his peers that the reason he was seeking a divorce was that he could not "get a hard on" in bed with his wife. "The choice is hers," Marsh claimed he told her attorneys. "Does she want me in public court, so testifying—or do you gentlemen care to advise her to stop with this whole silly business and keep our private lives to ourselves?" Leona agreed to settle, and Marsh got his divorce. During the extraordinarily nasty and protracted proceedings, however, the court tied up all his assets for years, and by the time he got out from under, he had signed away all his oil fields to his greedy partner, Sid Richardson, and a generous share of his fortune to provide for Leona and their children.

This still left Marsh with the difficult dilemma of how to arrange a shotgun marriage to the respectable daughter of a highly respectable country banker, a man of good standing who was known to many of his friends. This was Texas, after all, and the family honor was at stake. The elaborate escapade that Marsh planned to finesse this problem, Ingersoll recalled, showed the publisher at his most "ingenious and mischievous:

To have the baby Alice was sent on holiday to London. From there she wrote at once to her family that she had fallen in love with a wonderful Englishman, Major Manners. She had married him on the spur, because he was an officer in a regiment which was suddenly posted to India. She was to join him after he was settled. But he was hardly gone when Alice's family heard from their surprising daughter the happy news that she would be presenting him with a baby. She would stay in London, watched over by his country family, until the child came. Alas and alack, her doctors told her she was not up to a voyage home. But Major Manners got himself one leave and gallantly gave it up to journey all the way from the Himalayas to South Texas to present himself, in person, to his American bride's family and friends.

Alice's baby was born in England and duly christened Diana Manners. Shortly thereafter Alice wrote to her parents, informing them that her husband had been killed in a border battle, during "a skirmish with bandits." Four months later the widow Manners returned to America with her fatherless infant. As for the British character actor who played the part of the hapless major, Marsh himself hired and rehearsed him after spotting his mug in an advertisement for Arrow dress shirts in *The Saturday Evening Post*. The eye-catching, full-page ad featured the handsome young man modeling a new collared shirt called "Manners."

At Longlea, Charles' attempt to establish a new life with Alice was fraught with problems, and the Virginia estate quickly became her principal residence—family members always referred to it as "Alice's place"—while he seemed more like one of the guests. Alice had designed separate bedroom suites for herself and Charles and began to keep more and more to her own quarters. It did not help matters between them that when she gave birth to a son, Michael, two years after Diana, Charles knew the father was de Terrey, the charming decorator who had become her constant companion. Although he publicly acknowledged the boy as his own, he privately complained about her infidelity to close friends like Ingersoll and Dahl. (The baby had been conceived while Marsh was away on a long trip to California.) Alice, who was at best an indifferent mother, entrusted her children's care to the ever-efficient Rudolf and his wife, Margaret, who over time became devoted surrogate parents.

Alice held court at Longlea much the same way Marsh did in Washington, gathering her own salon and inviting the sort of gay, lively crowd she preferred. She loved to dance, knew all the steps, and liked partners like Lyndon Johnson, who were tall and good on their feet. Alice had a taste for champagne, which she freely indulged. A great deal of alcohol was consumed at Longlea, a disproportionate amount by its owners. Drinks accompanied every meal, beginning with breakfast, and punctuated every activity, from an afternoon ride to a dip in the pool, setting a hardworking pace for guests. Charles kept up his end, despite having been diagnosed with diabetes, which he controlled with medication, but the result was that he sometimes crashed early. Alice's parties tended to go well into the night and could get pretty wild. Long after Charles had retired to his bed, she would still be playing Gershwin tunes on the phonograph and looking for trouble. "She took on the privileges of a great beauty, and was very self-serving and demanding," said Antoinette. "She was a real courtesan. She knew what she was doing."

Inevitably, more than one man in Marsh's close circle of friends would become entangled with Alice. It was hardly surprising that among them was Lyndon Johnson, the brash, big-eared up-and-comer from the hill country outside Austin. Johnson was twenty-one years younger than Marsh and had a boundless enthusiasm and confident swagger that left little doubt that he was going far. He was a kid on the make, and his drive, ambition, and sense of mission were such that he could electrify a room with his presence. He was also an unabashed womanizer, given to crassly bragging about his masculinity and sexual prowess—the kind of man for whom Alice must have been an irresistible challenge. The strong physical attraction between Lyndon and Alice was undeniable, though they were so discreet in public that not even their closest friends could pinpoint exactly when in the late 1930s their relationship blossomed into a full affair.

Alice must have known that Marsh would see their affair as a double betrayal. He regarded Johnson as the most promising of his political protégés and, according to George Brown, another of LBJ's early backers, "loved Lyndon like a son." Marsh had known Johnson only since 1936, when he had phoned a mutual friend, Welly Hopkins, and asked him to arrange an introduction to the dark horse candidate from Austin's Tenth Congressional District. Johnson, who was then twenty-nine and a former schoolteacher ridiculed by the opposition as a "young, young man," was running for Congress on a New Deal platform. Marsh, who had a nose for talent, immediately recognized a man of destiny when he saw one and not only decided to back Johnson in the race but saw to it that Austin's two major dailies, the *American* and the *Statesman*, also backed him. Johnson ended up winning a ten-way runoff, and the following year he headed to Washington, in no small part thanks to Marsh's editorial support. "Marsh was effective because he put the power of his papers behind him openly," said Hopkins, who, although married to Alice's close friend and cousin, suspected that the high-rolling tycoon had helped Johnson only as a way of extending his own influence. "I think that Lyndon was smart enough to see through Marsh all the time. I don't think Marsh was ever out-thinking Lyndon a damn bit."

From then on Marsh inserted himself into Johnson's life, generously providing funds for his campaigns, as well as cash for his private needs, and offering advice on everything from political strategy and publicity to proper health care. What may have begun as a cynical attempt to influence politics evolved into a sincere friendship, with Marsh, in his self-appointed role as political godfather, doing everything in his power to help the junior congressman achieve his ambition of one day being elected to the highest office in the land. When Johnson arrived in Washington, Marsh offered to help ease his way and introduced the unknown freshman to powerful behind-the-scenes figures, arranged meetings with wealthy financiers and publishers, and, according to Martin Anderson, publisher of the *Orlando Sentinel,* who had once been the beneficiary of the same treatment, "tutored and groomed" Johnson during his "swaddling days" in politics.

At one point, Marsh even offered to bankroll Johnson for life. In 1940, Johnson was on vacation with Marsh and George Brown at the ritzy Greenbrier Hotel in West Virginia and had been worrying out loud about the difficulties of managing on an elected official's salary. Marsh, with typical bravado, offered to solve the problem with a simple wave of his hand. He proposed a deal that would make LBJ a millionaire many times over: Marsh had some oil wells that were already operating and pumping money out of the ground, and he would work it so Johnson could buy them for next to nothing, in exchange for a share in the future profits. Marsh had already passed a real estate deal Johnson's way, selling his wife nineteen acres on Lake Austin for $8,000, which he knew was in an area slated for development and would skyrocket in value; Lady Bird Johnson later sold the waterfront property for $330,000. This is to say nothing of the money-losing Fort Worth radio station he had talked Johnson into buying, arguing, "Some day it will be worth $3 million." Marsh's oil wells would eventually be worth far more than that and promised to make Johnson financially independent for the rest of his life. But looking ahead to the Senate and possibly the presidency, Johnson decided to steer clear of the oil interests, saying, "It could kill me politically."

There was no ignoring Charles Marsh, and Johnson was careful to always humor his loyal friend, seeking his counsel and deferring to his opinions, so that Marsh felt like a member of his team. If in private Johnson often dismissed Marsh's proposals as impractical or far-fetched, he never refused his calls or forgot the debt he owed the man who had helped launch his career. Recalling Marsh as "one of the most interesting human beings" she had ever met, Lady Bird, who was prim and painfully shy but a dedicated political spouse, wrote that "Charles had what I truly believe was an affectionate interest in enlarging Lyndon's life:

> He exuded what I can only describe as a life force—and even that is insufficient. He did a lot to educate Lyndon, and quite coincidentally me, about the breadth and strength of the rest of the world. . . . This was when the war clouds were gathering in Europe and we did not know how to appraise Hitler—what it meant in the long term to the American people.

When it came to Alice, whose Marlin, Texas, family she had known since childhood, Lady Bird held her tongue, as usual, subordinating her interests to her husband's. Her objective, she once confided to a journalist, was to make herself the "perfect wife." She spent many hours at Longlea in silent study of Alice, listening to her talk of music, literature, and politics, and was awed by her intellect, strong opinions, taste, and sense of style. It was a feminine confidence as foreign to her as her hostess's glittering emeralds and satin gowns. Alice was intimidating—"She's so tall and blonde she looks like a Valkyrie," she once observed—but if she ever sensed that Alice was also a threat, Lady Bird was too gracious to let on, acknowledging only that "she, too, helped 'educate' Lyndon and me, particularly about music and a more elegant lifestyle than he and I spent our early days enjoying."

Alice's illicit affair with Lyndon Johnson continued for years. While her marriage to Marsh seemed halfhearted at best and encompassed many partners, her passion for Lyndon was something deeper. Alice took a keen interest in politics dating back to her days in the Texas legislature, and even Marsh's political cronies acknowledged her instincts. Wallace liked to use her as a sounding board because she had the same kind of idealistic streak he did, and, as he put it, "seems to be the only person with enough imagination to know what I'm talking about." She recognized Johnson's potential early on and encouraged Marsh to use his newspapers to support his candidacy. When Johnson ran afoul of George Brown's hard-driving brother, Herman, during his first run for Congress, it was Alice who proposed the compromise that put an end to the hostilities. Instead of knocking heads over a condemned piece of land, she suggested divvying it up, "give Herman the dam and let Lyndon have the land," neatly avoiding a fight that could have prematurely ended Johnson's career. As Brown later conceded, she had "quite a bit of horse sense—for a girl."

Johnson may have won Alice's heart when he came to the rescue of Erich Leinsdorf, her young Jewish musician from Vienna, whom she had invited to stay with her when he had finished his engagement at the Met in the spring of 1938. Leinsdorf had been at Longlea only a short time when it suddenly came to him "with a terrific shock" that he had never received a reply to his application to extend his visa, and the temporary one he had been issued was due to expire in a week. He confided his problem to his hosts, and the next morning, even though it was a Sunday, Marsh drove him directly to Washington and took him to the suite he maintained at the Mayflower Hotel. Marsh had phoned Johnson, who met them at the hotel and listened "impassively" to the musician's problem. The young congressman, Leinsdorf observed, "treated Charles with the informal courtesy behooving a youngster toward an older man to whom he is in debt."

Johnson was happy to be of help, not only because of what he felt he owed Marsh but because he relished the opportunity to use his influence to save the talented young man from Nazi persecution. He also knew Alice held Leinsdorf in high regard and was worried that the numbers of Jewish refugees seeking asylum from Nazism would make it difficult for him to remain in the United States. "You have a great art and genius to console, uplift and support," Johnson told Leinsdorf, assuring him that he would do everything he could on his behalf. The next day Johnson called to say he was on the job and had made some progress: while the Immigration Department had rejected Leinsdorf's application, it seemed that as a result of a clerical oversight the paperwork had never been put through, and Johnson was able to use his influence to have the authorities change the customary seven-day grace period to six months.

Johnson, at Alice's urging, then set to work having Leinsdorf's status changed to that of a permanent resident. This took some doing, as it would require Leinsdorf to make a brief foray to Cuba to obtain the proper documentation. Johnson made all the necessary arrangements and pulled all the necessary strings, including having a staffer write an impassioned letter to the consul in Havana arguing something to the effect that "the United States had a holy mission to provide a peaceful haven for musical geniuses nervously exhausted from persecution and racial bias." Johnson, unaccompanied by Lady Bird, went to Longlea to personally deliver the young Austrian's letter and documents. As

Leinsdorf wrote in his memoir, that evening they all gathered on the terrace, and while sipping their fourth martini before dinner, listened as Johnson read aloud "his masterpiece of a letter."

Both Alice and Johnson took great pride in rescuing such a talented young musician. Leinsdorf had opened Johnson's eyes to the plight of refugees, and like Alice, who had been providing money to Jews fleeing Hitler, he began doing more on their behalf, eventually helping hundreds of Jewish refugees to reach safety in Texas through Cuba, Mexico, and other South American countries. Johnson also began making more solo visits to Longlea to see Alice, and not long after that they became lovers. They went to great lengths to keep their affair secret, sometimes even arranging to meet at her apartment in New York. They were almost found out one weekend when Johnson left the New York phone number with John Connolly, one of his aides, telling him not to give it out unless it was an emergency. Later, when Marsh called looking for Lyndon and insisted on speaking to him, Connolly, who was ignorant of the romantic triangle, relented and gave him the number. That Monday when Johnson saw Connolly, he reportedly told him of the narrow escape, saying, "Man, you almost ruined me."

Marsh was bound to find out eventually. Alice had confided in her sister Mary Louise, as well as her cousin Alice, who was married to Welly Hopkins. Various members of Marsh's staff, including the Kolingers and Claudia Haines, had observed them together one too many times and drawn their own conclusions. Although Marsh had finally extracted his divorce in 1938, he had not succeeded in getting Alice to the altar, though it was not for want of trying. "He was asking her and asking her and asking her to marry him," her sister Mary Louise recalled. If Alice was holding out hope that Lyndon would leave his wife for her, she underestimated his ambition. A divorce would have killed any chance he ever had for high office and was out of the question. In 1939–40 Johnson was eyeing a Senate seat, and his hopes of advancing his political career already looked doubtful in light of his close identification with Roosevelt, who by the seventh year of his presidency was facing an erosion in popularity and opposition to his running for an unprecedented third term.

Alice also misunderstood one of the most fundamental tenets of Johnson's worldview—loyalty. It was one thing to fool around with another man's mistress, quite another to wreck his home and carry off the mother of his children. The political society they moved in regarded adultery as no one's business—the lure of flesh was one of the things men sometimes succumbed to, along with liquor and cards. Divorce was something altogether different. It was a public affront to the rules of the church and conventions of society. Divorce was dishonor. According to Johnson's code, that would be an unforgivable transgression. "Everything was subordinate to loyalty," said Luther Jones, who worked for Johnson in his first term. "You must be loyal. That dominated Johnson's thinking." For Johnson, the shame was not in the affair, it was in being foolishly indiscreet. He had behaved like a cad and had gotten caught.

Marsh knew Alice had been unfaithful in the past, but to the extent that he was a possessive man, with an outsize ego, her involvement with Johnson infuriated him. He never revealed what tipped him off, but Antoinette recalled Claudia telling her about an angry confrontation between Marsh and Johnson late one night at Longlea. After loudly berating Johnson, Marsh threw him out. The next morning the chastened congressman returned to apologize and vowed to keep his hands off the lady of the house. The two men picked up their friendship where they had left off, and nothing more was ever said on the subject. "They didn't let her come between them," said Antoinette, noting that her father and Johnson, despite some memorable ups and downs, remained very close. "Men in power like that don't give a damn about women," she added. "They were not that important in the end. They treated women like toys. That's just the way it was."

Marsh chose to overlook Alice's lapse and married her in early 1940. He then adopted little Diana, endowing his natural child with the name that was rightfully hers. The exchange of vows did nothing for their relationship, which soured almost immediately. Marsh made no bones about his troubled marriage. He had few secrets from his close male friends and talked obsessively about women and sex, often in shockingly crude terms. "At a formal dinner, he was as apt to discuss his erections as he was to expound on Einstein's theory," recalled Ingersoll. "His non-stop conversation varied from the profane to the profound, and there is no evidence that he ever considered anything about himself secret."

For a long time, Marsh truly loved Alice and tried to make her happy, showering her with gifts and jewels, including a quarter-of-a-million-dollar necklace of emeralds fit for royalty. But in the end, Alice did not want to be kept. The age difference was too great, and no amount of expensive finery could prevent her from straying.* Complicating matters no end, her sister, Mary Louise, had some notion that she had become indispensable to Marsh and might succeed her libidinous sibling. Charles had other ideas. Not one to waste time on regret, he was already making plans to exit his second marriage much the same way as he had his first, with a fait accompli. He would free himself from both Glass sisters, he told Ingersoll, confiding his design for domestic tranquillity, and in their stead promote his pretty typist. "I will make that little Claudia my secretary *and* my mistress," he declared triumphantly.

By the time Dahl became a regular at Longlea in the summer of 1943, Charles and Alice barely made any pretense of being a couple. She lived in the country and had her apartment in New York. Marsh

---

*According to Johnson biographer Robert Caro, Alice continued to secretly see Johnson even after he became senator. Their relationship finally ended as a result of their bitter disagreement over the Vietnam War, which she passionately opposed.

was spending weeks on his own at the R Street house and ventured only occasionally to Virginia, and then only armed with a battery of friends. On his first few visits to Longlea, Dahl was treated as a welcome distraction, and Alice enjoyed engaging him in her teasing badinage. He was Charles' pet, but he and Alice had rubbed along just fine until he incurred her wrath. According to Antoinette, Dahl made the mistake of rejecting Alice's advances late one night and was subsequently banned from Longlea: "He turned her down, and that was it."

As it turned out, that was the least of his housing problems that summer. Finding decent lodging in wartime Washington was a perpetual nightmare and required constant perseverance and ingenuity. Dahl had spent weeks searching for a new place, when in mid-July he heard through the rumor mill of a house in Georgetown that was unexpectedly available following a grisly murder and suicide. What made it all rather awkward was that the house on 35th Street was occupied by several young female researchers at the OSS, some of whom he knew in passing, including the murder victim, a Chicago debutante by the name of Rosemary Sidley, who had inherited part of the Horlick malted milk fortune. Her roommate, a beauty from the north shore of Boston named Barbara Wendell Soule, had told friends that she could never set foot there again. Dahl was determined to have the place for himself, but he was a bit too keen for some people's taste, and in the end his eagerness backfired and became the source of macabre amusement around town. "It is an incredible story," Mary Louise Patten wrote Joe Alsop, explaining that Sidley had been murdered by "an ardent suitor" named William Chandler, who was her boss as well as the married father of two:

> It was a dreadful thing, as they both worked in the O.S.S. and she
> was very attractive and much liked, and he had been pursuing her for
> months and she would have none of him. Finally one night he came

to see her and her tactful girl friends left her alone with her beau and
he proceeded to shoot her and then kill himself. I didn't know either
of them, but everyone else in Washington seems to have and you can
imagine the excitement caused locally. . . . To show you how desperate
the real estate situation has become, the day after the murder there
were a line of people waiting to see if the house was going to be in the
market for rent, including several of our friends who shall be nameless.
Anyway, the first person to get there was one Dahl.

By all accounts, he was in such a hurry to rent the house that he failed to notice that there were still bloodstains on the carpet, not to mention a bullet hole in the ceiling and one in the floor. When Dahl went back later to take a closer look, he was horrified. "This was too much for his Nordic sensitive temperament," wrote Patten. "He told me the other day that he gets up at six every day to think over the problems of the postwar world for two hours before breakfast without even a twinkle in his eye so you can [see] the type he is." It just so happened that Isaiah Berlin and his friend Ed Prichard, a brilliant New Deal attorney, were hunting for a new bachelor pad and suffered from none of Dahl's misgivings. Apparently Dahl confessed to Berlin that he had returned to the house and "sat in the twilight to see if ghosts would occur—which as a creative writer he would find disturbing to cope with." The ghosts duly appeared. "So he hastily rented the house to the unfeeling Berlin, who is calmly moving in," Patten reported, "and has asked me to find a good cheap plasterer for him and where he can buy an inexpensive rug of some darkish color!"

Dahl spent the last weeks of August getting his life back in order and renewing his attention to his work. He had received some disappointing news from Disney. In July, Walt wrote that they would no longer be proceeding with the *Gremlins* as a feature and were instead planning to put it out as an animated short, "because of its timely nature and the fact that it should be out now." The truth, however, was that the studio had run into too many complications with the copyright and the RAF restrictions and was getting cold feet. Walt admitted to feeling "a little apprehensive" about Clause 12 of the contract, which stated that the air attaché could make suggestions and that the British Air Ministry had final approval over the picture: "With the amount of money that is required to spend on a feature of this type we cannot be subjected to the whims of certain people, including yourself." With so much risk involved, he concluded, "it simply is not good business."

Dahl had gone to considerable pains to arrange a tour for a Disney film crew of the Royal Canadian Air Force stations in Ottawa, Dartmouth, and Nova Scotia, including having Spitfires flown in for a demonstration, but the reduced budget meant the trip would have to be scrapped. After a year of story conferences and bicoastal meetings, Dahl could tell the project was stalling. Walt ended on an upbeat note, reassuring Dahl that he would try to make a trip to Canada himself "to look things over," adding that they should "get together for a cocktail" when he was in New York the following month. A few weeks later, when he heard that Lord Stansgate of the Air Ministry had paid Walt a visit in Burbank, Dahl felt every reason to be optimistic. A fat packet of gremlin material had arrived from Stansgate, who asked Dahl to forward it to Disney. Dahl dashed off a quick note advising Walt to ignore the Air Ministry's research, as it would only confuse him, but adding that he was sending it along anyway as "I must comply with orders."

In August another of his short stories, "The Sword," was published in the *Atlantic*. He was beginning to earn a reputation as a skilled raconteur. "The Sword" was autobiographical in tone and was set in Dar es Salaam in the autumn of 1939, "when the German armies were already mustering on the Polish frontier and when the whole of Europe was boiling and heaving under the threat of war." It was a poignant tale of a young African houseboy who, in his excitement at the news that England was at war with Germany, took his master's silver scabbard off the sitting room wall and ran over to a rich German merchant's home and chopped off his head. It was also good Nazi-bashing propaganda, which was more in demand than ever. Once again, the author's note gave the grisly tale a thrilling and romantic overlay of verisimilitude, explaining that Dahl had in fact been in East Africa with the Shell Oil Company when war broke out.

He also managed to sell another fictional story, called "Katina," to *Ladies' Home Journal*. Evoking the chaotic last days of the RAF fighters in Greece in 1941, it tells the story of a little blond girl who is wounded during a German bombing attack on the village of Paramythia. Two off-duty RAF pilots, who had spent hours digging around the ruins for the wounded, find her and take her back to the doctor at their fighter squadron, located in a muddy field on the out-skirts of the village. After learning that her family is buried beneath the rubble, they make her the camp mascot, and in a few days' time she knows the nickname of every pilot there. When they are told to move to Argos, in a futile attempt to give cover to the retreating ground forces, she comes with them. And when the German Messer-schmitts spot their makeshift aerodrome and move in with guns blaz-ing, she runs out onto the airfield "raising her fists at the planes," and is mowed down. The story is simply told, almost crudely executed in places, but is nonetheless effective. Dahl's anger at the waste of human life is palpable when he describes how the pilot turned away from her body to the burning wreckage of his plane and "stood star-ing hopelessly into the flames as they danced around the engine and licked the metal of the wings."

Marsh was convinced that Dahl had the makings of a serious writer and that he should begin planning bigger projects and forging the re-lationships that could help his career after the war. He thought Dahl would benefit from talking to someone in the business, and since there was nothing he could not fix with a phone call, he contacted the New York publisher Curtice Hitchcock and invited him to Longlea. Marsh had come to know Hitchcock through Henry Wallace, as Hitchcock and his partner, Russell Lord, were in the process of publishing a collection of the vice president's speeches. Hitchcock and Dahl spent the weekend deep in conversation, and shortly thereafter Marsh received a letter from the publisher thanking him for his hospitality and adding, "I was greatly taken with your young Dahl and I think I have some ideas based on his stuff which might result in a good book."

Dahl sought to repay Marsh's kindness by helping him reestablish his personal relationship with the president and to return in the capacity as a confidential adviser, something he knew his American benefactor desired but seemed strangely unable or unwilling to initiate. They had discussed the matter at length that August while vacationing together at Marsh's cottage in Cape Cod, and Marsh had worried aloud about his close association with Wallace and had theorized that perhaps that was one reason for Roosevelt's apparent ambivalence toward him. After Charles returned to Washington on business, Dahl sent him a long letter analyzing his situation and advising him on the best recipe for "a return ticket." In a role reversal of sorts, he provided a list of pointers that might help Marsh get his foot in the door. He counseled the publishing tycoon that "the Great White Indian Chief" thought of him only "as a man who owns a few newspapers," that FDR had even said as much to Dahl during his visit to Hyde Park, and that it was up to Marsh, by force of his personality and ideas, to persuade the president that he could be a useful member of his brain trust. He cautioned Marsh that when he got in to to see the president he should make every effort to modify his usual loud, overbearing style, to take a more "gentle" approach, and after making a brief presentation to "just stop talking and listen to what he has to say."

Dahl recommended that Marsh try one of two approaches. The easiest would be to simply ask his friend Sumner Welles, Hull's deputy at the State Department, if as a favor he would broker a meeting with FDR. If Welles seemed at all reluctant, however, Marsh should tell him not to bother, because if he only went through the motions, nothing would ever come of it. The alternative was to write directly to the president himself, preferably not more than a line or two, saying only that he would like to see him personally on an important matter. This second approach, Dahl concluded, was preferable, as it had the virtue of being quick and direct and could be done the next day should he so choose: "It is neat and fast, not clumsy or blundering, but it requires a little courage. I don't know whether you have it. You might like to find out." On August 17 Marsh, seldom a man of few words, sent Dahl a brief note saying that he would be in touch in a day or two, adding, "Considering your age, your wisdom passeth all understanding." Weeks went by, however, and Dahl heard no more on the subject. Marsh's courage failed him, and no letter to FDR was ever sent.

Taking a page from his own playbook, Dahl had also done his best to ingratiate himself with Halifax, even filling in as one of his tennis four on the embassy court. Despite his bad back, Dahl was still a very strong player, and his reach was so long it was hard to get the ball by him. He hoped that in helping Halifax to crush the opposition, he might score a few points for himself. As the ambassador had one bad arm—he was born with an atrophied limb and no left hand—this was easier said than done. He had developed a method of serving that involved gripping the ball and racket in his one good hand, with which he would then toss and hit the ball in a swiftly executed series of motions. As this move required precision timing, it was less than reliable and resulted in a great many double faults. A devout Anglo-Catholic, Halifax disapproved of any form of swearing and instead would let out a low groan of disgust every time he missed his serve. Dahl often had to struggle to keep his composure at these strangled outbursts and, harder still, had to remember to stifle the stream of four-letter words that rose to his own lips when he netted the ball. It was because of Halifax's piety at least as much as his love of hunting that Churchill had reportedly nicknamed him "the Holy Fox." Dahl thought he could not have come up with a better moniker himself and made free use of it when alone with Marsh.

Throughout the summer, the war news had steadily improved. Allied forces were beginning to take the offensive, and July saw the fall of Mussolini and the capitulation of Italy. U.S. ships had scored a major victory in the Battle of Midway in the year before and had inflicted heavy losses on the Japanese fleet at Guadalcanal. Dahl was most interested in the air war: the British had made a series of massive raids on Hamburg over four nights, and by August 2 the bombers had killed an estimated 50,000 civilians and created firestorms that reduced whole sections of the city to charred ruins. Churchill and Roosevelt had met in Quebec, and it was impossible not to feel heartened by reports that the fighting in Italy would intensify to overcome the last of the German resistance. Victory finally seemed at hand. Dahl had gone about his spying chores diligently, collecting rumors and scraps for the intelligence reports, but without fretting too much about his future or the world's. To his friend Creekmore Fath, who was unaware of his intelligence connections, it seemed like Dahl was taking a well-deserved break from the war. "I think he was glad to be carefree. He had done his bit and that was it. He didn't feel he owed any more to his country. He was having fun."

THE WAR
IN WASHINGTON

In those days it was the fashion for diplomats to regard
intelligence officers as unprincipled ruffians. We returned the compliment by regarding the diplomats as
ceremonial and gutless.

—DAVID OGILVY, *Blood, Brains and Beer*

Bᴠ ᴛʜᴇ ꜰᴀʟʟ of 1943, Dahl was in serious trouble. The loudest
complaints came from British air chief marshal Welch, who
called him on the carpet, roaring that it had come to his attention that
the airman's "outside activities were irregular." Dahl was warned "not
to stick his nose out of the embassy," and that unless he took immediate notice, he would be leaving Washington. The air chief marshal
proceeded to take up the matter with Halifax, reportedly expressing his
view that Dahl was "a very intelligent young man" but in need of "military discipline." He recommended that Dahl be transferred abroad, the
sooner the better for all concerned. Making matters worse, as Dahl later

framed his predicament for Marsh, this particular air chief marshal, who occupied a large suite at the Shoreham Hotel in Washington, was unusually well connected in civilian life and, as he put it, consorted with "big people." Marsh was sympathetic, as always, and offered his help. He immediately placed a number of calls to friends with influence with the American authorities, but he reported back that there was a general reluctance to intervene in internal embassy affairs. If the ambassador agreed that Dahl should go, there was little anyone could do. It was all rather disheartening.

The British Embassy was considered a plum assignment, and the staff was composed of future "diplomatic stars," according to Peter Smithers, who served as assistant naval attaché from 1941 to 1943 and was a close friend of Ian Fleming's. "Washington was the key to the future of Britain. If at the end of a couple of weeks a new member of the Embassy team seemed not to 'get on' with the Americans, he would find himself unceremoniously bundled onto the next transport back to Britain." Ironically, Dahl's problem was not that he had run afoul of his American hosts; rather he was not a good team player and had failed to get on with his own crowd, or as he told it, "mainly [the] Air Chief Marshall." While the situation was not without its absurdities, it had dire consequences for him. "I fell far, as one is bound to, of the diplomatic people," Dahl recalled. "And I got kicked out of the embassy."

Faced with this new censure and given his spotty record, Dahl foresaw a grim future. Resigned to his fate, he scrambled to find a new post and unofficially took service as a British-Greek liaison in Cairo. Before beginning his new job, he was granted permission to take a quick trip to England to see his mother and sisters. He was still making final arrangements and packing his bags prior to leaving when a message came down from BSC headquarters in New York. "When Bill heard I was going to be kicked out, as he always heard, he had ears everywhere, you see, through all these people," recalled Dahl, "he sent word to me: 'Go home. You'll be contacted and you'll come back immediately for me.'"

Dahl was pinning his hopes on Stephenson. He knew he had made a first-class muddle of things at the embassy. It would take someone with a lot of pull to put things right. As much as he wanted to believe it, however, he feared that not even the Big Chief himself would be able to get him a reprieve. "I thought, well, if he can do that, he must be a bloody magician, because there are very important people sending me home."

He left Washington under a dark cloud. It was an ignominious end to his diplomatic career. Then there was the dreary, crowded transatlantic air crossing, with everyone squeezed into uncomfortable bucket seats. Although he was excited at the prospect of seeing his family again, as he neared England and Mother, doubts about his future left him feeling fidgety and anxious. Fortunately, he did not have to wallow in uncertainty for long. The BSC made contact almost as soon as he touched ground in London, and after some backstairs machinations that he hardly dared speculate about, he returned to his job at the British Embassy, with a promotion to boot. "I went home a squadron leader," he recalled, "and I was back in a week as a Wing Commander."*

To outsiders, it probably appeared that he had received a well-deserved promotion, as he returned with the higher rank. Perhaps that was the impression the BSC intended to create. Dahl, for one, certainly

---

*In interviews after the war, Dahl always maintained that he was "kicked out of the embassy" and, thanks to Stephenson, returned as a wing commander. In recent years, however, this claim has been disputed. According to the biographer Jeremy Treglown, neither his RAF file nor the air force list had any record of the promotion. The RAF admits there has been some confusion about Dahl's service record, but Alan Thomas of the Air Historical Branch at Northolt confirms Dahl was appointed wing commander in 1943. In any case, Dahl was not telling tall tales, as has sometimes been implied. As Dahl was often vague about exact dates, and the records are not clear, it is hard to tell if he received this "promotion" in the fall of 1943 or several months later, after a subsequent trip to England.

enjoyed the impression it made on the air chief marshal who was responsible for giving him the sack. His first night back in Washington, Dahl attended a diplomatic function and spotted his old nemesis among the crowd. As soon as the air chief marshal saw Dahl, his face turned crimson, and he strode across the room and confronted the airman: "What the hell are you doing here?" Dahl said: "I'm afraid you'll have to ask Sir William Stephenson." At the mention of the BSC chief's name, the air chief marshal went even darker purple and walked away. "That shows the power of the man," recalled Dahl, relishing the moment. "The Air Chief Marshall was struck absolutely dumb. Couldn't say a word, and as a matter fact, wasn't able to do anything about it."

On his return to Washington, Dahl worked primarily for Bill Stephenson. He had looked forward to meeting the spy chief, if only to thank him in person for bringing him back to the United States, but he had yet to be honored with an invitation to the BSC headquarters. In fact, in all this time, despite everything that had transpired, he had never once had any direct contact with the elusive intelligence chief. For that matter, he had never been given any precise instructions as to how he was supposed to proceed in his new capacity as "one of theirs." Stephenson was confident that his boys were clever and would work it out. "He never outlined any role to anyone," recalled Dahl. "When he hired you he expected you to know what to think, what your role was going to be." It was more or less understood that he would carry on in his ostensible role as assistant air attaché at the British Embassy and use his official post to continue his "discreet indiscreet conversations" with his principal sources. On one issue, however, he was quite clear: no small part of these conversations would deal with the postwar air policies of the two countries, and he would henceforth be coordinating his efforts with Lord Beaverbrook.

While Dahl was cooling his heels in London, awaiting word on his future, Stephenson had arranged for him to meet with his friend Lord

Beaverbrook with the idea that the two men might be of help to each other. Beaverbrook was another small, tenacious Canadian tycoon and had risen to become England's wealthiest newspaper publisher and a powerful politician with ambitions to becoming the next prime minister. When Churchill ascended, he had to satisfy himself with playing second fiddle, agreeing to become minister of aircraft production (MAP) and take on the urgent task of rebuilding the country's beleaguered air force. The sixty-year-old Fleet Street dynamo rose to the challenge, overnight turning his ornate London mansion, Stornoway House, into the MAP headquarters and moving quickly to repair damaged aircraft and engines, turning around a desperate state of affairs in six weeks. Beaverbrook drove his senior staff with the same demonic energy he had once applied to his editors, sharing Stephenson's frustration at Whitehall's plodding pace and crippling departmentalism, which were impeding the war effort. As a result of his successful campaign—promoted endlessly in his own newspapers—Beaverbrook became a hero to weary Battle of Britain pilots (of which his son was one) and the factory workers who built their machines, who recognized that his contribution could be measured in lives saved. Stephenson, a former fighter pilot, was an unabashed admirer of his achievement: "But for the tremendous pressure that Beaverbrook exerted in his dynamic way, who could say whether the pitifully few aircraft that were flyable at the end of the battle in the air might not have been a minus zero force?"

Stephenson was so impressed with Beaverbrook that he even lobbied to have him replace Halifax as ambassador, but his efforts came to nothing. After a tempestuous year, having significantly boosted aircraft production, Beaverbrook resigned from the ministry for health reasons. He cited asthma as the cause, though his fifteen-hour days and fearful temper—he reportedly threatened to quit fourteen times in eleven months—may finally have gotten the better of him. He remained a member of Churchill's War Cabinet and was named minister of state, a title invented specially for him that was as vague and ill-defined as his responsibilities. After Hitler's attack on Russia June 22, 1941, and with America still dithering on the sidelines, Churchill called Beaverbrook back to action, this time making him minister of supply. He was soon working hand in hand with the American millionaire Averell Harriman, Roosevelt's emissary to London, not only on creating a supply line between their two countries but doing everything in their power to keep Communist Russia afloat.

In June 1943 Stephenson had asked Beaverbrook to help the BSC in its efforts "to neutralize" a particularly hostile American publisher named Roy Howard, who was president of the large chain of Scripps-Howard newspapers. The BSC's previous attempts to "tame" the politically ambitious publisher had failed, and he remained as vigorously anti-British and isolationist as ever. Stephenson decided that its best course of action was to flatter Howard, whom he regarded as a vain, overdressed little man, and he suggested that Beaverbrook should extend him a personal invitation to visit England as his guest. Howard accepted, and he, Beaverbrook, Stephenson, Donovan, and Harriman flew to London in Lord Beaverbrook's private plane. Apparently the visit went swimmingly, because shortly after his return to the United States, Howard sounded far more conciliatory and remarked to a BSC source that "most Americans, including myself, are now out of patience with criticism of British internal management."

By November 3, 1943, when Stephenson sent Dahl to see Beaverbrook in Whitehall at Gwydyr House, just a short walk from Downing Street, "the Beaver" was in fighting form. Churchill had made him Lord Privy Seal, charged with making sure that America, with its superior power and resources, did not corner the market in highly lucrative postwar air routes. Worried that the Americans were "grabbing the air traffic of the world," Beaverbrook worked assiduously to curry favor with Adolf Berle, the State Department negotiator. At one point, under the mistaken assumption that Berle was Catholic, Beaverbrook sent him a rare first edition of Cardinal Newman's *Occasional Hymns*. Berle responded sarcastically, replying that British intelligence had clearly goofed and that if he ever converted, "several generations of dissenting ancestors would turn in their graves." The British government was so concerned about the deteriorating air talks that it decided to create the War Cabinet Committee of Post-War Civil Air Transport, composed of leading members of the War Cabinet and chaired by Beaverbrook. It convened for the first time on November 11, 1943, and continued to meet on an almost weekly basis for the next fifteen months.

As Dahl was well versed in the American position, his report met with great interest. His information whetted Beaverbrook's appetite for more. Beaverbrook had a similarly low opinion of Lord Halifax's performance as ambassador to the United States, and believing the air attaché could be a useful presence in Washington, he agreed to put in a word on his behalf. Dahl, on his return to his post, would do everything he could to advance Beaverbrook's agenda with the Americans with an eye to reaching an agreement. Beaverbrook thought that national airlines should be allowed to fly any routes they wished, and that with proper regulation a workable compromise could be struck. While the old-empire types in the Air Ministry were affronted by the mere suggestion that America would have traffic rights on British routes, Beaverbrook was willing to be more flexible and was in favor of making "large concessions." Any general navigation agreement would have to rest on agreement between the United States and the British and the Commonwealth of Nations; practically all other countries—with the possible exception of Russia—would then accede. British and U.S. aviation experts had already agreed that without such a general understanding in place, neither side would negotiate exclusive or discriminatory pacts against the other.

As soon as he got back to town, Dahl went to Marsh's and gave him a full report. Marsh liked and respected the hardheaded British press lord, admired the publishing empire he had constructed, and told Dahl that with his forceful personality, there was little Beaverbrook could not accomplish. All in all, he was not a bad fellow to hitch his wagon to. Dahl, assured that he now answered to a higher authority than Halifax, took up his diplomatic duties with new enthusiasm and vigorously inserted himself in the ongoing debate over the postwar use of the American-constructed air bases on British possessions. As Marsh later summarized his activities in a letter to Wallace: "He believes that the fifty-fifty post war use . . . is a natural answer and should be offered voluntarily by the British. He has been working effectively with Beaverbrook, seeking to have Beaverbrook initiate the idea." Marsh continued:

> He [Dahl] sees that England's interest in global post war Air must be cooperation on a world basis. He believes in open decisions, openly arrived at. He particularly believes British-American-Russian Air interests are not conflicting, that each of course, should control Air over its own territory for interior and policing functions, but that the general policy of the greatest good to greatest number should be the over-all idea. He simply wants the maximum development of Air power for the human race.

Antoinette Marsh noticed a change in Dahl's demeanor. "He was very serious about his job [with the BSC]," she recalled. "He dedicated himself to it. He was at heart a big British patriot, but he did not go around waving the flag like some people did in those days. He was much too sophisticated for that."

Dahl fell back into his old routine of eating lunch regularly with Marsh and swapping political rumors and gossip: who was up or down in FDR's administration, who was out to get who and why. Now that he was getting to know some of his colleagues within the BSC, Dahl occasionally invited British intelligence operatives to join them. By the end of 1943, British concerns had begun to shift from doubts about America's commitment to fully prosecuting the war to the realization that there were powerful individuals and geopolitical groups in the United States who were supporting England's cause for postwar political and financial gain. Much of their attention that fall was focused on the deteriorating talks between the Americans and the British over international air policies.

Marsh argued that the initiative for the negotiations had been transferred to New York banking interests, and he claimed there was a close tie-up between General Breton B. Somervell, who commanded the Service of Supply, and Bernard Baruch. Taking a page straight out of the old Gould-Vanderbilt railroad tactics, Marsh believed Baruch was in bed with Wall Street moneymen and entrepreneurs like Juan Terry Trippe, the ambitious forty-four-year-old president and founder of Pan American Airways, who were greedily eyeing the future of civil aviation and wanted all the business for themselves. The press—particularly the Luce publications *Time, Life,* and *Fortune*—wrote admiringly of Trippe, who was invariably referred to as "America's arch strategist of foreign airways," and even savvy members of the administration fell sway to the legend of romantic pioneering that attached itself to the great Pan Am enterprise, so that some liked to think of it as America's "chosen instrument." Marsh distrusted Trippe, who was known as a ruthless competitor even by the standards of the relatively youthful, rough-and-tumble airline industry. He had almost single-handedly led his airline's rapid expansion into five continents and was suspected by some critics of carrying on a "high and devious diplomacy," preaching the patriotic function of building air bases in South America for the hemisphere's defense, while privately calculating their future benefit to his corporation's bottom line. "There will always be wars," Trippe maintained. "We must not just give things away for nothing. We must know our interests in the future as well as the British do."

According to Marsh, Trippe and his team of iron-willed monopolists wanted to get rid of British competition and "let their hearts bleed" about imperialism and oppressed subjects whenever they could. Pan Am already had the inside track over the other numerous American aviation interests and was working to make sure that when the bell rang they had a commanding position in the skies and would be the ones enjoying air sovereignty. Dahl, who favored free competition and worldwide freedom of transit, felt Marsh's appraisal of the situation was probably accurate and believed the scope of international aviation was far too great to be trusted to any single group or pool of interests.

An increasingly sensitive political issue before Congress was whether American foreign aviation would be in the hands of a monopoly company or divided among different commercial airline companies. Pan Am was, or already thought of itself as, the American air industry and had been very successful in making its case for monopoly ownership and control. Trippe and company wanted to seize the tremendous postwar assets of the government, namely the engine works and patents. They wanted a minimum of government regulation on the industry and a maximum of government protection through subsidies, policy, and pressure. There was plenty of support for the so-called New York plan among private financiers in London, who opposed the government control imposed after the blitz. As one of Marsh's London sources reported: "Entrenched position for the American private control plan post war is growing very rapidly. Berle's stature in the State Department is growing very rapidly. Over here we do not see how post war Air can be handled except by the official Governments of Russia, Great Britain, and the United States. But with Russia left out and American

Government policy being dictated by private interests we do not know where we are at."

Marsh did not fault Beaverbrook for the way things were unfolding, but he felt it was possible that as "a financial operator" he was naturally inclined toward private enterprise, and that these considerations may have distracted him from the "global outlook" with which the negotiations had opened. As usual Marsh was full of good ideas and leads that Dahl and his colleagues could follow up on in order to find out why the talks were bogging down. To show their gratitude for his help, at the end of one lunch Dahl and a fellow BSC agent "let it slip" that the president was unhappy with Admiral William Leahy, his chief of staff, and was planning to get rid of him. Marsh seemed inordinately pleased with this scoop, and Dahl was certain he would go home and straightaway telephone Wallace.

At the end of September, Dahl arranged a chaste lunch with Clare Luce, the great American expert in postwar air policy, and her husband, hoping to sound them out on a variety of topics. The congresswoman, while never admitting any fault, seemed to regret her "globaloney" speech and implied it had been "a mistake." She had apparently attracted strong support from isolationist groups—particularly after a glib put-down of the New Deal suggestions for global planning as "Dazzle-Dust"—which she said had never been her intention and which she had quickly disowned. After the heated controversy that had followed, she had been forced to retreat somewhat from her original position and was obliged to say that she hoped the British and the United Nations might come to fair agreements. Mrs. Luce made a point of heaping praise on Wallace, though the *Time* publisher was noticeably more reserved. Henry Luce knew that with the presidential election only a year away, and with Roosevelt possibly seeking an unprecedented fourth term, the controversial vice president had a rough road ahead of him. (Luce no doubt also knew that his magazine intended to throw its support behind FDR's old friend House Speaker Sam Rayburn.) When informed later by Marsh that Mrs. Luce had spoken very highly of him at lunch with the British air attaché, Wallace knew better than to believe the Republican mouthpiece had moderated her views. He told Marsh that Mrs. Luce was up to her old tricks and "had a purpose in talking to Dahl that way."

Marsh agreed. To his way of thinking, Clare Boothe Luce was a brassy interloper who had never had an original thought. She had once been "Baruch's girl," and he quoted a well-known Washington vulgarian to the effect that "Clare does not pee without asking Barney." Baruch, who liked to call himself an "adviser to presidents," with all the condescension that implied, was Clare's personal "brain trust," and her view of the world was cribbed from the Baruch view. Moreover, according to Marsh, one of Clare's biggest supporters during her first run for Congress was Sam Pryor, a vice president at Pan Am who worked for Trippe—both of them were Yale men, like her husband—which helped place her "globaloney" speech in its proper context. This was also why *Time* correspondents all flew Pan Am. Pryor was her Greenwich, Connecticut, neighbor and a wealthy patron of the Republican Party, and like many conservatives he disapproved of Wallace's advocacy of "internationalism" and efforts to spread the New Deal around the world. There was little doubt that Pryor had coached the congresswoman (a little spy reported having seen him delivering packets of Pan Am propaganda to her hotel room), which accounted for her sudden erudition in matters of aviation and her surprisingly sharp attack on Wallace. As always, this exhaustive reading of the tea leaves was Marsh at his best and the reason Dahl continued to consult him at every turn.

Keeping a close watch on Wallace in an election year involved a lot of nanny work and kept Dahl hopping. The British regarded the vice president as a growing political problem and wanted reports on all his activities and poll results. Adding to their grave misgivings about his postwar views, and their impatience with his frequent attacks on British imperialism and especially on Churchill, was the fact that Wallace's public image was increasingly becoming a handicap for FDR. Over the summer, Wallace had become embroiled in an ugly public brawl with Jesse Jones, the secretary of commerce, who ran the Reconstruction Finance Corporation (RFC), which shared authority over export and import licensing prerogatives with the State Department and several other wartime agencies. Wallace, as usual staking out the moral high ground, wanted the confusing division of powers to be clarified and demanded "clear-cut authority" for the Board of Economic Warfare (BEW), so it could carry out its war work effectively, provide loans to impoverished countries, and not be hampered by waste and inefficiency. Wallace was dedicated to bringing about economic and social development in Latin America, long exploited by American business, which might prepare the whole area for participation as equals in postwar regional and global organizations. He believed that the United States had to align itself with forces of democracy everywhere and had a responsibility to foster change, which in his view was the main purpose of the war.

Wallace's insistence on having the upper hand set off a bitter internal turf battle within the administration, arousing the opposition of Secretary of State Cordell Hull, who did not appreciate the vice president's intrusion into foreign policy, as well as Jesse Jones. Two of the most powerful conservatives in Washington, both disagreed with Wallace's political and social objectives. Hull complained that the political changes Wallace had in mind for Latin America might lead to revolution and constituted too much interference. Exacerbating tensions, Wallace and Jones were old rivals and had vied for the vice-presidential nomination at the last convention. Jones stubbornly defended his domain, and he and his bankers dug in, intentionally dragging their feet on loans and paperwork so as to impede the BEW's progress, making it impossible for the board to secure loans, acquire strategic materials, and acquire the necessary funding to aid underdeveloped nations in Latin America. Before long, allegations of bad faith and political smears of all kinds were being hurled back and forth between the heads of various federal agencies faster than the newspapers could print them. As the accusations escalated, the attacks became more personal, culminating in Wallace charging Jones with intentionally "hamstringing bureaucracy" and causing delays in a vital program, and Jones countercharging that Wallace had crossed the line by calling him "a traitor."

The protracted public feud created, in the words of Robert Sherwood, "an alarming sense of disunity and incompetence in very high places" and infuriated the president. On July 15 Roosevelt had finally had enough: he sent Wallace and Jones identical letters essentially relieving them of their war jobs and informing them that the BEW had been abolished and its myriad responsibilities, along with several RFC agencies, were being consolidated in the newly created Office of Economic Warfare, to be headed by Leo T. Crowley, a Wisconsin Democrat. Jones immediately declared himself the victor, and the press speculated that Wallace's firing marked the end of his political future. Wallace bore his punishment stoically, confining his public response to one sentence: "In wartime no one should question the overall wisdom of the Commander in Chief."

Speculation about whether or not FDR would run again in 1944, and how much Wallace's missteps had hurt his chances of remaining on the Democratic ticket, dominated the editorial pages and journals of opinion. By fall tempers had cooled considerably, and Roosevelt and Wallace were back on cordial terms, but his position was seen as tenuous at best. Wallace, with constant encouragement from Marsh, hoped that "the war in Washington" (as headline writers had dubbed the feud) could be put behind him and that he could begin to build support for his nomination.

Marsh was convinced FDR would seek a fourth term. FDR had also been slow to commit himself to running for a third time in 1940—it had never been done before—and there had been the same swirling rumors then that he was tired and unwell. Marsh told Wallace of a remark made by the president's son Elliott: "Pop has tried for twenty-five years to become president and he is going to keep on being president as long as he can." To a practical thinker like Marsh, the challenge was to make sure Wallace was still the one sitting next to the throne at the convention. Marsh knew Wallace was feeling uncertain and worried that most of FDR's close advisers were against him. To bolster his confidence, Marsh recounted a conversation that his friend Ralph Ingersoll had had with Mrs. Roosevelt at the end of October, during which she described the vice president in very positive terms, saying, "Henry Wallace has come out in the last year. He is showing signs of definite leadership. That pleases me."

Not surprisingly, in early November, British intelligence in Washington received word that the prime minister wanted a fresh check on the progress of the 1944 elections. Churchill wanted Roosevelt to run and win, but above all he did not want any surprises. As Dahl told Marsh, it was a safe bet that if the old man was asking, something was in the wind. In one of his many multipage memos to Wallace, Marsh reported that there was "some activity in the British Embassy extending to the New York office of British Intelligence seeking to determine Roosevelt's intentions regarding a fourth term." After checking with his own New York contacts, Marsh wrote Wallace:

The supposition is that Republican sources near Willkie may have sold British political Intelligence at New York the proposition that FDR might not stand fourth term if war is being concluded in Europe, and that Willkie deserves more attention. The Dewey statement favoring Anglo-American collaboration may have been loosely connected because it is obvious [sic] that uncertainty regarding FDR which would

---

cause British judgment to cover and contact Dewey and Willkie with increasing care.

For his part, Dahl needed to keep his superiors informed about the various contenders and track their respective odds. It was a wide field: on the Democratic side, there was Roosevelt, followed by Wallace, the former governor of Indiana Paul McNutt, James Byrnes of South Carolina, and Supreme Court justice William O. Douglas. On the Republican side there was Willkie, Dewey, Governor John Bricker of Ohio, and Senator Robert Taft, also of Ohio. The polls showed Roosevelt was more popular than Dewey, and Dewey more popular than Willkie. Of even more pressing concern was if FDR was up to it, who would be his running mate? Possible candidates included Wallace, Byrnes, Douglas, Rayburn, and Senator Harry Truman of Missouri. Wallace still had Roosevelt's tacit support, along with that of the party rank and file, but he was regarded as an extremist by so many senior congressional leaders that it was only a matter of time before they started pressuring FDR to dump him.

At the same time Dahl was monitoring Wallace's political temperature, he was supposed to continue cultivating Marsh, as well as other leading newspaper publishers. He needed to maintain their goodwill, as well as close links with their reporters and columnists, so he would be the first to hear if and when the president's loyalty to Wallace showed any signs of weakening. He was always hurrying off to press lunches at the Carlton, where half of Washington conducted its daily business, to drinks with Pearson at the men's bar of the Mayflower Hotel, and then on to the R Street house in time to catch the vice president paying his evening call. It was all grist for the mill.

To spare his feelings, Dahl may have been less than candid with Marsh about the extent of the anti-Wallace sentiment in the official British community. The vice president's infamous pamphlet, "Our Job in the Pacific," authored with the help of two State Department aides, John Carter Vincent and Owen Lattimore, was set to be published in the spring of 1944 by the very leftist Institute of Pacific Relations. It had deeply offended Churchill, as well as senior British officials in Washington. Thanks to Dahl's early interception of the document, British intelligence agents were already busy snooping around the institute, looking for any evidence that could be used to discredit it, as well as scouring the backgrounds of Vincent and Lattimore. As the breach took place on his turf, Stephenson went a step further. "I came to regard Wallace as a menace," he stated later, "and I took action to ensure that the White House was aware that the British government would view with concern Wallace's appearance on the ticket at the 1944 presidential elections." As usual, Stephenson's message was delivered to the White House by Ernest Cuneo, the trusted go-between, who had recently moved to New York and taken an apartment at the Dorset, the same building where Stephenson occupied the penthouse.

In the meantime, as one of the agents closest to Wallace, Dahl had his hands full. Rumors were rife about the existence of a group of letters written by Wallace while he was still a follower of the Russian mystic Roerich, which seemed to indicate that he received guidance on government policies from the spirit world. The so-called guru letters had surfaced at the end of the last campaign and fallen into the hands of the newspaper publisher Paul Block. The Democrats had managed to stop them from coming out by threatening to use a lot of dirt they had dug up on Willkie, so the letters remained under wraps, but they were still in the possession of the Republicans. Whispers around town had it that this was why the party could not dare consider Wallace for vice president again. Jonathan Daniels, a member of Roosevelt's palace guard, got an earful over dinner one night that August from Beanie Baldwin's wife, who disapproved of Wallace's religious ideas and his connection to other spiritualists. As he noted in his diary, "It seems like the big man in the whole business is a rich Texas oil man named Charles Marsh who some years ago put on the spiritualist play *The Ladder* in New York and let people come without any admission price." The "guru letters" further excited the British interest in stuff on Wallace.

Dahl thought his bosses, from Stephenson all the way up to "C," were positively obsessed with the vice president. "Menzies was always avid for everything he could get out of the White House and the Cabinet in regard to U.S. intentions," he recalled, "especially anything that had to do with U.S. intentions towards the Empire." Dahl was kept busy, and the months flew by.

Late that fall Dahl moved to another little house in Georgetown on P Street, a slightly less ramshackle affair than the last, which was one of a number rented by the British Embassy to house temporary staff. This time he shared his quarters with a remarkably handsome Scotsman named David Ogilvy, a pale, lean Lord Byron type, complete with flaming red hair and fashionable attire. Like Dahl, he had begun by freelancing for the BSC and in late 1942 joined the organization full-time. He had only recently signed on as a third secretary at the British Embassy. In the thirty-two-year-old Ogilvy, Dahl found an ideal fellow conspirator, clever, enthusiastic, and up for anything in the way of Stephenson's best young turks. A self-proclaimed expert on American public opinion, he had spent the last four years as an associate director at George Gallup's Audience Research Institute in Princeton, New Jersey, and boasted that he had conducted more than four hundred nationwide surveys measuring the country's pulse on every conceivable issue. Based on the Gallup polls, he claimed he could tell "what the natives want out of life, what they think about the main issues of the day, what their habits are."

Brimming with charm, the six-foot, blue-eyed Ogilvy was perfectly cast as a snoop. In addition to looking like a leading man, he had a genius for showmanship and gave the impression of grand lineage and connections, though he lacked the inheritance the part required. Nevertheless, he projected an air of affluence and, on the forty dollars a week he earned from Gallup, somehow managed to live in a splendid eighteenth-century house called Mansgrove, located in Princeton's leafy green academic enclave. His neighbor was the pharmaceutical tycoon Gerard B. Lambert, who had made a fortune advertising Listerine as a cure for halitosis. Lambert, an avid sailor and America's Cup contender, regularly took him on holidays on one of his many yachts, including his famous three-masted schooner *Atlantic*. Ogilvy had a very young American wife from one of the first families of Virginia, the lovely Melinda Street, who he had met and married in 1939 when she was an eighteen-year-old student at the Juilliard School of Music in New York. She and the baby, along with the four English refugee children in their care, still resided in the Princeton manor, and he was bunking with Dahl only until he could find someplace for them all to live. He was brisk to the point of being impatient and could be rather dismissive when he thought he was talking to someone who was a bit stupid, which he considered the case more often than not. There was nothing run-of-the-mill about Ogilvy, and while he was not to everyone's liking, Dahl thought his wit and originality outweighed his snobbishness, and they hit it off immediately.

Nothing if not eccentric, Ogilvy had come to the United States via a particularly circuitous route. Half Irish and half Scottish, he was the youngest of five, born into a genteel but impoverished family in West Horsley, England. His father, a classical scholar turned stockbroker, was forced to return to Edinburgh after being financially ruined in the market. His mother, Diana Fairfield, was a brainy beauty who read constantly, preferring to work her way from the last page of a book to the first, and was thoroughly bored by married life. Ogilvy was raised with great expectations and won a scholarship to Fettes, Scotland's leading preparatory school, and to Christ Church College at Oxford, but was by his own admission too distracted to do any work and was expelled. Neither a great scholar nor an athlete, he was by his own account "an irreconcilable rebel—a misfit."

Ashamed of his failure at Oxford, Ogilvy ran away from his family's cultured background and took menial jobs, anything that was "as far away from that fancy thing as [he] could possible get." He struggled at first to find his way and worked at various times as a chef at the Hotel Majestic in Paris, a social worker in the Edinburgh slums, and a door-to-door salesman of Aga stoves. He proved to be a natural-born salesman and sold so many stoves to tight-fisted Scots housewives that he was asked to write a sales manual for the company. "The good salesman combines the tenacity of a bulldog with the manners of a spaniel," Ogilvy instructed in his lively guide to snagging customers, adding by way of advice, "If you have any charm, ooze it." Having discovered his true calling, he joined his older brother Francis's advertising firm, Mather & Crowther, and quickly worked his way up from trainee to account executive. In 1938 he talked them into sending him across the pond to study American advertising techniques. At the end of his year's sojourn, he reported his findings to the London office and announced he was resigning to seek his fortune in America—"the most wonderful, delightful, marvelous country on earth"—where he figured he could make roughly three times as much money with the same amount of effort.

Armed with several letters of introduction, among them an endorsement from his cousin, the author Rebecca West, to Alexander Woollcott, one of the most influential drama critics in New York, he boarded a ship for the United States, traveling steerage. Ogilvy's glib humor proved his greatest asset, and he quickly enchanted Woollcott's theatrical circle, which included Ethel Barrymore, Ruth Gordon, Harpo Marx, George S. Kaufman, and Robert Sherwood. They opened doors for him, and in short order he was hired by Gallup's firm to apply his polling methods to the movie industry. Ogilvy, who needed a job in a hurry as he was staying at the St. Regis Hotel and was down to his last ten dollars, jumped at the chance. It turned out to be "the greatest break" of his life.

After spending a few weeks getting a solid grounding in opinion research, Ogilvy accompanied Gallup to Hollywood. They pitched their services to the head of RKO studios, pointing out the competitive advantages of measuring the popularity of movie stars, pretesting audience acceptance of movie ideas and titles, and forecasting trends. RKO awarded them a twelve-month contract, and other studios soon followed suit, noting that David Selznick "took to ordering surveys the way other people order groceries." Ogilvy admired Gallup immensely and gained a deep respect for the value of opinion research as a predictive tool in everything from marketing to politics. He found his time in Hollywood both entertaining and instructive and hobnobbed with some of the most famous movie stars of the day, almost all of whom he considered "repulsive egotists." As a result of his audience research, Ogilvy discovered that certain marquee names had a negative effect on a picture's earnings, and he assembled a classified list he called "box office poison" that prematurely ended many a career. "There is no great trick to doing research," Ogilvy later observed. "The problem is to get people to use it—particularly when the research reveals that you have been making mistakes." Most people, he found, had "a tendency to use research as a drunkard uses a lamppost—for support, not for illumination."

In the spring of 1940 Gallup organized the Public Opinion Research Project, financed by a grant from the Rockefeller Foundation, and appointed one of his colleagues, Hadley Cantril, as director. Gallup and Cantril sampled American attitudes toward the war in Europe using the fact-finding machinery he had developed at his institute. In June of that year, Gallup's polls revealed that the vast majority of Americans did not want the United States to declare war and send an army and navy to Europe. The most striking thing about the poll results was that while only about 7 percent of Americans wanted to declare war on Germany, when asked "Do you think the United States is giving too much help to England and France at this time, not enough help, or about the right amount of help?" nearly three-quarters of the respondents answered "Not enough." The polls also indicated a real desire to aid the British and French as much as possible: 64 percent of the American public believed the United States should do everything possible to help democracies short of going to war.

The British regarded Gallup's polls as extremely useful sources of information, and since many of the polls were kept secret, they set about penetrating the organization. It was to this end that Stephenson first approached Ogilvy, a British subject employed as one of Gallup's assistant directors, and he "readily agreed to cooperate." According to the official BSC history, from late 1941 on Ogilvy was "able to ensure a constant flow of intelligence on public opinion in the United States, since he had access not only to the questionnaires sent out by Gallup and Cantril and to the recommendations offered by the latter to the White House," but also to internal reports prepared by the Survey Division of the Office of War Information and by the Opinion Research Division of the U.S. Army.

As the official history study points out, "The mass of information which the BSC collected in this way was obviously of interest to London." Gallup's polls gave the British a real sense of the lag between the volume of desire on the part of American people to help them and the lack of congressional action necessary to fulfill this desire. The polls also indicated that as the possibility of a German victory was regarded as more likely, Americans felt a greater potential threat to their values and way of life. These findings were particularly valuable to the British in helping to determine what kinds of wartime propaganda would be most effective, and how to concentrate their efforts to subtly shift the balance of American opinion toward the idea that the British and French were fighting mainly to preserve democracy rather than protect their national wealth and power.

Ogilvy, by his own account, had been "moonlighting" as an adviser to the British government, passing along poll data that could influence political strategy, when Stephenson offered him a chance to take on a more active role. With U.S. intervention the key to Britain's survival, he quit his job and went to work for the BSC in Washington. Stephenson recognized that the same energy and daring that had led Ogilvy to jettison a burgeoning career and reinvent himself in America were qualities that would be of incalculable value in an intelligence agent. He promptly dispatched Ogilvy to Camp X, the BSC's secret training facility, which had been hastily established in the fall of 1941 on the north shore of Lake Ontario, twenty-five miles outside Toronto. Most of the 260-acre site consisted of flat, scrubby fields and rough woodland, with only an old eight-room farmhouse and a handful of outbuildings that served as storerooms once the camp was built. It was an ideal location, isolated enough to be secure but, with Toronto just two hours from New York by air, easily accessible.

Here in the frozen woods outside Oshawa, the BSC's raw agent recruits, a hundred or so at a time, received basic instruction in the conduct of operations in the field and information gathering, as well as useful skills such as housebreaking, safe blowing, and lock picking. They also received some special training in the use of various kinds of weapons and explosive devices. The school had a staff of thirty, all experts in their particular line, and was run with military efficiency by the commandant, Colonel Bill Brooker. According to Sweet-Escott, "Brooker was a born salesman. He was a brilliant and convincing lecturer, and an immense fund of stories from the real life of a secret agent to illustrate his points." Most of Brooker's guest visitors from the OSS who passed through the school left with "a much clearer idea of what secret operations were likely to involve than anything we could give them in Washington," even if Sweet-Escott could not vouch for "the exact truth" of all the anecdotes they heard.

Stephenson had sent Fleming there in 1942 and had been impressed with how well he had come through the course, recalling that he was "top of his section," though he lacked the killer's instinct, and had hesitated—a fatal error—during an exercise in which he was expected to "shoot a man in cold blood." While the camp schooled secret agents, spies, and guerrilla fighters who went on to carry out BSC missions in enemy-occupied Europe and Asia, most of the people sent on the course with Ogilvy had been recruited to do intelligence or propaganda work, had backgrounds in journalism and foreign relations, and knew little or nothing about spycraft beyond the jobs they were doing at their typewriters. At Camp X, Ogilvy and his fellow trainees donned army fatigues designed to help maintain the facility's cover as a regular army base, and attended lectures on the new high technology of espionage, from the use of codes and ciphers to listening devices, and observed awe-inspiring demonstrations of silent killing and underwater demolitions. They also received some limited practice in how to use a handgun and shoot quickly and accurately without hesitation. "I was taught the tricks of the trade," recalled Ogilvy. "How do you follow people without arousing their suspicion? Walk in *front* of them; if you also push a pram this will disarm their suspicions still further. I was taught to use a revolver, to blow up bridges and power lines with plastic, to cripple police dogs by grabbing their front legs and tearing their chests apart, and to kill a man with my bare hands."

Fully expecting to be parachuted behind enemy lines, he was a little let down when Stephenson assigned him to desk duty. Ogilvy was put in charge of collecting economic intelligence from Latin America, where the Germans were known to be very active and the BSC had a sizable number of agents. His primary function was to ruin the reputation of

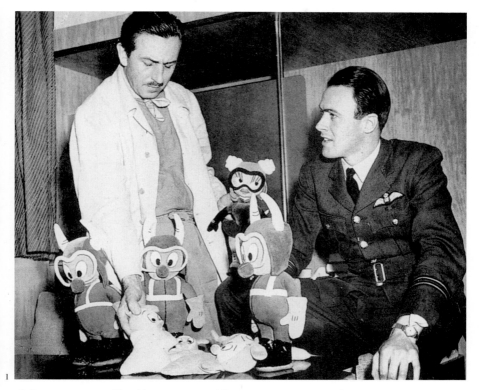

1

Flight Lieutenant Roald Dahl was so successful at writing wartime propaganda that one of his stories, "Gremlin Lore," attracted the attention of Walt Disney, who had his animators provide illustrations for a children's book and a planned movie about the RAF.

2

The self-styled Texas newspaper tycoon Charles Marsh became Dahl's mentor and volunteered his services to help the British cause.

3

Marsh's R Street mansion, Dahl's base of operations, was regarded by prominent New Dealers and journalists as a cross between a political salon and a private clubhouse.

Lord Halifax, the British ambassador, was "not of this century" and was frequently ridiculed in the press for engaging in such aristocratic pastimes as foxhunting.

Halifax often attended the famous parties at Friendship, the Georgetown mansion of Washington doyenne and archconservative Evalyn Walsh McLean (*far right, wearing glasses*), whose diverse guest lists included well-known isolationists as well as interventionists, such as her dinner partner Vice President Henry Wallace.

6

The shadowy Canadian millionaire William Stephenson became director of the BSC and oversaw a vast covert network of spies from his headquarters in Rockefeller Center.

Walter Winchell, the most powerful and feared gossip columnist of the day, was so convinced of the necessity of Anglo-American cooperation to win the war against the Nazis that he entered into a secret partnership with the BSC.

Ernest Cuneo, an American lawyer and member of FDR's palace guard, served as the intermediary between Winchell and the BSC. Margaret Watson, whom Cuneo married after the war, was one of Stephenson's loyal secretaries at the BSC's New York headquarters.

The influential newspaper columnists Walter Lippmann (*right*) and Drew Pearson (*below*) were important but delicate sources for the BSC to tap. Dahl was assigned to cultivate Pearson and their friendship became so close that Dahl was regarded as one of the family.

11

12

Commander Ian Fleming, on assignment with British naval intelligence, became one of Stephenson's special boys. He was given responsibility far above his rank and helped to draft an early memo on the OSS.

Stephenson also recruited Fleming's best friend, Ivar Bryce, a charming playboy, as a BSC agent and later made him a liaison officer with the OSS.

Fellow BSC operative David Ogilvy (*left*) was recruited from Gallup for his polling expertise and was Dahl's Georgetown roommate. Their colorful co-conspirators included the British film star Leslie Howard (*below, left*), who was killed when his plane was shot down by the Germans, and the playwright and composer Noël Coward (*below, right*), a determined patriot who used his celebrity as cover to carry out assorted intelligence duties for his country.

13

14

There was a shortage of men in wartime Washington and Dahl cut a wide swath. His conquests included Millicent Rogers (*top, left*), the Standard Oil heiress, and Clare Boothe Luce (*top, right*), the glamorous blond congresswoman from Connecticut. The beautiful Alice Glass (*bottom, left*), whom Dahl diplomatically rebuffed, was married to Marsh and carrying on an illicit affair with a young Texas congressman named Lyndon B. Johnson. The French actress Annabella (*bottom, right*) thought Dahl was too tall and handsome for undercover work: "You had to look at him!"

19

Congressman Johnson (*above right*) was a great admirer of President Roosevelt. (The man in the middle is Texas governor Jimmy Allred.) When he first came to Washington, Johnson was a frequent guest at Marsh's palatial Virginia estate, Longlea (*below*), where he fell in love with Alice Glass. For many years thereafter, he journeyed alone from Washington to Longlea for secret trysts.

Dahl ingratiated himself with First Lady Eleanor Roosevelt, who invited him to spend time with her and the president at the family retreat in Hyde Park. While the British supported Roosevelt, they regarded his running mate as "a menace," and Dahl was instructed to keep close tabs on Vice President Wallace (*below, left*) and his Communist friends.

23

Dahl reported back to the BSC on all his meetings with Roosevelt, who did not "glamour" him as much as he had expected, although he was much impressed by the paralyzed president's skill behind the wheel of his customized Ford.

24

Dahl's duties included monitoring the tense negotiations on the problem of which country would get the lion's share of the lucrative postwar business in transatlantic travel. Assistant Secretary of State Adolf Berle (*far left*) and Lord Beaverbrook (*second from left*) were at odds over Pan Am's political maneuvering and monopoly of air routes.

In 1946, former OSS chief William "Big Bill" Donovan pinned the Medal for Merit, America's highest civilian award, on BSC director "Little Bill" Stephenson for his "invaluable" assistance to the United States in the "fields of intelligence and special operations."

26

Dahl escorted the famous novelist and war correspondent Ernest Hemingway around London while they waited for the D-day invasion, which took place the following week.

businessmen who were known to be working with the Axis powers and to prevent them from supplying the Nazis with strategic materials, such as industrial diamonds, tungsten, vanadium, antimony, and the like. Since the middle 1930s, German businesses had been doing end runs around the Allies by finding international companies to run interference for them and sharing in the control of important industrial processes in other countries. In this fashion, Hitler had managed to keep the United States from manufacturing butyl rubber at the very moment the Japanese were preparing to cut America off from its supplies of crude rubber. Prior to Pearl Harbor, the Nazi chemical company I. G. Farben, through other economic arrangements, was able to achieve similar results. An agreement between Farben and Dow Chemical forbade the latter to manufacture more than 6,000 tons of magnesium a year—at a time when the Nazis were producing 75,000 tons—or to ship this metal to any European country other than Germany. As airplanes, to a large extent, were built from aluminum and magnesium, this restriction was of inestimable benefit to the German aircraft industry.

To combat their insidious influence, the BSC engaged in economic warfare. Damaging material about such unholy alliances could be leaked to newspaper outlets, supplying the U.S. government with the necessary pretext to take further action. According to the BSC history, "Rumors were spread. Articles were placed in newspapers and magazines. Radio talks and protest meetings were organized, and arrangements were made for picketing certain Farben properties." In 1942 the BSC, using this modus operandi, spread the rumor that the RAF had bombed Farben's factories in Germany and destroyed its drug supplies and formulas, "with the result that there have been many deaths from wrong prescriptions." Similarly, the BSC planted stories in the press exposing the German agent Kurt Rieth, whose father had become rich as a Standard Oil representative, and Nazi attempts to subvert the American oil industry to avoid the blockade. Rieth's unmasking made for scandalous headlines in the *New York Herald-Tribune*—"NAZI AGENT IS HERE ON SECRET MISSION SEEKS OIL HOLDINGS"—and led to his being deported. A quick study, Ogilvy turned himself into the BSC's analytical hitman and was a model of hard work and disciplined thoroughness. He became so adept at targeting pro-Axis operators and organizers, and learned so much about their clandestine activities, that he was soon supplying the OSS with "an average of forty reports a day."

As the military threat became less urgent, the BSC focused its attention increasingly on the industrial threat. In addition to the airlines, it also had grave concern about the oil business, and Stephenson had more than a shrewd suspicion that a number of the oil companies were not above doing a little business with the Nazis, including Standard Oil of New Jersey, which had close ties to Farben. By the time the BSC was finished, Standard Oil was subject to several lawsuits and a government investigation. Some of these large companies, as well as some banks, also served as "intelligence chains," providing cover for Nazi operations in the Western Hemisphere. There were German banks in South America that were "engaging in a little discreet blackmail of local politicians," recalled the BSC agent Gilbert Highet, who, like Ogilvy, researched suspect firms. Drawing on his scholarly background, Highet developed an index card system to identify and track individuals in these industries who might be vulnerable to blackmail. "This is really one of the purposes of espionage," he later observed. "Every human being has his weakness. In war, or in a very tight political struggle, both sides try to discover and to play on these weaknesses." By identifying those susceptible, "You can clearly become aware that the enemy will attempt to play on such weaknesses and take what steps you see fit to counterplay."

Ogilvy, like most of his BSC colleagues, counted himself as extremely fortunate to be working for Stephenson, whom he regarded as a man of "extraordinary fertility" and "one of the most effective operators in the long history of the Secret Service," in a class with such legends as Sir Francis Walsingham, Queen Elizabeth I's cunning spymaster, and Blinker Hall, director of Naval Intelligence in World War I, famous for intercepting the Zimmermann telegram, which had helped draw America into that conflict. Stephenson always seemed several steps ahead of everyone. Legend had it that a few days before Pearl Harbor, he sent a coded telegram to the London office that a Japanese attack was imminent. As the Foreign Office was not in possession of any corroborating reports from the embassy, they queried his source. Stephenson telegraphed his trademark terse reply: "The President of the United States."

Despite all the demands of the job, the BSC chief always listened to what his young subordinate had to say with interest, "a sympathetic grin flickering at the corner of his mouth." He was "quiet, ruthless, and loyal," and Ogilvy "stood in awe of his sagacity." He was only ever disappointed in his boss on one score—that Stephenson failed to fully exploit Ogilvy's expertise in public opinion. A fantastic self-promoter, Ogilvy talked endlessly about what he thought polling could do for the British war effort and was relentless in trying to find ways to apply Gallup's methods to secret intelligence. He argued that his findings could be used to Britain's advantage in guiding foreign policy, with the results of polls, secretly taken in other countries, used to shed light on the best way to settle internal political problems and determine what kinds of Allied propaganda would be most effective. During the summer of 1943, he set down his ideas in a detailed technical report, entitled "A Plan for Predetermining the Results of Plebiscites, Predicting the Reactions of People to the Impact of Projected Events, and Applying the Gallup Technique to Other Fields of Secret Intelligence." After reviewing it, Stephenson obliged his aide by forwarding the report both to the British Embassy in Washington and to SIS headquarters in London, where it reportedly got a lukewarm reception and languished in a filing cabinet for the rest of the war.* Ogilvy always looked back on it as a lost opportunity.

On Stephenson's orders, Ogilvy concentrated on analyzing the current state of American public opinion toward Britain. He conducted a series of polls that showed that the defeats Britain suffered at the start of 1942 had a damaging effect on public attitudes toward both Britain and the Roosevelt administration. In mid-February 1942, 63 percent of Americans believed that the British were doing all they could to win the war, but just three weeks later, after a string of crushing military losses had been reported in the press, this figure had fallen to 49 percent, the lowest point since the beginning of the war. Moreover, his samplings showed that the public had lost confidence in their own government: one out of three Americans believed that the Roosevelt administration was not doing enough to win a decisive victory over the enemy.

Ogilvy's findings confirmed Stephenson's worst fears. After Pearl Harbor he had cautioned Britons against a false sense of relief now that America was fighting at their side. Although he had largely accomplished what he had set out to do when he first came to New York, culminating in his role in the creation of the OSS, Stephenson had learned not to trust in the constancy of the American people. The Japanese had blasted U.S. neutrality to smithereens, but the country's new belligerent spirit had subsided as the Allies suffered setbacks and the war turned into a fight without a quick ending. While Britain no longer had to worry about winning sympathy for its cause, pro-German interests and American isolationism remained a problem. A few isolationist factions had become even more extreme, but their tone was so off-putting that they were on

---

*According to the intelligence historian Henry Hyde, the report was eventually picked up by General Eisenhower's Psychological Warfare Board, which successfully implemented some of Ogilvy's ideas in Europe during the last year of the war.

the verge of self-destructing, with very little help from the BSC. Lindbergh had begun demonizing the Jews as a powerful mob in cahoots with the British and Roosevelt in "pressing this country toward war," and his increasingly paranoid message left people cold. But the anti-Roosevelt forces railing against the president were as vitriolic as ever. While the BSC's mission had changed over the years, and the scope of its activities was not nearly what it had been, Stephenson remained convinced that British propaganda efforts were still required to make sure Roosevelt remained in office and to ensure British participation in formulating wartime policies as well as in the crucial postwar planning.

Meanwhile the British were facing the final critical stage of the war, and needed to be sure of their American ally's support. By the close of 1943, however, there was growing friction between the countries on a number of fronts. At the Allied summit in Tehran in November, Churchill, Roosevelt, and Stalin had sat around a big, round oak conference table for three days getting nowhere. Roosevelt and Stalin stood united on the subject of establishing a real second front, and in the end Churchill had no choice but to give them what they wanted, and it was agreed that Operation Overlord, code name for the Normandy invasion, would be launched on May 1. The British were increasingly nervous about the close relationship developing between America and Russia. America was weighing various courses of action, and at the British embassy in Washington there was a feeling that the crowded events of the past few months had jostled opinions in the wrong direction. On December 5, Marsh sent Wallace the following "British Intelligence Item"—presumably supplied by Dahl—noting that it was important only insofar as it went to Downing Street and Churchill "the night it was spoken":

The top diplomatic reporter for Downing Street has just returned from a swing of the country. He says: "Americans are uninterested in this war except as their personal affairs interest them. They want the war over and Roosevelt out, and want to get back to the peace time living basis with their families intact. They are job conscious but the rest of the post-war and world peace business has not gotten into their being. Your Pearl Harbor wasn't big enough. Our Dunkirk and London bombing woke us up. America is still playing and big-headedly proud of itself with bad information and little enthusiasm. You are too far away and provincial to get the point.

While the weather in Washington had cooled, events remained very hot. When Marsh headed down to Texas for a two-week vacation, he kept in close touch with Dahl by telegram, saying that he hoped to see him before Christmas, and he put in an order for one of Disney's gremlin dolls as a present for little Diana, "a mother in black hat, white gloves, white shoes." He had sent chocolate, ham, and other goodies to his poor mother and sisters in ration-starved England. Teasing Dahl that his last wire was "hopelessly vague" and "the work of an immature writer," Marsh told him that he was expected at Longlea for the holidays, adding that while he understood that the wing commander's "knowledge of geography is obscure, I humor him by saying Virginia is not a long way off and he ought to find his way that far."

8

DIRTY WORK

But many a king on a first-class throne,
If he wants to call his crown his own,
Must manage somehow to get through
More dirty work than I ever do.

—W.S. GILBERT, *The Pirates of Penzance*
quoted in David Ogilvy's memoir.

THE NEW YEAR did not get off to a good start. Dahl found himself in the doghouse again and was once more given his marching papers. It seemed the air chief marshal had not gone quietly. He had continued to agitate for Dahl's removal, and after Halifax had repeatedly ignored his recommendations for a change, he had gone over the ambassador's head and arranged another transfer, this time in the form of "Orders from Military Air" out of London. He reportedly did it quietly, while Beaverbrook was away in South Africa and his staff was too busy to take notice. The military orders meant that the ambassador's hands were effectively tied, so that even if he could be persuaded to show mercy, it would be too little too late. Moreover, as Dahl explained to Marsh, who had been down south most of December, it placed him in the awkward position of looking like a coward if he refused the wartime reassignment. Marsh once again turned to the vice president for help. "Probably this matter is not on the Portal [Sir Charles, commander in chief of the RAF] nor on the Churchill level," Marsh wrote Wallace on January 28, 1944, apologizing for the precipitate nature of his appeal, but he hastened to explain that Dahl might be "transferred from America within a very few weeks." He added that Dahl had decided "not to protest" the move, "although I am sure he wants to do his maximum on post war Air for Britain."

Realizing that the situation required extreme delicacy, Marsh devoted several pages of his letter to the vice president to demonstrating the critical nature of Dahl's role at the embassy and enumerating the many reasons he should remain in place. "It would be a considerable loss to American and British air accord post war if Dahl left without putting his maximum weight on the American constructed Air Base set up," Marsh began. "Undoubtedly Dahl, although a disabled flyer under thirty, is the purest and best brain on the British post war line up in this country. He has worked consistently at it. The British Air Marshall attached to Washington has many other duties. Dahl's immediate superior at the Embassy is ill and the position itself has undergone two or three changes." Marsh argued that it would be highly advantageous to keep Dahl involved in the negotiations: "Strange as it may seem, this young man has a vision of international communication in a peace time world involving sea and air travel, which is probably further ahead than anyone's in either British or American Government. Before he is checked out, someone should get him to put his stuff on paper."

In case Wallace missed his drift, Marsh proceeded to spell out a course of action that the vice president could pursue to stave off their friend's departure: "You might tell [the] proper person that you consider Dahl a very intelligent young man; that you generally check through him for accuracy of fact and viewpoint, on editorials pertaining to British matters. You understand that he is going abroad and you would like to know what other Britisher in America you can look to for accuracy and cooperation."

Anticipating the worst, Dahl wrote home that he might well be returning sooner than expected, explaining that he had asked to be "relieved." That may have been as much as he felt he could put in a letter, or as much as any wayward son ever wants to admit to his mother. In any case, he spent sleepless nights worrying, waiting for the boom to be lowered. Finally on March 10, word came from the Air Ministry that his tour of duty was over and that "every body has appreciated the good work you have put in as Assistant Air Attaché." Stephenson managed to secure his transfer to the BSC, and he was soon back in business.

Dahl quickly recovered his equilibrium. When he next met with Wallace at Marsh's home, he reciprocated by supplying the vice president with a full report on what the British saw as some of the preliminary stumbling blocks in the aviation talks. Dahl told Wallace that Beaverbrook and Eden were very disturbed about the American machinations with regard to postwar air and suspected that the Americans were trying to sew up the exclusive rights to air traffic in a number of South American countries. Pan American Airways had been secretly contracted by the U.S. military to build a number of airports in South America, and in addition to being handsomely compensated, they had the exclusive right to use the airfields and installations after the war— which, roughly speaking, was the reversion of $38 million worth of work. Dahl argued that it was important that the United States and Britain not get into a postwar air rights battle, but advised Wallace that he thought Britain could beat America at this game, though it was in everyone's interests to keep things on a cooperative basis.

Dahl also told the vice president that Halifax had been to see Berle at the State Department and had also called on Cordell Hull and the president. According to Halifax, Roosevelt had blamed the bottleneck on Bennett Champ Clark, a Democrat from Missouri, who was head of the Senate subcommittee that had been appointed to look into the question of whether American foreign aviation after the war should be in the hands of a monopoly company—that is, Pan Am—or divided among a number of companies, the more traditional form of regulated competition. An advisory committee on aviation had already submitted the view—with one vote dissenting—that foreign aviation rights should be apportioned among a select number of airlines, granting each a zone in which it could be dominant. The committee, in a subsequent report, had also warned of the growing conflict between Pan Am and sixteen other commercial airlines that favored free competition.

Armed with Dahl's report, Wallace phoned Berle the following day and passed on Dahl's intelligence without mentioning him by name. Berle agreed the problem was in the Senate, though he did not criticize Clark, whose wife had recently died after a long illness. "Berle said he was just as anxious to have conversations with the British on post-war air as the British themselves," Wallace noted in his diary. "Berle said he would welcome anything I could do to hasten the Senate hearings along. I then remembered that Dahl quoted Halifax to the effect that the President had said it would be good tactics to let Bennett Clark have his hearings before the British and Americans got too far in their negotiations. Berle says that some of the big American companies are disposed to think they can go ahead and handle the post-war situation more or less by themselves no matter what the British do. Berle thinks this attitude is bad."

During this period, Wallace's diary shows that on several occasions he forwarded Dahl's intelligence to interested parties in government as well as to the president. A brief unsigned memo, concerning the British ambassador's March visit to Moscow, during which Halifax met with Stalin and broached the subject of the British position on Poland, reports: "Stalin was very angry. He made no comment except to grunt repeatedly." Beneath this Wallace noted in pencil, "I passed the above which came through Dahl on to the President who had confirmatory evidence of his own."

Dahl continued to closely monitor the vice president's political fortunes. As the election year got under way, Marsh was increasingly inserting himself into the campaign. He regularly took his own informal polls by sounding out newspaper editors around the country, and he provided his own prognoses and recommendations in the form of an endless cascade of notes, letters, memos, and reports. Marsh was frustrated that he could not turn to his old friend Lyndon Johnson for insight and advice, but he knew he had been bitterly disappointed when Roosevelt passed over Rayburn for Wallace back in 1940. At the time Johnson had expressed disbelief that the president would select a man regarded by many as "an ex-republican with little political savvy and a reputation for mysticism."

Johnson, who had lost a hotly contested bid for the Senate in a special election in the summer of 1941, following the death of Morris Shepherd, the senior senator from Texas, had returned to the House and dedicated himself to the war effort. He had also devoted himself to working for Rayburn, who still had ambitions for the vice presidency and as Speaker of the House had a vast majority of congressmen favoring his elevation. Marsh was livid. He told Johnson that there was only a slight chance for the Roosevelt-Rayburn ticket. "The real fact," Marsh fumed, "is that Rayburn has neither the brain nor moral stamina to lead this country should he be called to the presidency and Roosevelt knows it." Even Johnson had privately conceded as much after a few drinks, telling Marsh, "I think I can say definitely that only Wallace could lose the nomination, as certainly the President will be for him."

As he had once done for Johnson, Marsh sent Wallace pep talks and inspirational notes on the campaign trail: "So as you go west and then swing back to Lincoln's tomb, I feel with great confidence that you are in the spirit of the thing to be done," he wrote. "I firmly feel you are a Crusader in the finest sense. I sense that you are an advance writer in the new religion of economic democracy."

Marsh did not restrict himself to campaign advice and frequently weighed in on British and U.S. foreign policy, penning furious memos on the shortcomings of American diplomacy. "It is most disquieting that our State Department apparently does not know the score," Marsh scolded in early 1944. "South America is primarily the job of our own State Department. Today we are getting most of our real information from British Intelligence and most of our policy direction from men who accept the governments of the United nations of the western world as spiritually democratic. Meanwhile, the road to fascism in South America is being made increasingly easy. Nationalism is growing under fascist over-lords. The common people south of the Rio Grande are confused and rapidly losing faith in the words of Roosevelt, Hull, Wallace and Welles." Dahl, who still regularly joined the two men for five o' clock cocktails, would do his best to egg Marsh on during these arguments with an eye to passing along the vice president's responses later.

By early 1944, London, and the prime minister in particular, were keenly interested in the progress of the presidential election. By using Ogilvy's method of analysis and drawing on the intelligence gathered by Dahl and other BSC agents, Stephenson kept them supplied with regular and reliable forecasts of the outcome. In the first week of February, Stephenson gave London a heads-up and reported that "Roosevelt has undertaken to the Party that he will jettison Wallace as vice-presidential candidate."* Stephenson

---

*This was prescient, to say the least, considering that Dahl later reported to the BSC that Wallace himself was unaware of the decision for another five months, until almost the day of the dramatic events of the Democratic convention, when Roosevelt acted to remove Wallace from the ticket and replace him with Truman.

was naturally quite pleased when Ogilvy's old employer, Gallup, began playing an unexpectedly prominent role in the election process, with his opinion polls replacing gambling odds as the best way to get a fix on the bandwagon vote. Stephenson was in an excellent position to keep London informed on this new development seeing as he already had an inside man.

Dahl continued to dribble British intelligence items to Marsh, including the delicious tidbit that Tom Dewey, who was trying to get the Republican nomination, was one of Gallup's principal clients. On January 24, Marsh reported to Wallace on Gallup's polling operation, sending a long memo that was clearly informed by Dahl, who had it straight from Ogilvy. Marsh explained that there was "much activity in Princeton," and this new science was, in the veteran newspaperman's opinion, "a final effort to seduce public opinion.

> It now takes the form of writing the political questions, putting the answers out at the right time, and furnishing by-product secret and possibly poisoned unofficial Gallup information to political and financial and labor leaders. In private, Gallup has committed himself as anti-Roosevelt, pro-Dewey, but says he must keep his business going and can't be wrong. Gallup knows that Roosevelt is unpredictable and largely makes his own trends of public opinion, and also knows that war and domestic events will be coming so fast this year that he will have to be careful both as to his questions and his political polls.

An additional Marsh memorandum to Wallace on Gallup—on which Dahl's name is scrawled at the top to indicate the actual source—details the pollster's political bias and rumors of double-dealing by his "disciples," including Hadley Cantril, whose Office of Public Opinion Research was being bankrolled by the "Listerine King" Jerry Lambert:

"Gallup is devoted intensely to Mr. Dewey but because of his Supreme Court of Virtue job he must be impartial before the American public. So Halitosis Lambert is unofficially delegated to the research job for the Dewey campaign. It is strongly suspected that he is paying Gallup a bit, directly or indirectly, for the use of his files." Even more incredible, according to Marsh, were rumors that the Princeton "gang" had been a bit sloppy: word had it that Cantril "is doing the same work for Wallace as Lambert is doing for Dewey. And Gallup is laughing as he feeds these boys."

Personally Ogilvy rather liked Lambert and considered him that "rare businessman with a first-class mind." He envied him his wealth, worldliness, and custom wardrobe, and developed a lasting friendship with the rich dilettante, who dabbled in cultural affairs at Princeton.[*] Never one to stand on principle, Ogilvy was amused by the cynical approach Lambert took to trying to nail down the nomination for Dewey during the run-up to the Republican convention. "When Dewey was to make a major speech on foreign policy," he recalled, "Jerry's pollsters prepared short statements which summarized every possible opinion on each major issue. They then showed these statements to a cross-section of voters and asked which most nearly reflected their views. The statement which received the most votes went into the speech." It was not the most inspiring approach to leadership, but Ogilvy believed it probably would have won the day for Dewey had he not looked, in the immortal phrase so often attributed to Alice Longworth, "like a little man on a wedding cake."

When he was not occupied with Marsh and Wallace, Dahl shared many of the press and propaganda chores with Ogilvy, who considered them "small beer." When all was said and done, intelligence work was for the most part fairly prosaic and involved a lot of tedious paperwork

---

[*]When Lambert died, Ogilvy inherited his clothes.

and shuttling back and forth between the various agencies, including the OSS, the FBI, the State Department, the Combined Chiefs, the Board of Economic Warfare, and so on. Nothing, however, was as appallingly dull as the routine tasks assigned by the British Embassy, which was judged to be a singularly ineffective institution. It was as if everyone there had taken to heart the Foreign Office's admonition "Above all, no zeal." Ogilvy shared Dahl's dim view of Halifax as a leader. He considered him "curiously lazy," observing that while the wartime ambassador found time every afternoon for a leisurely stroll with his wife and dachsund, he restricted meetings with the heads of the different British missions to once every two weeks, and then timed them to be sure they did not last longer than the allotted hour and a quarter. Halifax could not be bothered to meet with anyone below the rank of minister, and his diplomatic staff, which numbered fifty in all, "rarely set eyes on him."

As Halifax routinely failed to report the little of importance that he heard from the American officials who called on him, Ogilvy had the bright idea of installing a microphone in his office so that his staff could later transcribe the recordings and the summaries could be sent to London. "Needless to say," he later recalled, "this was considered ungentlemanly." Ogilvy, who had no such scruples, filed this quaint sentiment alongside the "prissy view" held by Roosevelt's secretary of war, Henry Stimson, that "gentlemen don't read each other's mail." To his mind, the Americans were determinedly naïve and preferred not to know when they were "the beneficiaries of such skullduggery." It was why so many BSC agents thought the Americans were hopeless when it came to espionage and why they dismissed the FBI as "flatfoots."

Ogilvy, who was promoted to second secretary in the spring of 1944, was bored silly by his official duties. He kept himself entertained by seeing how many telegrams he could get approved by the "hyper-critical levels" above him. His record was forty-two in one month. This was all the more impressive given the complexity of the material—everything from the correct official line regarding Russian requests for food, textiles, and other relief requirements to an analysis of Britain's postwar policy toward China—and that each telegram had to be encoded by hand before being sent, and then decoded in London. He took great pride in the fact that some of his finer compositions droned on for thousands of words, which his superiors found laudable. As a matter of policy, Ogilvy observed, "brevity was discouraged; it might cause misunderstanding." Bad as the British bureaucracy was, it did not compare to that of the State Department, which was largely staffed by Wall Street lawyers known for sending out instructions that were so unintelligible that the ambassadors were frequently at a loss to understand them and had to wire back for clarification. Ogilvy, however, could remember having no difficulty comprehending one "momentous communication" from Cordell Hull to Lord Halifax:

> *The Secretary of state presents his compliments to His Excellency the British Ambassador and takes pleasure in informing him that the appropriate Customs Officer has been authorized to admit free of duty three cases of whisky for the personal use of Mr. David Ogilvy.*

Because of their contacts in American journalism circles, Stephenson sometimes called on Dahl and Ogilvy to investigate leaks, which were a constant problem. "Our security was dreadful then," recalled Dahl. "We used to pass these telegrams all over the place." At the embassy, protocol dictated that incoming telegrams were earmarked for the most junior member of the diplomatic staff with oversight for that area. After he had read each telegram and written up his summary, or "minute," he passed them up to his superior, and they traveled in this fashion from desk to desk until the cables worked their way up to the ambassador, who added his two cents and then frequently passed them on to an even higher authority—Lady Halifax—for perusal. As a result, when a leak occurred, it was hard to know where to look first for the chink in the armor.

When Drew Pearson somehow got hold of a top-secret telegram from Churchill to the British commanding general in Greece and reprinted much of its contents in his "Merry-Go-Round" column, the Foreign Office became extremely exercised about the security of its confidential communications. London asked Stephenson to make immediate inquiries, and he promised to put one of his "ruffians" on the case. How was it that the text of Churchill's secret telegrams were finding their way into an American gossip column? Unlike Winchell, who had Cuneo serving as his lieutenant and sometime ghostwriter and hence could be counted on to march to the British tune, Pearson was cantankerous and hard to control. Isaiah Berlin considered him to be "one of the most malicious and irresponsible political muckrakers in the United States."

If Pearson thought he had a "hot" scoop, he ran with it, and the British could take their lumps along with everyone else—as he had demonstrated when he printed an item quoting Assistant Secretary of War John J. McCloy to the effect that he believed Britain was deliberately delaying the launching of the second front. He was not anti-British, however, and not intractable. In the past, Pearson had on occasion been persuaded to scratch stories that would have been damaging to the British cause and once even allowed the BSC to write a column publicizing the gallant role that British women were playing in the war. A staunch FDR supporter, he cared about the administration's war effort, and if he could be made to understand that something was potentially harmful to Anglo-American relations, such as the fact that their secure communications had been penetrated, he could be reasoned with. Ogilvy, who believed in low cunning and expediency, quickly pried loose the name of Pearson's "leaker," who turned out to be none other than Sumner Welles, the undersecretary of state.

With the war against Germany tapering off in the foreseeable future, the British were increasingly more engaged in clandestine politics than espionage against the enemy, so it was a matter of the utmost importance that Churchill's intelligence and policy—particularly where Russia was concerned—remained a closely guarded state secret, and kept out of American hands. Although America was Britain's firm ally, between them there was still "tremendous friction," as Dahl recalled, and the British could ill afford any further leaks. So when a subsequent problem with Pearson's column cropped up that summer, London asked Stephenson to give all possible assistance to the embassy. "The embassy waffled around with this for two or three days to try to find out what was going on," Dahl recalled. "They didn't, and then they went, of course, to Bill, who flashed one down to me, and said, 'find out at once.'"

The trouble had started with Pearson's publication in July 1944 of an extremely inflammatory confidential letter concerning the resignation of William Phillips, a highly regarded American diplomat and most recently the president's special envoy in India. The letter in question, which dated back more than a year to April 1943, was addressed to Roosevelt and had been sent from New Delhi, where Phillips was reporting on the situation in India, and was particularly unforgiving when it came to British colonial rule. The gist of his letter was that India was in shambles, and that resentment of the British, who had helped foster the divisiveness and helplessness that crippled the country, was deepening. The British had succeeded in their policy of "keeping a lid on" and had suppressed the independence movement among the Indians. Phillips went on to note that the British Army was there in force and to keep the peace had arrested political agitators; an estimated "twenty thousand Congress Party leaders remained in jail without trial." More to the point, he had been hard put to find any anti-Japanese sentiment in India, adding ominously that when it came time to fight, "We Americans should have to bear the burden of the coming campaign in that part of the world and not count on more than token assistance from the British in British India." Pearson alleged that Phillips had been declared persona non grata in London and was demanding an investigation by the Foreign Relations Committee.

As Isaiah Berlin reported in one of his weekly dispatches, Pearson had caused "a genuine flurry with his stories." The public airing of Britain's problems in India was the last thing the Foreign Office needed. Sir Ronald Campbell, the British minister, lodged a strongly worded protest, requesting that the U.S. government disavow any connection to the views expressed in Pearson's column. Campbell also met with Eugene Meyer, the publisher of the *Washington Post*, to express his outrage over the column, which turned out to be a waste of time because the *Post* was just one of the 616 papers that carried his column and had no particular influence over Pearson. Making matters worse, Campbell's report of his conversation with Meyer, sent to the Foreign Office in a secret telegram, was reprinted in full in Pearson's column just days later. The mischief-making Pearson privately claimed "to have collected a considerable dossier of facts on . . . India, publication of which would be unwelcome to His Majesty's Government," Berlin reported. "[He] has assured friends that he intends to print more and more Indian material likely to do us damage." The leak had turned into a flood. Dahl found the whole situation nothing short of farcical, and could not help enjoying the ambassador's humiliation: "Suddenly, in Drew Pearson's column in the *Washington Post* everyday, there appeared absolutely . . . Halifax's most secret telegrams to London."

Cordell Hull was beside himself. Phillips' letter had been copied to him, and he was determined to clear his office. Over the next three weeks he aggressively pushed the British to root out the source of the embarrassing leaks. According to the BSC history, their contact with Pearson in Washington "set to work, and, on 3 August, was able to report that he had received a copy of the Phillips letter from an Indian." Stephenson cabled London: "Man who gave Pearson Phillips memorandum was Chaman Lal, Indian nationalist."

This still did not explain how Pearson was regularly managing to get hold of bootleg embassy communications, including Campbell's recent telegram, which he was faithfully reprinting word for word. Stephenson sent Dahl back to work on the hard-nosed columnist, who put freedom of the press above any other interests, national or international. "Well, this wasn't too difficult for me because I knew Drew," recalled Dahl, who went directly to Pearson and brokered a deal for the culprit's identity. "I traded with him for this, and it turned out to be . . . an Indian in the Indian High Commissioner's Office." Major Altaf Quadir, a third secretary in the Washington office and another Indian agitator, had been copying telegrams and peddling them to Pearson as anti-British propaganda. The BSC saw to it that Quadir left the country, and Stephenson sent his completed report on the Washington leaks to London. "That stopped that," said Dahl, "but you see it meant that if that telegram was leaking, then any others they were sending could leak as well."

To the best of Dahl's knowledge, the only "absolutely secure" telegrams between the United States and England during the war were the ones sent by Stephenson from New York using his "fantastic coding machines." It was thanks to the BSC's communications division that Britain eventually adopted Stephenson's sophisticated code-making invention for ensuring the security of their top-secret communications traffic—including messages between Churchill and Roosevelt—and he liked to boast that they were handling up to a million characters a day. Dahl, who had only a nodding acquaintance with how the contraption worked, recalled Stephenson explaining how they intercepted wireless transmissions from German U-boats and deciphered them mechanically, before reciphering them and putting them on the wire to London, where they were again deciphered. "It took a whole roll of lavatory paper at one end," he recalled, waggishly describing the randomly perforated code tape, "and another at the other end with the same size and number of holes in them."

Dahl enjoyed having friends in the BSC, a sort of old boys' club for intelligence types comprised of an incongruous mixture of brass and brains, backgrounds and skills, who were always ready for a visit to a bar and a shared laugh at Halifax's expense, though that was about as much as they ever delved into their work. He liked the tribal manner-isms of his fellow sleuths, their friendly, low-key insults, studied indif-ference, and their nothing-sacred disposition toward all governments, institutions, and organizations, even their own. If he met up with them in New York, they invariably wound up at the 21 Club. In Washington they congregated at Billy Martin's, their local Georgetown pub, which was popular with the British and at night was thick with gold braid and mink.

During his off hours, Dahl spent a good deal of time with Ogilvy, who introduced him to his friend Ivar (John F. C.) Bryce. "Burglar" Bryce, one of the many names by which he was known, was an old school chum of Fleming's and quite a colorful character in his own right. Tall, dark, and handsome to the point of absurdity, he looked like an Aztec prince and was often mistaken for a film star. He was born to European nobility, counted the Marquess of Milford-Haven and the Earl of Medina as nephews, and radiated the languid ennui of some-one who never had to work for a living. His great-grandfather was the founder of W. R. Grace & Co., which he sold for a huge sum. As Lord Mountbatten reportedly said of his distant nephew, "It's terrible, the advantages he's had to overcome." Dahl found his good-mannered affa-bility "charming" and thought him "kind" if rather "lazy." Bryce had the splendid build and carriage of a natural athlete but had been barred from combat by a childhood sledding accident that left him with a bad knee, and a leg that was three inches shorter than it should have been. With his keen sense of adventure and wide-ranging curiosity, Stephenson, on Fleming's recommendation, had put him to work on all sorts of unusual schemes and operations.

When they were together, Fleming and Bryce acted like long-lost brothers, immediately squaring off for competitions, interrupting and insulting each other; they were obviously devoted. Ian had a way of entering a room and tossing out something faintly challenging that would wind Ivar up and get everyone going. He would never just say "hullo" but would start in right away with some taunt, but nothing so rude that anyone could really take offense. Lighting one of his gold-banded cigarettes, he would look down his nose and exclaim with a slight patronizing inflection: "My dear boy, that *ghastly* tie. Why can't you get yourself decently dressed." A "giant among name-droppers," as his colleague Donald Mclachlan once called him, he would breeze into town on some government propaganda business, and with a few well-placed phone calls would provoke instant action. Thereafter, his friends would find themselves in the company of very senior officers who were forever inquiring after the health of Ian Fleming. As Dahl would note fondly many years later, "There was a great red glow when Ian came into the room."

Fleming and Bryce were opposites in almost every way: Ian, intense and industrious, was regarded by his colleagues as something of a workaholic, while Ivar was supremely indolent and saved from complete inertia only by his instinctive, lightning-quick grasp of facts and events, which lent him an air of command in any situation. His linguistic dexterity, the result of an ill-spent youth cavorting around Paris, São Paulo, Kitzbühel, and Capri, covered the languages of the principal European powers and made him exceptionally well equipped for espionage work. He was well connected in New York and Washington and was recently married to Sheila Byrne, who brought to the union a hefty trust fund and Walter Lippmann as a brother-in-law. Bryce, who moved in fashionable circles on both sides of the Atlantic and seemed to know every girl with a private fortune, was without doubt one of the BSC's most aristocratic and elegant operatives.

While they generally observed the traditional taboo of not talking shop, Bryce had a hilarious store of tales from the early days of his apprenticeship in the intelligence service, which he later described as "misfires in the cloak-and-dagger machinery." Early in his tenure at the BSC, he had received orders from London to "make contact" with an agent who was due to arrive in New York the following day. His instructions were to be at the bar at Delmonico's at noon, and he was told he would be able to spot his man because the fellow would be carrying a folded copy of the *Daily Express* in his left hand. "In traditional spy-story style, I was to accost him with, 'I always think November is the best month in New York.'" Bryce recalled. "To which he would reply, 'The only time I came here before was March.'" After they had gotten these pleasantries out of the way, all Bryce had to do was escort him to the BSC's headquarters, and mission accomplished.

Needless to say, nothing went according to plan. Bryce made his way to the rendezvous spot, only to discover to his horror that his cousin, Bunny Phillips, a member of the Coldstream Guards, whom he had not seen since his escape from Dunkirk, happened to be at the bar. Terrified that his cousin would recognize him and that he would, in expressing his delight and surprise at seeing him again, completely blow his cover, Bryce made an elaborate effort to avoid eye contact. He sidled awkwardly up to the counter as his cousin moved to the far end. At six foot five, Colonel A. M. Phillips was hard to miss, but Bryce studiously looked past him. It was several minutes before he noticed the newspaper in Phillips' hand, and "the penny dropped." Not knowing what else to do, Bryce went up to him and, wearing a sheepish grin, said, "Hullo, Bunny. New York is wonderful in November, isn't it?" Mortified, Phillips said, "March, you fool," and they made a hasty exit.

It turned out Phillips had been temporarily posted to Stephenson's staff in New York. A few months later Bryce moved to Washington, where he was attached to the British Embassy and the Combined Chiefs of Staff. By a stroke of luck, "the Rabbit" was assigned to Donovan, and he and Bryce took a lease on a Georgetown house at Volta Place that belonged to a distinguished American general who was doing a tour in Europe. As Bryce soon discovered, his baptism by fire into special operations was not over. Soon another set of orders arrived, under top-secret seal, together with a small pill box and a thin cardboard packet. As Bryce recalled, the decoded instructions read: "To be opened by G140 or G142, when alone in secure quarters together." Filled with curiosity, the cousins hurried back to Volta Place and emptied the contents of the two packages onto the kitchen table. They contained one ampoule full of a yellow viscous liquid, one hospital syringe, and a set of directions for their use:

> *You are to run a test between you to familiarize yourselves on the effectiveness of the accompanying drug: a drug newly developed by London Science Section which, when properly administered, is capable of causing the subject to answer questions addressed to him, truthfully, immediately, and with complete frankness.*

There followed some complicated instructions about how to administer the drug (to be injected in a fatty substance, such as butter or bacon, just prior to being consumed by the unwitting subject); how to gauge the correct dosage according to the size, age, and health of the subject (a half gram was recommended); and a list of expected side effects. Under normal circumstances, five minutes after ingesting the drug, the subject should begin to exhibit increased animation, excitability, laughter, and uncontrollable hilarity accompanied by tears, followed ten minutes later by a relaxed, sometimes even affectionate, state. This final phase, known as "co-operative humour," was the prime period during which the subject should be interrogated. As the duration of this state was uncertain, and varied from subject to subject, time was short and no questions should be wasted.

Phillips was enthralled with the potential of the top-secret drug. He theorized that just as some German general was snuggling up to his mistress at the Ritz, she would feed him the stuff and then extract the organization plan for the whole German garrison in Paris. "What we could do with that!" he mused aloud. "Just think." They tossed a coin to see who would be the victim, and Bunny lost. Bryce filled the syringe with a demigram of the truth serum and injected one of the bacon and egg sandwiches the housekeeper had left for their supper. Preparing to play the interrogator, he gathered up a notebook and pencil. He watched his cousin swallow the doctored food, and then studied him closely for the first sign of the giggles. After a few minutes, Bunny was shaking with laughter and soon seemed on the verge of revealing the deepest secrets of his love life—he was in the midst of a prolonged affair with Lord Mountbatten's wife, Edwina—when he suddenly turned white as a sheet and collapsed. Bryce was sure he had poisoned him with an overdose. As he watched, his cousin's face became "lettuce green," and he did not appear to be breathing.

Terrified, he frantically felt for a pulse and tried to work out what to do: "Running to the telephone to make an emergency call was out. Security. Even unearthing the most reliable and security-checked medical man in Washington was out of the question. The drug was top secret and could under no circumstances be observed or described by anyone but us." The night passed, "filled with horror." Finally, around dawn, his cousin regained consciousness. He woke up with a splitting headache but otherwise seemed to suffer no adverse effects. Dutifully following their orders, they told no one but Stephenson about their ill-fated experiment. Stephenson informed them that the wartime drug was a prototype of the "wonder anaesthetic pentathol" and was being developed as a useful tool in extracting secrets from the enemy. Not long thereafter Phillips left to do intelligence work in the Far East.

While none of Bryce's exploits with his cousin compared to the "map affair," these wild adventures were by no means unusual. No idea was too crazy or too far-fetched to be considered useful by the BSC in its dirty tricks campaign against Britain's Nazi and fascist foes. The fact that a great many of their provocative efforts amounted to nothing, and that some even went terribly awry, was no deterrent. Some of the tactics seemed lifted straight out of a fraternity house handbook on freshman hazing. Bryce, who helped to set up the Camp X training facility, would have been familiar with BSC's preferred methods of harassment, as outlined in this how-to memo suggesting that it should be possible to invent "at least 500 ways of persecuting a victim" without the persecutor compromising his identity:

> *[The individual] can be telephoned at all hours of the day and night and when awakened can be apologetically assured that it is the wrong number; the air can mysteriously disappear out of his motor car tyres; shops can be telephoned on his behalf and asked to deliver large quantities of useless and cumbersome goods—payment on delivery; masses of useless correspondence can reach him without stamps so that he is constantly having to pay out petty sums of money; his lady friend can receive anonymous letters stating that he is suffering from mysterious diseases or that he is keeping a woman and six children in Detroit; he can be cabled apparently genuine instructions to make long, expensive journeys; a rat might die in his water tank; street musicians might play "God save the King" outside his house all night; his favorite dog might get lost.*

If the U.S. State Department and FBI had winked at the BSC's undercover activities during its first year, by 1943 they had become a major point of tension. Berle wanted Stephenson's organization, which was an amalgamation of at least nine different branches of the British secret services, curtailed. The previous winter he had pushed for the McKellar Bill, which would outlaw the BSC's counterespionage and propaganda activities in the United States and require the registration of all its foreign agents, effectively placing them under the supervision of the Justice Department. The bill was aimed directly at Stephenson and kicked off what Berle described as "no end of a row, though it was all covert." Berle provided a summary of the ensuing disturbance in his diary:

> *Briefly, the British Intelligence who maintain a lively if not too creditable spy system (masked under the name Security Coordination Police) don't want any such act because they don't want their spy system interrupted. They intervened with the Embassy but the Embassy said they could do nothing about it. Thereupon they intervened with Bill Donovan, who promptly put in a memorandum to the President asking him to veto the bill which was on his desk. I am impressed by Donovan's courage though I don't think much of it in terms of national wisdom. Why should anybody have a spy system in the United States? And what will anyone look like a little later when someone finds out about it?*

Much to Berle's dismay, FDR chose to modify the bill, adjusting it to allow agents of foreign powers allied to the United States to operate within its borders. In the weeks that followed, however, Berle's antagonism toward the BSC chief deepened to a grudge after he received a tip from the FBI that their people had discovered that a British intelligence agent, Denis Paine, was out to "get the dirt" on him. If the information was then leaked to the press, it could be used to force

Berle's removal from the State Department. According to the FBI, they had accumulated sufficient proof of Paine's sleuthing to call in Stephenson, who, as Berle recounted in his diary, professed "surprise and horror that any of his men should do such a thing." The FBI told the BSC chief that they wanted his spy out of the country by six o'clock "or else," and after some mild protestations Stephenson put Paine on a plane for Montreal. As Berle noted in his diary, the only dubious information the British had succeeded in digging up was an old newspaper clipping reporting that he had "twin bath tubs" in his house, which had long since earned him the absurd nickname Two Bathtubs Berle.

Incensed by the BSC's blatant meddling in domestic affairs, Berle was determined to see Stephenson taken to task. His outrage may have stemmed in part from his simmering antagonism toward the British, which some colleagues traced back to the grudge he bore Britain for its harsh treatment of Germany at the end of World War I. A Harvard prodigy, he had attended the Paris Peace Conference as a delegate at the age of twenty-four but resigned over the terms of the treaty. Berle's family was of German origin, and he had been tormented during his student years for having the same christian name as Hitler, and for his refusal to sign manifestos denouncing the Hun. The experience had left lasting scars. He remained bitter and convinced that the British saw him as "the easiest mark." Berle believed that the legacy of British intelligence in the United States, from Wiseman through Stephenson, was one of "half truths and broken faith." This latest incident involving the BSC's trickery only illustrated "the precise danger which is run from having these foreigners operate":

I plan to call the British Embassy and tell them that I am sufficiently experienced not to be influenced by this sort of thing, but that I think they should take it up with Lord Halifax and arrange to have this kind of thing stopped.

As promised, Berle raised a fuss about the BSC's attempts to discredit him and complained that Stephenson and his subversive agents were giving British intelligence a bad name. Having caught Stephenson in a rare blunder, Berle was determined to make the most of it. He demanded that the British ambassador informally provide "his personal word" that the BSC would never undertake such an action again. He subsequently met with Halifax; Sir Ronald Campbell, the embassy counsel; Hoover; and Attorney General Francis Biddle to review the regrettable situation. Afterward he noted with satisfaction that Hoover had indicated that "the President and the Cabinet were unhappy about Stephenson's activities and presence in their country." Their conclusion was that British intelligence in the United States should be confined to liaison and that they probably "needed a different type of man to head it."

When the press got wind of the dispute, the controversy escalated dangerously. As the undercover debate threatened to boil over, the BSC chief dropped out of sight for a while and avoided his Rockefeller Plaza office. The embassy and State Department spent the next few weeks dickering over the future of British propaganda and intelligence organizations in the United States. Ultimately Halifax—reportedly on orders from "C" and possibly even Churchill—backed Stephenson up. The British took the line that everything Stephenson had done had been duly submitted to Hoover and that he had at all times operated "with the direct authority and cooperation of the American officials." To mollify the indignant Berle, Halifax agreed that Stephenson's position should be "liaison, pure and simple." He also agreed that none of the 137 British intelligence agents (or so he claimed) in the United States would carry out any operations without passing them by Hoover first. In the meantime, Donovan had continued to defend the BIS and BSC, and Roosevelt was ultimately persuaded not to sign the bill. A watered-down version, one that the British could live with, was reintroduced as the Foreign Agents Registration Bill and several months later was signed into law. After the dust settled, Stephenson resurfaced, and took up exactly where he left off, with the slight inconvenience that his agents would now be working for (however nominally) the OSS. The overall effect of Berle's new measures was to drive Stephenson even further underground.

Hoover, like Berle, was not happy that Stephenson's interloping outfit would be allowed to continue to operate. "The implication that the FBI was not capable of dealing with sabotage on American soil was wounding to a man of his raging vanity," Philby later observed. "But the real reason for his suspicious resentment, which he never lost, was that Stephenson was playing politics in his own yard, and playing them pretty well." Hoover had never forgiven Stephenson for the part he played as "midwife and nurse to the OSS." According to Philby, "the creation and survival of the new organization was the only serious defeat suffered by Hoover in his political career—and his career had been all politics."

From time to time there would be another round of rumors that Stephenson was in trouble and "C" wanted him replaced. While nothing ever seemed to come of them, it did not auger well for the BSC's operations, which were being queried and second-guessed at every turn. Between the end of 1943 and the spring of 1944, Stephenson suspected "C" of sending a number of deputies to spy on him and perhaps even gather evidence against him should they at any point choose to recall him. When at one point Stephenson learned that Beaverbrook had dispatched a man to Washington to check up on him, he felt sufficiently threatened to take action. Stephenson, who had an instinct for the jugular, decided to turn the tables on their out-of-town guest. Dahl was reportedly instructed to lay the trap. The only implements he needed were a length of wire and a small microphone. He then invited Beaverbrook's sleuth to lunch at his Georgetown residence, plied him with drink, and got him talking, while the hidden mike he had rigged earlier in the day captured every word of their conversation. In a particularly cunning twist, Dahl encouraged the fellow to gossip about his employer, and he was predictably indiscreet. After listening to the damning tape, Stephenson forwarded it to Beaverbrook, confident it was the last he would hear of the matter. Dahl later used the incident as the basis of a short story entitled "My Lady Love, My Dove," about a husband who agrees to bug the bedroom of houseguests, but only after telling his wife, "That's the nastiest trick I ever heard of." In the story he conceals the mike in the springs of a sofa and runs the lead wire under the carpet to the door, at which point he makes "a little groove in the wood so that it was almost invisible."*

In the end, it appears "C" decided he did not want to risk a major showdown with the BSC chief. Stephenson was a dangerous opponent, and his ruthless tactics ensured his survival. He did not fool around. "If he told me a double agent was being 'naughty,'" recalled Cuneo, "well, the fellow could probably use a couple of bodyguards." Stephenson was an extraordinarily shrewd political infighter who, when not fending off detractors within his own intelligence community or deftly managing the resentful Hoover, was capable of cutting through thickets of red tape and improvising all kinds of action against the enemy with stunning speed and results. He managed to survive the internecine intelligence wars that flared between the SIS, OSS, FBI, and other branches of the Allied intelligence community because he was protected by powerful defenders, flanked on either side by Churchill and Roosevelt, and by all accounts had done such a magnificent job of shoring up his relationship with Donovan that he was almost unassailable. "His position was therefore exceedingly strong," recalled Sweet-

*The story was first published in *The New Yorker* in 1953 and later collected in *Someone Like You*.

Escott. "For one or possibly two of his masters in London might just conceivably be gunning for him at any one time, but it was most unlikely that they would all be doing so at the same moment, and so he could always get support from a third."

By April 1944 the air talks had progressed to a better phase, and it appeared likely that there would be a series of trilateral conversations among the British, Americans, and Canadians, all leading up to a United Nations conference to be held later in the year. There would also be exploratory conversations with the Russians and the Chinese, if they cared to join in. At the time of the international conference, the British Embassy would be sending a group of officials, assisted by experts and technicians, though Dahl did not know if he would be among the party, as the ambassador had not yet decided who would be going. Berle made a quiet trip to London with the idea of moving things forward, though purely for the purpose of exchanging views and not making any commitments.

Among the things on Berle's agenda was to tactfully let the British know that the United States intended to keep the Soviets informed of the progress of the air talks and of their intention to include them in the discussions, either in London or Washington. The meeting between Berle and Beaverbrook in London did not go well. Wallace heard a bitter summary of the conference from Marsh, who most likely had it from Dahl: "Both Berle and Beaverbrook approached the problem from a competitive, nationalistic standpoint of profits for big air companies, and from the standpoint of reconciling competitive positions between the different companies so that they might make the most money." The "tragedy," as Wallace later reflected in his diary, was that both countries were focused on the coming defense boom, and the consumer point of view was not represented. Some of the vice president's idealism must have rubbed off on Dahl—along with his oft-repeated phrase "the greatest good to the greatest number"—because the young airman was outraged that private greed would trump public interest. Dahl had become fiercely committed to the idea that this clash of air imperialists had to be eliminated so that civilization could reap the full benefits of modern aviation.

In the end, the Senate subcommittee never got anywhere. It turned out Pan Am had a stooge on the committee, Senator Ralph Brewster, a Republican from Maine, who openly favored a monopoly and whose job it was to line up enough noses for the airline to secure the right to handle American air interests in foreign negotiations. Brewster miscalculated, however, in part because Bennett Clark, after waffling, chose not to side with the monopoly lobby and stayed with the president's position. Then the independent airlines started a nationwide publicity campaign to oppose Pan Am, so that a number of senators who had previously been persuaded to vote for the monopoly declined to go along with the program, and a majority vote was never reached.

Dahl was immensely pleased with the small part he had played in foiling Pan American's monopolistic scheme. Even then the punishment of greed was a salient theme. From the very beginning, the American airline company had behaved dishonorably and had tried to acquire landing rights and develop commercial interests on the back of its wartime contracts. In its relentless quest for worldwide air supremacy, Pan Am had pitted one government against the other, driven its own bargains for exclusive agreements, operated under the "closed sky" system to its own advantage, and engaged in all manner of aerial skullduggery. The net result had been diplomatic chaos, which in turn had discouraged international cooperation, competition, and progress.

There was no sign, however, that America's "chosen instrument" intended to reform its ways. Even after the setback on the subcommittee, Pan Am continued its thinly concealed campaign for control of

American foreign aviation. Aware of this, the BSC kept the company under close scrutiny. British intelligence would later present Beaverbrook with evidence showing that Pan Am president Juan Trippe had negotiated a secret deal with Alfred Cecil Critchley, the managing director of BOAC, during his visit to the United States some months earlier. The two men were conspiring to perpetuate the cartel system and had struck a deal essentially giving Pan Am the cream of the North Atlantic routes, while agreeing to stay out of Europe, with BOAC getting the Continent and agreeing to stay out of South America. As this was not declared policy, and neither of the two companies had the authority to negotiate such a deal, Beaverbrook immediately put an end to it.

9

GOOD VALUE

As you often say, you get much out of your visits to my
house of ill fame.

—CHARLES MARSH to Dahl

BY THE SPRING of 1944, Dahl had less to occupy him than usual and
was at loose ends. His primary target, Henry Wallace, had departed
for a long trip through Asia on May 20 and was not expected back until
early July. The First Lady was also away traveling the world, which meant
that his White House invitations had dried up. Deprived of his high-level
sources, Dahl's supply of gossip, rumors, and political intrigue was reduced
to a trickle. While he waited for his prey to return, he spent his days troll-
ing Capitol Hill watering holes, trading mundane intelligence items with
Marsh, Pearson, Lippmann, and company. He was amused to learn that
his friend Creekmore Fath, who had been drafted and sent to the West
Coast, had landed a job with American intelligence. He had reportedly
used his close ties to Mrs. Roosevelt to get her to ask the president to have
him transferred. He was now in New York working for the OSS in civilian
clothes and might prove a fount of information.

Fortunately, the Georgetown social scene continued unabated. Dahl made the rounds of his weekly poker games and played bridge with everyone from Commerce Secretary Jesse Jones and the celebrated shipbuilder Henry Kaiser (whose amazing war production was one of the miracles of American know-how) to the popular Brazilian ambassador Carlos Martins. Evalyn Walsh McLean kept up her sparkling entertainments, despite the fact that most hostesses exercised restraint and had cut back on parties and frivolous spending, bearing in mind that their small sacrifices at home were nothing compared to the hardships of the front.

Dahl had rather a soft spot for the plucky dowager, who served as a volunteer air-raid warden and wore her uniform, helmet and all, to dinner on nights when alerts were expected. Since January the War Department had ordered practice alerts along the eastern seaboard, and periodically air-raid sirens would sound the warning of a blackout. On those occasions, she allowed plane spotters to stomp through her ornate mansion to take their positions on the roof, while she patrolled the streets of Georgetown, the Hope diamond tucked inside her shirt, the two-inch-wide diamond cuffs on her wrists gleaming even in the dark. Dahl always accepted her invitations with alacrity and relished his undercover role as house detective. In his letters home, Dahl noted that dining at Mrs. McLean's was always "good value," as he put it, because it was "like going to the circus and getting a free meal served into the bargain." As he could not write about what he was really up to, Dahl instead sought to amuse his mother with descriptions of the gaudy excesses of Mrs. McLean's soirées, where "everything was gold"—from the candelabras and place settings to the cutlery.

Pearson, who like Dahl was a regular at Friendship, reported that one night their irrepressible hostess informed the table that Henry Wallace attended "mystic séances." Apparently she also attended said séances, but not at the same time as the vice president, so she had never actually laid eyes on him "under the spell." Pearson regarded her testimony as complete hearsay but said it was being repeated all over Washington in the vein of another weird Wallace story. When Dahl passed this amusing morsel on to Marsh, he was none too pleased. He was incensed that McLean would go about maligning the vice president's reputation in his absence and snapped that it was "further evidence of what a lovely lady she is."

Even when he was out of the country, Wallace managed to be controversial. His pamphlet on the Pacific was published that spring and brought forth the expected cries of outrage from British officialdom. Lord Halifax, on orders from Churchill, registered a formal protest with Cordell Hull, the secretary of state, objecting to the "regrettable" statements made by the vice president. Halifax reportedly stressed that Wallace's timing could not have been worse: major joint military operations were under way, and Overlord was on the verge of being launched. Other British military representatives in Washington were quick to point out that Wallace's statements raised serious security issues. The Dutch ambassador, Alexander Loudon, was much disturbed by Wallace's demand that the date of "liberation" of colonial subjects should be specifically announced, and he arranged a meeting with Hull to discuss it. When Dr. Loudon arrived at his office, he spotted Wallace's pamphlet on the desk, but before the ambassador could utter a single word, Hull reportedly asked him whether he had read that "bunk." (It may have been "junk.") In any case, this went a long way to assuaging the ambassador's pique.

When the first intimations of trouble reached Wallace, he asked Marsh what if any reaction he had heard from his British friends. Marsh, laughing, reported that Dahl "had been very much excited" by the whole business. As Wallace observed in his diary, "Apparently while I was gone, the entire British Secret Service was shaking with indignation as well as the British Foreign Office. Dahl said to Marsh at the height of his indignation, 'This is very serious. You know

Churchill is likely to ask the President to get a new Vice President.' Charles replied merely by saying, 'Don't be a child. Grow up. Don't you know that the most certain way to be sure that Wallace will continue to be Vice President is for the word to get around that Churchill is against him?'" Marsh, who had oddly mismatched blue eyes, which could switch in an instant from warm to coldly objective, dismissed the episode as just another diplomatic tempest in a teapot. While the future of the empire was a topic dear to the British heart, he did not think it warranted the degree of melodrama the air attaché invested in it and told him as much. Dahl only wished he could be half as sanguine about the BSC's response and what it might bode for the vice president's future.

A few weeks later Dahl attended a dinner at Friendship during which Evalyn Walsh McLean entered into a spirited debate about the British secret service with Congressman Martin Dies, a big, burly, sharp-tongued Texan who was chairman of the House Un-American Activities Committee. Dies, who despised FDR and his liberal administration, liked to position himself as a superpatriot committed to rooting out subversives, and his committee had barraged the Justice Department with hundreds of documents aiding in the prosecution of Nazis, fascists, and Japanese agents. Dies had been holding forth about the extent to which Churchill was kept well informed by his secret service when Mrs. McLean indignantly interrupted him and protested that he should not "talk nonsense." J. Edgar Hoover was her best friend, and he always maintained that the American intelligence service was far superior. Insisting that the British secret service was "no damn good," she stared directly at Dahl.

Trying to sound blasé, Dahl, who was seated next to the actress Constance Bennett, commented offhandedly that he had always heard that British intelligence "was the best in the world." Dies wholeheartedly agreed, and told Evalyn she did not know what she was talking about and was wrong on all counts. Mrs. McLean refused to back down and claimed she had it on good authority that the British did not know "half of what is going on." They argued the issue back and forth until Mrs. McLean thirstily called for more champagne, and Dahl maneuvered the conversation onto less dangerous terrain.

Afterward Dahl wrote up the priceless exchange, adding it to his weekly compilation of material, and passed it on to be disseminated to higher authorities. He could not resist entertaining Marsh with his vivid account and gave him a copy of his Friendship revue, which he had artfully composed in the form of a musical comedy, featuring Constance Bennett drunkenly chorusing "Oh balls!" at regular intervals. Marsh invariably shared Dahl's snatches of gossip with Wallace and other close friends, so that the stories enjoyed remarkably swift and wide circulation in Washington.

Dahl's lack of discretion was dangerous. Once he started playing childish games, he could never help wanting to play them to the hilt. It had gotten him into trouble before, and Marsh should have cautioned him about being too free with his inside reports, lest his trademark sarcasm and pungent one-liners betray his identity. The American publisher, however, enjoyed it all far too much to want to discourage Dahl, and if anything he was guilty of encouraging him. Throughout that winter, they had merrily carried on their intemperate correspondence, regularly exchanging letters ridiculing Anglo-American relations, impugning each other's characters and credibility, and savaging all those in their incestuous Georgetown circle—from Evalyn Walsh McLean and Cissie Patterson to Isaiah Berlin—as imposters and potential enemy agents. Dahl had continued his practice of using British Embassy stationery, composing colorful little notes that positively oozed condescension on every page, and gleefully sending them in the ambassador's name, typing at the end of each one, "Yours Very truly, HALIFAX." He stopped short of actually forging the ambassador's name, however, and omitted a handwritten signature. For added effect, he secured the heavy buff-colored envelopes with red wax and the embossed embassy seal and wrote "SECRET" or "BY HAND/CONFIDENTIAL" on the front. It was pure escapism, all cheap satire, lewd insinuations, and swaggering sexuality—a way to lampoon a war that had dragged on too long and was far more arduous than anyone had thought possible. That it might be regarded as very bad form for a BSC operative to pen such foolishness seems not to have troubled Dahl in the least.

Dahl and Marsh constantly teased, taxed, and challenged each other. In a tongue-in-cheek letter dated February 12, 1944, and addressed to "The Mother of Roald," sent to him at the British Embassy, Marsh wrote that it had come to his attention that the "more-or-less infamous" author of *The Gremlins* had copied his ideas from an obscure book of Japanese fairy tales. He was apprehensive that plagiarism might be the least of his transgressions, and that Dahl, "seduced a bit for fame," might be guilty of "trafficking mentally with the enemy":

I've had some slight acquaintance with your son and his face seems open and kind. His personality is not one which would suggest any fraud. . . . Can you enlighten me somewhat about his childhood. Did he, between the age of two and twelve, display flights of fancy which a mother would call plain lies? Did the family by any chance have Japanese connections? Obviously your son is too inarticulate to be a student of Japanese.

Ten days later Marsh received a tart reply, purportedly from Halifax, informing him that his letter to Mrs. Dahl had been intercepted by the British Embassy's censors and was a matter of serious concern. The letter went on to say that the ambassador shared his suspicions about the airman and had ordered an investigation to be conducted along the very lines Marsh had suggested. A preliminary report had already revealed that Dahl had once engaged in a "tawdry affair" with a Japanese girl whom he had met on a coastal steamer in 1939, while traveling from Zanzibar to Dar es Salaam, and that he had been observed "to pinch her twice on the afterdeck." Clearly, this was evidence that he had been consorting with the enemy, and further investigation was warranted. . . .

Marsh's even more facetious follow-up, addressed to "My Dear Lord Halifax," opens with an apology for his being an "ignorant American," but hastens to add that he is confident that any lapse in manners on his part will be overlooked because "you, as a great gentleman, have an innate sense of democracy and are not a stickler for form and ceremony":

> To get to the nuts of the thing: You have a fellow named Dahl working at your shop who has had his points. In fact, he has been of slight use here and there due largely to his personal belief in himself. I am reminded of the quote, "Fools often go in where angels fear to tread. . . ."
>
> I attach here the proof that this ex-patriot of Norway, a mercenary for pay of his Majesty's, the King, has used your name in a most fraudulent manner. He has even plagiarized your character and expressions. He has, of course, feloniously used the EMBASSY STAMP.

At the bottom of the page, Marsh added a postscript in ink: "I leave this entirely to your intelligence. I deny emphatically the broad American viewpoint that you have no imagination."

The indignant rejoinder arrived four days later. Written on pale blue embassy letterhead, it defends His Majesty's employee against all spurious accusations and instead charges that Marsh is obviously a "troublemaker" and an "evil influence." After throwing down this gauntlet, Dahl has the ambassador pulling his investigators off his assistant air attaché's case and putting them to work looking into

Marsh's "murky career." Their early reports suggest that Charles E. Marsh, with homes in Washington, Culpepper County, Virginia, and Cape Cod, is "a sinister character who is known to operate from his home on R Street." Furthermore, Marsh is regarded as someone who is easily "hoodwinked" and to this end is regularly visited by a parade of German spies disguised as leading American politicians, most notably one who bears an uncanny resemblance to Vice President Wallace and is in fact an agent by the name of Kurt Schweinhogger. Marsh is also known to surround himself with attractive women, and "it is probable he is subject to some form of blackmail by at least one of these ladies." The letter goes on to say that the FBI is aware of this matter, and the only reason it has not stepped in is that all the information passed on by Marsh is so "misleading and garbled" as to be nearly incomprehensible and consequently poses no real threat. Halifax concludes the letter by saying that he will be forwarding a copy of his investigators' report to the secretary of commerce, Jesse Jones.

One evening just before Wallace left for China, Marsh, who was in a particularly expansive mood, showed the vice president samples of the illicit correspondence he had been carrying on with their mutual friend at the British Embassy. "The views attributed to Halifax were most amusing," Wallace noted in his diary, adding, "I am afraid Dahl has been rather irreverent."

Dahl and Marsh were so pleased with their humorous send-up of international diplomacy and espionage that they approached the New York publisher Curtice Hitchcock about possibly collaborating on a book together. The movie project with Wallace had long since petered out, and Dahl, always on the lookout for money-making enterprises and eager to retain the support of his generous patron, was casting about for a new joint venture. On April 22 Hitchcock wrote Dahl that he was sure the book would be "a tremendous hit," and if it went over as big in both England and the United States as he expected it would, "we shall be able to laugh ourselves out of some of the pain and casualties of this war":

> *Perhaps the nearest thing which has approached it in fantasy is your own* Gremlins, *but think of the wave of laughter across the Atlantic from both shores when the hoax is discovered and Halifax shows what a good sport he is.*

Hitchcock went on to say that he was "rather surprised" to learn that Dahl had managed to obtain Lord Halifax's consent for the book but was reassured by Marsh's explanation that His Lordship had a "statesman's mind" and "clear sense of humor." He understood, of course, the need to protect Dahl's position at the embassy and agreed with Marsh that for the time being the air attaché's part in the project "should be observed as a secret." Outlining the terms of the deal for Dahl, Hitchcock wrote that Marsh had agreed to be listed as the sole author of the spoof and would "take the full responsibility of having written it all." As a further precaution, Hitchcock promised to see to it that any trace of Dahl's participation was either "destroyed or hidden."

It seems highly unlikely that Halifax was ever consulted. Instead, Marsh sent Dahl an extremely crude, over-the-top letter requesting that he seek the ambassador's assistance on a sex manual for boys' preparatory schools that he was writing for Hitchcock, as he regarded "his Lordship as the purest English type of sex manhood," and "only a past master in the theory and practice of sex life can qualify as a collaborator." Marsh, who relished any opportunity to descend into vulgarity, went on to poke fun at Halifax's distinguished ancestry, disgusting sexual practices, and desiccated balls, culminating in the inevitable "dong" jokes. That said, he told Dahl that the ambassador was probably unique in the annals of literature and that his name as a coauthor would mean much: "My chapter on English public schools will need careful editing. I have never attended an English public school . . . Halifax could supply the equivalent English experience finishing with the dead end of the Oxford don—page Berlin." Marsh placed an asterisk by Berlin's name and tacked on a scathing addendum in which he ripped into the embassy's London liaison, a fixture at Georgetown dinner parties, who had rebuffed him once too often:

> Berlin is not a city nor does it refer to a music writer named "Irving." It refers to Isaiah the Great, the Ouija Board operator who forecasts the political scene for Churchill—Berlin, alias THE WHITE SLUG, the volcano of a mind, the cannibalistic brain that ate up a body at the age of two, the genius of sex sublimation, the perfect virgin. So give me Halifax the Pure but I trust the imperfect. Rather a dumb bunny of dignity rather than a genius of nonperformance. Always the practical man for mine.

And so their epistolary circle jerk continued. Dahl sent a reply in his own name stating that he had taken the liberty of showing Halifax Marsh's letter of the seventeenth of that month. After mulling it over in silence for what seemed like an eternity, he had called for his secretary and dictated a reply. Enclosed was another fake letter from Halifax to Marsh, expressing his great excitement at being asked to help with the sex book: "I have long played with the idea of how I could best give the world the benefit of my profound and widespread knowledge on this subject." Not one to be outdone in print, Dahl then launched into a lengthy discussion of His Lordhip's "extreme virility," the secret of his amazing performance, manifold experience, and subtlety of operation. The ambassador concludes the letter by stating that he cannot wait to have at the subject, adding, "I shall not fail to consult my chambermaid."

The war interrupted their schoolboy games, bringing their correspondence temporarily to a close. That spring Dahl did a good deal of traveling for the BSC—the exact nature of these missions is never specified—while Stephenson maneuvered to get the air marshal off his new recruit's back by having him officially transferred. Dahl also spent a lot of time and effort brokering a deal for his friend Ernest Hemingway to visit England. Martha "Marty" Gellhorn had called him at the embassy and asked if as a personal favor he could possibly help them arrange air passage across the Atlantic, which was next to impossible to obtain for civilians not engaged in priority war business. Gellhorn had begged Dahl to see what he could do, as she felt Hemingway had spent enough time in the bars of Havana and it was time he got back in the field. She was desperate to get out of Cuba herself and made no secret of the fact their life of drunken domesticity was driving her mad. Finally, in late 1943, she had traveled to Europe alone to report on the fighting for *Collier's* and ever since had been sending Ernest letters filled with all the news from London in an effort to entice him to join her. The saturation bombing of the coastal defenses in France had begun preparatory to the big push— to be called D-day—and her only thought was to be there in time for the invasion.

Dahl had no trouble convincing British authorities of the propaganda value of inviting Hemingway, the celebrated American author and war correspondent, to visit their embattled island. By March, he had worked out a compromise: If Hemingway would be willing to report on the RAF's heroic feats in one of the popular American magazines, the Air Ministry could be persuaded to allocate him a seat on a seaplane. Hemingway immediately agreed to the proposal and talked *Collier's* into giving him the assignment, effectively big-footing Gellhorn's work for the magazine. She was understandably miffed that after penning twenty-six articles for the magazine, her byline was to be eclipsed by her husband's. Making matters worse, Gellhorn, who had flown back to Cuba to help pry Ernest away from his hard-drinking buddies, now found herself stranded in the United States with no way to get back to England. In mid-April Britain tightened security in advance of the invasion and for the first time during the war imposed travel restrictions, including forbidding all neutral and Allied diplomats from leaving the country.

With no assurances from Dahl that a second seat could be allocated for her, Gellhorn went to Washington to see what strings she could pull, and she stayed at the White House for several days at the invitation of her old friend Eleanor Roosevelt. At the end of April, she wrote the First Lady thanking her for the swell accommodations and confided that she "had been a fool to come back from Europe" to fetch Ernest. She was almost "sick with fear" that she would miss out on the coming invasion and lose out on the one thing she cared most about seeing and writing about in her whole life. "Anyhow, due to Roald Dahl—who has been angelically helpful—Ernest will get off to England at the end of next week," she added. "But I have been shoved back and back, on the American export plane passenger list, and we do not know if the RAF will consent to fly me over (it's different for Ernest) and there I am." In the end, Dahl was not able to secure her a seat, and Gellhorn ended up being left behind and feeling badly used. A friend finally found her a berth on a Norwegian freighter, and she traveled to England as the sole passenger on a ship loaded with a cargo of amphibious personnel carriers and dynamite.

While the Hemingways were still in New York awaiting word of their passage, Dahl came up from Washington to raise a glass and see them off in style. They spent a drunken evening at the Hotel Gladstone, spooning caviar from a two-kilo tin and downing magnums of champagne. They were joined by the boxing coach George

Brown, who owned a gymnasium in New York where the macho author liked to work out when he was in town. Hemingway was sporting a long salt-and-pepper beard, which he claimed he could not
shave on doctor's orders. His story was that he was suffering from a
form of benign skin cancer due to years of exposure to the sun, but
he told so many different versions of the tale that it seemed likely he
had grown attached to the luxuriant growth. Gellhorn shipped out on
May 13, and four days later Hemingway took off on a Pan American
flying boat.

The Air Ministry, in its infinite wisdom, decided Hemingway needed
looking after during his tour of duty as an observer with the RAF and
assigned various officers to oversee his program and make sure the trip
went off without a hitch. It was the famous American author's first visit
to the city he insisted on calling "dear old London town," and his arrival
was expected to make news. Dahl, who was already on good terms with
the writer, was assigned to be one of Hemingway's RAF escorts. After
the isolation of Washington, Dahl welcomed the opportunity to get
back to London, despite the renewed bombings known as the "Little
Blitz," which the Luftwaffe was treating the city to that spring. There
had already been thirteen major raids, with as many as three hundred
bombers in each, and the nights were full of the sound of barking guns
and wailing sirens. He worried about the strikes being awfully close to
his mother's village and about his youngest sister, Asta, who was in the
WAAF (the women's branch of the RAF) and dangerously close to the
frontline radar stations on the south coast. For the most part, however,
the bombings seemed like a last hurrah. The Allies were about to invade
Europe and win the war. If he was lucky, he would have a grandstand
view of not only the military victory but, much more than that, the long
overdue triumph of a people who had refused against tremendous odds
to give up.

He had been very moved by a story he had recently heard about an old Scottish dowager who had lost three sons in the war. All three had been in the RAF. She was the sort of "fossilized" creature with a centuries-old manor house that one would normally stear clear of, but this Lady MacRobert, upon being told of the death of her last boy, gave a tremendous sum of money to the RAF to pay for the construction of a new Sterling bomber. When the plane was completed, she asked them to paint on its side, "Lady MacRobert's Reply." It struck Dahl as "something really dauntless, really indomitable," and he remembered thinking, "You really cannot defeat such people."

Dahl made his way through the scarred but still familiar streets to the Dorchester Hotel, which had survived five years of bombing remarkably unscathed, and knocked on the door of Ernest's suite. He found the great man preoccupied with an eyedropper and a bottle of hair-growing lotion, which, as it emerged, had something to do with the heavily bearded author's concern about the thinning white halo on his crown. "Why the eyedropper, Ernest?" Dahl inquired. "To get the stuff through the hair and onto the scalp," Hemingway explained. "But you don't have much hair to get through," Dahl pointed out. "I have enough," he retorted crossly.

His RAF guards notwithstanding, there was no keeping Hemingway out of trouble. With Gellhorn still on the high seas, making the arduous two-week crossing by boat, the writer was free to spend his nights drinking with old friends. After one especially rambunctious late-night party at the home of the photographer Robert Capa, a drunken Ernest and his kid brother Leicester (who was there as part of an army documentary unit) insisted on giving a sweaty demonstration of their boxing prowess for their fellow revelers. In the wee hours of the morning, Peter Gorer, a doctor at Guy's Hospital, and his German refugee wife offered to drive Hemingway back to his hotel. They made it less than a mile in the blacked-out streets before crashing into a steel water tank. Hemingway's head collided with the windshield, and he had to be pried from the wreckage. He and the car's other passengers were rushed to St. George's Hospital at Hyde Park corner, two blocks from the hotel. Hemingway suffered a concussion and later boasted that the doctors needed fifty-seven stitches "to tidy him up." A British dispatch reported that the famous author had been killed in a blackout accident in London, and the story was picked up by the major wire services. It was a whole day before the correction went out, during which Bumby, Hemingway's son by a previous marriage, who was stationed in Italy, mourned his father's loss by going on a serious bender.

When Gellhorn arrived in Liverpool, she was sandbagged at the dock by a throng of reporters demanding to know her view of her husband's accident. She was not amused by their colorful accounts of the boozy escapades that preceded the collision, which she considered contemptible at such a tense moment in the war. When she finally paid a sick call to the London clinic where he was recovering, she burst into laughter at the sight of his big head swathed in a giant white turban of bandages. Instead of being sympathetic, she ridiculed his appearance to all their friends. Her response brought little comfort to the bruised author, with his wounded pride, and they quarreled nonstop in the days that followed. While still at sea, Gellhorn had written to her oldest friend that she feared their relationship was "over"—she was "wrong for him," he was "bad" for her—and their hospital reunion only reaffirmed her conviction that it "would never work between [them] again." She did not yet know, but surely suspected, that Ernest had already moved on. Shortly after his arrival, he had begun avidly courting a tiny, buxom blond American reporter named Mary Welsh, who, although married at the time, proved amenable.*

Hemingway had originally planned to accompany some RAF pilots on their missions to the Continent, but his injuries forced him to post-

---

*Mary Welsh would become Hemingway's fourth wife.

pone the flights. He checked out of the clinic on May 29 and, despite bad headaches from the concussion, took up drinking and carousing where he left off. Ten days after his accident, he insisted on going on a low-level bombing mission against France, riding along in a Mosquito fighter, even though his head was throbbing and the sudden changes in altitude could bring on bleeding where he had been stitched up. Embarrassed by his bandages, Hemingway told Peter Wykeham Barnes, the group captain in command of the attack wing of Mosquitoes, a cock and bull story about stumbling and banging his head on the fountain outside the RAF Club in Piccadilly. The RAF was none too happy about taking him up, but Hemingway had come to see the war and would not be talked out of it. To the poet John Pudney, an RAF public relations officer, "He was a fellow obsessed with playing the part of Ernest Hemingway and 'hamming' it to boot." Compared with the many brave young soldiers, "who walked so modestly and stylishly with death," the swaggering American appeared to Pudney "a bizarre cardboard figure."

As D-day approached, the RAF issued the combat reporters a heavy blue woollen uniform with a shoulder patch marked "Correspondent" and a regulation escape kit that came equipped with such life-saving essentials as a map sketched on a silk handkerchief, cash, a compass, pills, and chocolate. On the weekend of June 2, Hemingway, along with several hundred other war correspondents, was briefed on the long-expected invasion by young British military officers and then assigned to various outfits. They were then taken to the south coast to wait for word that the invasion flotilla was on the move. In the early dawn hours of June 6, Hemingway, despite his still swollen knees, managed to clamber down the ropes with the others onto one of the landing craft going ashore at Omaha Beach, one of the beaches where the Allied landings had taken place. When they reached the French coast, he saw that the beach at the foot of the cliffs was strewn with burning tanks and the bodies of the dead, who "lay where they had fallen, looking like so many heavily laden bundles on the flat pebbly stretch between the sea and the first cover." They were the human cost incurred by the first six assault waves. The seventh was just getting under way, and a megaphone-wielding lieutenant in a control boat was wishing them good luck. Hemingway's landing craft stayed only long enough to put its troops and munitions ashore and help rescue the wounded from another swamped boat. Once the wounded had been lifted onto a destroyer, they pulled out.

Not long after the Normandy landings, Dahl stopped by the Dorchester and found Hemingway hammering away at his typewriter, putting the finishing touches on his D-day story, "Voyage to Victory." Looking it over, Dahl did not think it particularly good but kept his opinion to himself. To gloss over his disappointment, Dahl observed, "But Ernest, you've left out that marvelous bit you told me about the expression on the man's face as he tried to get out of the burning tank." Ernest looked at him in astonishment. "My God," he told Dahl, "you don't think I'd give that to *Collier's*, do you?"

Gellhorn, who was technically barred from covering D-day by U.S. Army regulations forbidding female correspondents access to the front, secretly made her way across the Channel in a hospital ship. As it stood in the shallows taking on wounded during the night of June 6, she managed to slip ashore and wrote a moving piece that ran in the same issue of *Collier's* as Hemingway's. She was still put out with Dahl when she caught up with him in London, but they eventually patched up their friendship. Her relationship with Hemingway, however, was beyond repair. The rift between them that Dahl had first detected in New York, and that had noticeably deepened during their stay in London, proved real and permanent. Before departing for Italy, Gellhorn sent Hemingway a brief but pointed note of farewell saying she was off to cover the war, "not live at the Dorchester."

Hemingway stayed on at the Dorch and devoted his time to chronicling the activities of the RAF. The first German buzz bomb, the flying V-1 rocket, landed in London on June 13. Hemingway wrote about the deadly new weapons, which Fleet Street had dubbed "the doodlebug" and "robot bombs," names he rejected as too coy; he persisted in calling them "pilotless aircraft" in his story for *Collier's*. The one-ton warheads inflicted massive damage on whatever poor pocket of the city they struck, and everyone in London quickly became attuned to the moment of danger when the motor suddenly cut off, signaling that the explosive warhead was about to drop. Hemingway waxed lyrical in his account of the RAF's valiant efforts to destroy the V-1s, attempting to intercept them midair "in that fine 400-mile-an-hour airplane, the Mosquito," and attacking their launch sites, hunting down "these monsters in their hellish lairs."

It was midsummer by the time Dahl made his way back to Washington, via a circuitous route that took him first to Montreal and New York. It was oppressively hot, hotter than anything he recalled in Africa or Iraq, with record-setting temperatures that July in the high nineties. The humidity made the air heavy, and everyone outside on the street moved as slowly as possible to keep from sweating profusely. He suffered sufficiently to move downstairs and sleep on the living room sofa. Adding to his discomfort, Dahl had injured his leg in London and was limping badly. The long transatlantic flight home had been spent in an agony of discomfort. His back ached, and his right leg was painful, and he thought the sciatic nerve was probably infected. He would have to see a doctor about it, which was "a nuisance" when he was so busy.

In the interim, Stephenson had finally contrived to have Dahl formally appointed to the British intelligence service. He was finished with his embassy duties and was now assigned to the BSC's Washington bureau as a liaison officer with the OSS. It would mean he would be doing a good deal more traveling, in addition to shuttling back and forth to the New York headquarters for meetings at least once a week. His replacement as assistant air attaché at the embassy was Squadron Leader William Roxburgh, and it fell to Dahl to show him around town and introduce him to Washington society.

Dahl was so preoccupied with his new job at the BSC and settling into his downtown office that he had given little thought to Marsh, who was away for the summer. A reproachful letter from his old friend pointed out this lapse: "Rumor from the Great Peeping Tom of American Journalism has it that you returned." Sounding put out at Dahl's long absence, Marsh immediately started in by needling him about his former boss, the ambassador. "Viscount Halifax has been upped in the peerage," he gloated, referring to recent stories in the papers. "Evidently great work was done for him by his loyal assistants which enlengthened the stature of his place in history regardless of the condition of the extremities of the body."*

As he plowed through Marsh's rambling, multipage discourse on the dismal state of American politics, which paled only in comparison to the appalling state of affairs in his own personal life, Dahl realized his old friend was deeply depressed and feeling lonely and neglected. Marsh was writing to him from Austin, following the Democratic revolt at the Texas convention, in which the anti-Roosevelt faction had overwhelmed the proceedings and the state party had been persuaded to throw its vote for Senator Harry Byrd for president. A riot had almost broken out, and even Lyndon Johnson had found himself caught in the cross fire between the loyalists and the renegades and heckled as one of FDR's "Yes-men" and "Pin-up Boys." Marsh had taken the southern Democrats' defection personally and was stunned that they broke faith with their president. While Roosevelt already had enough pledged del-

---

*The letter makes reference to a running joke between them that they crudely called the "Joy Through Length Project."

egates to get the renomination, Marsh worried that it could lead to a fight over the vice presidency and a crisis in the coming election:

> *Our electoral college has busted. Had you been here to advise me and report all that Isaiah [Berlin] knew in advance, I would not have been caught short (an American expression meaning a slight digestive inconvenience caused by a green melon) and permitted the kind of people you run with from stealing the Texas electoral vote from your friend Roosevelt. . . .*
>
> *I missed the Texas significance. The Duponts, and Pews and Gannetts ganged up on me. Republican money, carpetbagged (you don't know what carpetbagged means but I will tell you sometime) into the deep South with stacks of gold and bought up my loyal Texans so that now it looks as if Byrd, the Apple King of Virginia, will get the votes of Texas from the poor saps who think they are voting for Roosevelt.*

Now that Dahl had abandoned him in his hour of need, "I can only depend on Churchill himself to save Roosevelt from the meatball visage—Dewey the Great," Marsh sulked. "I will give you anything, anytime, anywhere, if you will only come and save America, America for me, me for America." Marsh maintained that it was Dahl's fault that he had been distracted and allowed the Texas delegates to slip through his fingers. He should not have thrown him a curve. "I was trying to entertain a female that you had introduced me to, a fifth column gal posing as an artist," he griped. "Had you been here, my dear sir, or had you not by design left others to appeal to my baser nature, I would have been on the job and not on a job."

By the end of the letter, Marsh's mood had improved, and he was back to his usual blend of profanity, political analyses, and rolling oratorical flourishes. While he may have been outsmarted and outspent in Texas, he was not going to take it lying down. He knew Texas like the back of his hand, and he knew the state's love of Roosevelt ran deep. Once they woke up to the presence of the carpetbaggers and understood that they had been duped into voting for Byrd instead of Roosevelt, Marsh was convinced there would be hell to pay. The down and dirty tactics of the anti–New Dealers and Roosevelt haters had spurred him into action: "I am about to start a revolution to eliminate the appendix of the electoral college from the Constitution, and reestablish the equality of the common man in blood, sweat and tears." When he was through, that gang of southern conservatives would not be leaving town with any Byrd-for-president racket. Eager to have his sidekick join him, Marsh promised Dahl it would be "a great show" and definitely worth his while. "If you get here and travel in a train deluxe," he wrote, "we will see a sort of wild west shooting . . . which you can tell to your children and grandchildren, even to the great Halifax."

10

ENEMY MANEUVERS

There was this rather ingenious RAF wing commander,
which was me you see.

— ROALD DAHL

DAHL'S DOUBLE LIFE was sorely tested that summer. By July, British
authorities were becoming increasingly alarmed by the "whispering campaign about the President's health," as Isaiah Berlin reported
in one of his weekly dispatches, as well as "the horrid prospect of Wallace." The Democratic National Convention in Chicago was to open in
just nine days. Dahl, who anxiously awaited the vice president's return,
had to report every comment or utterance that might in any way con-
firm the rumors that Democratic operatives were trying to persuade
Roosevelt to commit to another running mate, while at the same time
reassure Marsh that everything he heard confirmed that Wallace was
still the party favorite. It was a difficult situation. To Marsh, Wallace
was an irreplaceable asset to his country; to the British, he was just a
liability. Dahl's loyalties were divided, and he could see no happy reso-
lution to the problem.

When Wallace finally arrived in Washington on July 10, the wolves were already circling. He had been out of the country for fifty-one days on his Asian tour, and his enemies had been busy in his absence. The first warning came from Wallace's old friend and supporter Senator Joe Guffey, an influential Pennsylvania Democrat, whom he spoke to by phone when he touched down in Fairbanks, Alaska. "Things are not going well," Guffey warned him. "Some people around the White House are saying, 'We need a new face.'" A telephone call from Judge Sam Rosenman, the last of the original members of FDR's brain trust, was still more worrisome: Secretary Harold Ickes wanted to see Wallace at the earliest possible moment, by which he meant lunch on Monday, July 10. The urgency was that Ickes had a date on the West Coast and was leaving town on the night train. As Wallace, who had logged 27,000 miles and had circled the globe, recalled: "Ickes does not fly and so it was proposed that I fly all night in order to make it possible for Ickes not to fly at all." As he made his way back to the capital, Wallace thought better of Ickes' invitation and sent a wire stating that he thought it advisable for him to see the president first. After traveling all night and arriving in the capital at 9:30 A.M., he phoned the White House at ten, only to be informed that the president was bathing. Wallace then received word that Roosevelt wanted him to meet with Ickes and Rosenman before meeting with him at 4:30 in an "on-the-record conference."

While he had come to expect a certain amount of "intrigue" from the White House, and from Roosevelt's palace guard in particular, Wallace braced for the worst. He took the precaution of asking Ickes and Rosenman to meet him for a private lunch at his apartment at the Wardman Park Hotel, where he could be sure to avoid reporters. After a half hour of pleasantries, they got down to business: Wallace had made too many enemies and had become "a bone of contention" in the party and ought not let his name be presented at the Democratic National Convention in Chicago on July 18. Before Ickes lowered the hatchet, Rosenman, who was diligent without being ruthless, explained that the president preferred Wallace as a running mate but agreed with the consensus that he could not win in Chicago and would do nothing to help him win in the fall. Before they could go any further, Wallace slammed the door closed on the conversation, abruptly telling them he had to make a report on his China mission that afternoon and had no time to talk politics. He would not be bullied into withdrawing from the race.

Wallace's meeting with the president began on a cordial note, and they spent some two hours discussing his China trip. Then Roosevelt brought up politics, but before saying his piece he told Wallace that when he left he should say no politics were discussed. As the president put it, "I am now talking to the ceiling." Roosevelt began by saying that Wallace was his choice for a running mate, and he said he was willing to make a statement to that effect. He then proceeded to voice doubts about the idea, however, explaining that "a great many people" had cautioned him against it, arguing that it would be a repeat of the bruising battle in 1940, when Wallace was roundly booed at the convention, and Roosevelt had to force his deeply unpopular choice of a running mate on the unhappy delegates. Wallace immediately replied that he did not want to be "pushed down anybody's throat" and wanted to know if the president definitely wanted him in the second spot on the ticket. Roosevelt, Wallace recalled, "was very ready with his assurance."

Yet in the next breath the president allowed as how he had been told that Wallace could cost the Democratic ticket from one to three million votes. Changing tacks, Roosevelt then said he could not bear the thought of the vice president being put up before the convention and publicly rejected. "You have your family to think of," he said. "Think of the cat calls and jeers and the definiteness of rejection." Wallace told him he was not worried about his family and later noted that at the time he was thinking, "I much more worried about the Democratic party and you than I am about myself and my family." Roosevelt asked him to come back for lunch two more times that week to talk. Wallace, who had been gone for a long time and wanted to find out where he stood, agreed to do some checking and report back.

He immediately got in touch with Charles Marsh, who in his absence had volunteered to undertake a lengthy state-by-state election report on what he called "Wallace's Pre-Convention Situation." Reading it over, Wallace agreed with Marsh that the results "looked very good." The following morning, Tuesday, July 11, Roosevelt finally confirmed what the papers had been presaging for months—he would be seeking a fourth term. When they met for lunch later that day, Wallace gave Roosevelt an elegant Uzbek robe, a gift from Tashkent officials, along with the lengthy memorandum by Marsh on the vice presidency. Roosevelt methodically thumbed through Marsh's report, as well as the state-by-state tabulation of the vote he had prepared with help from Sydney Hillman, the labor leader who was head of the Political Action Committee and solidly behind Wallace. As the president would not be at the convention—he would be on a ship bound for Hawaii and a meeting with his Pacific commanders, which Republicans labeled a political ploy to remind voters he was commander in chief—Wallace gave Roosevelt a statement, drafted by Senator Guffey, designed to seal his nomination on the first ballot. Before he left, the president mentioned that many people looked on Wallace "as a Communist—or worse." He seemed worried about some of the more infamous Wallaceisms of the recent past, specifically mentioning his much-derided comment that he wanted "to give a quart of milk to every hottentot." Wallace flatly denied ever making such a statement, and the president seemed genuinely surprised.

That afternoon Marsh phoned Wallace to report on the latest "enemy maneuvers." Of the half dozen ambitious men vying for his job,

three had emerged as potential threats. According to Marsh's information, Wall Street was lining up behind the progressive southerner Al-
ben Barkley from Kentucky, though he was even older than Roosevelt.
Ickes was pushing hard for the Supreme Court justice William O.
Douglas. Then there was Robert Hannegan, a gregarious former professional baseball player who was the party chairman, whose game,
according to Marsh, was "to knock Wallace at every possible turn" in
hopes that his man Truman ultimately got the nod.

It turned out Marsh was right on the last two counts. The president
had given Wallace every assurance that they were still the "same old
team" at their last lunch meeting on Thursday, July 13, explaining that
he would settle the vice-presidential matter by sending a letter of endorsement to the convention chairman saying that he would vote for
Wallace if he were a delegate. But Roosevelt had in fact already made a
separate promise to Hannegan. During a meeting with his top advisers
the previous evening, the president had agreed to run with either one of
two alternate candidates—Douglas or Truman—hastily scrawling their
names in that order on the back of an envelope. Hannegan, who would
not rest until he had nailed down the nomination, tried to browbeat Wallace into not going to Chicago and withdrawing then and there. Failing
at that, Hannegan finagled another meeting with the president, corner-
ing him in his railroad car in Chicago's Rock Island railroad yards while
en route from Hyde Park to San Diego, and hammered on about Truman
until an exhausted Roosevelt, who was sicker than anyone knew, finally
acquiesced. Roosevelt had equivocated to the end, giving Hannegan the
opening he needed, and he left with a personal note from FDR, written
in longhand, first endorsing the modest, hardworking Truman, who had
no real enemies, followed by Douglas, who was generally admired on the
Hill. The president probably conceived of it as a private document, to be
circulated by Hannegan in the event Wallace bombed or the convention
became deadlocked.

Although rumors of a secret White House conference dumping Wallace from the ticket rippled across Washington, Marsh refused to give credence to the idea. Then on July 17, the day before the convention opened, Roosevelt's letter putting Wallace's name into nomination was read into the record. It was so lukewarm as to be almost indifferent:

> *I have been associated with Henry Wallace during his past four years as Vice President, for eight years earlier while he was Secretary of Agriculture, and well before that. I like him and I respect him, and he is my personal friend. For these reason, I personally would vote for his renomination if I were a delegate to the Convention.*
>
> *At the same time, I do not wish to appear in any way as dictating to the Convention. Obviously the Convention must do the deciding. And it should—and I am sure will—give great consideration to the pros and cons of its choice.*

The veteran reporter Allen Drury, political correspondent for United Press, later summed up FDR's letter in his journal: "If you want him, well, OK. If you don't, well, OK. Suit yourself. And so long, Henry."

Wallace vowed he would "fight to the finish." Marsh, realizing they were facing long odds, rose to the challenge. The Texas publisher, an old hand at last-ditch political plays, knew that if Wallace was positioned as the underdog going in, they might be able to capture the sympathy of the press and possibly pick up steam for his nomination. Marsh gathered a large, colorful contingent to fight for Wallace at the convention and help round up delegates. He took a special trainload of supporters from New York to Chicago, filling it with labor people, mostly from the Garment Workers Union, and booked a full floor of the Sherman Hotel. He and his crusading "seamsters" swamped the hotel, the overflow squatting in the hallways and staircases, while others scurried around Chicago and made plans to stampede the convention hall.

On the afternoon of Thursday, July 20, Wallace took to the podium and delivered the speech of a lifetime, electrifying the huge crowd packing the sweltering stadium. "The strength of the Democratic Party has always been the people," Wallace began, "plain people like so many here in this convention—ordinary folks, farmers, workers, and businessman along main street." The delegates loved it and responded with a rousing ovation, the cheering reverberating through the hall. Wallace loyalists, led by Joe Guffey, smoked out the back-room conspiracy to bounce Wallace from the ticket and forced Hannegan to divulge Roosevelt's secret handwritten note naming Truman and Douglas at 6:30 P.M., just as the delegates were gathering for the evening session. The press was scandalized, and although Wallace was disappointed by the news, nothing could have induced him to walk away at that point.

That night, after Roosevelt delivered his solemn acceptance speech from a West Coast naval base, his disembodied voice echoing from the loudspeakers, the galleries suddenly erupted with hundreds of loyal delegates waving Wallace placards and demanding their candidate's nomination. The convention organist struck up the "Iowa Corn Song," his homespun theme, and the hall reverberated with the deafening chant "WE WANT WALLACE! WE WANT WALLACE!" For a brief moment, Marsh's friend Senator Claude Pepper, who was with the Florida delegation, thought the Wallace parade had pulled it off. From what he could see, standing on his chair and looking down at the forest of state standards raised in the air, it appeared that "if a vote was taken that evening, Wallace could be nominated." The Wallace demonstrators looked like they were about to riot. Hannegan, realizing that emotions had become too hot, hastily yelled at the party chairman to adjourn the night session. Pepper tried to reach the platform, to appeal to the floor not to adjourn. With a bang of his gavel, it was over. The crowd groaned in protest, but the police were already ushering them toward the exits.

The next day, inside Chicago Stadium, the mood had altered. The party bosses had regained control of the convention, and the Democratic machine had the delegates back in hand. In due course Truman was nominated. After a sweaty, interminable nine-hour session, the reading clerk announced the final count over the loudspeaker system: "For Truman, 1,031; for Wallace, 105; for Douglas, 4."

Marsh, who had stayed at the hotel and was getting reports by the minute, was crushed. He had put his heart and soul into seeing his principled friend reelected and was overcome with anger and grief at the outcome. Vanquished, he left Chicago on the night train. The union workers had to be back at work the next morning and had no choice but to abandon their seats to the delegates and head home. Wallace took the loss better than Marsh did. He had never been a popular candidate and was unbowed in defeat, saying, "It was a fine fight, and everything is all right." In the end, the thing that bothered him most was Roosevelt's strange betrayal. Why had he not simply asked Wallace to pull out and saved them all a lot of time and trouble? Why bother with the empty endorsement? It was especially puzzling in light of the president's last words to him at the White House, uttered in the friendliest tone and accompanied by a full smile and hearty handclasp: "Even though they do beat you out in Chicago, we will have a job for you in world economic affairs."

All this, of course, Marsh relayed to Dahl in gory detail. His anger grew in the retelling. Marsh blamed the defeat on an underhanded plot by party professionals who put compromise above "character, enterprise, conviction and public virtue." He wrote a cascade of postconvention memorandums in the following days and weeks, all of them suffused with bitterness toward the president. "When a 'dark horse' like Truman comes through, the simplest explanation is to say that he had a good jockey," Marsh wrote on July 28. "In this case the bosses and Roosevelt did not want Wallace. The second 'secret'

letter of Roosevelt was the whip at the finish that nosed out Wallace."
As angry as he was, Marsh rejected the idea that the president had
deliberately set out to double-cross the vice president and instead saw
it as a sign of "political feebleness rather than political leadership"—a
sign that FDR was finally losing his grip. Roosevelt was no "Richelieu,"
he concluded in yet another memo analyzing the president's mind-set.
"It is extremely difficult, even distressing, for us to see Roosevelt as an
aging and vacillating man:

> It shows Roosevelt as a liberal under such heavy pressure that he himself
> went into temporary collapse. It is reasonable to believe that he sincerely
> sacrificed Wallace; that his soul was in a torment of uncertainty; and
> that he was in great pain emotionally. Roosevelt perhaps saw the world
> and peace and himself as a necessary agent. He traded his country's in-
> surance policy in order to insure a continuation of himself.

Marsh told Dahl he would work for the president's election because
he was afraid of what the Dewey alternative might mean, but then he
was finished. He was disgusted with the party pros. The friends of
liberalism might well continue to serve and fight under Roosevelt, but
they would go forward with a "heavy, uncertain step." After November 7,
he would rethink his role. "When Wallace got defeated it broke Dad's
heart," said Antoinette.

It was a dirty convention and made for a lot of hard feelings all
around. Roosevelt tried to be conciliatory and asked Wallace to remain
part of his administration, telling him he could have his pick of jobs
with the exception of secretary of state. That job was reserved for his
dear friend Cordell Hull, his secretary of state for the past ten years,
who was in his last stint of public service. Roosevelt hastened to assure
Wallace that he wanted him to take an active role in postwar planning
and to sit on "some international conferences." Wallace felt that as one

of the strongest leaders in the Democratic Party, he should by rights have the State Department, the most important cabinet post. Out of deference to the president's wishes, however, he settled for secretary of commerce, the seat currently occupied by his bitter adversary Jesse Jones. The president had already indicated that after the election one of the first people he wanted to boot from his administration was the arrogant "Jesus H. Jones." The ambitious commerce secretary had been a thorn in Roosevelt's side as well, and it suited him to allow Wallace to replace him, thereby exacting a measure of revenge on both their behalfs.

Everything about the 1944 presidential campaign aggravated Marsh, and he quarreled with old friends and allies. He had a falling out with his old friend Mrs. Ogden Reid, upon learning that she had recently gone to England to sell Churchill, Eden, and Brendan Bracken, minister of information, on Dewey as the man to best further the cause of Britain in the United States. Marsh was disgusted and agreed with Wallace that she had become an obnoxious woman and had lost the charm that once covered her claws. Dahl, as he did for all Marsh's foes, gave her the unflattering nickname "Horse-whip Helen" and made a point of deriding her in his subsequent letters.

Dahl knew that Marsh's real beef with Helen Reid was that he blamed her for preventing him from seeing Lord Beaverbrook during his recent visit to Washington. Beaverbrook, accompanied by a battalion of advisers, had come to advance the talks on aviation and for three weeks had been the toast of Georgetown society. His presence, coinciding with a visit by the Duke and Duchess of Windsor, created a flurry of excitement, and as Marsh wrote Dahl, Mrs. Reid, "the great female agent of the British Empire in America," could hardly contain herself:

The great social humiliation of my short life occurred when the great adventuress Mrs. Reid, who beavered her way into control of the Her-

ald Tribune—"beavered" did I say—broke an engagement for me to dine with her, said to her secretary that she was out of town, and by postponing my dinner to the following Monday bootlegged the Duke and Duchess into her home.

It was only by the merest accident the following day, when Marsh called upon one of Mrs. Reid's favored guests, that he happened upon the truth. She had quietly gone behind his back and informed British intelligence that he was "too loud" for the duke and arranged for his place to be given to one Major George Fielding Eliot, a military historian and major player in the British front organization Fight for Freedom. All this, Marsh explained in his long-winded fashion, added to his "great regret at not having seen the Beaver."

With Wallace out of the running, the tension in Dahl's daily life was greatly relieved. At the end of the summer, Dahl decided to throw a party at his Georgetown residence. As gloomy as Marsh might be about the future of America, there was only good news from Europe. Just days earlier they had heard that the Nazis had finally been chased out of Paris, and the Allied armies had them on the run. There were rumors of attacks on Hitler's life and revolt inside Germany. Dahl had heard that the flying bombs had stopped landing on London, and his family was finally safe. The end of the war was in sight. He had even managed to sell his last unsold story, "Missing Believed Killed," to a magazine called *Tomorrow*. He was in a mood to celebrate.

The buffet dinner hosted by "Wing Commander Dahl" was written up in Hope Ridings Miller's gossip column and sung the praises of the British pilot-turned-author who "made all of us Gremlin-conscious." The guest list included Charles Marsh; the Brazilian ambassador, Carlos Martins; Walter Lippmann and his wife, Helen Byrne (Armstrong) Lippmann; and Archibald MacLeish, a poet and former colleague of Ingersoll's at *Time* who was the librarian of Congress and had been assistant director of the Office of War Information supervising American propaganda. There were a fair number of high-ranking British officials, including Mr. and Mrs. Paul Gore-Booth, the air commodores Blackford and Lydford and their wives, and Captain Abel-Smith of the Royal Navy. Among the many young colleagues Dahl invited was Donald Maclean, a good-looking thirty-one-year-old Scotsman who was first secretary at the embassy and chief of the cipher room.*

Dahl had also been seeing rather a lot of Millicent Rogers, which was an occupation in itself. He had spent the Easter holidays at her estate in Virginia, and they had gone on a number of weekend getaways. She had been kind enough to invite him to stay with her while his Georgetown house was being redecorated, so he spent the latter part of the summer living in splendor. He was terribly impressed with her art collection, which he studied closely in his spare time. Dahl took no small amount of pride in the fact that he had managed to acquire a Matisse, picked up comparatively cheaply during his last trip to the war-ravaged Continent, and two paintings by Matthew Smith, an English disciple of Matisse's and a friend since 1941. Both of Smith's sons had been in the RAF and had been killed in the war, and he had taken a liking to Dahl, who was then just back from North Africa. One of the Smith paintings was a striking portrait of Dahl in uniform, his tan face framed by a vivid orange drapery, staring off into the middle distance. It was the centerpiece of his own modest collection, which he planned to display in his newly refurbished living room.

Marsh was greatly amused by Dahl's relationship with the Stan-

---

*Unbeknownst to Dahl, Maclean was also a Soviet agent and a member of the Cambridge spy ring. He became head of the American department of the Foreign Office and passed on classified information about the development of the atomic bomb, before defecting to Moscow with Guy Burgess in 1951. Dahl later wrote a short story about Maclean entitled "The Vanishing Act." It was never published.

dard Oil heiress, and professed an interest in examining "the beautiful home of the lady of the curvature of the spine," as he dubbed his eminent Virginia neighbor, "even if I am not a great art collector, and am a mere homebody." Rogers had recently graced the pages of *Vogue*, and Marsh teased Dahl for dating "the great international society highlight of the month of August 1944." Given his own romantic difficulties at the moment, he was actually quite jealous of Dahl's many female admirers and the fuss they all made over him. In honor of Dahl's birthday that September—he turned twenty-eight on the thirteenth—Rogers threw him a fancy party and invited the usual cast of ambassadors, diplomats, undersecretaries of state, and assorted socialites and sycophants. Everyone sipped champagne and made polite chatter, and Dahl later complained that he found the whole thing a crashing bore.

On September 18 Dahl paid a courtesy call on the vice president at his office and offered his heartfelt condolences. He was sorry the convention had ended so unhappily for Wallace, though it went without saying that his superiors had no cause for regret. With his lame-duck status, Wallace would now have limited access to secret information, and Dahl knew he would be less and less use to him in his undercover activities. Perhaps with that in mind, Dahl, speaking frankly for the first time, informed the vice president that he was now with the British secret service. With the European war winding down, security was somewhat relaxed, and those in the BSC could officially introduce themselves to colleagues and friends. Showing off a little, Dahl told him that for a time the British government had been "scared to death" that Roosevelt would offer Wallace the State Department and had raised strong objections. Dahl claimed that British authorities already knew that the president, if he won, would be putting Wallace in the cabinet but had been reassured that it would not be as secretary of state. Beyond that, he indicated that his superiors did not much care what happened to the vice president. Dahl made no mention of the controversial pamphlet, or his private concerns about the part the BSC, and Stephenson in particular, may have played in Wallace's fall from power.

Since Dahl was putting his cards on the table, Wallace decided to venture a few questions about the clandestine intelligence organization of which the airman was now a member. Who exactly was he working for? Dahl answered cautiously that the head of the BSC was "a secret" and known to only a handful. "I asked if he knew his name," Wallace recorded in his diary. "He said 'yes.' He says this secret and powerful gentleman can go right in to see the King or Prime Minister day or night, unannounced, any time he wants. I asked if he himself could blow in on this high-powered gentleman unannounced? Dahl was shocked at the thought."

Wallace, who was not as wholly naïve as Dahl supposed, was somewhat bemused by the extent to which the novice spy seemed to be in awe of his employer, especially when Dahl began boasting about the BSC's vast covert network, claiming the British had had "10,000 agents in Germany all through the war." Wallace found some of his claims strained credulity. If he was shocked by any of Dahl's revelations, however, he did not let on. It would be surprising, though, if he did not feel somewhat disappointed that the young man he had grown so close to, even sending him a little bag of his special plant fertilizer at Christmas, had not been entirely on the up-and-up. As Wallace's diary discloses, there was a new note of skepticism in his assessment of his British colleague. "Dahl is an awfully nice boy of whom I am very fond," Wallace observed. "Undoubtedly at times he pulls Charles Marsh's leg by telling him things that are not true."

In early October, Dahl consulted a specialist in New York about the recurring pain in his back. In the three years since his accident, he had become accustomed to a constant dull ache and even periodic bouts of real discomfort, but with the arrival of the cold weather it had become measurably worse. On the doctor's recommendation, he went into the hospital for a series of X-rays and tests. After suffering a bad reaction to a lumbar puncture, he was laid up for nine days and left the hospital feeling "just the same as before." He was no sooner back on his feet and buttoned into his blue winter uniform than he found himself caught up in the swirl of events and traveling almost constantly. Roosevelt had surprised the British by announcing plans for a large international air conference in Chicago, which threw the Foreign Office and Air Ministry into turmoil. When he heard the news, Beaverbrook had reportedly "laughed loud and long," but mirthlessly, and informed Churchill that the peremptory strike was a clear indication that America "was determined to call the tune." Preparations for such a meeting would normally take weeks of planning and effort, and Beaverbrook, who was tired of the minutiae of the civil aviation negotiations, declared it "not his cup of tea" and handed the job off to Lord Swinton.

Dahl, who was part of the British delegation, first went to Toronto for a meeting with Swinton and the Canadian delegation, before proceeding on to the International Civil Aviation Conference, which began in Chicago on November 1. At the luncheon on opening day, Lord Swinton argued bitterly with Berle, the chairman of the U.S. delegation, which also included Senator Owen Brewster, Pan Am's "stooge." Swinton a stiff old-empire type, was in favor of an equitable "parceling out" of the air traffic among nations, while Berle wanted a free-for-all. Berle took Swinton's supercilious attitude to mean he was returning to their old position "that controls be applied dividing traffic between Britain and the United States on a fifty-fifty basis," which at this point meant America would have to divert traffic to the British lines out of the goodness of its heart. Swinton said he thought that this sounded fair. Berle, whose animosity toward Swinton caused him to take a harder line, insisted that it was "as impossible now as when it was broached last spring," and that America was not in the business of supporting British aviation. There would be no turning back the clock to the glory days of British mercantilism. "In other words," Berle declared impatiently, "there is no excuse for a modern air British East India Company or Portugese Trading Monopoly or 'Spanish Main' conception."

The conference got off to a rocky start and more than once came close to derailing in face of insurmountable obstacles. Juan Trippe kept his distance from the proceedings, but Pan American agents were everywhere, stirring the pot and feeding stories to the *Chicago Tribune,* the leading Roosevelt-baiting paper, making it seem as though the Americans were giving too much away. Both countries kept up stiff propaganda campaigns, but little else could be expected under such strained circumstances. As Berle observed in his diary, "This is merely a note, the only moral of which is that politics is nasty." Nevertheless by day ten there was reason to hope that both sides would eventually be able to reach an accord and start the ghastly process of putting the policy resolutions into agreed-on texts. In a weary letter to his mother, Dahl wrote that he was so befuddled by the many days of dashing between airports and meetings that unless he glanced at a newspaper, he had no idea what day it was.

The conference dragged on for nearly a month. The talks threatened to break down again when the British, in secret meetings, balked at the idea of putting their bases all over the world at the disposal of other nations—primarily the United States. Again the conference became bogged down in controversy and was saved only by Roosevelt's pointed intervention, when he told Churchill that people would wonder at the chances of their two countries "working together to keep the peace if we can not even get together an aviation agreement."

Several days later Roosevelt received a conciliatory message from the British prime minister, who blamed Berle for any apparent misunderstanding. Even so, his letter seemed to sum up the accumulated hurt of a war that had placed the United States in "an incomparably better position," and not just when it came to the aircraft industry:

> You will have the greatest Navy in the world. You will have, I hope, the greatest Air Force. You will have the greatest trade. You have all the gold. But these things do not oppress my mind with fear because I am sure the American people under your reacclaimed leadership will not give themselves over to vainglorious ambitions, and that justice and fair play will be the lights that guide them.

While the conference ground on, the British still expected the hoped-for Roosevelt landslide on November 7. No matter how often they were told that the election results were a foregone conclusion, Dahl's superiors found new grounds for concern. Dewey, who had tapped John Bricker as his running mate, was garnering a lot of press attention and gaining ground. Roosevelt's absence at Chicago, along with the haggard photo of him that appeared in the newspapers the day after his acceptance speech, was vivid proof of his decline in health and had been the talk of the convention hall. Dewey, meanwhile, was busy acting presidential and impressed reporters in a postconvention press conference by following up a question about the danger of "changing horses" midstream with an uncharacteristically clever quip about how the Democrats had already "changed half a horse" at Chicago. It was the sort of playful joust Roosevelt had once been known for, and it reinforced the impression that the sixty-two-year-old president was tired and spent. Jittery British officials worried that the president was fading fast.

As Election Day drew near, London asked Stephenson to undertake an independent voter survey. Stephenson conferred with Donovan, who first cleared the project with the president. Roosevelt, who paid close attention to opinion polls and had consulted them in determining political strategy on everything from the First Lady's public profile to Lend-Lease, reportedly gave his approval and asked to be apprised of the results. Donovan then brought in David Seiferheld, one of the OSS's top statisticians, to prepare "a clinical analysis" of the election polls. Seiferheld reevaluated Gallup's calculations and found that in the 1940 election there had been a 4 percent margin of error in his poll. By correcting for that error in the system that he used, Seiferheld maintained that his predictions would be much closer to the actual outcome than Gallup's. London was naturally interested to learn that the custodian of America's leading polls was privately a Republican and, according to some reports, might be deliberately adjusting his figures in favor of the Dewey-Bricker ticket in hopes of "stampeding the electorate." If the Gallup poll was "tainted," it could have major implications for the coming election. Ernest Cuneo carried news of this startling development to the BSC chief. "It's unbelievable," he told Stephenson. "There are going to be some white-faced boys in this country. . . . Dewey is calling Gallup up so often they have to have a clerk to answer him. . . . Imagine a guy shaking so much."

A week before the election Stephenson sent London a telegram containing his latest electoral predictions and told Cuneo that the forecast would forever brand him "either an idiot or a genius":

MY ESTIMATES HAVE CONSISTENTLY CONFLICTED MARKEDLY WITH THOSE OF GALLUP AND OTHER POLLSTERS AND POLITICAL PUNDITS . . . AND NOW SHOW EVEN GREATER DIVERGENCE FROM LARGELY ACCEPTED VIEW THAN PREVIOUSLY. . . .

MY CURRENT ANALYSES INDICATE VICTORY FOR FDR IN MINIMUM REPEAT MINIMUM OF 32 STATES WITH 370 ELECTORAL VOTES AND MAXIMUM OF 40 WITH 487 ELECTORAL VOTES. . . .

DEWEY MINIMUM COMPRISES NORTH DAKOTA, SOUTH DAKOTA, NE-

BRASKA, COLORADO, KANSAS, WYOMING, VERMONT AND IOWA. . . . .
MAXIMUM INCLUDES FORGOING PLUS MAINE, IDAHO, WISCONSIN,
INDIANA, MICHIGAN, OHIO, MINNESOTA, AND ILLINOIS. . . . LAST FOUR
ARE DEWEY'S MOST DOUBTFUL ONES AND NOT IMPROBABLE RESULT
ANTICIPATES HIS LOSING THREE OR ALL FOUR.

Stephenson's election prophecies were right on the mark. Roosevelt carried thirty-six states, and Dewey the eight states listed in his forecast as his minimum, as well as four of the questionable ones. In the Electoral College vote, Roosevelt won 432 to Dewey's 99, nothing less than a landslide. His popular vote edge was significantly reduced, however, the majority being only 3.5 million. The party gained twenty-two seats in the House and lost one in the Senate, too small a change to alter the political course of the country. Roosevelt could continue to be his own man during the fourth term. In the end, the professional polls were nowhere near as accurate a guide as the BSC's private tally. Gallup ended up with only 51.5 percent voting for Roosevelt, where in fact—with the soldiers' ballots still waiting to be counted—more than 53 percent had. The results, as Isaiah Berlin observed in his November 11 dispatch, "although undeniably within Gallup's admitted margin of error (of 3–4 per cent), does not serve to strengthen the faith of the unconverted in the complete dependability of his polls. Perhaps his alleged Republican sympathies led him to underestimate the size of the total vote on which the percentages were based."[*]

In any event, Ogilvy had served them well. Stephenson regarded him as a superior talent in the field of covert warfare and later praised his performance in Washington, singling out his "keen analytical powers

---

[*]It was later shown that Gallup was not guilty of tampering, and that the margin of error in his election forecasts was the result of a genuine miscalculation, or as Isaiah Berlin put it, "unavoidable human fallibility."

and special aptitude for handling problems of extreme delicacy . . . not only a good intelligence officer, but a brilliant one."

Dahl spent election night at Mrs. McLean's traditional gala. The crowd of Washington leaders, legislators, diplomats, and notables were more raucous than usual, arguing and debating noisily among themselves, falling silent only long enough to hear the latest report on the radio. People's appetites were either ruined or improved depending on the voting trends, though most had only an absentminded regard for the food. Dahl stayed well into the night listening to the reactions as the final returns poured in over the airwaves. The next day he sat down and wrote Eleanor Roosevelt a congratulatory letter telling her

BRITISH SECURITY CO-ORDINATION

November 13, 1944.

Dear Wing Commander Dahl:

Thank you so much for your letter. I deeply appreciate your writing and the very kind things you say.

Now that you are back here I shall hope to see you soon.

Very sincerely yours,

how pleased he was that the president was the winner and confessing that he gave "a sigh of unofficial relief" when he heard the news. He went on to explain that he had been back in Washington for some time and was happy to hear that the First Lady was feeling well and was in good spirits. He sent his regards to Tommy, signing the letter "Wing Commander Roald Dahl." He typed the brief note on his new British Security Coordination letterhead, with the official crest on the top, crossing out the BSC's address at Sixteenth Street and typing in the new office address at 1106 Connecticut Avenue. Eleanor promptly replied, thanking Dahl for his letter, adding, "I deeply appreciate your writing and the very kind things you say. Now that you are back here I shall hope to see you soon." A few days later he was invited to dine with her at the White House.

Marsh was vastly amused when shortly after the election someone—Dahl claimed to be the culprit—painted the balls of the giant bronze bison by the Q Street bridge bright red. It was quite a shocking sight. The ornamental statue, which was near Dahl's house, now stood out more than ever, its "prominent personal organs" in bold relief for all to see. To commemorate this historic event, Marsh penned one of his fake letters for Dahl's amusement, this time addressing it to Cissie Patterson. He demanded that she take a bucket and brush and "do a job on the balls of the bison," but not before satisfying herself that what had been done was not unnatural: "Have you, my dear Cissie, ever in your long and variegated experience, observed a bison, or even an ordinary man, with a gray or gray-green scrotum?" He went on to implore her to take pity on "the small man" who must walk to work each morning over the Q Street bridge, and back again at night, faced with this rude sight. After all, despite running "a scandal sheet," he continued, "I realize that the purpose of your life has been for the public welfare and nothing has been too small or too large for you to observe." The bull became Marsh and Dahl's de facto mascot, a favorite joke between them, and an emblem of all they been through in that awful campaign.

With the election over, Dahl could relax. His superiors were overjoyed by Roosevelt's thumping victory over Dewey and no doubt congratulated themselves that they had had a hand in seeing that he got in. The embassy was buzzing with rumors that the war in Europe was nearing an end and might be over by Christmas. Soon they would all be going home. The British were not alone in feeling cheered. The whole of voteless Washington, which had swelled to massive proportions during Roosevelt's incumbency, seemed in a mood to celebrate. The long months of uncertainty were over, government employees could stop worrying if their jobs were safe, and administration loyalists would be rewarded. Even the campaign-weary press corps was glad it was finally finished and done with and toasted FDR in their customary fashion, three deep at the Mayflower bar.

On December 7 the aviation conference finally adjourned. In light of all that had preceded it, a surprisingly simple document was drawn up. A uniform set of rules for air navigation had been established, as well as a permanent international authority to promote the development of air transport. But both sides had been forced to concede key points, and the result was an uneasy compromise. Neither London nor Washington was happy. Addressing the convention for the last time, Berle tried to affirm the new spirit of cooperation and seized on the symbolism of the third anniversary of Pearl Harbor. "We met in an era of diplomatic intrigue and private and monopolistic privilege," he told the restless crowd. "We close in an era of open covenants and equal opportunity and status." Dahl doubted anyone believed him.

Dahl took advantage of his free time to see more of his new love interest, a French actress known as Annabella, née Suzanne Georgette Charpentier. Dahl had first met her in February, at the opening night dinner in honor of Franz Werfel's and S. N. Behrman's comedy *Jaco-*

bowsky and the Colonel, which was playing in Washington for several weeks during its break-in tour. Delighted to find himself seated next to the glamorous blonde, who was married to the matinee idol Tyrone Power, he did his best to impress her with his literary flair, spinning a macabre tale about a stranger who bets his Cadillac that a young man can't coax a flame from his cigarette lighter ten times in a row. The catch was that should he win the bet, the loser would have to surrender the little finger of his left hand. Accustomed to cowing listeners with his arrogance and barbed wit, Dahl was somewhat taken aback when the petite actress eyed him coolly and asked, "What happened next?" He saw her back to her suite that night and the next day returned for lunch in the hotel's dining room, tipping the maitre d' to make sure that he was placed across from her regular table.

Dahl made fast work of their courtship, but then he had plenty of encouragement. Annabella was an adventuresome spirit and was at the time estranged from her husband, who had enlisted as a private in the Marine Corps and was away at a combat training camp. Several years older than Dahl, she was beautiful, intelligent, and endowed with enormous charm. She was warm and down to earth and had no interest in associating with big Hollywood stars, preferring to surround herself with a lively mixture of American and European creative people, including playwrights, screenwriters, and theatrical directors. For Dahl, Annabella was more than just another wartime fling—she became his confidante and close friend. She was worldly in ways he was not, and as always, he was irresistibly drawn to fame and sophistication.

Annabella had begun her career as a dancer and at sixteen was cast as Violine Fleuri in the French director Abel Gance's silent classic *Napoléon*. She rose to become a star of French cinema, appearing in three classics: the René Clair films *Le Million* and *Quatorze Juillet* and Marcel Carné's *Hôtel du Nord*. When she came to Hollywood in 1938, she was twenty-nine and had already been married twice—to the French writer Albert Sorre, who died, and to the much older French actor Jean Murat, with whom she had a daughter. Later that year the volatile actress made news with her divorce and snapped at an interviewer: "It is not always good to be a film star in America . . . they want to know what I eat, what I think, they even want to know whom I love—and that I tell no one."

She had met Tyrone Power on Twentieth Century–Fox's back lot shortly after arriving in America. Annabella had just appeared opposite Henry Fonda in *Wings of the Morning*, Britain's first full-length color film, in which she wore her blond hair cropped short and masqueraded as a bewitching young boy. After seeing her at a screening of the film, the bisexual Power was smitten. Hoping to turn her into the next Greta Garbo, Darryl Zanuck, the head of Twentieth Century–Fox, cast her in *Suez*, a big-budget quasi-historical drama that was designed to be a vehicle for Power. Much to his dismay, however, the two fell in love during the production. Power was then one of Fox's most bankable stars, and Annabella—a foreigner, a divorcée, and several years senior to the twenty-five-year-old Power—was a far cry from the all-American sweetheart the studio had in mind for their golden boy. After communicating his disapproval to the pair, Zanuck attempted to get rid of Annabella by shipping her to London to work on a picture. Annabella refused to go and wed Power in April 1939 in the garden of her friend and compatriot, Charles Boyer. Zanuck was incensed. Studio chiefs thought nothing of rearranging the lives of their contract stars to conform to Hollywood press releases—ordering abortions and ending affairs—and her defiance cost her countless roles.

By the time Power reported to boot camp in January 1943, he was trying to escape a stalled career and rocky marriage, strained by his more than passing interest in male companionship. In an effort to protect the image of their valuable star and avoid potentially ruinous gossip, the studio pressured them to keep up the facade of a happy couple. The continental Annabella quickly accommodated herself to the arrangement. While Power continued his protracted training— after officer's training school at Quantico, Virginia, he did a stint at a command school, then received advanced flight training before finally being shipped to the Pacific more than eighteen months later—Annabella became a U.S. citizen and threw herself into a war-bond-selling tour. She gave rousing speeches in cities across the country, entertaining small crowds at post offices, factories, and insurance buildings. She also starred in a series of propaganda films, including *The French Underground* and *Tonight We Raid Calais*. Both pursued a succession of outside relationships: Power, between men, fell madly in love with Judy Garland; Annabella, in retaliation, took up with a well-known British actor, a writer, and a wealthy scion of an old New York family. Dahl knew he was by no means her only paramour and vice versa. As this was an arrangement that suited them both, they carried on a clandestine love affair.

Jacobowsky and the Colonel opened on Broadway in March 1944 to rave reviews and went on to a hugely successful six-month run. Dahl often took the train up to New York to be with her and waited for her backstage at the Martin Beck Theater, and afterward they would go to dinner. One night, not long after his return from England, he and Annabella ran into Marsh's daughter, Antoinette, and her husband at the Plaza Hotel. "I went to the Oak Room after the theater and ran into them," recalled Antoinette. "She was very pretty, and Roald looked pleased as punch." On the night of August 22, after being told in the wings that the radio had just announced the news that Paris had been liberated, Annabella took to the stage alone and, tears streaming down her face, announced to the audience that her native city had been freed. The whole audience got to its feet and joined her in singing "La Marseillaise."

When Dahl was in New York, he usually stayed at Marsh's town house, on 92nd Street just off Fifth Avenue. Antoinette and her husband had an apartment in the building and often invited Dahl to parties: "Roald would bring Annabella to dinner—he'd come whenever he couldn't get reservations." Dahl also stayed at Annabella's hotel suite. On one occasion, when Dahl was in town on BSC business, he had a plainclothes assignment and asked if he could leave his uniform at her place until his return. He told her not to press him for any explanation because he had already told her more than he should. Annabella was greatly amused at the idea that Dahl could go anywhere incognito. "He was so tall and good-looking," she recalled. "You had to look at him!"

As much as she enjoyed her liaison with Dahl, Annabella had not entirely given up on her marriage with Power, whom she later described as "the one great love of her life." They saw each other for brief, intense visits during a few days' leave, while he waited—and wondered if the marines would ever send a movie star into battle—for his orders. Despite everything that had happened, there was still something between them. The war had broken up a great many marriages, and Annabella knew their future together was doubtful at best, but she was willing to give it another go when his tour of duty was over. She was old enough to know that Dahl was not the kind of man you marry, in the end summing him up as "kind of impossible." They clicked, physically and emotionally, and that was enough. She always regarded Dahl as a genuine hero but knew in her heart that "the crazy thing" with the handsome British pilot was not going to last. At all times, things were clear between them. "We had a complete understanding," she said, "and he trusted me."

Annabella was one of the few women Dahl did not quickly tire of and discard. They continued their friendship and their on-again-off-again sexual relationship. It was the rare exception to a pattern of short, tempestuous affairs that even his closest friends at the time, like the happily married Antoinette, found distressing. Dahl could be incredibly insensitive where women were concerned, to the point of utter heartlessness. She could recall being shocked by the occasional callousness of his conversation and by the sight of his intended victim across the table, white and shaken. "He could be mean, just awful," she recalled. "When he got bored, he could lay into them, and be very, very sarcastic." To Ogilvy, he appeared to pursue women more for the sake of sexual conquest than from any real interest, and "when they fell in love with him, as a lot did, I don't think he was nice to them."

The last few weeks of 1944 were chaotic and filled with uncertainty. Cordell Hull fell ill and tendered his resignation. Roosevelt failed to offer his job to Wallace and instead, without so much as a hint about what he was up to, completely reorganized the State Department and nominated Undersecretary of State Edward Stettinius Jr. to succeed Hull. He promoted Will Clayton, the assistant secretary of commerce, to be his number two. In effect, this meant that Berle was out of a job. Dahl and his BSC colleagues were happy to see the back of him, and delighted in the *Time* story announcing the resignation of the "gnome-like, greying Boy Prodigy. " There were rumors that Berle would be awarded the ambassadorship to Brazil, but at least they would be free of his watchful presence in Washington.

Marsh, however, was infuriated by FDR's calculated ambivalence toward Wallace, whose future was still uncertain. Roosevelt had departed for Warm Springs without a word, leaving the vice president in an embarrassing limbo. There was only the vague promise of the commerce job, which Roosevelt appeared reluctant to formalize. Eleanor Roosevelt told Wallace she regarded him as "the outstanding symbol of liberalism in the United States" and put in a plea for him to lead a greatly expanded liberal political action committee. Dahl heard the British were pushing for Wallace to be appointed to the UN, as head of the Food and Agriculture Organization, which would effectively keep him out of government for three years. Others within the administration, like Sidney Hillman, were trying to relegate Wallace to the less important post of labor secretary and were adamant that he should not be given the commerce job.

Marsh and Wallace spent hours holed up in his study plotting their next move, fearing that if they did nothing the opposition would use the situation to their advantage and try to oust him from the cabinet altogether. On the morning of December 5, Marsh gave Wallace a lengthy strategy memo to read before meeting with Ickes about his going to bat for him with the president. Marsh interpreted the news that the president was returning to Washington as "favorable" and predicted that the next ten days would see "very fast action with Roosevelt on the job." He cautioned Wallace not to trust Ickes, that he was merely "fishing," and that anything he told him would be passed up the food chain—to Baruch, Hopkins, and the president—"within the hour."

Late that same evening, Marsh got a call from Drew Pearson, who reported that Ickes had given him a detailed account of his meeting with the vice president over the telephone and had said Wallace appeared "sad" and that there wasn't any "fight" left in him. When Marsh got off the phone with the "Merry-Go-Round" columnist, he was mad, and he stayed mad for the rest of the month.

The mood at the R Street house that Christmas was bleak. They were all in for a rough winter. Dahl, who usually filled the role of Marsh's "favorite court jester," as Ingersoll described him, was in no condition to lift their spirits. He was in quite a lot of pain and was resigned to the fact that there would probably be no avoiding another operation on his back. Once again his old war injuries were spoiling his fun and threatening to put him out of action. After seeing him limp across the room one afternoon, Marsh observed that the classic horror actor Lon Chaney, who starred as *The Hunchback of Notre Dame*, "never dragged his crippled body along more beautifully that you did when extracting sympathy." An expert on all things, Marsh was of the opinion that the doctors at the wartime hospital in Alexandria may not have done the best job of patching him up. There was something very much amiss in his thin body. After New Year's, Marsh packed Dahl off to the Scott and White Clinic in Temple, Texas, to see its leading specialist, Dr. Arthur Scott, who was his friend and personal physician. Scott determined that an operation on his spine was necessary. It was not happy news for Dahl, who dreaded the thought of more surgery. He came through it well, however, and spent the next several weeks recuperating at the Texas clinic. Marsh saw that he had a splendid room all to himself and footed the bills.

Marsh, as usual, wrote constantly, sending him bulletins from the front lines of the long, lonely fight over Wallace's nomination as secretary of commerce. Jesse Jones had told a newspaper reporter that Roosevelt would have to dynamite him out, and he was as good as his word, galvanizing Senate conservatives to block Wallace's appointment. Jones and his mob of like-minded senators, many of whom had worked to dump Wallace from the national ticket, banded together again to defeat their old adversary and argued that the vice president lacked the business acumen to handle the Reconstruction Finance Corporation and other important lending agencies. The *New York Sun* summed up the collective outrage: "The fourth term was scarcely twenty-four hours old before it thus became known that into the hands of the most radical, impractical, and idealistic dreamer in his entourage, Mr. Franklin D. Roosevelt has placed a large measure of responsibility for the ultimate liquidation of billions of dollars' worth of industrial property now under the control of the Federal government."

Determined not to lose this battle, Marsh helped Wallace mount a defense. He worked the phones, urging old friends like Lyndon Johnson and Claude Pepper to join the fray. Ironically, they were somewhat helped by the fact that some southern Democrats were beginning to worry that the extreme opposition to Wallace might create a backlash and actually work in his favor with the Democratic Party rank and file for the presidential nomination of 1948. If that was the case, it might be better to take the pressure off him now, before they created a martyr. On January 22, just before Wallace was set to testify before the Senate committee to contest allegations that he lacked the necessary competence to administer the agency, Dahl sent a telegram to his apartment at the Wardman Park wishing him good luck. He had followed the proceedings carefully, and despite his superiors' objections to Wallace, he did not want to see that crowd of jackals on the Hill drive a good man out of government. Finally, on March 1, the Senate confirmed Wallace's appointment. But it had been a near thing, and before giving the commerce job to the former vice president, the Senate stripped it of all the lending powers that his predecessor had exercised. Several weeks passed before Wallace responded to Dahl's wire. Apologizing for the delay due to an overwhelming amount of work, he wrote, "Nevertheless, even at this late date, I want you to know I am personally grateful to you for your support, especially in the days before my confirmation," adding, "I hope I always merit your kind opinion of me."

To keep his bedridden friend amused, Marsh sent a stream of comic letters, each one wilder and more nonsensical than the last, most of which centered on their activities as spies in the employ of an outfit called "Screwball, Unincorporated International." Dahl, who had spent far too long in the wilds of Texas with far too little in the way of diversion, happily took up their imprudent correspondence, again impersonating Halifax and inventing his own plots and subplots. He wrote of "placing" an agent in the R Street house to keep him informed of all Marsh's movements and to monitor the comings and goings of his friends, assorted statesmen, amateur politicos, and highbrow writers who were all members of a gang of notorious spies. Marsh's longtime black butler, Mr. Clinton, was in fact a tracker of enemy agents and had them all under investigation: "This man reports to me each day, and you will know how important his information is to me."

After two and a half weeks flat on his back, Dahl was able to leave the hospital and moved into Dr. Scott's house for the remainder of his stay. As soon as he was able to sit up again, he began working on new short stories and "wrote like a madman." In the last few months, he had managed to sell several more short stories to magazines and was hoping to have enough for a book. Curtice Hitchcock had sent him a letter stating that his firm, Reynal & Hitchcock, would be interested in publishing the collection.

In early February, Dahl was called back to Washington on "urgent business" that he could not divulge, but as soon as it was taken care of, he retreated to Marsh's house in Virginia to continue his recuperation. With both Marsh and Alice away, there was no one at Longlea besides Marsh's two young children, who had been left in the care of the household servants, so he was more or less on his own, living "in solitary opulence." With its breathtaking view of the Blue Ridge Mountains, it was an ideal setting in which to rest and regain his strength. His recovery was taking rather longer than he expected, and he still could not bend down to tie his shoes. But he had his writing to occupy him and still had a great deal to do, including reworking "A Piece of Cake" and several earlier stories to include in his short story collection. He dashed off a note to his mother filling her in on his progress and suggested she phone Stephenson, "my boss," who was in London, to get "all the news."

By early March, Dahl had taken a turn for the worse and was feeling sufficiently unwell to worry Dr. Scott. On his advice, Dahl caught an RAF plane back to Texas and returned to the clinic for further examination. Scott immediately diagnosed the problem and scheduled Dahl

for a small secondary operation to remove a substance from his spine
that had been injected back in January to enable them to take X-rays.
Dahl spent a week in traction and then moved back into Dr. Scott's
house. He was soon up and about and feeling much better and wrote
his mother that he was confident that the last procedure "did the trick"
and he was finally cured.

During his absence, Marsh kept Dahl abreast of matters of diplomatic
and domestic consequence and on March 7 sent him a letter alerting
him that the personal press spokesman for Representative Clare Luce
had "privately communicated" that she would be making a speech
upon her return from her travels from the Middle East and that she
hoped that the wing commander would be present. Addressing Dahl as
"My Dear Lord," Marsh continued:

> Naturally the people concerned with air routes and oil are educating
> her. It has been suggested that she confine her remarks to love in order
> to be accurate in her standard role as a Narcissus actor.
>
> Attached are a few of the highlights of her speech on love from the
> Orient to the Occident, from the front to the back, from the head to the
> foot, on the axis of thought. The attached speech is not in her exact lan-
> guage, but is provocative and suggestive of what might be said by this
> lady Congresswoman to all these men in Congress who will hear her.

Dahl had been back in Washington less than a week when he learned
of the president's death from a massive cerebral hemorrhage on the afternoon of April 12. It was just as his superiors had feared—Roosevelt
had died in office, and his vice president would be imposed on a grieving nation. Only it would be Truman, not Wallace. All the old American warhorses were dropping in their tracks. Pa Watson, a member of
FDR's inner circle, had passed away during the return trip from the
Yalta conference. Hull had heart problems and had retired. Hopkins

was in and out of the hospital. Soon there would be a complete changing of the guard, and Churchill might have trouble finding a friendly
face among the country's new leadership. It was unlikely that Truman,
whom Marsh categorized as a man of "small brain and great ambition"
and wholly ignorant of foreign affairs, would be as kindly disposed toward Great Britain as his predecessor. Roosevelt would be missed by
the English at least as much as by his own people, maybe more.

On April 14 Dahl debriefed Pearson on Truman's first cabinet meeting, held just before he was sworn in—which the columnist had directly from a cabinet member—and filed the following intelligence
report with the BSC:

> He [Truman] said he wanted them all to continue serving. Stettin-
> ius said he would be glad to. . . . Stimson said he was a soldier and
> would serve so long as the war lasted. . . . Mrs Perkins started weep-
> ing. . . . Truman lunched with Senators on the Hill yesterday; they
> all endeavored to persuade him to make following changes in his
> staff . . . Byrnes Secretary of State . . . remove Madame Perkins as
> Secretary of Labor . . . decision already taken make Spruille Braden
> Ambassador to Argentine. . . . You should know that conversations
> are going on at present between Army, Navy, State Department and
> Department of Interior re Roosevelt's proposal make conquered Jap
> islands in Pacific trusteeships. This . . . one of the first problems con-
> fronting Truman. . . .

Later that day Dahl was stricken with acute appendicitis and un-
derwent emergency surgery. Marsh wired his family in England that
Roald was doing fine and that hopefully this would be "the last of his
troubles." On a more reassuring note, he explained that before this
last hiccup, Dahl's back was almost completely better and that he had
been getting ready to play tennis, adding drolly, "I am so very happy to

report that I believe your son is going to be a normal physical young man before the year is over."

When Dahl finally limped out of the hospital, Marsh installed him in the R Street house, where Claudia Haines, his "perennially efficient secretary," as she wryly referred to herself, nursed him back to health. Claudia doted on Dahl, and treated him like a second son. Moreover, her own nineteen-year-old son, Davis, and twenty-one-year-old daughter, known as young Claudia, had become extremely close to him over the past three years. Young Claudia, who had always worshipped the handsome pilot, waited on him hand and foot. In the past year, she had blossomed into an exceedingly attractive young woman, with shiny dark hair, a well-developed figure, and a sultry air that Charles always said gave her the exotic looks of "a Hawaiian princess." Young Claudia was sweet and affectionate, and Dahl soon convinced himself that he was in love, and he surprised them both by proposing. Despite having an enormous crush on Dahl, she knew him to be a tireless bird dog and, as Antoinette recalled, "quite sensibly turned him down."

THE GLAMOUR SET

We almost suffered emotional bends the day the war ended.

— Ernest Cuneo

D AHL HAD BEEN working for the BSC for what seemed to him like "quite a long time" without ever meeting the big chief. By his own estimate, it had been over a year and a half since his first contact with Stephenson's agents and the beginning of his work along counter-espionage lines. Now that he had formally joined the outfit and was considered a staff member as opposed to just another freelance agent, it seems he was finally being honored with a summons to the New York headquarters. He already knew, of course, that the large suite of offices the spy chief had chosen for the nucleus of his American operation occupied the thirty-fifth and thirty-sixth floors of a New York skyscraper, but he was not prepared for the black marble grandeur of Rockefeller Center or the dizzying speed of the state-of-the-art elevators, which, he later recalled, moved "faster than I have ever dived in any aeroplane." Over the years, the office had functioned under a variety of covers, from the United Kingdom Commercial Corporation and

British Purchasing Commission to the British Library of Information. At the moment, the small plaque by the door indicated that he had arrived at the British Passport Control Office.

Dahl could not help feeling just a little bit nervous at penetrating the much-vaunted veil of secrecy that separated the secret world from regular society—the "insiders" from the "outsiders." At the same time, he was unaccountably pleased that he had made it through an arduous trial period without raising any red flags and was about to be invited into an elite corps. As he was led through the bustling premises, he could not help noticing the many comely young women, a pool of fifty or more Canadian secretaries whom, rumor had it, the BSC chief personally recruited and swore to secrecy. When he was finally ushered into Stephenson's large office and the man behind the desk rose to greet him, Dahl received "quite a shock." The legendary director of the BSC was surprisingly diminutive—all the more so from Dahl's perspective of six feet six inches. "The first impression of Stephenson was a small man of immense power, nothing indecisive about him at all," he recalled. "I liked him instantly. There was bound to be at first trepidation and fear because you were right in the lion's den."

Everything about Stephenson was compact and efficient. He was a slim, brisk man in his late forties, with the springy step of a boxer, cropped graying hair, and a pair of penetrating eyes. Unlike most short men, Dahl noticed that Stephenson never raised his head in order to meet his gaze but instead kept his chin tucked in so that "only his eyes, which were very, very pale, looked up at you." He was dressed in plain clothes, lit his next cigarette from the one still planted in the corner of his mouth, and talked in short, clipped sentences. He could speak with authority about science, economics, and politics and in the next breath expertly lay out the latest technology for secret coding and surveillance, seamlessly switching from one subject to the other with the ease of someone adjusting the wireless. What was most striking about him was his imperturbable calm, an aura of absolute control that allowed him to offer only the occasional comment while eliciting from others a flood of nervous chatter, a talent that prompted Robert Sherwood to dub him the "quiet Canadian," a moniker that stuck with him throughout the war. "He never raised his voice, ever," recalled Dahl. "He had this extraordinary quality. You knew that in that head of his, as he was listening to you and watching you, something was ticking about twice as fast as it was in your head, and every facet and angle was being weighed up, and then one question would come out which would just about cover the whole lot, and you would answer it."

It was typical of his temperment that he insisted on taking part in Operation Overload. On D-day, Stephenson, who would not be denied a front-row seat, had flown as a rear gunner over the Normandy coast. The old World War One fighter pilot had not lost his appetite for battle. He was disappointed not to have cornered a German in his crosshairs but was immensely proud to have been part of the greatest invasion force in history. It was a longing for action that Dahl understood and frankly admired, but no longer felt himself.

It was ironic that by the time Dahl started seeing a lot of Stephenson and learning firsthand the details of his masterful clandestine role, his far-reaching counterespionage apparatus was already in the process of being dismantled. The BSC had done what it set out to do—push America toward intervention and secure the defeat of the Nazis—and now, with the war drawing to a close, it was no longer needed. Their covert operation had been of inestimable value, but as is usually the case in espionage on foreign soil, gratitude was in short supply. Most of what the BSC had done within the United States could not be publicly acknowledged, and Stephenson's cavalier disregard for the law of the land had long outraged the head of the FBI and senior State Department officials, who could not wait to clip his wings. During his five years in Washington he had been far too vigorous and independent, and the new generation ascending to power, both in America and England, favored executives who could be counted on more for their restraint than for their initiative. Stephenson, whose strength lay in his intuitive grasp of politics, could feel the tide in Washington turning against him.

While he was by no means ready to relinquish his power and probably felt he still had a firm hold on the situation, he knew the awarding of laurels always signaled that a warrior was near the end of his run. He had received the knighthood in January, his name included in the New Year's honors list. He was more proud of the comment, written in Churchill's signature green ink, next to his name on the list of candidates being recommended to King George VI. It read: "This one is dear to my heart." He was later awarded the Medal for Merit by President Truman, the first foreigner to receive the honor from the United States government.

If Stephenson had been content to retire then and fade into the sunset, it probably would have been better. But it never happened that way. A particular hazard facing secret service officials was paranoia— the toxic by-product of their profession. It went way beyond the normal fear of being eclipsed. They never trust their successors not to do them in, and Sir William was no exception. He suspected that his rivals within the service would inevitably seek to rewrite history, taking credit for his accomplishments and reapportioning the blame. With this in mind, he moved to secure his legacy and commissioned a history of the BSC's wartime achievements. As in the past, he banked on this "official" record of his agency's activities to protect him against future criticism. He assigned the task to one of his brightest subordinates, Gilbert Highet, the brains behind their political counterpropaganda activities in Latin America. A classics professor in his prewar life, he seemed ideally suited to cataloging the BSC's triumphs. Highet had begun work on the project early in the spring of 1945, but in mid-June, after rejecting an early draft as less than satisfactory, Stephenson called for reinforcements.

The first Dahl heard of this new assignment was an unequivocal request from the chief himself. He wanted the acclaimed young writer to apply his storytelling skills to render the material a little more palatable than Highet's dry, academic text. Stephenson reportedly had something considerably more dramatic in mind and expected them to somehow condense the hundreds of thousands of wartime documents into a colorful, compelling narrative. He had already tapped another BSC staffer by the name of Thomas H. Hill. A journalist by training, Hill had edited trade publications in Canada and had been drafted by the BSC to edit the *Western Hemisphere Weekly Bulletin*, a sort of in-house organ that trumpeted the BSC's unclassified successes in various countries and made the case for their importance to SIS in London.

Stephenson also brought in an editor named Giles Playfair, the son of actor-producer Sir Nigel Playfair, who had been a radio journalist for the Malaysian Broadcasting Company. Playfair had escaped during the fall of Singapore and had written an exciting eyewitness account of the Japanese invasion entitled *Singapore Goes Off the Air*. He had subsequently been recruited by the BSC and worked on counterespionage in the New York office. Stephenson thought he was just the man to punch up the copy. As soon as each chapter was finished, it was handed off to Playfair for a final polish before being submitted to Stephenson for approval. To this odd assortment of talents, Stephenson added two of his Canadian secretaries, Grace Garner and Eleanor Fleming, who had worked for him for most of the war. The head of his filing section, Merle Cameron, rounded out the team.

Dahl was amazed at the extraordinarily elaborate security precautions Stephenson ordered to safeguard his secret history. He insisted that all the work be done at their isolated Camp X site, on the northern shore of Lake Ontario, where he could guarantee that both his papers and personnel were protected. "The thing I always remember," said Dahl, "was how Bill had all these archives sent up from New York in some sort of wonderful security truck with an escort." The operation was vintage Stephenson, taking place under the cover of darkness, with the armed guards stealthily transferring hundreds of cartons of files into trucks waiting outside Rockefeller Plaza sometime after midnight. Ten hours later, a Canadian army captain handed the border guards his name and code number, and the convoy was waved across the border into Canada, where it proceeded to the Oshawa training facility. Stephenson had already been using some of the school's outbuildings as cold storage for some BSC records, so in his mind it was a logical place to set up shop.

Having only just returned to Washington, Dahl did not relish spending the summer in the Canadian wilderness, surrounded by flat, gray scrub brush and marshlands. He quickly grew bored in the cloistered environs of Oshawa and Whitby, where a night out consisted of dinner at the Genosha Hotel. The job of cataloging the BSC's myriad operations proved laborious and dull, and in his own words, he "copped out" and left the majority of the work to Hill. Whenever possible, he sneaked back to New York for a few days, always on the pretext of business.

In early July, Dahl dashed off a quick note to Claudia, making no reference to his mysterious work and furnishing no details of his whereabouts beyond a post office box in Toronto. He reported that he was working too hard to do any writing of his own, but that he hoped to be finished by the end of August. Adding to his impatience to be off was that Hitchcock had accepted ten stories based on his combat experiences in the RAF and would be publishing them in a collection to be entitled *Over to You*. The book was already in galleys, and fairly crowing with excitement, Dahl told Marsh that as the "official go-between" between himself and his literary editor, he should be the first to hear the news, and he proudly enclosed copies of the advertising pulls that were soon to appear in the *Times Literary Supplement*.

After complaining of a dearth of letters from R Street during his exile in Canada, Dahl received his due the following week. Marsh wrote that he had spent the previous ten days in New York and that Dahl had been in his thoughts much of the time, as he was involved in work "which you would have so very much enjoyed being around." He referred obliquely to a meeting at the Hay Adams, where he finally worked out a divorce settlement that, at long last, "may help the flickering light of a liberal life."*

Just as he had earlier vowed, Marsh had freed himself of both Glass sisters: Alice got Longlea and a large cut of his net worth; Mary Louise, who reportedly quit in a fit of pique over a rude comment of Charles', eventually married Wallace's assistant, Harold Young. Marsh made it clear in his own distinctive way that Claudia was graduating from secretary to mistress, at one point even stopping to acknowledge the lady faithfully taking down his every word: "She is a martinet, she is a cruel and decisive woman, we all look for them, don't we?" Instructing Dahl that he should henceforth write to her at a separate address—for the sake of propriety, she insisted on having her own place until they could be married—Marsh added: "Claudia is too conceited to call herself your Mother. She will settle on the Aunt position. But I strongly suspect that she wants to be more than a big sister. No woman will settle for anything less than being a woman."

By late summer, Hill, Dahl, and Playfair had completed a five-hundred-page manuscript. Stephenson, who was obsessed with safe-

---

*Alice Glass was married a total of five times. After divorcing Marsh, she wed two of his friends, and frequent Longlea guests, in rapid succession: Palmer Weber and Zadel Skolovsky. After a brief fourth union, her fifth marriage, to Colonel Richard J. Kirkpatrick, lasted from 1959 to his death in 1974. Alice died of cancer in Marlin, Texas, in December 1976.

guarding the manuscript, contracted a small Oshawa printing company, located four miles from the camp, to do the job, but not before the place was carefully vetted by the Royal Canadian Mounted Police. "It became quite a little feat of logistics," recalled Hill, describing how they proofread the galley pages by day and then at night would take the typescript back to the printer's under armed guard, shuttling back and forth in military vehicles. The entire print run was restricted to twenty copies, and as soon as the last set of signatures was boxed and sealed, they were taken directly to a bookbinder in Toronto. Stephenson had arranged for each leather-bound volume to be carefully placed in an individual locked box of his own design. Believing the original records too sensitive to risk preserving—particularly the details of British intelligence's activities prior to America's entry into the war, during a period of neutrality, which if ever made public would seriously damage Anglo-American relations—he ordered Hill and his wife to burn the lot. Thousands of tons of BSC documents were heaped into a homemade concrete furnace at the camp, specially outfitted with grate to prevent any partially charred pages from escaping, and went up in flames.

Needless to say, Dahl did not get to take home a sample of his handiwork. Stephenson personally took charge of all twenty volumes of the official history, which was referred to from then on as "the bible" but which he gave the riveting title, *British Security Coordination (BSC): An Account of Secret Activities in the Western Hemisphere, 1940–45*. It was understood that he would be keeping two for himself, and distributing copies to Roosevelt, Churchill, and "C," along with a handful of other high officials in the SIS and SOE in London. The remaining ten were reportedly locked in a bank vault in Montreal.*

---

*As with almost everything to do with Stephenson, the fate of the twenty volumes, if there were in fact twenty, is shrouded in mystery. Stephenson claimed he gave Roosevelt a copy, but as the president died long before the book was completed, and as there is no record of it at the Roosevelt Library, this does not seem likely. In 1946 he

By the time Dahl got back to Washington, the war was over. It was a strangely blank sensation. The tension, which had been a constant in his life for so long, was suddenly gone. Cuneo put it best when he said it felt like the power had been "switched off." For more than four years, the rotund White House liaison had called on Stephenson on practically a daily basis, so the following afternoon he stopped by the BSC chief's Rockefeller Plaza office as usual. Without a word, Stephenson shoved a copy of the London *Times* across his desk and pointed with a finger to a single line: "The Home Secretary told the Commons last night that the emergency having ended, habeas corpus was restored." Stephenson remarked, "I guess that's what it was all about." "I guess it was," Cuneo agreed, and because there was nothing else to be said, they headed to the 21 Club for a drink.

Dahl found that the euphoria of V-E Day and V-J Day had quickly passed and given way to a mood of nervous distrust. Victory in Europe, so long anticipated, had come in May. Then in August, victory over

---

ordered Hill to destroy the ten copies collecting dust in the Montreal safe. What happened to the rest? Stephenson made a copy available to his handpicked biographer, Harford Montgomery Hyde, who had served under him at the BSC from 1941 to 1944 and quoted extensively from it for his book *The Quiet Canadian,* which was published in 1962. Stephenson similarly encouraged his subordinate Dick Ellis in his efforts to chronicle his tenure as head of the BSC, but later rejected his two-hundred-page draft. His subsequent biographer William Stevenson also obtained a copy of the BSC chief's official history for his 1976 best seller *A Man Called Intrepid.* There followed what Thomas Troy, the American intelligence historian, called "a literary strip-tease," with various journalists and authors, including himself, managing a peek at the bible, if only briefly. No one knows for certain how many of the original volumes exist, or where they are all located. Fifty-three years later, this "remarkable document," as Nigel West calls it in his introduction, was finally made public by St. Ermin's Press in Britain, which published it in its "complete and unexpurgated format." This 1998 edition, *British Security Coordination: The Secret History of British Intelligence in the Americas, 1940–1945,* carries the following disclaimer: "This publication has not been officially endorsed by Her Majesty's Government."

Japan was achieved with shocking finality by the atom bomb. America was already looking to the future and was tired of feeling Britain's hand at their back. The mounting differences between Russia and the West, exacerbated by America's possession of the A-bomb, did not bode well for postwar cooperation. The Georgetown drawing rooms that Dahl frequented echoed with anti-Russian talk. The Truman administration had adopted a view of Russia as aggressive and expansionist and blamed it for the breakdown of the wartime alliance. The administration was following an increasingly hard line, abruptly terminating Lend-Lease the minute the European war was over, paring down the loans to Britain for reconstruction, and repudiating Russia's request for funds to help jump-start its shattered economy. Ships bearing Lend-Lease cargoes to Britain remained docked, and those already under way had to be recalled.

America was letting it be known that there would be no unconditional postwar handouts—not to Britain, not to anyone. Uncle Sam was not going to play "Uncle Sucker" a second time. As the British Embassy cabled London: "The dollar sign is back in the Anglo-American equation." The sudden loss of Lend-Lease funds shocked Britain, and relations between the two countries became increasingly strained and contentious. Churchill, who had been assured of ongoing American support by Roosevelt, was deeply disappointed, and, believing Truman reneged on their deal, called the move "rough and harsh." Clement Attlee, who had just been made prime minister in the recent British elections, echoed regret at Truman's precipitate action with no prior consultation and voiced concerns about the degree to which the Americans planned to work with their allies in the future. Stalin made it clear that Russia regarded Truman's cut-off of rehabilitation funds as a deliberately hostile act.

In this atmosphere of mutual suspicion, Donovan and his people had wasted no time in turning the OSS, which still had the temporary status of a wartime agency, into a far more hawkish outfit, letting go many of Roosevelt's more liberal appointments and weeding out the British officers brought in during the formative days of the organization. In doing so, Donovan was not only trying to assert his independence but also seeking to silence the critics who were uncomfortable with the OSS's dependence on British intelligence. There was a sizable anti-British element within the FBI and State Department, as well as military intelligence, who felt it was time for sweeping change. Those who had long nursed a grudge against the BSC were quick to revive old complaints about the competition between the American and British intelligence agencies and fears that the British wanted to limit the OSS's operations and reduce them to a lesser role, or "Cinderella status." Part of their new adversarial attitude toward their British allies stemmed from the growing conviction that only America was somehow strong and true enough to command the powerful new arsenal of atomic weapons. While the British had initially shared their scientific knowledge with the Americans, it had become an essentially American effort—an American breakthrough, an American bomb. Fears that any breach in security could lead to the Soviets acquiring nuclear secrets drove the president and military planners to adopt an increasingly fortresslike mentality.

Donovan, however, still had a high regard for Stephenson and the British and was pushing for a permanent, coordinated overseas intelligence service under his direction. Dahl and Marsh, who had debated the postwar future of the BSC and the OSS dozens of times over, producing the usual trail of reports and memos, fancied themselves experts on the subject. Now that the administration was at last "catching up" with this idea, Marsh sent Wallace a memorandum on what he termed "the matter of the President's eyes and ears," advocating Donovan's "set up" and including a second unsigned report, presumably furnished by Dahl, representing the British point of view. Dahl, who was by then completely in Stephenson's thrall, was convinced that the United States should approve a peacetime extension of Donovan's organization and urged "the establishment of a world wide secret economic and political intelligence organization." Writing from his "experience of the British government in the intelligence field," Dahl argued that the new organization should not be under the authority of either the Foreign Office or the Board of Trade but should instead function as an independent agency reporting directly to the prime minister, so that he could have some "check" on his diplomatic and consular representatives abroad. (No doubt Halifax was foremost in his mind.) Dahl also contended that the FBI was not qualified to take over for the OSS and that while their policing was above reproach, the training for their "cops and robbers" role was inadequate for the investigation of "intricate economic and political situations" in the foreign field. The OSS, in its present form, was admittedly less than perfect, he concluded, but was a temporary solution and could be expected to evolve in the months after the war, especially since so many top personnel would be returning to private life.

The much-decorated Donovan, who had up until then always enjoyed good publicity, was not prepared for the storm of controversy that greeted his efforts to preserve his wartime agency. Most of it was stirred up by the die-hard isolationist press. Blazing the way, as usual, were the McCormick-Patterson papers—the *Times-Herald*, the *Daily News*, and the *Tribune*—in a series of sensational front-page stories by Walter Trohan. The OSS-bashing campaign had begun back in January when copies of Donovan's proposals were mysteriously leaked to Trohan, who painted a frightening picture of "an all-powerful intelligence service to spy on the postwar world and pry into the lives of ordinary citizens at home." Inflammatory headlines accused Donovan of trying to create a "Super Spy System" and "Super Gestapo Agency." There were more damning details: it was rumored the OSS would have "secret funds for spy work along the lines of bribing, and luxury living described in novels." British Embassy sources suggested the information was leaked deliberately, if not "maliciously," by military intelligence, which had long been jealous of the OSS. Hoover, who also had no use for the OSS, was causing trouble and wanted a "piece of the action" for his agency.

Donovan's plan for a postwar intelligence organization had continued to be the subject of rumors and speculation in the press until May, when Trohan launched another major attack, this time "exposing" serious flaws within the OSS, tagging it "the glamour set," composed of members who took "oaths of secrecy 'as awesome as [those in] a fraternity institution.'" Two stories took direct aim at the so-called tie-up between the OSS and the British: the *Washington Times-Herald* charged that the "OSS Is Branded British Agency to Legislators," and the next day the *Chicago Tribune* proclaimed that "British Control of OSS Bared In Congress Probe." Trohan, quoting unidentified members of Congress, provided ample evidence of the "tie-up": the facts that OSS agents were trained in England, that the British had access to OSS information otherwise denied to them by the United States, and that the OSS and the British Passport Control Office in New York, known to be "the headquarters of British intelligence in the U.S.," had a close relationship.

The final nail in the coffin was Trohan's claim that the OSS had spent "more than $125,000,000 in propagandizing and intelligence work around the world" but was "scarcely more than an arm of the British Intelligence Service." Trohan's timing was impeccable. The House Appropriations Committee was in the midst of hashing out the OSS budget for 1946, and every day the papers put another black mark next to the agency's name, printing allegations of Communist infiltration and the ultraliberal bias that repeatedly brought Donovan to Capitol Hill to defend his staff.

By September, Donovan, tired of being on the defensive, came out swinging. An Irish charmer with many friends in the press, he met personally with dozens of reporters and columnists and gave rousing public statements in support of his plan for a new unified agency. He argued that the OSS concept was new only in America and that both Britain and Russia had possessed good intelligence agencies before the war and continued to retain their services as a matter of course. As one of the largest, most responsible, and influential nations in the world, America, he maintained, could no longer afford the mistakes of the past—that is, Pearl Harbor—or the kind of mistakes that might arise from bad information or bad judgment. Donovan pledged that the intelligence-gathering part of the OSS would be as valuable in peacetime as it had been during the war, not as a means to investigate the folks at home, or to spy on and destroy the enemy, but as a vital measure of defense. His counteroffensive worked, up to a point. The *New York Times* ran stories on the OSS's "cloak and dagger" heroics, and the *Washington Post* reported on a mission to rescue "4000 stranded fliers" and other bold exploits. On September 12 Donovan released the names of twenty-seven OSS men whom he decorated for outstanding service to their country.

Although Donovan had succeeded in subduing his most vocal critics, Cuneo doubted the cease-fire would last for long. Even before this last skirmish, he knew there was entrenched opposition to Donovan's unit in the Joint Chiefs of Staff. Cuneo liked and admired Donovan and had worked hand in glove with the OSS and the BSC throughout the war, but even he was not convinced that the coordinated service was a marriage made in heaven. "To put it mildly, I was chary," he recalled. Since the British taught in their intelligence-training schools that all neutrals could be enemies, he "naturally drew the corollary that all allies could be potential enemies." He told Donovan that as far as he could ascertain, "England was not a country but a religion, and that where England was concerned, every Englishman was a Jesuit who believed the end justifies the means."

One fall morning, as Dahl walked downtown with Wallace, who now worked in the massive gray Department of Commerce Building, he took advantage of their time together to lobby for the postwar alliance with the OSS. Dahl was "very complimentary about the high quality of the work done by the OSS under Donovan" and spoke warmly of "the very close friendship" that had continued since the beginning of the war between Donovan and Stephenson. Dahl told Wallace that America had benefited greatly from their close cooperation, pointing out that of the twenty German saboteurs discovered by the FBI, seventeen of them were apprehended because of advance information given to the FBI by the British secret service. He felt certain that such a reciprocal relationship would only help their countries in the future.

Wallace listened courteously and did not voice any real objections, though he was privately of the opinion that integrating the intelligence services had "dangerous implications." When Donovan had pushed for this move the previous October, Roosevelt had demurred, saying that he would first have to get clearance from the other agencies. Wallace did not believe that the departments of State, Army, Treasury, and Navy, to say nothing of his own Commerce Department, would all sign off on it, and he recorded his misgivings in his diary:

> [Dahl] *thinks a combined American-English Secret Service is necessary to prevent the destructive possibilities of the bomb. In other words, Dahl envisions the United States and England working together to prevent Russia from blowing up Anglo-Saxon civilization and wants an American Secret Service which in fact will be under the thumb of the British Secret Service organization.*

At one point in their conversation, Dahl admitted to Wallace that he had become susceptible to the argument that the Soviets were intent on military expansion and was now "something of a Russophobe." Wallace, who thought the hardliners were inviting conflict, told him: "Well, if you fear the Russians, it won't be long until your fears are well founded." He later reflected again in his diary on "how fond" he was of Dahl, and what "a nice boy" he was, but that he was necessarily biased: "He is working out problems from the standpoint of British policy, and British policy clearly is to provoke the maximum distrust between the United States and Russia and thus prepare the groundwork for World War III."

On a more conciliatory note, Dahl told Wallace a humorous tale about Churchill that he had recently heard from the navigator on one of the PM's flights. Apparently Churchill was under doctor's orders not to fly too high. So when the plane climbed to nine thousand feet, he naturally became concerned and asked someone onboard to check his pulse. One of the pilots, who had only a dim recollection of how this was done, went to the forward cabin in search of a stopwatch when a colleague took him aside and whispered in his ear, "Seventy-two." So the pilot went back and took Churchill's wrist, and when the stop-watch showed sixty seconds were up, he announced, "Seventy-two." As Dahl told it, "Churchill grinned happily and said, 'Pretty good for an old man, isn't it?'" Wallace laughed and said that he "didn't know of any story which better typified the spirit of England."

Dahl, who was worried he might be sent back to Canada, seized the opportunity to take a few weeks' home leave. On October 19, he sailed on the *Queen Elizabeth* for England. It was a chance to celebrate the war's end with his loved ones and catch up with his mother and sisters, who were hungry for news of his activities in America. For security reasons, he had not been able to tell them what he was doing. There was also a great deal of practical business that had to be attended to. The reality was that life in England after the war was not easy. The hard times and shortages were far from over, and he worried about his mother's finances. They would all have to begin picking up the pieces of their lives and find a way forward. In theory, he could probably go back to work for Shell, but that was not in the cards. His younger sister, Asta, had accepted a posting in Norway and had written that Roald had been invited to apply as an assistant air attaché in Oslo. He told her he was not remotely interested. He was planning to leave the RAF altogether on what he considered "very reasonable medical grounds."

When he got back to Washington in early December, Dahl discovered he had sorely underestimated the new administration's suspicions of the wily and unscrupulous British. The prevailing opinion was that if the British advocated a policy, it was because they had some ulterior and probably sinister motive. Donovan's OSS never stood a chance. Just as in the movies, when the FBI called in the IRS to nab a particularly slippery villain, the administration used the Budget Bureau to finish off the OSS. It seemed that in the name of cutbacks, the government could do away with almost anything—especially when the president had given them the go-ahead. Donovan had been relieved of his command by executive order, and the OSS was abolished, its functions distributed between the departments of State and War. Truman wanted a "broad" service that was "attached to the President's office." The new Central Intelligence Agency, entrusted to new hands, was speedily approved.

The former OSS director was given a pat on the back and a letter from Truman addressed to "My Dear General Donovan." It acknowledged his "capable leadership" and assured him that America's permanent intelligence services were "being erected on the foundation of the facilities and resources mobilized through the OSS during the war." Before scattering to the winds, Donovan and his talented recruits assembled for a last time in the Riverside Skating Rink, one of the many Washington buildings the agency had taken over during the war. It was a subdued occasion, marked by proud speeches, tearful farewells, and that odd American penchant for hugging.

Thankfully, the English did not go in for such sentimental displays. In any event, by late fall, most of Dahl's BSC colleagues and old embassy pals had already packed up and cleared out. Stephenson had been tarred by the same brush as Donovan, and any hopes he may have had of carving out a postwar fiefdom died with the OSS. The atmosphere in Washington had soured. The general feeling was, the sooner they were all gone, the better. Dahl's former roommate, Richard Miles, was happy to be leaving. He was excited about the victory of the Labour Party and hoped the new prime minister would follow through on his promise to steer the country, exhausted from so many years of war, to "a planned society" with better opportunity for all. England was undergoing dramatic changes on the domestic front, all of which spelled doom to the old class hierarchy. Miles thought Wallace should go to England and expressed the belief that the Prophet of the Common Man could "do a great deal of good with the new crowd."

Dahl's pals Bryce and Ogilvy had been demobilized and were already busy planning their return to civilian life. Bryce had immediately fallen back on his indolent ways. After being let out of the BSC shortly after VJ Day, he and his wife had decamped to Jamaica, where some years earlier she had purchased a small plantation. The property, located in an area known as Red Hills, included a handsome eighteenth-century stone "great house" called Bellevue, which once belonged to Admiral Nelson and, according to legend, was haunted. Beautifully situated atop a small mountain, it looked down over the green Jamaican hills and, in the distance, the glimmering outline of Kingston and the Port Royal peninsula. Bryce had a natural affinity for the slow pace of island life and decided to settle there permanently, passing his days socializing, fussing over his fruit trees, and doing a bit of farming. He had what Cuneo called "a violent addiction to being left undisturbed," and there was no place more undisturbed on earth than Bellevue.

As it happened, Stephenson also regarded the island as an ideal hideout and made use of it throughout the war. On one occasion, he borrowed Bryce's villa, sending an ill and overworked Noël Coward there for a badly needed rest cure. In December 1942 the singer-composer was, according to his diary, "exhausted and almost voiceless" after a strenuous tour of troop concerts in Europe and a series of Christmas broadcasts in New York, made at the special request of Henry Morgenthau. Stephenson, who had invited Coward to spend Christmas with him and his wife in New York, worried that he was on the verge of a breakdown and insisted he take a holiday to restore his health. As in everything the BSC chief did, Coward's stay on Jamaica was arranged with "impeccable secrecy": he was met at the airport by a naval officer who whisked him off to Bryce's mountaintop retreat and, after fourteen luxurious days of semiseclusion, was driven back in the still-dark early-morning hours to the airport. "The spell was cast," recalled Coward, "and I knew I should come back."

The island had the same romantic hold on Fleming, though Bryce never quite understood why. In the middle of the war, the two friends discovered that they were both scheduled to attend the same high-level Anglo-American naval intelligence conference in Jamaica and were overjoyed at the idea of escaping their respective cubicles for a brief rendezvous in the Caribbean. Four dismal, rain-choked days later they had boarded the plane back to Washington. Bryce, who had long wanted to show Fleming his "magic island," was thoroughly disgusted. It had rained ceaselessly, the sun never once appeared, and they spent their nights trapped in his barely furnished plantation house, sipping pink grenadine—the only bottle of booze in the place—and listening to the steady, drumming downpour and dreaming of someplace dry. As a result, he had been nothing short of dumbfounded when Ian, who had said little on the return journey, suddenly turned to him and announced, "You know, Ivar, I've made a great decision. When we have won this blasted war, I am going to live in Jamaica. Just live in Jamaica and lap it up, and swim in the sea and write books."

As soon as Bryce was reestablished at Bellevue, he fulfilled the promise he had made to Fleming to help him find "the right bit of Jamaica" to buy. He scoured the beaches and byroads to no avail, until an old acquaintance told him he had just the spot. Bryce cabled "the Commander" in London saying he had found his paradise retreat, if he was still interested. Fleming's reply came the next day: "PRAY PAUSE NOT IAN." Several months later Fleming flew out to take a look at the land. It was a fourteen-acre plot high above the water on the north shore at Orcabessa, down the coast from Bellevue, in an area the locals called Racehorse because of an old donkey track that had been there for more years than anyone could remember. The seaward view was lovely, with an aquamarine bay, a protected harbor, and a small sliver of sand that served as a private beach. Fleming loved it and decided after some debate to call the place Goldeneye after the code name of a SIS operation he had helped plan in occupied France. He paid two thousand pounds for the property and spent the next few months sketching the design of the house he planned to build, on blotters in his Admiralty office in London.

In November, Fleming was released from His Majesty's service and took a job as a journalist. He had toyed briefly with the idea of returning to his former career in banking, but after seven years in intelligence it struck him as depressingly humdrum. Instead, he accepted an offer from the British press baron Lord Kemsley, whom he had gotten to know well during the war, to start a foreign news service for his chain of newspapers. Kemsley, a friend of Stephenson's, owned by far the largest newspaper empire in England, including the prestigious *Sunday Times*. The salary was more than generous, and Fleming somehow managed to have it written into his contract that he was guaranteed two months' paid vacation a year, which meant he could regularly slip away to his new house in Jamaica.

Ogilvy was offered a job with the peacetime MI6 that he politely declined. He was a capitalist at heart and still had it in mind to make some serious money. It had occurred to him that the BSC's wartime net-work of talented British, American, and Canadian businessmen should not go to waste, and on a whim he wrote up a prospectus in which his "colleagues in economic warfare could be converted into a profitable company of merchant adventurers." Stephenson was impressed, and the new company of merchant adventurers. the World Commerce Corp., was formed, with many leading figures from the intelligence community signing on as shareholders, including General Donovan, David Bruce, and Charles Hambro. John Pepper, the prime mover in all the BSC's economic and industrial subversion, was president. Ed Stettinius Jr., the former secretary of state, signed on as a director. Ogilvy, who was vice president of the new company, lasted in the job for only a few weeks before becoming bored. He resigned and headed for greener pastures, plunking down $23,500 for a hundred-acre tobacco farm in Lancaster, Pennsylvania, in the heart of Amish country.

The new company flourished without him. With help from Hambro's bank, Stephenson and his ex-intelligence cohorts quickly raised $1 million in capital, which they stated was to "help bridge over the breakdown in foreign exchange." Their plan was to export American know-how and capital to other countries and to help develop untapped resources. One of their first big deals was in Jamaica, which was rich in gypsum and lime-stone but had no cement plant, forcing them to import it from England at great expense. Stephenson, who was already on good terms with the local government, negotiated a nineteen-year monopoly on Jamaican cement, and the company began making plans to build a large industrial plant at Kingston harbor. He bought one of the finest homes on the island, called Hillowtown, overlooking Montego Bay, and turned his back on Washington and the world of secret intelligence. It was an odd sort of semiexile for the powerful spymaster, who was not yet fifty. He invited Dahl, his admiring subordinate, to visit, and Dahl promised that he would.

When all was said and done, however, Dahl could not help thinking it was an unfitting end for a man of Stephenson's remarkable ability. "The sad thing was that when the war finished, they didn't put him straight in the British cabinet," he said many years later. "To me, this was an absolute tragedy." He supposed that while Churchill knew all that the BSC chief had contributed to the war effort, he must also have recognized that Stephenson was not cut out for government work. Stephenson was too clever by half and would have run rings around the new prime minister and other cabinet members. It was probably also the case that he had alienated too many people along the way and would have undoubtedly been given "a very rough ride" had his name ever been put forward. "Although Bill had tremendous political sense, he wasn't a political animal," reflected Dahl. "I think they were frightened that he would have been a terrible nuisance to them in one way or another."

As the war receded from the front pages and dimmed in people's memories, Stephenson's former recruits could not help noticing an increased tendency on the part of many people, even the "otherwise well-informed," to think anyone connected with black propaganda and special operations could not have been "quite nice," in the words of Bickham Sweet-Escott. "Some," he recalled, went "a great deal farther, and will tell you that the SOE was a racket, peopled by wrongheaded and irresponsible young men, by *embusques* or by crypto-communists, if not by out-and-out traitors." Given half a chance, they would add that all their undercover actions had not only failed to produce "any results worth speaking about" but had made life "immeasurably more difficult" for their country now that the war was over. Inevitably, this fashionable view took hold and was expressed everywhere from Georgetown soirées to Mayfair dinner parties. In peacetime, intelligence work—eavesdropping and peering over people's shoulders—seemed ruthless and dishonest. No one seemed to remember that this villainy was practiced for their collective security; the buggers, forgers, safe-busters, document thieves, information-sifters, and propagandists had all been on the side of the angels. Small wonder that Dahl and his BSC colleagues, who had all been in the game, were increasingly circumspect about discussing their "diplomatic" service. There was no place for espionage in polite society.

Dahl's wartime duties also came to an end that fall. He was mustered out of the RAF, and amateur that he was, there was no chance of a position with any postwar agency. He was spending most of his time in New York and was working temporarily out of the BSC offices at 630 Rockefeller Plaza, Room 3553. When he was in town, he stayed in Millicent Rogers' "luxurious apartment" in Sutton Place, which had windows overlooking the East River and was very grand and full of marvelous Biedermeier furniture. He usually had the place to himself as she was often away.

He, too, would soon be leaving, striking out on his own. At that moment, however, the future looked very uncertain. As blithe and unconcerned as he pretended to be, Dahl was not at all confident of his chosen career as a writer. The occasional checks he pocketed from *The Saturday Evening Post* and other American magazines had been a welcome supplement to his regular salary, but he wondered how he would ever manage to support himself writing full-time. At the same time, Forester's early praise, and the popularity of his first efforts, had nurtured his ego and ambitions. Thanks in large part to Marsh, he had also come to enjoy an extravagant lifestyle, influential friends, and all the beautiful things money can buy, from expensive paintings to expensive women. For an unemployed twenty-nine-year-old, reconciling these seemingly disparate elements of his life was not easy. Instead of being able to kick up his heels and bask in those first heady days of freedom, Dahl felt the weight of expectations bearing down on him.

He drove four hundred frozen miles from New York to Virginia to spend Christmas with Marsh as usual. His castle, Longlea, was now in the queen's possession, so Charles had bought a new farm in Rappahannock County called Jessamine Hill, not too far down the road from his old place. He had also moved out of the R Street house in Washington, and relocated to somewhat smaller digs at 1711 22nd Street. They spent most of the holiday talking about their future plans. Marsh, whose riches had been greatly reduced by his divorce, was planning to make another fortune in newspapers. He had taken back control of his company, General Newspapers, and was already casually assembling another mini-empire. Making money came to him as naturally as breathing and was seemingly just as effortless. Dahl, who was very much concerned with his own prospects, talked about his determination to write a novel. Too many of the New York publishing types Marsh had introduced him to had advised him that there was no market for short stories. They all said books were the thing, so he would just have to have a go at it. The legendary Maxwell Perkins, Hemingway's editor at Scribner's, had agreed to take him on and offered him a contract for his first foray into long-form fiction. Hoping to capitalize on his early success, or perhaps just hedging his bets a little, the story Dahl had in mind was an adult fantasy that once again featured that tiny scourge of the RAF and was tentatively entitled *The Gremlins*.

Marsh never doubted his protégé's potential. The American tycoon, who over the past three years had formed the habit of running Dahl's life, decided to fully realize his role as mentor and loaned Roald the funds to help finance his beginnings as an author. "My father knew he didn't have any money," explained Antoinette. "He had complete faith in him, and wanted to help him get his start." According to Ingersoll, Marsh also felt strongly that Dahl had been wronged, "when having served his bosses so conscientiously for so long, they dropped him without a pension or further interest." In the end, Ingersoll observed, "It was Charles and not his own government that paid off Roald."*

---

*Dahl was actually listed as 60 percent disabled and pensioned off for the paltry sum of 160 pounds.

Dahl put off his return to England until after the New Year so he could be present for the publication of his new book. He wanted to make the rounds and take his farewell bows before heading home for good. *Over to You* appeared in early January to great acclaim. Nona Balakian, a critic for the *New York Times,* hailed Dahl as an exceptionally promising short-story writer who captured the RAF pilots' "mad abandon with marvelous subtle insight and genuine humor." In his spare constructions, she continued, "One senses the touch of a craftsman who weighs the effects of his words and phrasing. He has, what is essential, an acute awareness of the narrow margin separating shadow and substance. He has not been afraid to venture into the realm of vision, where not only gremlins are born, but the very stuff of literature."

Wallace, who had received a copy as a Christmas gift, dropped Dahl a line at the Hay Adams Hotel, where he was staying, thanking him for the book and the personal dedication. He wrote that he had spent the holiday reading the book and "especially enjoyed the high, disinterested British courtesy which is employed by the officers of the RAF in faraway lands when they rescue damsels in distress."

Eager for approval, Dahl approached Hemingway, who he counted as one of his heroes and early influences, for an opinion of *Over to You.* As Hemingway had shown him a draft of his D-day article in London, Dahl thought it only appropriate to reciprocate by giving him an advance copy of the book. Hemingway kept it for two days, and then handed it back. When Dahl asked if he liked the stories, Hemingway replied, "I didn't understand them," and then strode down the corridor without looking back.

Most of Dahl's wartime colleagues found his fictionalized memoirs very moving. Noël Coward read the slim volume while on vacation in Jamaica and was powerfully reminded of the desperate times they all had been through—"in hospitals and messes and ships"—and barely survived. "These stories pieced the layers of my consciousness and stirred up the very deep feelings I had during the war and have since, almost deliberately, been in danger of losing," he noted in his diary. "If I forget these feelings or allow them to be obscured because they are uncomfortable, I shall be lost."

They were all a little lost that first, unsteady year of peace. After his peculiar service to his country, Dahl knew he was bound to feel unsettled and unsatisfied. Leaving the BSC was like removing a heavy coat. It would be a while before he stopped missing it. Marsh understood this strange depression—or was it just the inverse of so much high excitement?—better than anyone. After seeing a glowing review of *Over to You* in the February 18 *Herald Tribune*, Marsh sent Dahl his congratulations, uncharacteristically compressing his unruly emotions into a single jubilant word: "Hurrah!" The thrust of his message, however, was sober and cautionary. There was a stubborn boyish streak in his flying friend that had Marsh worried. More than ever now he felt it was important that Dahl not become distracted or sidetracked by other whims and enthusiasms. He knew him far too well not to know the danger of his suddenly becoming bored with a project and abandoning it in favor of something new and exciting, to say nothing of the entanglements of his large, extended Norwegian family, which always threatened to drag him away from his desk and interfere with his sense of purpose. If Dahl truly wanted to be a writer, he would have to devote himself to it wholeheartedly, without reservation. "Work hard," Marsh exhorted him. "Talk little. Be truly a miser of time. And then the novel when the Gremlins get an honest publishing job."

On February 7, Dahl headed home. He would be stopping off in London, at the Dorchester, while he tried to drum up some writing assignments and met with Hamish Hamilton, the publisher of the British edition of *Over to You*. Then it would be on to his mother's house, where he planned to live and work. Marsh refused to say a final good-bye and instead threw himself into planning a joint trip to Scandinavia that spring, with Dahl serving as tour guide in his native land.

In an earlier letter, tinged with melancholy, Marsh, in a sort of farewell salute, wrote with pride and affection of the deep bond they had forged during the war. His tone was warm, ruminative, and full of goodwill. With rare insight and understanding, he acknowledged that their relationship had altered in recent months and would inevitably change even more as their paths crossed less often in the years to come. He was resigned to the fact that they would be separated by work and distance. But their allegiance to each other would never end. They were too close for that, closer than any "mere papa" and son. Despite their occasional differences, and the disappointments of that last tumultuous year, nothing had ever happened to diminish his opinion of the young man who had entered his life in the winter of 1942. "Your presence struck me intensely as you first walked into the R Street house living room," Marsh wrote. "In the wear and tear there has been some abrasion, as you have seen my clay feet and I have seen yours. But by measure, as the Eighth Symphony closes, and as I go into the beef stew, I know that your spirit is with me now, and tomorrow, and yesterday."

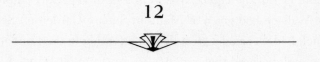

12

FULL LIVES

Gamblers just before they die are often given a great
golden streak of luck.

—IAN FLEMING

BY THE FALL of 1946 Dahl had settled at Grange Farm, his mother's
new house near Great Missenden, set up a makeshift office in the
barn, and knuckled down to work. He had finished the first draft of his
new novel over the summer, but he was not satisfied with it and knew
it needed work. A painfully slow wordsmith for whom the pages did not
come easily, he found it difficult to maintain his focus. He tried to write
most mornings, but something always seemed to come up. Once interrupted, he would declare the working day ruined and abandon his desk.
Moreover, the novel was a dramatic departure from anything he had
attempted before and it felt long and unwieldy. Doubts crept up on him
like the morning damp. Unlike his war stories, which had a detached, almost dreamlike quality, there was a distinct new bitterness to his tone.

The war, and four years in Washington, had changed him. The bomb
weighed heavily on his mind. He had little faith in the brokered peace

and was dismayed by the growing divide between England and the United States. America's return to isolationism filled him with despair: "YOU ARE STILL THE SAME OLD BUNCH OF INTERNATIONAL COWARDS YOU WERE IN '39," he cabled Marsh in a fit of anger over a pro-Russia speech Wallace had given at Madison Square Garden on September 10, which had received a great deal of attention in the London papers. Wallace had declared that Americans "must not let British balance of power manipulations determine whether and when the United States gets into war," and while criticizing England's continuing "imperialistic policy," he had advocated flexible give-and-take" with Stalin's Russia. "In this connection, I want one thing clearly understood. I am neither anti-British or pro-British—neither anti-Russian or pro-Russian." As usual with Wallace, however, nothing was clearly understood, and his remarks were endlessly twisted and exaggerated and elicited a flood of criticism.

To Dahl's ears, it was exactly the same kind of naïve grandstanding that had led to the last war, and just as before, a complement of small European countries would fall while the United States postured. He told Marsh he was "through forever" with Wallace, whom he blasted as a "semi-sincere misinformed oaf." (He took small comfort in the fact that ten days after his controversial Madison Square Garden remarks, Truman asked his commerce secretary to resign from the cabinet. Wallace went home to his farm in South Salem, New York, and spent his days breeding corn and chickens and became editor of *The New Republic*.) Dahl's anxieties about the future found expression in his writing and took the form of an antiwar fantasy for adults, in which his weird, foot-high cartoon characters impatiently wait for mankind to finish destroying what is left of their civilization so the gremlins can inherit the empty earth. This book would not be another benign Disney fable but a savage, postapocalyptic vision of life after World War III and IV, with the accompanying devastation and massive loss of life.

His solid Norwegian family was not all sure they thought filling notepads with his mad scribbling was any kind of a proper career for a young man and clucked with disapproval. After Dahl persuaded his sister Asta to help with the typing, she pounded out some early pages of his manuscript. When she had finished, she gave him a piece of her mind. "I don't know what you think you're doing, Roald," she told him, "but it's absolute baloney." He did not disagree and promised to do better.

Dahl's gloom was further aggravated by the recurrent problems caused by his debilitating war injuries. Although Dr. Arthur Scott had managed to fix his right leg, his left leg had been troubling him all fall and had now given out. He wrote Marsh that he was hobbled by the intense pain and was unable to walk. In December he went into the military hospital in Wheatley, Oxford, for yet another operation, followed by another long recuperation. After so many successive surgeries, it was difficult to summon up much hope in his chances for a full recovery. He was not the depressive type but was increasingly resigned to the fact that he would never be "cured." He had nightmares that he would end up lame—or worse yet, a cripple. Charles and Claudia were so worried by his wretched state of mind over Christmas that they wrote they could not possibly enjoy the holidays and would not rest easy until "we hear that your body is improving or at least in intelligent hands." They offered to "fly over at once" but realized they would be more of a burden than a help.

Dahl's homecoming did not have the expected salutary effect. With every cold, gray month of English winter, he grew more sullen and despondent. In some ways, he seemed to be suffering from the same kind of strain, both physical and emotional, that he had earlier discerned in battle-worn RAF pilots. In "Someone Like You," a short story that was included in *Over to You*, he wrote of seeing a colleague he had known early in the war but who was almost unrecognizable after five years of fighting: "From being a young, bouncing boy, he had become someone old and wise and gentle. He had become gentle like a wounded child. He had become old like a tired man of seventy years. He had become so different and he had changed so much that at first it was embarrassing for both of us and it was not easy to know what to say."

It is clear from both his stories and his letters that he was wrestling not only with his sorrow and fatigue, but also with his grave doubts about war as a form of murder and his own complicity in the senseless killing. In "The Soldier," which he wrote over the winter of 1947 and later rewrote, he described a returning veteran who is haunted by his combat experiences, reflexively ducking when planes fly overhead, and suffers from a progressive deadening of the senses—he can no longer feel the difference between hot and cold, or between the prick of a pin and the touch of a feather. The neurosurgeon who is treating him is baffled by his deterioration, and fails to realize it is the by-product of the young man's deliberate exertion, an attempt to blot out "the noise of the gunfire" at dawn and "whistle-shriek of the bomb." It does not occur to the doctor that his patient prefers to be numb.

Dahl's body slowly mended, but his outlook did not improve. After working hard on the final draft of the gremlins novel, he wrote Marsh in the fall of 1947 that it was finally finished and was to be published in a four months' time under the title *Some Time Never: A Fable for Supermen*. He knew that the dark subject matter probably doomed its chances in the market, noting, "Not many will read it." Nevertheless, it accurately reflected his grim assessment of the world, and the inevitability of another war in their lifetime, probably within the next twelve years. "I'm not frightened of Communism, I'm frightened of war," he confided. "Not frightened of it, just appalled by it and its coming." *Some Time Never* came out in early 1948 and as predicted was not well received and scarcely sold any copies. He later disowned it. The American critics thought it was disappointing, dull and wordy, and would have worked better had it been shorter. The reception in England was not any kinder. The bad reviews hurt him deeply, and he swore off novels for good.[*]

He rededicated himself to short stories, but there was no money in it. At his laborious pace, the longer magazine pieces took at least four to six months. He was lucky to do two a year. Making matters worse, he grew short-tempered and difficult. He quarreled with editors who tried to cut his work, in one case ranting to Marsh that he had sent *The Saturday Evening Post* back their check and told them "what they could do with it."

The postwar climate in England was even less hospitable to short story writers than in America, and Dahl had trouble finding takers. Wounded RAF pilots were a dime a dozen, and the public had tired of their tales of derring-do. A reviewer in the London *Observer,* in the course of panning Hemingway's latest war novel, *Across the River*, complained that his heroes familiar "posture"—"despair held bolt upright by courage and virility"—was overdone and out of vogue. As more than one critic had identified Dahl as following in Hemingway's footsteps, it did not augur well for his future. While the BBC eventually bought "The Soldier," it turned down several other pieces. The rejections rankled. Dahl, who had no university degree, and little or no cachet in London literary circles, began to question whether it made sense to continue trying to eke out a living as a writer. He blamed the country's ongoing economic woes on the new prime minister and the bungling Labour government, telling Marsh scornfully, "I wish them dead."

Dahl retreated from the outside world and lost himself in the familiar, comforting rhythms of rural life. He managed his mother's farm,

---

[*]It was thirty years before he attempted another novel with *My Uncle Oswald*. He would similarly renounce the theater after the disastrous Broadway debut of his first play, *The Honeys,* in 1955.

tended the livestock, and loafed. To relieve the boredom, he fell back on his old habit of gambling, placing daily bets on the races. He became a dog-racing enthusiast, and started breeding and schooling his own greyhounds with help from the local butcher, Claud Taylor. He began spending his afternoons at the scruffy little local courses laid out with posts and cord in nearby fields, along which an accelerating dummy hare was pulled with the dogs in hot pursuit. He loved hanging out with the bookies and poachers and other rough customers who gathered at the track, claiming it was "cheap for the thrill [he got] out of it." He was so enamored of Claud that he featured him in a number of gruesome stories about English country life, painting an anything but quaint picture of shifty-eyed neighbors, rat-infested farms, sewage-lined roads, and vicious gypsy dogs whose specialty was "to tear another one to pieces at the end of the race." He could not resist biting parody, even when it came to his own personal haven.

When Dahl squandered a modest inheritance on dog losses, his family grew concerned. After four years in England, he was brooding and lacked direction. More than a few of his friends wondered what the formerly freewheeling bachelor was doing buried in a sleepy village in Buckinghamshire, living back at home with his mother. Martha Gellhorn, who came for a visit, met the family matriarch (referred to in her native Norwegian as Mumu or Mormor) and what she later remembered as "*a thousand* sisters." In her view, Dahl gave new meaning to the term "Mama's boy." Sofie Dahl was a formidable personality who kept a tight grip on her brood. Several daughters had already settled nearby, and she clearly intended to keep her son close to hand. It was quite clear that no woman could ever measure up to her exacting standards or be "good enough" for her precious Roald. Given the "suffocating atmosphere of adoration of him," which struck Gellhorn as unhealthy in all its many implications, she came away thinking it was a miracle Dahl was not worse than he was.

By the fall of 1950, Marsh had independently arrived at much the same conclusion. He decided it was time to pry Dahl loose from his mother's clutches and persuaded him to return to New York for a brief stay, during which time he could drum up some work and catch up with old friends. Marsh still had his Manhattan town house on 92nd Street, and he lured Dahl with the promise of one of the apartments. It went without saying that he would happily underwrite most of his expenses. "It was Charles who picked up Dahl's life," recalled Ingersoll, who was party to Marsh's plan to free Dahl from the "Lady Board of Managers" who had him under lock and key. "Roald's establishmentary sisters, all establishmentarily married, had long since concluded that their brother had turned out to be hopelessly impractical and generally bewildering. Charlie Marsh, this strange American he had suddenly become so enthusiastic about after the war, I think they instinctively mistrusted as Roald's latest folly. But Charles did set him free, psychologically."

Dahl grasped the lifeline Marsh threw him. It was not an offer he could refuse. Max Perkins, the editor who commissioned *Some Time Never*, had died six months before it was published, and Scribner's had subsequently turned down his idea for a new collection of stories. While Dahl seldom let his debonair facade drop, Marsh could see that his protégé was floundering. Mindful of the young man's pride, he approached the problem with unusual care and tact. Rather than offering Dahl another loan to tide him over, Marsh made noises about needing to get his estate in order and established a $25,000 trust fund in Roald's name.

Marsh also found Dahl a role in his entourage he knew he would enjoy, entrusting him to buy art and antiques for his new homes to replenish those lost in the divorce. Dahl had taste and a good eye and even with his meager resources had managed to acquire some very good paintings: Bonnards, Boudins, Cézanne watercolors, a Renoir, a Sisley, and a Degas seascape. His only problem was that it took him so long to finish a story, he would invariably have to sell the pictures six months after he bought them. Over the next few years, thanks in part to the booming postwar art market, he would locate a variety of treasures for both Marsh's collection and his own. More often than not Marsh rewarded Dahl's efforts by presenting him with a sculpture or painting he knew Dahl especially coveted.

To help him get his career back on track, Marsh also pressed Ingersoll into service and asked him to make some helpful calls and provide guidance. "Charles got me, Harold Ross's onetime editor at *The New Yorker*, to turn Roald in that direction, to start his post-war life as a writer," recalled Ingersoll. "The macabre pieces that came from Roald's depths were anything but typical '*New Yorker* material' but they captured Ross's enthusiasm instanta—and overnight Roald became a known *New Yorker* writer with a following of his own."

The New Yorker bought several stories in quick succession, including "Taste," about a famous gourmet who bets that if he can correctly name his wealthy host's rare wine, he will claim his young daughter's hand in marriage; and "Skin," about the gruesome dilemma facing an impoverished old man who is offered large sums for the painting that he had had tattooed on his back on a drunken dare in his youth, which has since become an extremely valuable and coveted work of art. When Knopf brought out a collection of his vengeful, teasing tales, *Someone Like You*, the *New York Herald Tribune* reported that there was "something like a cult" centering on the former RAF wing commander, whose new stories were notable for the strain of Lardner-like bitterness running through them. Most involved morbidly suspenseful plots about the punishment of greed and tied up with a nasty trick ending. Dahl told the paper, "It's not true that I dislike people," and he insisted his loathing was reserved for phonies and cheats. Still, some of his old admirers found the undercurrent of sadism and misanthropy disturbing. After a dinner with Dahl shortly after the publication of

Someone Like You, Noël Coward observed, "the stories are brilliant and his imagination is fabulous. Unfortunately, there is, in all of them, an underlying streak of cruelty and macabre unpleasantness, and a curiously adolescent emphasis on sex. This is strange because he is a sensitive and gentle creature."

Being in New York was a tonic for Dahl. He reconnected with his band of wartime colleagues, and they immediately resumed their boisterous, ribbing banter. During the four years in England, he had forgotten how much he needed the consolation of friendship. It was also reassuring to know that he was not the only one who had gotten off to a bumpy start. After almost going broke, Ogilvy had sold the tobacco farm in 1948. Certain that a thirty-seven-year-old unemployed university dropout would never find employment, he had opened his own small advertising business and was using his public opinion expertise to target unsuspecting consumers. He had gotten a helping hand from his brother, Francis, a highly successful advertising executive in England, who saw that expansion and greater earnings lay in America. Together with a colleague, Robert Bevan of S. H. Benson, they arranged for David to set up their New York agency. Ogilvy decided he needed an American business partner and recruited Anderson Hewitt from the J. Walter Thompson Company's Chicago office, and Hewitt, Ogilvy, Benson and Mather was formed.

Starting with only $6,000 in capital, no credentials, and no experience in advertising other than a finely honed sense of what made Americans tick, Ogilvy quickly built a reputation for originality and salesmanship. He played the part of the misplaced English country gentleman to the hilt. Much to his friends' amusement, he took to dressing as if he had just come back from a long tramp in the woods and went around New York with a wool cape thrown over his British tweeds, striped shirts, and red suspenders. He was rarely seen without his trademark pipe in hand. "I'd got a gimmick—my English accent, which helped to differentiate me from the ordinary," Ogilvy admitted in later years. With so many agencies and so much competition, his carefully created persona gave him a "terrific advantage."

By 1950 he had two major clients, Guinness and Wedgwood, two fusty British brands that he had helped to establish a new identity for the American market. The following year he scored his biggest hit by effectively popularizing stereotypes drawn from his years with British intelligence. The September 22, 1951, issue of *The New Yorker* carried an ad showing a dashing figure in a black eye patch, along with the slogan "The Man in the Hathaway Shirt." The mysterious image of Baron George Wrangell, a Russian aristocrat (whose eyes were perfectly good) immediately caught the imagination of the public, along with the five paragraphs of inspired copy that included the word "ineffably." The hugely successful ad campaign ended 116 years of obscurity for Hathaway and made Ogilvy famous overnight. The formula was so successful, he used it again in a campaign for Schweppes, featuring the company owner and veteran of Her Majesty's navy commander Edward Whitehead, who called his beverage "curiously refreshing" and caused sales to skyrocket. Known as "the Ambassador from Schweppes," Whitehead was a walking caricature of the priggish Foreign Office types whom Ogilvy had had to put up with during the war, and now he had his just revenge. The cheerful, red-whiskered commander was so popular, he became the most widely recognized Englishman in America after Churchill.

Dahl also caught up with Bryce, who had been through another bruising divorce and was minus the beautiful wife and beautiful house in Jamaica. After digging himself out of that hole, England's most indefatigable playboy had finally found a woman who made marriage worth his while. He was newly wed to Marie-Josephine (Jo) Hartford, the granddaughter of George Huntington Hartford, the founder of the Great Atlantic and Pacific Tea Company, the sister of A&P tycoon

Huntington Hartford, and one of the richest women in the world. She was a big, beefy blonde, and in Dahl's view decidedly plain, but wore the most fantastic jewels. She owned a number of homes, including a magnificent villa in Nassau, and kept a string of racehorses. Then there was Back Hole Hollow Farm, her country estate near Saratoga, on the border of Vermont and New York, where she kept more horses. The scale of her wealth was tremendous, quite staggering after the austerity of England, and she lavished enormous sums on her households, making them incredibly luxurious and inviting, not just for herself but also her guests. At her dinner parties, the food was always superb, the service perfection, and the choice greater than that found in most first-class restaurants.

The Bryces had become the center of a rather swell social circle in New York, surrounding themselves with colorful European aristocrats and American millionaires, including "Honey" and Alex Hohenlohe, a former Texas showgirl who was married to an Austrian prince with a sporting lodge called Schloss Mittersill that catered to the idle rich, and Tommy Leiter, the hard-drinking scion of the Marshall Field fortune. Bryce's cousin, Bunny Phillips, was also in town and had married Gina Wernher, a close friend of the queen's, whose wealthy family was descended from the grand duke of Russia, brother of the czar. Dahl was simultaneously drawn to their moneyed set and repelled by it. "In the Bryce world," he later sniffed, "all you needed was a dinner jacket and the ability to amuse people to make the grade."

In 1951 Bryce, who was in need of an occupation more than a job, invested in Ernest Cuneo's new venture, the North American Newspaper Alliance (NANA), a wire service and syndicator of well-known columnists and cartoonists. The agency had originally been formed by a group of newspapers to allow them to pool their resources when they needed to buy expensive serial rights to any really big book coming on the market. Cuneo's plan was to buy the down-at-the heels company and restore it to its former glory. Cuneo and Bryce also bought a weekly paper, the *Maryland News,* and put their old pal Drew Pearson in charge of managing it. For the dissolute Bryce, it was a diverting if not particularly profitable pastime. "There was always something going on and interesting people to be met," he recalled, "loveable old newsmen living on a shoestring, their reward and all they asked the by-line; celebrities of stage and screen who needed the friendship of the press; callers with original ideas; eccentrics." After five years, his attention flagged and he sold his interest to Cuneo.

Whenever Fleming was in New York, he could always be found in the company of Cuneo or the Bryces. Conveniently, Ernie had a country house a mile and a quarter from Black Hole Hollow Farm, so during the summers they all saw quite a lot of one another. Cuneo and Bryce had convinced Fleming to become European vice president of NANA, which essentially gave him unlimited expense account and an endless excuse to travel. Dahl had kept up with Fleming in London after the war, as well as in Jamaica, when he had visited Stephenson in the winter of 1948 at his house in Montego Bay. Lord Beaverbrook had bought a home, called Cromarty, eight hundred yards down the hill, and they had all dined together and talked of old times. Dahl and Fleming had not gotten on well because of Ian's affair with Millicent Rogers, who also was also a regular visitor to the island. Their dalliance had reportedly not ended well, and the two men had words over it. At the time, Fleming was carrying on a long, tortured affair with Lady Anne Rothermere, the wife of the *Daily Mail* proprietor Esmond Rothermere, and Dahl, probably out of envy as much as principle, was piqued by his caddish behavior. When Anne later became pregnant, however, Fleming stepped up and did "the right thing." After a quick divorce from Rothermere, Ian and Anne were married in Jamaica in March 1952. After a celebration at Goldeneye, complete with serenade by Noël Coward, they flew to Nassau, and then New York, to be feted by the Bryces.

By the time Dahl and Fleming met up again in New York, they had long since patched up their friendship. Fleming never talked about his own literary ambitions but took an active interest in Dahl's work, read everything he published, and always had words of praise. One evening at the Bryces, just as they were making their way into dinner, after a great many martinis, Fleming took Dahl aside and proposed the perfect murder plot: "Why don't you have someone murder their husband with a frozen leg of mutton which she then serves to the detectives who come to investigate the murder?" Dahl liked the idea so much he used it as the basis of a grisly *New Yorker* story entitled "Lamb to the Slaughter," which he published in 1952. Alfred Hitchcock later turned it into an episode for his television series. Fleming kept suggesting story ideas, some of them quite clever, but Dahl later maintained none of them quite fit his formula.

Later, when Fleming limned his years in intelligence for *Casino Royale*, which he completed in early 1952 and published the following year, he was very self-deprecating and would always say, "Of course, I'm just playing about. My stuff is nothing, despicable stuff, but yours is literature." According to Dahl, however, Fleming "never missed a trick." Everything was grist for the mill. "A good fifty percent of the Bond thing—the luxury, the atmosphere—came directly from Bryce," he recalled. Everything that interested Fleming eventually wound up in his books: Ivar (whose middle name was Felix) and Tommy Leiter were the basis for 007's CIA counterpart Felix Leiter, while Hohenlohe and Schloss Mittersill (which was used by the Nazis for scientific research during the war) were the models for Ernst Blofeld and his hideout in the Alps.

Cuneo became Fleming's American tour guide, tutoring him on crime and taking him to nightclubs in Harlem to provide material for *Live and Let Die*. Fleming dedicated the book to him—"To Ernest Cuneo, Muse." Cuneo later led him on expeditions to Chicago, Las

Vegas, and California and was a main source of ideas, expertise, and arcane information for years to come. This offhand method of collaboration later came back to haunt Fleming, when he and Bryce were sued by two screenwriters, Steve McClory and Jack Whittingham, for not crediting their original ideas in their film version of *Thunderball* or in Fleming's subsequent novel. After the case dragged on for ten days, Bryce decided to settle and put an end to the embarrassing headlines, and Fleming had little choice but to go along. Bryce footed the bill, but the expensive legal wrangle strained their friendship.

In the meantime, Cuneo had married Margaret Watson, one of Stephenson's handpicked BSC secretaries and a great favorite of Dahl's from the old days. They had two babies and were blissfully happy. Once part of his intelligence fraternity, they now became extended family. Cuneo had become firm friends with Marsh, and they had embarked on a number of joint business ventures, including the purchase of Universal Newsreel. Another project was the acquisition of the palatial, five-story former Rockerfeller residence at 9 East 62nd Street, which had until recently served as the Iranian Embassy and which they remodeled to provide office space for themselves as well as gracious living quarters. Charles occupied an elegant duplex on the first and second floors, Ingersoll and his new wife were above, and Dahl was tucked away in a small apartment on the top floor.

Marsh involved Dahl in his myriad business plans and schemes, and even in his declining years, his prodigious energy and zest for life were contagious. His optimism was quintessentially American, and he remained convinced that there was no problem that a combination of hard work and money could not solve. Finished with politics—he had broken with Wallace, who in 1948 ran for president as part of a third-party Progressive platform, which was endorsed by the Communist Party—Marsh decided to spend his remaining time on earth exercising what he called his "humanitarian instincts." In the years after the war, he had been profoundly moved by the poverty and scarcity he saw in Europe, and he wanted to find a way as a private citizen to help meet those urgent needs, coming up with a small-scale version of the Lend-Lease aid he had earlier helped foster. It began, in typical fashion, as a spur-of-the-moment gesture while traveling with Dahl in Norway in the spring of 1946. Marsh started giving away money to poor laborers they met on the roads, at times literally jumping out of the limousine to make cash "handouts," or turning to Claudia and commanding, "Right, give him $200," as the astonished locals looked on. On that trip, Marsh's benevolence also extended to Dahl's relatives. After Roald made the case that his family's timber business might be able to help the American publisher's newspaper business by supplying badly needed paper, Marsh wired $10,000 to keep the struggling operation going.

In England, where Charles and Claudia often traveled to visit Dahl in the late 1940s, Marsh's grants became larger and more frequent. Since Dahl's first visit home after the war, Marsh had been sending money as directed, in one case arranging for the parish rector in Limehouse, East London, to identify two hundred of the neediest families to receive a $200-a-month stipend for six months from the wealthy American. The parish was quickly overwhelmed with demand, and for political reasons Dahl wrote Marsh requesting that the project be extended to the neighboring village of Rotherhithe. Dahl's letters were filled with details of the appalling conditions in the countryside, and Marsh, whose new cattle farm in Virginia was already producing a considerable income, sent surplus apples and other foods that were in short supply in England. When he sent a supply of vitamins, however, which Dahl had earlier sought for his mother, his generosity met with scorn. Dahl wrote back that simple country folk "do not give a fuck for vitamins" and would not take them even if told they were aphrodisiacs.

Marsh persisted in his humanitarian endeavors, and over time it became clear that what had begun as a charitable impulse needed to be organized as a permanent philanthropy. The Public Welfare Foundation, which Marsh first conceived of in 1945—he cavalierly announced that he intended to give all his money away and "die broke"—was formally established in Texas in 1947. Two years later, with the help of newly elected Senator Lyndon Johnson, it received tax exemption status.

Taking a leaf out of Stephenson's book, Marsh employed a network of "agents" to carry out his philanthropic work, recruiting friends and acquaintances around the world to give away his money to needy individuals and projects. Dahl, of course, was one of the first of these well-funded agents, though the ranks swelled to more than 130 and came to include everyone from Mother Teresa and Indira Gandhi to Noël Coward and to Clare Boothe Luce.[*] Ingersoll recalled that his recruitment style was typically capricious: "If he chanced upon a man or woman whose face he liked he asked a single direct question, 'Do you know anyone who needs money?' From the questionee's reaction, he made up his mind, instantly." The list of agents extended to a taxi driver in New York, a jewel merchant in India, and a travel agent in Thailand. He would simply instruct Claudia to take their name and put them down for small monthly checks of $10 to $200.

Throughout the latter period of Marsh's life, Dahl was his constant companion and muse, traveling with him on business trips and pleasure cruises as well as frequent sun-seeking getaways to Jamaica.

---

[*]As Marsh's philanthropy grew, the agents shrank in number and were phased out altogether in 1961 after the Internal Revenue Service raised questions about the practice. The Public Welfare Foundation continues to this day and, with assets of over $600 million, ranks as one of the nation's 150 wealthiest private philanthropies, with annual grants of $21.4 million.

When the hotel they frequented on the north side of the island burned to the ground, Marsh spotted a business opportunity that would benefit both himself and the local economy. He took out a ninety-year lease on a beautiful stretch of beachfront property and set about building a gracious new facility that would serve as their winter retreat and provide work and decent wages for the community year-round. Marsh appointed his son John overseer, and the new Mediterranean-style hotel was designed to his specifications, with thirteen bedrooms, each with a big balcony facing the ocean. They decided to call it the Jamaica Inn, borrowing the name from the best-selling Daphne du Maurier novel. Dahl wrote his mother that Marsh's new hotel was "lovely" and the perfect paradise retreat. Noël Coward's place, Blue Harbor, was only fifteen miles away in Porta Maria, and he frequently joined them for dinner.

When Dahl got back from a holiday in England at the end of the summer of 1952, Marsh's East 62nd Street mansion was almost finished and "looked marvelous." Dahl and his new neighbors had regular dinners, and the men often sat up late into the night smoking and talking about the strange, unpredictable turn their lives had taken. In the course of these drunken evenings, Dahl endured many a sermon on the joys of domesticity. Marsh was contemplating a third marriage, this one to Claudia, and wanted the support of his favorite partner in crime. Dahl was by then thirty-five years old, with all the incipient signs of middle age, most notably his receding hairline. According to Ingersoll, Marsh "got it in his head that it was high time for his gay blade to pick himself a wife."

When Dahl went to his old friend Lillian Hellman's for dinner in the fall of 1952, he was very much on the prowl. He was seated beside a beautiful, husky-voiced brunette named Patricia Neal, who was slated to star with Kim Hunter in the revival of Hellman's play *The Children's Hour*, which she was mounting on Broadway. With characteristic arrogance, Dahl spent the whole night deep in discussion with Leonard Bernstein, who was seated across the table, and gave no indication he had taken any notice of her until he called a day or two later and asked her out. Famous actresses do not like to be trifled with, and Neal, who had no idea who Dahl was until she queried her hostess, was not amused. "I didn't like him at all," she recalled. She declined his first invitation, but when he called back two days later, she relented. He took her to dinner at a wonderful Italian restaurant that was owned by John Huston's father-in-law and won her over with his curiosity, clever conversation, and passion for paintings and antiques.

Before the evening was over, Dahl told Neal that there was some-one he wanted her to meet. He took her up to Marsh's penthouse suite at the Pierre, where he was staying while his new apartment was being decorated, and introduced her to his magnanimous patron. "I met Charles Marsh, an old man with a strange face," Neal wrote in a memoir. "With him was a lovely woman named Claudia. While we were there she didn't say a word, but heeded his every beck and call with the trained eye of a geisha, then quietly returned to her needle-work." Even though this was their first date, Neal could see that Dahl and Marsh had an unusual relationship; "Charles just adored him, he would do anything for him." As they rose to leave, Marsh conveyed his approval of Dahl's choice with characteristic bluntness. "Charles knew what pleased him in a woman," recalled Neal. "He told Roald, 'Drop the other baggage. I like this one!'"

All that fall, Dahl frequented the theater, attending rehearsals and giving notes to Hellman. Afterward he and Neal would often go out with friends and various members of the cast. After the play opened in December, he began calling for her backstage every night after her performance. While she found his "consistent but dispassionate in-terest" intriguing, she was far from being swept off her feet. She had already had that, by her own account, with Gary Cooper and was still "ragged from bitterness" at the end of their long affair. They had met and fallen madly in love in 1947 while filming *The Fountainhead* and had carried on their relationship, which was an open secret in Hollywood, for four years. When the Coopers briefly separated in 1951, the gossip columns had had a field day, branding Neal as the other woman. One headline read: "THE GARY COOPERS PART: IS PATRICIA NEAL NEXT?" To escape Cooper, whose Catholic wife was never going to grant him a divorce, and the insinuating Hollywood press, Neal had relocated to New York. She was determined to make a fresh start and at twenty-seven badly wanted to settle down and have a family, but she still pined for Cooper.

Dahl courted her with patient deliberation, introducing her to his friends and gradually incorporating her into his life in New York. "I got to know them all," recalled Neal. "Ivar and Jo, Ian, David, Bunny, who was very tall and thin like Roald, and just sensational looking. They were really something, these Englishmen. And Ernie Cuneo, who was short and fat, and fantastically chatty. They had this great bond from being in the war together, and talked and joked about it a lot, though I didn't really understand most of it." Dahl was also eager for her to get to know Stephenson, to whom he was very close. "It was easy to see why he liked him so much," said Neal. "He was a super man. I loved the man. I loved them all." Dahl never divulged what he did for Stephenson during the war. "He honored the code," she said, "but he was very proud of his secret service work." What he did tell her is "what fun he had" in Washington: "Roald was a fabulous storyteller. He would talk about how he used to play poker with Harry Truman. He knew all these very important people and liked to tell stories about them."

When Dahl proposed to her one night in her dressing room at the theater, however, she was so taken aback that she turned him down flat. She had seen him turn on people at parties and pick fights for no reason. "He could be the most charming man in the world when he wanted to be," she recalled, "and then he could be just terrible, terrible, terrible." Some of her friends had already been burned, and they begged her to break it off, including Hellman's longtime partner, Dashiell Hammett, who took exception to Dahl's rudeness and bullying humor. They had had a particularly bad row at Lillian's one night and were no longer on speaking terms. "Dahl couldn't stand him," she said. "He had a great crush on me at one time, and really cared about me."

Despite her misgivings, Neal's desire to have children got the better of her. She told Dahl she had reconsidered, and shortly thereafter Marsh surprised her with a ring. "[He] suddenly produced a large marquise diamond ring and offered it to us. It was not a gift, as I later found out. Charles expected Roald to pay for it eventually, but he was obviously anxious for his favorite couple to get moving." At a previous meeting Charles had quizzed her on her movie earnings, at one point asking her directly how much she had in the bank. He was clearly disappointed by her answer. While Dahl was working for the top-paying magazine in New York, he was earning only $3,000 per story, and at the rate of two a year was far from well off. Neal could see that Dahl's sponsor was concerned that he had no money and was hoping he would "find a rich girl."

They were married on July 2, 1953, in the little chapel of Trinity Church in lower Manhattan. Marsh was Dahl's best man, and all their closest friends were in attendance, including the Bryces, Ogilvys, Cuneos, and Ingersolls. Hellman, proud of her matchmaking, accepted congratulations. Afterward everyone went back to Marsh's home for a champagne reception. Exactly two weeks later Charles and Claudia tied the knot in France. The two couples honeymooned separately. Roald and Pat took off for a six-week tour of the Italian seacoast and the French Riviera in a secondhand Jaguar that Dahl had managed to pick up cheaply. Then they crossed the Channel to England, as it was Roald's wish that they end their sojourn with a grand meeting of the Dahl family. Since returning to New York, Dahl had been spending part of every summer in Great Missenden and hoped his new bride would want to do the same. He asked his sisters to help them find a place of their own, and they eventually bought a lovely Georgian farmhouse on five acres, which according to the original deed was known as Gipsy House.

Neal adored the lush pastoral setting but found Dahl's mother cold and critical. Dahl, in turn, had nothing but disdain for her Kentucky clan, whom he considered dull and uncultivated. The marriage got off to a rocky start. While Neal went on the road with *The Children's Hour*, Dahl continued his social rounds in New York and kept company with Gloria Vanderbilt. He told Neal that the heiress was infatuated with him but that he had managed to "cool her ardor" by reminding her he was a married man. (Years later Vanderbilt would confess to an affair and described the love letters he wrote to her as "very well done.") There were more tense moments than happy ones. After less than eight months, Dahl announced he wanted a divorce.

Marsh intervened and invited Neal to Jamaica for an emergency summit. "Charles was a friend, teacher, and Father Confessor," Neal recalled. They spent days walking the beach and talking about what went wrong. Marsh felt that as a successful actress, Neal overshadowed her husband and that she needed to assume a more traditional housewife role. Marsh advised her in no uncertain terms to drop the diva act, quit lying in bed all morning, and start making breakfast and washing dishes. "Boy, he told me off," she said ruefully.

Marsh was convinced that money was at the heart of the problem. He told her that Dahl was having difficulty handling the fact that she was the breadwinner, and if she wanted to save their marriage, she should turn the checkbook over to him. "You don't understand men, Pat," he counseled her. "When it's a question of sex, not all of them want to be on top. When it comes to money, they all do. You can't have the balls in the family. You can make the money, but Roald must handle it." Assured it was that simple, Neal promised her husband, who had come to join her, that she would try harder.

The next morning they woke up to shocking news. During the night, the sixty-six-year-old Marsh had been bitten by a mosquito and contracted a grave form of malaria. By the time the doctor arrived, he was near death. Marsh refused to let go. Although he rallied, the high fevers, followed by a series of devastating strokes, damaged his brain. He was never again able to speak more than a few words. To see such a dynamic force struck down broke Dahl's heart. The following week Dahl and Neal left Jamaica saddened and deeply shaken. In a strange way, the tragedy brought them closer together. Neal always believed that Dahl intuited the lecture that Marsh would have given him had he not been robbed of his voice, and straightened up according to his mentor's wishes. From that moment on, it was decided: they were vulnerable and would have to stick together.

Marsh lingered on for another ten years. On Sunday morning, December 1, 1963, just six days after John F. Kennedy had been laid to rest at Arlington National Cemetery, Lyndon Johnson went to the gravesite to lay a wreath before heading to the Oval Office. On November 23 he had been sworn in as the country's thirty-sixth president in a hasty proceeding aboard *Air Force One*, using Kennedy's own Bible, while the body lay in a casket in the back of the plane. On his way to the White House, which he had yet to occupy out of respect for the grieving family, Johnson instructed his driver to make a short, unscheduled stop at Marsh's home. He bounded up the familiar stairs and, with only a quick nod to his hostess at the door, went in search of his old friend. He found the Texas publisher stretched out beneath a sheet, being pummeled by a masseur. Unaware of how far Marsh had slipped, Johnson tried a self-deprecating joke about his "new eminence." As Antoinette later recounted, when "he got no reply, and as the silence lengthened, he blanched." Johnson stared at the long, limp body. Stunned, he descended to the foot of the stairs where Claudia waited and, with tears in his eyes, asked, "Where are Mr. Sam [Rayburn] and Charles now, when I need them?" Then he turned and left. The next day the *Washington Star* reported that the mysterious detour held up the new president's motorcade only "four or five minutes."

Dahl and Neal made New York their home for seven years, until another calamity sent them reeling: a speeding taxi ran over their infant son in his carriage, smashing his skull and nearly killing him. Dahl decided he had had enough of city life. In the summer of 1961, he moved his family back to England, where his two young daughters, Olivia and Tessa, would be safe, and Theo could heal. Both Dahl and Neal had been rocked by the deaths of close friends: Gary Cooper from cancer in May, followed by Hemingway's suicide in July.

Dahl was sure life in Great Missenden would be good for them. He devoted himself to caring for his children, particularly his son, who had developed hydrocephalus, a dangerous swelling of the brain. He could not bear to watch the boy suffer and spent months working with a friend, Stanley Wade, the inventor of hydraulic pumps, to design a nonblocking valve to drain fluid from the brain that could replace the primitive shunts that kept clogging and necessitated repeated cranial operations. He finally succeeded, with the help of a neurosurgeon named Kenneth Till, and the DWT (Wade-Dahl-Till) valve was developed and put into use; thousands of other injured children became the ultimate beneficiaries. Ivar Bryce, who was Theo's godfather, did everything he could to help. He and Jo had bought Moyns Park, an idyllic seventy-room Elizabethan mansion on the Essex-Suffolk border, and invited the Dahls to come and relax, as Neal recalled, "weekend, after weekend, after weekend."

In the fall of 1962, just as Theo began to come into his own, their eldest daughter, Olivia, caught the German measles; four days later she was dead, the result of encephalitis, a rare complication of the disease. Although a measles epidemic had swept through their village earlier in the year, Olivia was never vaccinated because the gamma globulin that would have saved her life was not readily available in England after the war. Dahl, whose sister Astri had also died at the age of seven, was overwhelmed by a sense of doom.

Although nothing would replace the little girl they had lost, they were thrilled at the birth of another daughter, Ophelia, in May 1964. Dahl's depression lifted. He managed to pick up the pieces of his life again and even took in stride the untimely death of his friend Ian Fleming, from a heart attack, that August. Months went by in calm, comforting monotony. Then during a stay in California while working on a film, Neal was felled by a series of cerebral hemorrhages, the last one massive. After undergoing surgery to remove the clots in her brain, she lay in a coma for days. As fate would have it, the aneurysm was preordained: it was a congenital weakness. It had always been just a matter of time. When she finally regained consciousness, Neal's right side was completely paralyzed, and her memory, fine motor control, and power of speech were impaired. She was three months pregnant. She felt her belly, but "could not remember what the roundness meant."

Again Dahl refused to give up without a fight. He took her back to Gipsy House and commandeered her rehabilitation, instituting a daunting regimen of physical therapy at the RAF military hospital nearby, followed by laps in the pool and lessons in everything from speech to reading and writing. With his deeply ingrained Nordic stoicism, Dahl could be a cruel taskmaster, and there were times when she hated him. Nevertheless the grueling daily routine worked, and she improved. Less than six months after her stroke, Neal gave birth to a healthy baby girl, Lucy. *Life* magazine sent a reporter to do a piece on her recovery or, as Neal put it, to profile "the Greek tragedians of Great Missenden."

Through all this, Dahl, by necessity, had to keep writing, as he was now the family's sole means of support. In an unexpected twist worthy of one of his own creations, his children's books, which he had turned to again in the early 1960s to help pay the bills for his growing family, suddenly caught on. *James and the Giant Peach* became an international success and was followed in the same year by *Charlie and the Chocolate Factory,* which became an even bigger success, and was made into a movie. The books were blackly humorous, grotesque even, but enormously appealing to the young, in part because of their complete irreverence for authority. Dahl also took to writing screenplays, which he considered a "beastly job" and only did for the money. Albert "Cubby" Broccoli, the producer of the James Bond films, asked him to write the script for *You Only Live Twice*. That led to his doing an adaptation of Fleming's fanciful novel *Chitty Chitty Bang Bang*. For the first time in his life, Dahl was not only making a living, he was earning large sums, and he gloried in his fame and fortune.

Still, he was in a hurry for his wife to go back to work, whether for her own good or to allow him a little respite. Neal felt in no shape to return to acting. Her speech was still slow and halting, and she had a limp and often stumbled. In her memoir, she maintains that Dahl badgered her into accepting the few roles she was offered, and there followed a string of forgettable films about women coping with illness and adversity. In 1972 Dahl negotiated a deal with David Ogilvy's agency for Neal to serve as Maxim Coffee's spokeswoman for a year. The campaign was a hit, and she was asked to do more, flying regularly to New York to shoot the commercials. Felicity Crosland, a freelance fashion coordinator for Ogilvy & Mather and a divorced mother of three, became a family friend and a fixture in their lives. Before long she also became Dahl's mistress and in 1983, after a bitter tabloid divorce, his wife.

Dahl stayed in the garden shed where he wrote and never waivered from his routine. When the furor died down, he presented his new wife to the world as if his thirty-year union to Neal had never existed.

In a cookbook entitled *Memories with Food at Gipsy House,* written with Crosland and published posthumously, the family tree omits any mention of their previous spouses, so that Roald and Felicity appear to be the parents of all seven children. Despite his tempestuous personal life, he was remarkably productive, writing nine books of short stories in all and nineteen children's books, many of which were best sellers and are now considered classics. In the mid-1980s he penned two brief, beautiful remembrances of his youth, *Boy* and *Going Solo.* Together he and Felicity turned his literary legacy into a lucrative cottage industry, repackaging stories and putting out cute cartoon versions of his stories. Last year approximately 10 million copies of his books sold in the United States and abroad.

In his declining years, Dahl was made to seem like a slightly grumpy English version of Mr. Rogers, complete with grandfatherly cardigan. His snide humor continued to get him into trouble, however, and a number of reckless remarks about Israel, expressed to interviewers and in written reviews, earned him a reputation for anti-Semitism. He grew bitter that he never received the knighthood he felt his work warranted, particularly his charitable endeavors in neurology, hematology, and literacy. Dahl never lost his taste for the good life acquired at Marsh's elbow, demanding to the end that his publisher dispatch a Rolls-Royce to collect manuscripts from his home. He died of leukemia on November 23, 1990, at the age of seventy-four. Dahl appointed his second wife, who still resides at Gipsy House, executor of his literary estate. She reportedly divides half the income generated by his estate among his four children and uses her share to fund his charity, the Roald Dahl Foundation. In 2005 the Roald Dahl Museum and Story Centre opened in Great Missenden.

Through all the vicissitudes of the postwar years, Dahl remained lifelong friends with his fellow spies. He never wrote about his time in the BSC, even after numerous books about Stephenson and Fleming delved into its activities in America, and both Ogilvy and Bryce penned jaunty memoirs. Dahl touched on his experiences in Washington only once, in an autobiographical short story called "Lucky Break," in which he recounted his beginnings as a writer while employed at the British Embassy. Whatever secret oath they swore, Stephenson's recruits remained fiercely loyal to him and stood by one another, even when luck played havoc with their lives, arbitrarily doling out mortal disasters and phenomenal successes. They saw less and less of one another as time went on but were never out of touch.

In July 1969, just a few days after Neil Armstrong took his first steps on the moon, Dahl received a cable from his old boss, like a bolt out of the blue. It was in reference to an intelligence report he had filed in late 1944, stating that a government source had revealed a U.S. plan to plant the American flag on the surface of the moon. "It was a proper and accurate piece of information that I'd gotten," recalled Dahl, but he had been told at the time that when his message was read in the New York office, it was greeted with hoots of laughter. "Then I got the telegram from Bermuda [where Stephenson ultimately retired] saying 'Congratulations, you were right.' You think of all the messages he got through the war years," marveled Dahl, "and he remembered."

When the television movie of *A Man Called Intrepid* came out in the spring of 1979, based on the best-selling biography and starring David Niven—who had done a few favors for Stephenson during the war and coincidentally played the part of James Bond in the film version of *Casino Royale*—the surviving members of the old gang all traded letters. Sir William, then a frail eighty-three, had recovered from a devastating stroke, and they wanted to congratulate him on making it that far and tease him a bit about his Hollywood fame. They were all in their final lap and given to cataloging complaints about their various aches and pains and looking back with nostalgia "on the days when we were in the summer of our lives," as Cuneo wrote to "Intrepid," still playing the part of the faithful aide-de-camp twenty-four years later. Quoting his favorite Spanish proverb, "No one can steal the dance you've danced," he added, "For full lives, particularly the ones of world crises, which we shared, we must admit we've had a hell of a ball."

NOTES

ABBREVIATIONS

AH   Antoinette Marsh Haskell, oldest daughter of Charles Marsh, interview.

BBB   David Ogilvy, *Blood, Brains and Beer: The Autobiography of David Ogilvy* (New York: Atheneum, 1978).

BSI   Bickham Sweet-Escott, *Baker Street Irregular* (London: Methuen, 1965).

BOY   Roald Dahl, *Boy–Tales of Childhood* (New York: Puffin, 1984).

CF   Creekmore Fath, interview with author.

CBC   The Canadian Broadcasting Corporation's "Tuesday Night" documentary *A Man Called Intrepid,* which inspired the best-selling book by the same name by William Stevenson. During the preparation of this 1972 documentary, the CBC conducted in-depth interviews with Sir William Stephenson, as well as a number of his BSC operatives, including Roald Dahl, Dick Ellis, and Bickham Sweet-Escott. Transcripts of these interviews are housed in the William Stevenson Papers, University of Regina Archives, and were made available with the permission of the author, William Stevenson. Parts of these interviews have been quoted elsewhere, but in all cases I have used the original transcripts.

CMC   Charles Marsh correspondence with Roald Dahl, uncataloged family papers, viewed and quoted with permission of Marsh's grandson and literary executor, Robert Haskell III.

CMP   Charles E. Marsh Papers, Lyndon B. Johnson Library, University of Texas, Austin.

ECP   Ernest L. Cuneo Papers, Franklin D. Roosevelt Library, Hyde Park, N.Y.

ERP   Eleanor Roosevelt Papers, Franklin D. Roosevelt Library, Hyde Park, N.Y.

GS   Roald Dahl, *Going Solo* (New York: Puffin 1986).

HWD   Diaries of Henry Agard Wallace, 1935–1946, Special Collections, University of Iowa Library.

LB   Roald Dahl, "Lucky Break: How I Became a Writer," 1977, in *The Wonderful Story of Henry Sugar and Six More* (New York: Knopf, 2001).

LBJ   Oral History Collection, Lyndon B. Johnson Library, University of Texas, Austin.

NR   Adolf A. Berle, *Navigating the Rapids, 1918–1971: From the Papers of Adolf A. Berle*, ed. Beatrice Bishop Berle and Travis Beal Jacobs (New York: Harcourt Brace Jovanovich, 1973).

NYT   *New York Times*

NYTBR   *New York Times Book Review*

OH   Official History of the BSC British Security Coordination. *British Security Coordination: The Secret History of British Intelligence in the Americas, 1940–45.* Introduction by Nigel West (London: St. Ermin's Press, 1998). A top-secret document prepared in 1945 by William Stephenson and a handful of BSC agents, including Roald Dahl. Since then, as West explains in his introduction, it was "deliberately kept from the public," with a few photocopied versions of Sir William's personal edition made available to a small circle of intelligence historians and journalists. This "remarkable document," as West calls it, in its complete and unexpurgated form, was finally made available to the public in 1998, though the publication still carries the caveat that it "has not been officially endorsed by Her Majesty's Government."

QC   H. Montgomery Hyde, *The Quiet Canadian: The Secret Service Story of Sir William Stephenson* (London: Hamish Hamilton, 1962). Published in the United States as *Room 3603: The Story of the British Intelligence Center in New York During World War II* (New York: Farrar, Straus and Giroux, 1962).

RDM   Roald Dahl Museum and Story Centre, Archives, Great Missenden, Buckinghamshire, England.

RIP   Ralph Ingersoll Papers, Howard Gotlieb Archival Research Center, Boston University. Includes an unfinished memoir of Charles Marsh, *But in the Main It's True*.

WD   H. G. Nicholas, ed., *Washington Despatches, 1941–45: Weekly Political Reports from the British Embassy* (Chicago: University of Chicago Press, 1981).

WDA   Walt Disney Archive, Burbank, California.

WP   *Washington Post*

WTH   *Washington Times-Herald*
YOLO Ivar Bryce, *You Only Live Once: Memories of Ian Fleming* (London: Weidenfeld & Nicolson, 1975 and 1984).

PREFACE

   xiv   "to do all that . . .": OH.
    xv   "invisible fortress": Stevenson, *Man Called Intrepid,* p. 101.
   xvi   "man in Washington": Troy, *Donovan and CIA,* p. 62.
  xviii "ignited controversies": Troy, *Wild Bill and Intrepid,* p. 150.
    xx   "Truth is far too . . .": Stafford, *Camp X,* p. 20.

CHAPTER 1: THE USUAL DRILL

   2   "a rotten job": CBC, Dahl, take 1–2.
   2   "the ideal height": GS, p. 82.
   3   "was marvelous fun": Ibid, p. 88.
   4   "Who wants to be invalided home . . .": Ibid., p. 116.
   8   "palm-trees and coconuts . . .": BOY, p. 175.
   9   "very fit" and "fun": GS, p. 204.
   9   "She'll probably have been . . .": lbid., p. 205.
  10   "flew down the steps . . .": Ibid., p. 210.
  10   "Oh no, sir . . .": CBC, Dahl, take 3.
  13   "wave of the future": Steel, *Walter Lippman and the American Century,* p. 386.
  14   "flung in at the deep end": GS, p. 96.
  16   "a most unimportant . . .": CBC, Dahl, take 3.
  16   "the inward excitement": Astley, *The Inner Circle,* p. 85.
  16   "[I'd] just come from the war . . .": Ibid.
  18   "unpredictable . . .": BOY, p. 162.
  20   "a very vivacious . . .": Drew Pearson, Oral History Interview, LBJ.
  20   "Charles was able . . .": CF.
  23   "Hawk-beaked Charles . . .": RIP.
  23   "Charles always had a group . . .": CF.
  23   "his wit . . .": RIP.
  23   "We all just adored him . . .": AH.
  24   "bit of divine . . .": CMC.
  25   "being not of this century": Ignatieff, *Isaiah Berlin,* p. 111.

25 "very grand": Treglown, *Roald Dahl*, p. 56.
26 "For Transmission to the King": CMC.
27 "Roald could be like sand . . .": Neal, *As I Am*, p. 166.
27 "In a game of one-upmanship . . .": AH.
27 "I started nosing around . . .": CBC, Dahl, take 1–2.
28 "It was a very strange . . .": Peter Viertel, interview by author.
29 "I knew who he was . . .": CBC, Dahl, take 1–2.
30 "I had been contacted . . .": Ibid., take 3.
30 "For security reasons . . .": BSI, p. 17.
31 "This meant that recruiting . . .": Ibid., p. 32.
32 "I'd slip him a couple of bits . . .": CBC, Dahl, take 3.
33 "an RAF uniform with wings . . .": GS, p. 207.

CHAPTER 2: PIECE OF CAKE

35 "Becoming a writer . . ." : *NYTBR,* December 25, 1977.
36 "rare bird . . . been in combat": LB, p. 195.
39 "detail, that's what counts . . .": LB, p. 197.
39 "You were meant . . .": Ibid., p. 198.
39 "He [Donovan] was lying in bed . . .": C. S. Forester letters, Thayer Hobson Papers, Harry Ransom Center, University of Texas, Austin.
41 "progressively less realistic . . .": *NYTBR,* December 25, 1977.
42 "It's almost impossible . . .": *Twilight Zone Magazine,* February 1983.
43 "BELIEVE IT HAS . . .": WDA.
43 "overcome the difficulties . . .": Ibid.
43 "Gremlinologist . . . because I really do . . .": Ibid.
44 "It will seem strange . . .": *Observer* (London), November 8, 1942, p. 6.
44 "We would want . . .": WDA.
45 "We're doing this . . .": *WP,* November 18, 1942.
45 "the whole subject . . .": WDA.
45 "remarkable adeptness . . .": *NYT,* June 13, 1942.
46 "He was terribly pleased . . .": AH.
46 "the problems facing all humanity . . .": *NYT,* January 10, 1943.
48 "a libel on the staid . . .": *WTH,* January. 11, 1943.
49 "Europeans who hate Hitler . . .": HWD, memo from CM to HW, December 15, 1942.
50 "danger justified privilege": Waugh, *The End of the Battle.*
50 "very, very attractive . . .": Treglown, *Roald Dahl,* p. 61.

51 "man across the sea": *The New Yorker*, May 2, 1942.

53 "isolation ends . . .": Gabler, *Walter Winchell*, p. 294.

55 "The conduct of . . .": OH.

55 "Of course, my father knew . . .": AH.

56 "I want this message . . .": RIP.

56 "staccato, disjointed . . .": Treglown, *Roald Dahl*, p. 280.

57 "You woke me . . .": CMC.

58 "airplane of the future": HWD.

58 "persona non grata": Ibid.

59 "is our best . . .": CMC.

60 "Eden is respected . . .": Ibid.

61 "Berle may go to England . . .": Ibid.

62 "that menace": Brown, *Secret Life of Menzies*, p. 482.

63 "crazy": Culver and Hyde, *American Dreamer*, p. 342.

63 "Henry Wallace is now . . .": *NYT*, October 12, 1941.

63 "With no source as frank . . .": RIP.

CHAPTER 3: ENTHUSIASTIC AMATEURS

65 "this mythical, magical name . . .": CBC, Dahl, take 3.

66 "hiding in the back . . .": Ibid.

71 "He [Stephenson] had such immense . . .": Ibid.

72 "to establish relations on the highest . . .": Troy, *Donovan and CIA*, p. 34.

72 "Sir William did not want to make . . .": Troy, *Wild Bill and Intrepid*, p. 39.

73 "broken-down boarding house": Ibid., p. 63.

73 "A true top-level operator . . .": Philby, *Silent War*, p. 73.

74 "Realizing what a task . . .": CBC, Dahl, take 1–2.

75 "that gang at Broadway": Brown, *Secret Life of Menzies*, p. 263.

75 "thumb-twiddlers . . .": Stevenson, *Man Called Intrepid*, p. 99.

76 "to do all that was not being done . . .": OH.

76 "Six months before . . .": Sherwood, *Roosevelt and Hopkins*, p. 270.

76 "indefinite": Troy, *Donovan and CIA*, p. 34.

77 "cramped and depressing": QC, p. 35.

78 "Our best information . . .": Downes, *Scarlet Thread*, p. 61.

79 "threat to the American way . . .": QC, pp. 80–82.

80 "It is unlikely . . .": OH.

82 "He was small . . .": Coward, *Future Indefinite*, p. 167.

83 "I waited in this . . .": Hoare, *Noël Coward,* p. 310.

83 "I was to go as an entertainer . . .": Coward, *Letters,* p. 403.

84 "It took eleven secretaries . . .": BBB, p. 90.

84 "a man of few words . . .": Pearson, *Life of Fleming,* p. 98.

84 "by far the largest": CBC.

85 "one of the great secret agents . . .": Hyde, *Room 3603,* pp. x–xi.

85 "the chocolate sailor": Pearson, *Life of Fleming,* p. 84.

86 "innumerable services . . .": Hyde, *Room 3603,* p. xii.

86 "with the air . . .": Pearson, *Life of Fleming,* p. 97.

87 "It is certainly a bit difficult . . .": Astor Letters to FDR, April 1940, Roosevelt Papers.

88 "real object": Troy, *Donovan and CIA,* p. 33.

88 "read history backwards . . .": Troy, *Wild Bill and Intrepid,* p. 44.

89 "supplying our friend . . .": QC, p. 152.

89 "pressed his view": Troy, *Wild Bill and Intrepid,* p. 67.

89 "the earliest collaborator . . .": Ibid.

90 "$3,000,000 to play with . . .": McLachlan, *Room 39,* p. 230.

90 "Ian got on well . . .": Ibid.

91 "splendid American": Hyde, *Room 3603,* p. xi.

91 "original charter of the OSS": Pearson, *Life of Fleming,* pp. 101–2.

91 "my memorandum . . . the cornerstone . . .": Ibid.

91 "as a sort of imaginary exercise . . .": Ibid.

91 "[He] must have trained powers . . .": Lycett, *Ian Fleming,* p. 130.

92 "if you are willing . . .": YOLO, p. 50.

93 "the dreadful responsibility . . .": Ibid., p. 52.

93 "jealousies and petty rivalries . . .": Ibid., p. 61.

93 "If you felt": Mahl, *Depererate Deception,* p. 55.

94 "The obvious aggrandizement . . .": YOLO, p. 65.

94 "Were a German map . . .": Ibid.

94 "the Reich's chief": Ibid.

95 "I have in my . . .": Weber, "'Secret Map' Speech."

95 "a sky-high reputation . . .": Ibid.

95 "The item was made . . .": YOLO, p. 67.

96 "on our guard" and "false scares": Weber, "'Secret Map' Speech."

96 "full size secret police . . .": Troy, *Wild Bill and Intrepid,* p. 74.

98 "all but blind adoration . . .": ECP.

98 "all against an atmosphere . . .": Ibid.

98 "Bill knew this very well . . .": CBC, Dahl, take 3.

CHAPTER 4: SPECIAL RELATIONSHIPS

99 "He's a killer with women": Patricia Neal, interview by author.

99 "a roaring time": Dahl, to a *Time* magazine correspondent, unpublished interview.

100 "They were having a ball . . .": AH.

100 "parties for a purpose": Brinkley, *Washington Goes,* p. 141.

101 "racketeers": CMC.

101 "paid to throw parties": CMC.

102 "Dahl, an R.A.F. man . . .": Susan Mary Patten to Joseph Alsop, July 30, 1943. Courtesy of Elizabeth Winthrop, reprinted with permission of Anne Milliken and Bill Patten.

103 "The truth is": OH.

104 "A good rumour": Ibid.

106 "She absolutely hated . . .": AH.

106 "Don't touch it, bad luck . . .": "Town Talk," *WP,* December 23, 1944.

107 "parasite": Brinkley, *Washington Goes,* p. 139.

109 "Just why are you . . .": HWD.

110 "Be sure and come back . . .": Ibid.

111 "Her basic thought . . .": Ibid.

111 "She runs a good saloon . . .": Ibid.

111 "Come back . . .": Ibid.

112 "cut quite a local swath": "The Magazine Rack," *WP* September 21, 1947.

112 "Girls just fell . . .": Treglown, *Roald Dahl,* p. 59.

112 "There was a parade . . .": AH.

112 "one of the biggest . . .": Treglown, *Roald Dahl,* p. 59.

115 "She went for Roald . . .": CF.

116 "She is a clever . . .": Brown, *Secret Life of Menzies,* p. 479.

116 "Clare, you just can't be that way": CMP.

116 "But much of what Mr. Wallace . . .": Henley, *Au Clare de Luce,* p. 172.

117 "spheres of influence": Josephson, *Empire of Air,* p. 12.

117 "Freedom of the air . . .": Ibid.

118 "The future of every nation . . ." Henle, *Au Clare de Luce,* p. 174.

118 "clarification of loose thinking": WD, p. 153.

119 "Some have spoken . . .": Culver and Hyde, *American Dreamer,* p. 277.

119 "to assume leadership . . .": Ibid.

119 "All bets are off . . .": Josephson, *Empire of Air,* p. 214.

120 "Otherwise there will be friction . . .": Ibid., p. 11.

120   "in stirring up strife . . .": WD, p. 151.

120   "I am all fucked out . . .": Treglown, *Roald Dahl*, p. 60; reconfirmed by CF.

121   "She was something else . . .": AH.

121   "a lucky stroke": CBC, Dahl, take 1–2.

121   "You're a flying chap . . .": Ibid.

121   "an immensely secret . . .": Ibid.

121   "I thought, my goodness . . .": Ibid.

121   "the emancipation . . .": Brown, *Secret Life of Menzies;* p. 483.

121   "hair stand on end": Ibid.

122   "He flashed off . . .": CBC, Dahl, take 1–2.

122   "a bit of a stir": Ibid.

122   "could hardly believe what . . .": Ibid.

122   "people like Adolf Berle . . .": Brown, *Secret Life of Menzies*, p. 483.

123   "Anglo-Saxon superiority": HWD.

123   "Charley Marsh told me . . .": HWD.

123   "some chap in Washington . . .": CBC, Dahl, take 1–2.

124   "could be very devious": Brown, *Secret Life of Menzies*, p. 484.

124   "a lovely man . . .": Ibid.

124   "You have shown . . .": CMC.

125   "You have had the wisdom . . .": Ibid.

CHAPTER 5: BUFFERS

127   "rather lucky thing": CBC, Dahl, take 1–2.

128   "took a liking . . .": HWD.

128   "So I went to dinner . . .": CBC, Dahl, take 1–2.

128   "the excellent photograph": ERP, Eleanor Roosevelt to Dahl, June 29, 1943.

130   "she was not in his bedroom": Dahl intelligence report: "Visit to Hyde Park, July 2nd to 4th," July 6, 1943, CMP.

132   "You must be pretty tired . . .": Ibid.

132   "He did not 'glamor' me . . .": Transcript of Dahl's private verbal report to Marsh, "Comments of Week-End Reporter—Hyde Park," July 7, 1943, CMP.

132   "with a wave of the hand . . .": Dahl report, "Visit to Hyde Park, July 2nd to 4th," CMP.

133   "but only if he is not busy . . .": Ibid.

133   "took delight . . .": Ibid.

134 "a very nice man": Ibid.
134 "would do anything for a change": Ibid.
135 "the President's attitude . . .": "Comments," July 7, 1943, CMP.
135 "too old a hand . . . to sit back . . .": Ibid.
136 "like diving into the sea . . .": Dahl to Eleanor Roosevelt, July 8, 1943, ERP.
136 "Miss Thompson and I . . .": Eleanor Roosevelt to Dahl, July 21, 1943, ERP.
137 "I think it is 50–50 . . .": "Comments," July 7, 1943, CMP.
137 "The Crown Princess . . .": Ibid.
137 "entirely under the influence . . .": Ibid.
138 "He is truthful . . .": CMP.
138 "The name of Wallace . . .": Ibid.
138 "This young observer . . ." "Comments," July 7, 1943, CMP.
139 "I remember once . . .": CBC, Dahl, take 1–2.
140 "to prepare London": Ibid.
140 "buffers": Ibid.
140 "discreet indiscreet conversations": ECP.
140 "My job really was to try": CBC, take 1–2.
141 "With unstinted and constant . . .": BBB, p. 89.
141 "You never spoke directly . . .": CBC, take 1–2.
142 "Although it was in a way bleeding . . .": Ibid.
142 "If the isolationists had known . . .": BBB, p. 89.
143 "The very considerable espionage": NR, p. 400.
143 "That's why our side . . .": Stevenson, "A Piece of Cake in Tinseltown." *TV Guide*, May 5, 1979, p. 3.

CHAPTER 6: ONE LONG LOAF

145 "pretty careful tabs . . .": Brown, *Secret Life of Menzies*, p. 482.
146 "Henry Wallace was . . .": Haines, *Private Philanthropist*, p. 13. Excerpts courtesy of the Public Welfare Foundation and quoted with permission of Davis Haines.
146 "He had a direct pipeline . . .": CBC, Dahl, take 1–2.
146 "We became very good friends . . .": Ibid.
148 "For all I know . . .": Ibid.
149 "malicious rumors . . .": Daniels, *White House Witness*, p. 210.
149 "I don't even own . . .": Ibid.
149 "It's all nonsense. . .": Ibid.
149 "is still circulating . . .": WD.

150 "out to get Hopkins . . .": HWD.

150 "high-level stuff": Haines, *Philanthropist,* p. 19.

151 "What does he . . .": Ibid.

152 "Dear Governor . . .": Kopper, *Giver,* p. 50.

152 "Men do not make . . .": Haines, *Philanthropist,* p. 18; Kopper, *Giver,* p. 59.

153 "He and Roosevelt . . .": AH.

153 "positively sick to his stomach": HWD.

154 "the Preceptor": CMC.

154 "He always wanted to be . . .": Welly Hopkins, Oral History Interview, LBJ.

154 "He could be rude . . .": Ibid.

155 "As I listened . . .": HWD. The detailed description of life at Longlea was furnished by Antoinette Haskell, both in interviews and in the form of written reminiscences provided with her permission by the Public Welfare Foundation.

158 "Alice was a beautiful . . .": CF.

158 "There was a constant stream . . .": Leinsdorf, *Cadenza,* p. 75.

159 "her long blond hair . . .": RIP.

159 "You are not for Austin, Texas . . .": Ibid.

160 "The choice is hers . . .": Ibid.

161 "ingenious and mischievous . . .": Ibid.

161 "a skirmish with bandits": Ibid.

162 "She took on the privileges . . .": AH.

163 "loved Lyndon like a son": Kopper, *Giver,* p. 64.

163 "a young, young man": Dallek, *Lone Star Rising,* p. 150.

163 "Marsh was effective . . .": Welly Hopkins, Oral History Interview, LBJ.

164 "tutored . . . swaddling days": "Millionaire-Maker C. E. Marsh Dies," *Orlando Sentinel,* December 31, 1964.

165 "It could kill me politically": Caro, *Years of Johnson,* vol. 2, p. 25.

165 "one of the most interesting . . .": Kopper, *Giver,* p. 66.

166 "She's so tall and blonde . . .": Caro, *Years of Johnson,* vol. 1, p. 491.

166 "she, too, helped 'educate' . . .": Kopper, *Giver,* p. 69.

166 "seems to be the only person . . .": Caro, *Years of Johnson,* vol. 1, p. 480.

166 "give Herman the dam . . .": Ibid., vol. 1, p. 483.

166 "quite a bit of horse sense . . .": Ibid., vol. 1, p. 480.

166 "with a terrific shock": Leinsdorf, *Cadenza,* p. 76.

167 "treated Charles with the . . .": Ibid.

167 "You have a great art . . .": Dallek, *Lone Star Rising,* p. 169.

167 "The United States had a holy . . .": Leinsdorf, *Cadenza,* p. 77.

168 "his masterpiece of a letter": Ibid.

168 "Man, you almost . . .": Dallek, *Lone Star Rising*, p. 190.

168 "He was asking her and asking . . .": Caro, *Years of Johnson*, vol. 1, p. 485.

169 "Everything was subordinate . . .": Reston, *Lone Star*, p. 41.

169 "They didn't let her . . .": AH.

170 "At a formal dinner . . .": RIP.

170 "I will make that little Claudia . . .": Ibid.

171 "He turned her down . . .": AH.

171 "It is an incredible story . . .": Susan Mary Patten to Joseph Alsop, July 30, 1943.

172 "because of its timely . . .": WDA.

172 "With the amount of money . . .": Ibid.

172 "to look things over . . .": Ibid.

172 "I must comply . . .": Ibid.

172 "when the German armies . . .": Roald Dahl, "The Sword," *Atlantic Monthly*, July 1943.

174 "raising her fists . . .": Roald Dahl, "Katina," *Ladies' Home Journal*, March 1944.

175 "I was greatly taken . . .": CMP.

175 "a return ticket . . .": Ibid.

176 "Considering your age . . .": Ibid.

177 "I think he was glad . . .": CF.

CHAPTER 7: THE WAR IN WASHINGTON

179 "outside activities . . .": CMP.

180 "big people": Ibid.

180 "Washington was the key . . .": Peter Smithers, *Adventures of Gardener*, p. 19.

180 "mainly [the] Air Chief Marshall": CBC, Dahl, take 1–2.

180 "I fell far, as one is bound to . . .": Ibid.

180 "When Bill heard . . .": Ibid.

181 "I thought, well, if he can . . .": Ibid., take 3.

181 "I went home . . .": Ibid., take 1–2.

182 "What the hell . . .": Ibid.

182 "He never outlined . . .": Ibid.

183 "But for the tremendous pressure . . .": Hyde, *Room 3603*, p. 54.

184 "to neutralize": Ibid.

184 "most Americans . . .": OH.

184 "the Beaver" was in fighting form: Beaverbrook Archives, House of Lords Records Office, Engagement diaries, 1922–1964.

184 "grabbing the air traffic . . .": Chisholm and Davie, *Beaverbrook,* p. 447.

185 "several generations . . .": Ibid., p. 448.

185 "large concessions": Ibid.

186 "He believes that . . .": CMP.

186 "He was very serious . . .": AH.

187 "America's arch strategist . . .": Josephson, *Empire of Air*, p. 21.

187 "chosen instrument": Ibid., p. 156.

187 "high and devious diplomacy": Ibid., p. 196.

188 "There will always be wars . . .": Ibid., p. 202.

188 "let their hearts bleed": CMP.

188 "Entrenched position . . .": HWD.

189 "let it slip": Ibid.

189 "a mistake": Ibid.

190 "had a purpose . . .": Ibid.

190 "Clare does not pee . . .": Ibid.

192 "hamstringing bureaucracy": Culver and Hyde, *American Dreamer,* p. 305.

192 "an alarming sense . . .": Ibid., p. 306.

192 "In wartime no one . . .": HWD.

193 "Pop has tried for . . .": Ibid.

193 "Henry Wallace has . . .": Ibid.

193 "some activity in the British . . .": Ibid.

193 "The supposition is that . . .": Ibid.

195 "I came to regard Wallace . . .": Brown, *Secret Life of Menzies,* p. 484.

196 "Menzies was always . . .": Ibid.

196 "what the natives . . .": BBB, p. 73.

198 "an irreconcilable rebel . . .": Ogilvy, *The Unpublished David Ogilvy*, p. 101.

198 "The good salesman . . .": *Fortune*, April 1965.

198 "the most wonderful . . .": *Current Biography*.

199 "took to ordering . . .": BBB, p. 81.

199 "repulsive egotists": Ibid., p. 80.

199 "There is no great trick . . .": Ogilvy, *The Unpublished David Ogilvy*, p. 90.

200 "Do you think the . . .": Cull, *Selling War,* p. 109.

200 "readily agreed": OH.

201 "moonlighting": BBB, p. 86.

201 "Brooker was a born . . .": BSI, p. 143.

202 "shoot a man . . .": Stevenson, *Man Called Intrepid,* p. 194.

202 "I was taught . . .": BBB, p. 90.

203 "Rumors were spread . . .": OH.

204 "an average of forty . . .": BBB, p. 91.

204 "engaging in a little . . .": CBC, Gilbert Highet, take 1.

204 "This is really one of . . .": Ibid.

205 "extraordinary fertility": BBB, p. 90

205 "one of the most effective . . .": Ibid., p. 88.

205 "The President of the . . .": Ibid., p. 90.

205 "a sympathetic grin . . .": Ibid.

207 "pressing this country . . .": Hyde, *Room 3603*, p. 80.

207 "British Intelligence Item": CMP.

208 "a mother in black hat . . .": CMC.

208 "knowledge of geography . . .": Ibid.

CHAPTER 8: DIRTY WORK

209 "Orders from Military Air": CMP.

210 "Probably this matter . . .": Ibid.

210 "It would be . . .": Ibid.

210 "You might tell . . .": Ibid.

211 "relieved": RDM.

212 "Berle said he was . . .": HWD.

213 "Stalin was very angry . . .": Ibid.

213 "an ex-republican . . .": Dallek, *Lone Star Rising*, p. 197.

213 "The real fact . . .": CMP.

213 "I think I can say . . .": Ibid.

213 "So as you go west . . .": HWD.

214 "It is most disquieting . . .": CMP.

214 "Roosevelt has undertaken . . .": Hyde, *Room 3603*, p. 212.

215 "much activity in Princeton . . .": HWD.

216 "Gallup is devoted intensely . . .": Ibid.

216 "rare businessman with . . .": BBB, p. 85.

216 "When Dewey was . . .": Ibid.

216 "small beer": Ibid., p. 92.

217 "curiously lazy": Ibid., p. 98.

217 "Needless to say . . .": Ibid., p. 99.

217 "gentlemen don't read . . .": Troy, *Wild Bill and Intrepid*, p. 208.

217 "the beneficiaries of such . . .": BBB, p. 99.

218   "hyper-critical levels": Ibid., p. 93.
218   "brevity was discouraged . . .": Ibid., p. 94.
218   "The Secretary of state . . .": Ibid., p. 97.
218   "Our security was dreadful . . .": CBC, Dahl, take 3.
219   "one of the most malicious . . .": WD, p. 241.
220   "tremendous friction": CBC, Dahl, take 1–2.
220   "The embassy waffled . . .": Ibid.
220   "keeping a lid on": Hyde, *Room 3603*, p. 229.
221   "We Americans should have to . . .": Ibid., p. 230.
221   "a genuine flurry . . .": WD, p. 412.
221   "to have collected . . .": Ibid.
221   "Suddenly, in Drew Pearson's . . ." CBC, Dahl, take 1–2.
222   "Man who gave . . .": OH.
222   "Well, this wasn't too . . .": Ibid.
222   "That stopped that . . .": Ibid.
222   "absolutely secure . . .": Ibid.
223   "It took a whole roll . . .": Ibid.
223   "It's terrible, the advantages . . .": ECP.
223   "charming . . . lazy": Interview with Dahl, John Pearson Papers, Manuscripts Department, Lilly Library, Indiana University, Bloomington; by permission of J. Pearson.
224   "My dear boy . . .": Ibid.
224   "A giant among . . .": McLachlan, *Room 39*, p. 9.
224   "There was a great red glow . . .": Pearson, *Life of Fleming*, p. 207.
225   "misfires in the cloak-and-dagger . . .": YOLO, p. 55.
225   "In traditional spy-story style . . .": Ibid.
226   "Hullo Bunny . . .": Ibid., p. 56.
226   "To be opened . . .": Ibid., p. 57.
226   "You are to run a test . . ." Ibid.
227   "Running to the telephone . . .": Ibid., p. 59.
228   "wonder anaesthetic . . .": Ibid., p. 60.
228   "at least 500 ways of persecuting": WP, September 17, 1989.
229   "no end of a row . . .": NR, p. 400.
229   "get the dirt": Ibid., p. 402.
230   "surprise and horror . . .": Ibid.
230   "the easiest mark . . .": Troy, *Wild Bill and Intrepid*, p. 145.
230   "the precise danger which is run . . .": NR, p. 402.
231   "his personal word": Brown, *Life of Menzies*, p. 391.

231 "the President and the . . .": Ibid.
231 "needed a different type . . .": Troy, *Wild Bill and Intrepid*, p. 75.
231 "with the direct authority . . .": Brown, *Life of Menzies*, p. 392.
231 "liaison, pure and . . .": Ibid.
232 "The implication that the FBI . . .": Philby, *Silent War*, p. 73.
233 "That's the nastiest . . .": Roald Dahl, "My Lady Love, My Dove," *New Yorker*, June 21, 1952, p. 20.
233 "If he told me a double agent . . .": ECP.
233 "His position was therefore . . .": BSI, p. 130.
234 "Both Berle and Beaverbrook . . .": HWD.
234 "tragedy": Ibid.

CHAPTER 9: GOOD VALUE

237 "As you often say . . .": CMC.
238 "good value . . .": RDM.
238 "everything was gold": Ibid.
238 "mystic séances": HWD.
239 "further evidence . . .": Ibid.
239 "regrettable": Ibid.
239 "bunk": WD, p. 376.
239 "had been very much . . .": HWD.
239 "This is very serious . . .": Ibid.
240 "talk nonsense": CMC.
240 "was the best in the world": Ibid.
242 "The Mother of Roald . . .": CMC.
243 "tawdry affair . . .": Ibid.
243 "you, as a great gentlemen . . .": Ibid.
243 "troublemaker . . .": Ibid.
244 "The views attributed to . . .": HWD.
244 "a tremendous hit . . .": CMP.
245 "his Lordship as the purest . . .": CMC.
246 "I have long played . . .": Ibid.
248 "had been a fool . . .": Gellhorn, *Selected Letters*, p. 160.
248 "Anyhow, due to Roald . . .": Ibid., p.161.
250 "something something really dauntless . . .": Farrell, *Pat and Roald*, p. 137.
250 "Why the eyedropper . . .": Baker, *Hemingway*, p. 390.
251 "to tidy him up": Ibid., p. 391.

251 "would never work . . .": Gellhorn, *Selected Letters*, p. 163.

252 "He was a fellow . . .": Baker, *Hemingway*, p. 392.

253 "lay where they had fallen . . .": Ernest Hemingway, "Voyage to Victory," *Collier's*, July 22, 1944.

253 "But Ernest . . .": Baker, *Hemingway*, p. 395.

253 "not live at the Dorchester": Ibid.

254 "in that fine 400-mile . . .": Ernest Hemingway, "London Fights the Robots," *Collier's*, August 9, 1944.

254 "a nuisance": CMC.

255 "Rumor from that Great . . .": Ibid.

255 "Yes-men," "Pin-up Boys": Dallek, *Lone Star Rising*, p. 261.

255 "Joy Through Length Project": Treglown, *Roald Dahl*, p. 99.

256 "Our electoral college . . .": Ibid.

256 "I can only depend . . .": Ibid.

CHAPTER 10: ENEMY MANEUVERS

259 "There was this rather . . .": CBC, Dahl, take 1–2.

259 "whispering campaign . . .": WD, p. 381.

260 "Things are not going well . . .": HWD.

260 "Ickes does not fly . . .": Ibid.

260 "on-the-record conference": Ibid.

260 "a bone of contention": Ibid.

261 "I am talking to the ceiling . . .": Ibid.

261 "pushed down anybody's . . .": Ibid.

262 "Wallace's Pre-Convention . . .": CMP, HWD.

262 "as a Communist . . .": HWD.

262 "enemy maneuvers": CMP, HWD.

264 "I have been associated . . .": Culver and Hyde, *American Dreamer*, p. 351.

264 "If you want him . . .": Ibid.

264 "fight to the finish": CMP, HWD.

265 "The strength of the . . .": Culver and Hyde, *American Dreamer*, p. 359.

265 "if a vote was taken . . .": Ibid., p. 363.

266 "For Truman . . .": Hart, *Washington at War*, p. 216.

266 "It was a fine fight . . .": Culver and Hyde, *American Dreamer*, p. 366.

266 "Even though they do . . .": HWD.

266 "character, enterprise . . .": CMP, HWD.

266 "When a 'dark horse' . . .": Ibid.

267 "heavy, uncertain step": CMP.

267 "When Wallace . . .": AH.

267 "some international . . .": Culver and Hyde, *American Dreamer*, p. 373.

268 "Horse-whip Helen": CMP, HWD.

268 "the great female agent . . .": CMC.

269 "too loud": Ibid.

269 "great regret . . .": Ibid.

269 "made us all Gremlin . . .": WP, August 24, 1944.

271 "the beautiful home . . .": CMC.

271 "scared to death": HWD.

272 "I asked if he knew . . .": Ibid.

272 "10,000 agents . . .": Ibid.

272 "Dahl is an awfully nice boy . . ." Ibid.

273 "just the same as before": RDM.

273 "laughed loud and long": Chisholm and Davie, *Beaverbrook,* p. 450.

273 "parceling out": NR, pp. 498–99.

273 "as impossible now . . .": Ibid.

274 "In other words . . .": Ibid., p. 502.

274 "This merely a note . . .": Ibid.

274 "working together to keep . . .": Bender and Altschul, *Chosen Instrument,* p. 389.

275 "an incomparably better . . .": Ibid.

275 "changing horses . . .": Hart, *Washington at War*, p. 218.

276 "a clinical analysis": Hyde, *Room 3603*, p. 212.

276 "It's unbelievable . . .": Ibid., p. 213.

276 "either an idiot or a genius . . .": Ibid.

277 "although undeniably . . .": WD, p. 454.

277 "keen analytical powers . . .": BBB, p. 103.

277 "unavoidable human fallibility": WD, p. 454.

279 "a sigh of unofficial . . .": Dahl to Eleanor Roosevelt, November 8, 1944, ERP.

279 "I deeply appreciate . . .": Eleanor Roosevelt to Dahl, November 13, 1944, ERP.

279 "do a job on the balls . . .": CMC.

280 "We met in an era . . .": Bender and Altschul, *The Chosen Instrument*, p. 392.

281 "What happened next?": Treglown, *Roald Dahl,* p. 78.

282 "it is not always good . . .": *NYT*, September 21, 1996.

283 "I went to the Oak Room . . .": AH.

284   "Roald would bring . . .": Ibid.

284   "He was so tall . . .": Treglown, *Roald Dahl*, p. 79.

284   "the one great love . . .": *NYT*, September 23, 1996.

284   "kind of impossible . . .": Treglown, *Roald Dahl*, p. 79.

285   "He could be mean . . .": AH.

285   "when they fell in love . . .": Treglown, *Roald Dahl*, p. 77.

285   "gnome-like, greying . . .": Bender and Altschul, *Chosen Instrument*, p. 390.

285   "the outstanding symbol . . .": HWD.

286   "favorable . . .": Ibid.

286   "sad": Ibid.

286   "favorite court jester": RIP.

287   "never dragged his . . .": CMC.

287   "The fourth term was . . .": Culver and Hyde, *American Dreamer*, p. 380.

288   "Nevertheless, even at . . .": CMC.

288   "Screwball, Unincorporated . . .": Ibid.

289   "This man reports . . .": Ibid.

289   "wrote like a madman": RDM.

289   "urgent business": Ibid.

289   "in solitary opulence": Ibid.

290   "did the trick": Ibid.

290   "privately communicated": CMC.

290   "My Dear Lord . . .": Ibid.

291   "small brain . . .": CMP.

291   "He said he wanted . . .": OH.

291   "the last of his troubles": CMC.

292   "perennially efficient . . .": Ibid.

292   "a Hawaiian Princess": AH.

292   "quite sensibly . . .": Ibid.

CHAPTER 11: THE GLAMOUR SET

293   "We almost suffered . . .": ECP.

293   "quite a long time": CBC, Dahl, take 3.

293   "faster than I . . .": RDM.

294   "quite a shock": CBC, Dahl, take 3.

294   "The first impression . . .": Ibid.

294   "only his eyes . . .": Ibid.

295   "quiet Canadian": Sherwood, *Roosevelt and Hopkins*, p. 270.

295 "He never raised . . .": Ibid.
296 "This one is dear . . .": Hyde, *Room 3603*, p. xii.
298 "The thing I always . . .": Stafford, *Camp X*, p. 253.
298 "copped out": Ibid.
298 "official go-between": CMC.
299 "which you would . . .": Ibid.
299 "She is a martinet . . .": Ibid.
300 "It became quite . . .": Stafford, *Camp X*, p. 256.
301 "switched off": ECP.
301 "The Home Secretary . . .": Ibid.
301 "a literary striptease": Troy, *Wild Bill and Intrepid*, p. 153.
302 "Uncle Sucker": Blum, *Victory*, p. 303.
302 "The dollar sign . . .": Ibid., p. 312.
302 "rough and harsh": Ibid.
303 "catching up": CMP.
303 "the matter of the President's . . .": CMP, HWD.
304 "the establishment . . .": Ibid.
304 "an all-powerful . . .": Troy, *Donovan and CIA*, p. 255.
304 "secret funds for . . .": Ibid.
305 "maliciously . . .": WD, p. 518.
305 "exposing" and "the glamour set . . .": Troy, *Donovan and CIA*, p. 280.
306 "To put it mildly . . .": ECP.
307 "very complimentary . . ." HWD.
307 "dangerous implications . . .": Ibid.
307 "something of a Russophobe . . .": Ibid.
308 "Seventy-two . . .": Ibid.
309 "very reasonable medical grounds": RDM.
309 "attached to the President's . . .": Troy, *Donovan and CIA*, p. 296.
309 "My Dear General . . .": Ibid., p. 303.
310 "do a great deal of good . . .": HWD.
310 "a violent addiction . . .": ECP.
311 "exhausted and almost . . .": Coward, *Future Indefinite*, p. 275.
311 "impeccable secrecy . . .": Ibid.
311 "You know, Ivar . . .": YOLO, p. 74.
312 "the right bit . . .": Ibid.
312 "PRAY PAUSE NOT . . .": Ibid., p. 81.
313 "colleagues in economic . . .": BBB, p.103.
313 "help bridge over . . .": *Time*, June 6, 1949.

314 "The sad thing . . .": CBC, Dahl, take 3.

314 "a very rough ride": Ibid.

314 "Although Bill . . .": Ibid.

314 "quite nice": BSI, pp. 13–14.

315 "luxurious apartment": RDM.

316 "My father knew . . .": AH.

316 "It was Charles . . .": RIP.

317 "mad abandon . . .": *NYT,* February 10, 1946.

317 "especially enjoyed . . .": CMC.

317 "I didn't understand . . .": Baker, *Hemingway,* p. 637.

317 "in hospitals and . . .": Coward, *Diaries,* p. 50.

318 "These stories . . .": Ibid.

318 "Hurrah!": CMC.

318 "Talk little . . .": Ibid.

319 "mere papa": Ibid.

319 "Your presence . . .": Ibid.

CHAPTER 12: FULL LIVES

321 "Gamblers just before . . .": Pearson, *Life of Fleming,* p. 299.

322 "must not let British . . .": Schapmeier and Schapmeier, *Prophet in Politics,* p. 155.

322 "through forever": CMC.

323 "I don't know what . . .": BBC/NVC Roald Dahl documentary, produced and directed by Donald Sturrock.

323 "cured": CMC.

323 "we hear that . . .": Ibid.

324 "From being a . . .": Dahl, *Over to You,* p. 151.

324 "the noise of gunfire . . .": Roald Dahl, "The Soldier," *Someone Like You.*

324 "Not many will read it . . .": CMC.

325 "what they could do with it": Ibid.

325 "despair held bolt upright . . .": Baker, *Hemingway,* p. 486.

325 "I wish them dead": CMC.

326 "cheap for the thrill . . .": Ibid.

326 "to tear one another . . .": Dahl, "Claud's Dog," *Someone Like You.*

326 "a *thousand* sisters . . .": Treglown, *Roald Dahl,* p. 84.

327 "It was Charles . . .": RIP.

328 "Charles got me . . .": Ibid.

328 "something like a cult . . .": *NYHT,* December 13, 1953.

328 "It's not that I dislike . . .": Ibid.

329 "the stories are brilliant . . .": Coward, *Future Indefinite*, p. 231.

329 "I'd got a gimmick . . .": Ogilvy, *The Unpublished David Ogilvy*, p. 174.

330 "curiously refreshing . . .": *Advertising Age*, July 6, 1999.

331 "In the Bryce world . . .": Interview with Dahl, John Pearson Papers, Manuscripts Department, Lilly Library, Indiana University, Bloomington.

332 "There was always . . .": YOLO, p. 93.

333 "Why don't you . . .": Interview with Dahl, John Pearson Papers.

333 "Of course, I'm just playing . . .": Ibid.

335 "humanitarian instincts": CMC.

335 "Right, give him $200": Haines, *Philanthropist,* p. 35.

335 "do not give a fuck . . .": CMC.

336 "humanitarian endeavors": Ibid.

336 "die broke": *Newsweek*, January 13, 1947.

336 "If he chanced . . .": RIP.

337 "looked marvelous": CMC.

337 "got it in his head . . .": RIP.

338 "I didn't like him at all": Patricia Neal, interview by author.

338 "I met Charles . . .": Neal, *As I Am,* p. 156.

338 "consistent but dispassionate . . .": Ibid., p. 159.

339 "I got to know them all . . .": Neal interview.

340 "He could be the most . . .": Ibid.

340 "Dahl couldn't stand . . .": Ibid.

340 "[He] suddenly produced . . .": Neal, *As I Am,* p. 166.

340 "find a rich girl": Ibid., p. 158.

341 "cool her ardor": Ibid., p. 179.

341 "very well done": Ibid.

341 "Charles was a . . .": Ibid., p. 181.

341 "Boy, he told me . . .": Neal interview.

341 "You don't understand men . . .": Neal, *As I Am,* p. 181.

342 "new eminence . . .": Kopper, *Giver.*

343 "weekend, after weekend . . .": Neal interview.

344 "could not remember . . .": Neal, *As I Am,* p. 259.

344 "the Greek tragedians . . .": Ibid., p. 273.

345 "beastly job": *Twilight Zone Magazine,* February 1983.

347 "It was a proper . . .": CBC, Dahl, take 3.

348 "no one can steal . . .": ECP.

BIBLIOGRAPHY

Arce, Hector. *The Secret Life of Tyrone Power*. New York: Bantam, 1979.

Astley, Joan Bright. *The Inner Circle: A View of the War at the Top*. Boston: Atlantic–Little, Brown, 1971.

Baker, Carlos. *Ernest Hemingway: A Life Story*. New York: Scribner's, 1969.

Beard, Charles A. *President Roosevelt and the Coming of the War, 1941*. New York: Transaction Publishers, 2003.

Bender, Marylin, and Selig Altschul. *The Chosen Instrument: Pan Am, Juan Rippe, the Rise and Fall of an American Entrepeneur*. New York: Simon & Schuster, 1982.

Benson, Raymond. *The James Bond Bedside Companion*. London: Sinclair-Stevenson, 1994.

Berle, Adolf A. *Navigating the Rapids, 1918–1971: From the Papers of Adolf A. Berle*. Edited by Beatrice Bishop Berle and Travis Beale Jacobs. New York: Harcourt Brace Jovanovich, 1973.

Berlin, Isaiah. *Personal Impressions*. Edited by Henry Handy. New York: Viking, 1981.

———. *Washington Despatches, 1941–1945: Weekly Political Reports from the British Embassy*. Edited by H. G. Nicholas. Chicago: University of Chicago Press, 1981.

Bjaaland, Patricia C. *The Norwegian Royal Family*. Oslo: Tano, 1986.

Blum, John Morton. *V Was for Victory: Politics and American Culture During World War II*. New York: Harcourt Brace Jovanovich, 1976.

Brinkley, David. *Washington Goes to War*. New York: Alfred A. Knopf, 1988.

British Security Coordination. *British Security Coordination: The Secret History of British Intelligence in the Americas, 1940–1945*. Introduction by Nigel West. London: St. Ermin's Press. 1998.

Brown, Anthony Cave. *"C": The Secret Life of Sir Stewart Menzies*. New York: Macmillan, 1987.

Bryce, Ivar. *You Only Live Once: Memories of Ian Fleming*. London: Weidenfeld & Nicolson, 1975, 1984.

———. *Wild Bill Donovan: The Last Hero*. New York: Times Books, 1982.

BIBLIOGRAPHY

Caro, Robert A. *The Years of Lyndon Johnson*. 3 vols. New York: Alfred A. Knopf, 1990–2002.

Chisholm, Anne, and Michael Davie. *Lord Beaverbrook: A Life*. New York: Alfred A. Knopf, 1993.

Conally, John Bowden, with Mickey Herkowitz. *In History's Shadow: An American Odyssey*. New York: Hyperion, 1993.

Conkin, Paul K. *Big Daddy from the Pedernales: Lyndon Baines Johnson*. Boston: Twayne, 1986.

Coward, Noël. *Future Indefinite*. New York: Doubleday, 1954.

———. *The Noël Coward Diaries*. Edited by Graham Payne and Sheridan Morley. London: Weidenfeld & Nicolson, 1982.

———. *The Letters of Noël Coward*. Edited by Barry Day. New York: Alfred A. Knopf, 2007.

Churchill, Winston S. *The Second World War*, vols. 1–4. London: Cassell, 1951.

Cookridge, E. H. *Inside SOE*. London: Arthur Baker, 1966.

Cooper, Duff. *The Duff Cooper Diaries, 1915–1951*. Edited and introduced by John Julius Norwich. London: Weidenfeld & Nicolson, 2005.

Cull, Nicholas John. *Selling War: The British Propaganda Campaign Against American "Neutrality" in World War II*. Oxford: Oxford University Press, 1995.

Culver, John C., and John Hyde. *American Dreamer: A Life of Henry A. Wallace*. New York: W. W. Norton, 2000.

Cuneo, Ernest. *A Life with Fiorello*. New York: Macmillan, 1955.

Dahl, Felicity, and Roald Dahl. *Memories with Food at Gipsy House*. New York: Viking, 1991.

Dahl, Roald. *The Gremlins: A Royal Air Force Story*. New York: Random House, 1943.

———. *Over to You: Ten Stories of Flyers and Flying*. New York: Reynal and Hitchcock, 1946.

———. *Someone Like You*. New York: Alfred A. Knopf, 1953.

———. *Boy—Tales of Childhood*. New York: Puffin, 1984.

———. *Some Time Never*. New York: Scribner's, 1984.

———. *Going Solo*. New York: Puffin, 1986.

———. *The Best of Roald Dahl*. New York: Vintage, 1990.

———. *Ah, Sweet Mystery of Life*. London: Penguin, 1990.

———. *The Collected Short Stories of Roald Dahl*. London: Penguin, 1992.

———. *The Wonderful Story of Henry Sugar and Six More*. New York: Alfred A. Knopf, 2001.

Daley, Robert. *An American Saga: Juan Trippe and His Pan Am Empire*. New York: Random House, 1980.

Dallek, Robert. *Lone Star Rising: Lyndon Johnson and His Times, 1908–1960.* New York and Oxford: Oxford University Press, 1991.

Daniels, Jonathan. *Frontier on the Potomac.* New York: Macmillan, 1946.

———. *White House Witness, 1942–1945.* New York: Doubleday, 1975.

Deacon, Richard. *A History of the British Secret Service.* London: Muller, 1969.

Downes, Donald. *The Scarlet Thread.* London: Verschoyle, 1953.

Farrell, Barry. *Pat and Roald.* New York: Random House, 1969.

Fleming, Ian. *Casino Royale.* London: Penguin, 1953.

Foot, M.R.D. *SOE: The Special Operations Executive, 1940–46.* London: BBC, 1984.

Ford, Corey. *Donovan of OSS.* Boston: Little, Brown, 1975.

Gabler, Neal. *Walter Winchell: Gossip, Power, and the Culture of Celebrity.* New York: Alfred A. Knopf, 1994.

Gellhorn, Martha. *The Selected Letters of Martha Gellhorn.* Edited by Caroline Moorehead. New York: Henry Holt, 2006.

Goodwin, Doris Kearns. *No Ordinary Time: Franklin and Eleanor Roosevelt: The Home Front in World War II.* New York: Simon & Schuster, 1994.

Guiles, Fred Lawrence. *Tyrone Power: The Last Idol.* San Francisco: Mercury House, 1979.

Haines, Davis. *The Private Philanthropist: The Story of Charles Edward Marsh and the Public Welfare Foundation, 1947–1987.* Unpublished manuscript. Excerpts courtesy of the Public Welfare Foundation.

Hart, Scott. *Washington at War, 1941–1945.* Englewood Cliffs, N.J.: Prentice-Hall, 1970.

Hart-Davis, Duff. *Peter Fleming: A Biography.* Oxford: Oxford University Press, 1987.

Henle, Faye. *Au Clare de Luce: Portrait of a Luminous Lady.* New York: Stephen Daye, 1943.

Hinsley, F. H., et al. *British Intelligence in the Second World War.* Vol. 1–5. Her Majesty's Stationery Office, 1997–1990.

Hitchens, Christopher. *Blood, Class and Nostalgia: Anglo-American Ironies.* New York: Farrar, Straus and Giroux, 1990.

Hoare, Philip. *Noël Coward: A Biography.* Chicago: University of Chicago Press, 1995.

Hodgson, Lynn-Philip. *Inside Camp X.* Oakville, Ontario: Blake Books, 1999.

Hoopes, Roy. *Ralph Ingersoll: A Biography.* Foreword by Max Lerner. New York: Atheneum, 1985.

Hull, Cordell. *Memoirs.* 2 vols. London: Hodder and Stoughton, 1948.

Hyde, H. Montgomery. *Cynthia.* London: Hamish Hamilton, 1966.

———. *The Quiet Canadian: The Secret Service Story of Sir William Stephenson.*

London: Hamish Hamilton, 1962. Published in the United States as *Room 3603: The Story of the British Intelligence Center in New York During World War II*. New York: Ballantine, 1962.

―――. *Secret Intelligence Agent*. New York: St. Martin's Press, 1982.

Ickes, Harold L. *The Secret Diary of Harold L. Ickes*. 3 vols. New York: Simon & Schuster, 1953–54.

Ignatieff, Michael. *Isaiah Berlin: A Life*. New York: Henry Holt, 1998.

Ignatius, David. "Britain's War in America: How Churchill's Agents Secretly Manipulated the U.S. Before Pearl Harbor." *Washington Post*, Sept. 17, 1989, pp. C1–2.

Irving, David. *Churchill's War*. Vol. 1. Australia: Veritas Publishing Co., 1987.

Jones, R. V. *Most Secret War*. London: Hamish Hamilton, 1978.

Josephson, Matthew. *Empire of the Air: Juan Trippe and the Struggle for World Airways*. New York: Harcourt Brace, 1944.

Kimball, Warren F. "World War II's 'Intrepid' and the Pitfalls of Popular History." Letter, *New York Times*, Aug. 5, 1981, p. A22.

Kiplinger, W. M. *Washington Is Like That*. New York: Harper, 1942.

Kopper, Philip. *Anonymous Giver: A Life of Charles E. Marsh*. Washington, D.C.: Public Welfare Foundation, 2000.

Lash, Joseph P. *Roosevelt and Churchill*. New York: W. W. Norton, 1976.

Leinsdorf, Erich. *Cadenza: A Musical Career*. Boston: Houghton Mifflin, 1976.

Lovell, Mary S. *Cast No Shadow: The Life of the American Spy Who Changed the Course of World War II*. New York: Pantheon, 1992.

Lycett, Andrew. *Ian Fleming: The Man Behind James Bond*. Atlanta: Turner Publishing, 1995.

Macdonald, Bill. *The True Intrepid: Sir William Stephenson and the Unknown Agents*. Vancouver: Raincoast Books, 2001.

Mahl, Thomas E. *Desperate Deception: British Covert Operations in the United States, 1939–44*. Herndon, Va.: Brassey's, 1998.

McCormick, Donald. *The Life of Ian Fleming*. London: Peter Owen, 1993.

McCullough, David G. *Truman*. New York: Simon & Schuster, 1992.

McLachlan, Donald. *Room 39: A Study in Naval Intelligence*. New York: Atheneum, 1968.

McLean, Evalyn Walsh, with Boyden Sparks. *Father Struck It Rich*. Ouray, Co.: Bear Creek Publishing, 1981.

―――. *Queen of Diamonds: The Fabled Legacy of Evalyn Walsh McLean*. Franklin, Tenn.: Hillsboro Press, 2000.

Meacham, Jon, *Franklin and Winston: An Intimate Portrait of an Epic Friendship*. New York: Random House, 2003.

Miller, Hope Ridings. *Embassy Row.* New York: Holt, Rinehart and Winston, 1969.

Morgan, Janet. *Edwina Mountbatten: A Life of Her Own.* London: Fontana, 1991.

Naftali, Timothy J. "Intrepid's Last Deception: Documenting the Career of Sir William Stephenson." *Intelligence and National Security* 8 (July 1999): 72–92.

Nicholson, Harold. *The War Years, 1939–1945.* Vol. 2 of *Diaries and Letters.* Edited by Nigel Nicholson. New York: Atheneum, 1967.

Neal, Patricia. *As I Am: An Autobiography.* New York: Simon & Schuster, 1988.

Ogilvy, David. *Confessions of an Advertising Man.* New York: Atheneum, 1976.

———. *Blood, Brains and Beer: The Autobiography of David Ogilvy.* New York: Atheneum, 1978.

———. *The Unpublished David Ogilvy.* Edited by Joel Raphaelson. New York: Crown, 1986.

Pearson, John. *The Life of Ian Fleming.* New York: McGraw-Hill, 1966.

Pepper, Claude, with Hays Gorey. *Pepper: Eyewitness to a Century.* San Diego: Harcourt Brace Jovanovich, 1987.

Persico, Joseph E. *Roosevelt's Secret War: FDR and World War II Espionage.* New York: Random House, 2001.

Philby, Kim. *My Silent War.* New York: Modern Library, 1968.

Porter, McKenzie. "The Biggest Private Eye of All." *Maclean's Magazine,* Dec.1, 1952, p. 7.

Powling, Chris. *Roald Dahl.* Minneapolis: Carolrhoda Books, 1998.

Pulliam, Russell. *Publisher: Gene Pulliam, Last of the Newspaper Titans.* Ottawa, Ill.: Jameson, 1984.

Reston, James. *The Lone Star: The Life of John Connally.* New York: Harper and Row, 1989.

Roosevelt, James, with Bill Libby. *My Parents: A Differing View.* New York: Playboy Press, 1976.

Schapmeier, Edward L., and Frederick Schapmeier. *Prophet in Politics: Henry A. Wallace and the War Years, 1940–65.* Ames: Iowa State University Press, 1970.

Schwartz, Jordan A. *The Speculator: Bernard M. Baruch in Washington, 1917–1965.* Chapel Hill: University of North Carolina Press, 1981.

Shadegg, Stephen. *Clare Boothe Luce: A Biography.* New York; Simon & Schuster, 1970.

Shale, Richard. *Donald Duck Joins Up: The Walt Disney Studio During World War II.* Ann Arbor, Mich.: UMI Research Press, 1982.

Sheed, Wilfrid. *Clare Boothe Luce.* Thorndike, Me.: Thorndike Press, 1982.

Sherwood, Robert R. *Roosevelt and Hopkins: An Intimate History*. New York; Harper, 1948.

Smithers, Peter. *Adventures of Gardener*. London: Harvill Press and the Royal Horticultural Society, 1995.

Stafford, David. *Camp X*. New York: Viking Press, 1986.

———. *Churchill and Secret Service*. London: Abacus, 1995.

———. *Roosevelt and Churchill: Men of Secrets*. New York: Overlook Press, 1999.

Steel, Ronald. *Walter Lippmann and the American Century*. Boston: Atlantic–Little Brown, 1980.

Stevenson, William. "A Piece of Cake in Tinseltown." *TV Guide*, May 5, 1975.

———. *A Man Called Intrepid: The Secret War*. New York: Harcourt Brace Jovanovich, 1976.

———. *Intrepid's Last Case*. New York: Ballantine, 1983.

Straight, Michael. *After Long Silence*. London: Collins, 1983.

Sweet-Escott, Bickham. *Baker Street Irregular*. London: Methuen, 1965.

Tapert, Annette, and Diana Edkins. *The Power of Style*. New York: Crown, 1994.

Treglown, Jeremy. *Roald Dahl: A Biography*. New York: Farrar, Straus and Giroux, 1994.

Trohan, Walter. *Political Animals: Memoirs of a Sentimental Cynic*. New York: Doubleday, 1975.

Troy, Thomas F. *Donovan and CIA*. New York: University Publications of America, 1981.

———. *Wild Bill and Intrepid: Donovan, Stephenson and the Origin of the CIA*. New Haven and London: Yale University Press, 1996.

Wallace, Henry Agard, and John Morton Blum. *The Price of Vision: The Diary of Henry A. Wallace, 1942–1946*. Edited and with an introduction by John Morton Blum. Boston: Houghton Mifflin, 1973.

Waugh, Evelyn. *The End of the Battle*. Boston: Little, Brown, 1961.

Mark Weber, "Roosevelt's 'Secret Map' Speech," *Journal of Historial Review* 6 (1985): 125.

West Nigel. *A Thread of Deceit: Espionage Myths of World War II*. New York: Random House, 1985.

———. *MI5: British Security Service Operations, 1909–1945*. New York: Stein and Day, 1982.

———. *MI6: British Secret Intelligence Operations, 1909–1945*. London: Weidenfeld & Nicolson, 1983.

———. *Unreliable Witness*. London: Weidenfeld & Nicholson, 1986.

Bibliography

Winant, John Gilbert. *Letter from Grosvenor Square*. Boston: Houghton Mifflin, 1947.

Winchell, Walter. *Winchell Exclusive*. New Jersey: Prentice-Hall, 1975.

Winder, Simon. *The Man Who Saved Britain: A Personal Journey into the Disturbing World of James Bond*. New York: Farrar, Straus and Giroux, 2006.

Wright, Peter. *Spycatcher: The Candid Autobiography of a Senior Intelligence Officer*. New York: Viking, 1987.

ACKNOWLEDGMENTS

THIS ACCOUNT OF Roald Dahl's wartime adventures could not have been written without the encouragement of Robert Haskell III, heir to Charles Marsh's passion for politics and journalism, and publisher in his own right of the family-owned *Martinsville Bulletin,* who gave me unrestricted access to the mass of correspondence between his grandfather and Roald Dahl, as well as to additional Marsh letters, family papers, and photographs. It is impossible for me to adequately express my gratitude to Robert and his wife, Elizabeth, for their extraordinary hospitality, generosity, and kindness. Not only did they provide bed and board at their beautiful Virginia farm, answer endless questions about the family, no matter how frank, but also somehow arranged for me to be allowed inside Marsh's beloved Longlea, which is presently owned by the religious sect Opus Dei. I am also deeply grateful to Robert's mother, Antoinette Marsh Haskell, for sharing with me her detailed memories of the young RAF officer who frequented her father's house on R Street.

In pursuing firsthand sources, I was helped immensely by the author William Stevenson, who granted me access to his archive at the University of Regina in Canada, which includes the unedited and unpublished transcripts of interviews with members of the BSC conducted by the CBC for the 1972 documentary *A Man Called Intrepid,* which led to Stevenson's best-selling book by the same name, as well as interviews and related correspondence for the radio programs *The Two Bills, The Great Canadian Spy* and *Martin Bormann*. William Stevenson was a wry and thoughtful guide to navigating this complicated and controversial material, which over the years has spawned a mini-industry of Intrepid critics and debunkers. I am also greatly indebted to the writer John Pearson for making available interviews he did for his authoritative 1966 biography of Ian Fleming, which provided rare insight into the complex friendship between Dahl, Fleming, Bryce, Cuneo, Ogilvy, and their collective hero, Bill Stephenson.

For research assistance, I would like to record my gratitude to the Roald Dahl Estate, which is administered by his widow from his second marriage, Felicity Dahl, and Amanda Conquy. Pinning down wartime dates can be a tricky business, and I greatly appreciate the contribution of Jane Branfield, archivist at the Roald Dahl Museum and Story Centre in Great Missenden, Buckinghamshire, which houses the bulk of Dahl's papers and correspondence.

I would also like to thank the following for their recollections, family letters, diaries, photographs, and documents: Patricia Neal, Beth Warner, Davis Haines, Creekmore Fath, John Forester, Jonathan W. Cuneo, Elizabeth Winthrop, Annette Tapert, and the late Peter Viertel. For their Jamaican hospitality and tales of island life, I must pay tribute to my hosts Michael Thomas, Chris Blackwell, and Nigel Pemberton. My thanks also to several former members of the OSS who agreed to reminisce a little for my benefit but asked not to be named, and to the mutual friends who made the introductions.

Too many individuals and organizations provided assistance to mention them all, but special recognition is due to John Huey, editor in chief of Time Inc. At the Public Welfare Foundation, Elaine Shannon was exceptionally resourceful and hunted down obscure facts and old pictures and, when all else failed, turned photographer. For his assistance with the Ralph Ingersoll Collection at the Howard Gotlieb Archival Research Center at Boston University, I want to thank Charles Nile. I also benefited from the hard work of a number of researchers: Paul Veneziano of

ACKNOWLEDGMENTS

History Associates, Donna Coates, Katharine Dale, Ruth Tenenbaum, and in Britain, Christopher Werth. Cavelle Sukhai manages everything, and I would be lost without her. For their unflagging support and friendship, which means so much more than this small mention can convey, I am beholden to Barbara Kantrowitz, Mary Tavener Holmes, Perri Peltz, and Toni Goodale.

I owe an enormous debt of gratitude to Kris Dahl, my literary agent, who was especially helpful to me in focusing this project, and first planted the kernel of an idea that became *The Irregulars*. She, too, is a distant descendant of brilliant, blue-eyed Viking stock, though there is no evidence she is related to Roald. This is my third book for Alice Mayhew, my editor, whose intelligence, patience, and boundless enthusiasm make all things—even finishing—seem possible. There are so many at Simon & Schuster who have contributed to this book, beginning with David Rosenthal, an exuberant champion of his writers, on whom Dahl, who was most particular about people, would doubtlessly have bestowed his favorite adjective, "sparky." I would also like to acknowledge Roger Labrie's careful shepherding, Janet Biehl's painstaking copyediting, and Michael Accordino's inspired art direction.

Finally, I dedicate this book to my boys—my husband, Steve Kroft, and son, John—who are my best friends and favorite coconspirators. You have braved years of war stories, and I am deeply grateful to you both.

Jennet Conant
Sag Harbor, 2008

INDEX

British Security Coordination (*cont.*)
  criticism of, xviii, 143, 314–15
  Dahl's work for, 30, 55–64, 103–106,
    120–25, 138–43, 146–50, 181–82,
    186–87, 214–22, 237–46, 254, 272,
    293, 346–48
  economic warfare, 203–204
  history of wartime achievements, xix, 147
    and *n.*, 296–301 and *n.*
  intelligence on U.S. public opinion,
    199–206, 215, 276
  postwar, 302–315
  recruiting agents for, 30–31, 80–83,
    201–202
  Rockefeller Center headquarters, 28–29,
    141, 293–94, 298
  role in 1944 presidential election, 214–16,
    275–77
  Rumor Factory, 104–105
  turf battles with American authorities,
    96–97, 229–33, 295, 303
  "Wallace affair," 121–24
  war propaganda, 30, 65, 77–98
  See also specific agents
British Security Coordination (BSC): An Ac-
  count of Secret Activities in the Western
  Hemisphere, 1940–45 (book), xix, 300
    and *n.*, 301*n.*
British War Relief, 83
Broccoli, Albert "Cubby," 345
Brooker, Bill, 201–202
Broun, Heywood, 50
Brown, George, 163, 164, 166, 248–49
Brown, Herman, 166
Bruce, David, 141, 313
Bryce, Ivar, xvii, 91–95, 223–28, 343, 347
  background of, 223–24
  BSC intelligence work, 91–95, 224–28
  "map affair," 94–96, 228
  postwar life, 310–12, 330–32
Bryce, Jo Hartford, 330–31
Byrd, Harry, 255
Byrne, Sheila, 225
Byrnes, Jimmy, 150, 194

Campbell, Sir Ronald, 221, 231
Camp X, 201–203, 228, 297–99
Canada, 10, 66 and *n.*, 67, 80, 94, 173, 201,
  234, 298
Cantril, Hadley, 199, 215
Capa, Robert, 250
Chamberlain, Neville, 25, 75
Chicago Sun, 51
Chicago Tribune, 105, 150*n.*, 274, 305
Churchill, Winston, xv, xvi, 11, 25, 60, 120,
  122, 183, 184, 191, 300, 302, 308, 314

  becomes Prime Minister, 75 and *n.*
  British secret operations in U.S. and, 65,
    69–75, 207, 219–20, 231, 240
  encourages U.S. entry into war, 29, 71
  Roosevelt and, 11–12, 21–22, 122–23, 132,
    134, 137, 140–42, 177, 193–95, 207,
    222, 274, 291
Civil aviation, postwar, 117–22, 131, 184–89,
  212–13, 234–36
  British-U.S. negotiations, 120, 185, 186–89,
    213, 234–35, 273–75, 280
  1944 conference, 273–75, 280
  Roosevelt on, 132–33, 212, 273, 274
  Henry Wallace on, 116–23, 191, 211–12,
    234
Clark, Bennett, 212, 235
Clark, Joseph, 108
Clayton, Will, 50, 285
Cohen, Ben, 21
COI, 89, 141
Coit, Richard, 81, 92
Coke, David, 9 and *n.*
Collier's, 41, 50, 247, 253, 254
Communism, 50, 62, 305, 334
Congress, U.S., 22, 47, 79, 101, 116, 163, 188,
  277, 288, 305
Connolly, John, 168
Cooper, Gary, 102, 338–39, 343
Corbett, Leonora, 115
Cosmopolitan, 45
Coughlin, Father Charles, 109
Coward, Noël, xvii, 82–83, 108, 310–11,
  317–18, 329, 332, 336, 337
  BSC intelligence work, 82–83
  Future Indefinite, 65
Critchley, Alfred Cecil, 236
Crosland, Felicity, 345–46
Crowley, Leo T., 192
Cuba, 92, 94, 167, 168, 247
Cuneo, Ernest, 54–55, 195, 219, 276, 301,
  306, 347
  BSC ties, 54–55, 97–98
  postwar life, 331–34

Dahl, Asta, 249, 309, 323
Dahl, Harald, 7, 8
Dahl, Lucy, 344
Dahl, Olivia, 343, 344
Dahl, Ophelia, 344
Dahl, Roald, xvi–xvii
  assigned to intelligence service, 30–33, 55
  Beaverbrook and, 182, 184–86
  Boy, 346
  as British Embassy envoy in Washington,
    D.C., xvi, 10–17, 27–33, 102, 179–81,
    183, 210, 241–44, 254, 347

INDEX

INDEX

ILLUSTRATION CREDITS

Numbers in roman type refer to photos in the insert; italics refer to book pages.

Walt Disney Studios/Dahl Estate: 1
Courtesy of Haskell Family: 2
Courtesy of Elaine Shannon: 3, 20
Historical Society of Washington, D.C.: 4, 5
AP Photo: 6, 25
Hulton Archive/Getty Images: 7, 9
Courtesy of Jonathan W. Cuneo: 8
Time & Life Pictures/Getty Images: 10, 24
Weidenfeld & Nicholson Archive: iv *(bottom left and bottom right)*, 11, 12
Bettmann/Corbis: iv *(top left and top right)*, 13, 14, 16, 21, 26
Serge Balkin, originally published in Vogue: 15
Casson Studio/Lyndon B. Johnson Library: 17
Hulton-Deutsch Collection/Corbis: 18
Lyndon B. Johnson Library: 19
Corbis: 22
Franklin D. Roosevelt Library: 23, 278 *(both letters)*

ABOUT THE AUTHOR

JENNET CONANT is the author of the *New York Times* best seller *Tuxedo Park: A Wall Street Tycoon and the Secret Palace of Science That Changed the Course of World War II* and *109 East Palace: Robert Oppenheimer and the Secret City of Los Alamos*. A former journalist who has written profiles for *Vanity Fair, Esquire, GQ, Newsweek,* and the *New York Times*, she lives in New York City and Sag Harbor, New York.